SOMETHING ABOUT THE AUTHOR

SOMETHING ABOUT THE AUTHOR

Facts and Pictures about Authors

and Illustrators of Books for Young People

Anne Commire

VOLUME 19

GALE RESEARCH
BOOK TOWER
DETROIT, MICHIGAN
48226

Also Published by Gale

CONTEMPORARY AUTHORS

*A Bio-Bibliographical Guide to Current Writers in
Fiction, General Nonfiction, Poetry, Journalism,
Drama, Motion Pictures, Television,
and Other Fields*

(Now Covers Nearly 57,000 Authors)

Associate Editors: Agnes Garrett, Helga P. McCue

Assistant Editors: Dianne H. Anderson, Kathryn T. Floch, Mary F. Glahn,
D. Jayne Higo, Linda Shedd, Susan L. Stetler

Consultant: Adele Sarkissian

Sketchwriters: Rosemary DeAngelis Bridges,
Mark Eisman, Gail Schermer

Research Assistant: Kathleen Betsko

Editorial Assistants: Lisa Bryon, Susan Pfanner, Elisa Ann Sawchuk

Table of Contents

Introduction

Beginning with Volume 15, the time span covered by *Something about the Author* was broadened to include major children's writers who died before 1961, which was the former cut-off point for writers covered in this series. This change will make *SATA* even more helpful to its many thousands of student and professional users.

Authors who did not come within the scope of *SATA* have formerly been included in *Yesterday's Authors of Books for Children,* of which Gale has published two volumes.

It has been pointed out by users, however, that it is inconvenient to have a body of related materials broken up by an arbitrary criterion such as the date of a person's death. Also, some libraries are not able to afford both series, and are therefore denied access to material on some of the most important writers in the juvenile field.

It has been decided, therefore, to discontinue the *YABC* series, and to include in *SATA* at least the most outstanding among the older writers who had been selected for listing in *YABC*. Volumes 1 and 2 of *YABC* will be kept in print, and the listings in those two volumes will be included in the cumulative *SATA* index.

GRATEFUL ACKNOWLEDGMENT

is made to the following publishers, authors, and artists,
for their kind permission to reproduce copyrighted material.

ABELARD-SCHUMAN (London). Illustration by S.E. Ellacott from *The Norman Invasion* by S.E. Ellacott. Reprinted by permission of Abelard-Schuman.

ALADDIN BOOKS. Illustration by L.F. Bjorklund from *Cochise of Arizona* by Oliver La Farge. Copyright 1953 by Oliver La Farge. Reprinted by permission of Aladdin Books.

ALLEN & UNWIN, LTD. Illustration by Pauline Baynes from "Fastitocalon," in *The Adventures of Tom Bombadil* by J.R.R. Tolkien. Copyright © 1962 by Allen & Unwin, Ltd./ Illustration by Pauline Baynes from *Smith of Wooten Major* by J.R.R. Tolkien. Copyright © 1967 by Allen & Unwin, Ltd. Both reprinted by permission of Allen & Unwin, Ltd.

AMERICAN LIBRARY ASSOCIATION. Sidelight excerpts from "Memories of Arna Bontemps," in *American Libraries* by Jack Conroy. Copyright © 1974 by Jack Conroy. Reprinted by permission of American Library Association.

ATHENEUM PUBLISHERS. Illustration by Peter Boston from *The Guardians of the House* by L.M. Boston. Copyright © 1974 by L.M. Boston. Illustrations copyright © 1974 by Peter Boston./ Illustration by Gustave Dore from *The Enchanted Forest* retold and adapted by Beatrice Schenk deRegniers. Copyright © 1974 by Beatrice Schenk deRegniers. Both reprinted by permission of Atheneum Publishers.

THE ATLANTIC MONTHLY PRESS. Sidelight excerpts from *Jungle Days* by William Beebe. Copyright © by The Atlantic Monthly Press. Reprinted by permission of *The Atlantic Monthly Press.*

ERNEST BENN, LTD. Illustration by Edmund Dulac from *Treasure Island* by Robert Louis Stevenson. Reprinted by permission of Ernest Benn, Ltd.

BILLBOARD PUBLICATIONS, INC. Sidelight excerpts from an article by Nick Meglin, March, 1977 in *American Artist*. Copyright © 1977 by Billboard Publications, Inc. Reprinted by permission of Billboard Publications, Inc.

THE BODLEY HEAD, LTD. Photographs by A.F. Kersting, J. Oldknow, and others and sidelight excerpts from *Memory in a House* by L.M. Boston. Copyright © L.M. Boston, 1973. All reprinted by permission of The Bodley Head, Ltd.

R.R. BOWKER CO. Sidelight excerpts from "Some Books I've Illustrated," by Reginald Birch, October 19, 1935 in *Publishers Weekly*. Copyright © 1935 by R.R. Bowker Co. Reprinted by permission of R.R. Bowker Co.

CURTIS BROWN, LTD. Sidelight excerpts from *Books Are By People* by Lee Bennett Hopkins./ Sidelight excerpts from *Jonathan Swift* by A.L. Rowse. Copyright © 1975 by A.L. Rowse. Both reprinted by permission of Curtis Brown, Ltd.

THE CAXTON PRINTERS, LTD. Illustration by Dell J. McCormick from *Paul Bunyan Swings His Axe* by Dell J. McCormick. Copyright 1936 by the Caxton Printers, Ltd./ Illustration by Lorna Lively from *Tall Timber Tales* by Dell J. McCormick. Copyright 1939 by the Caxton Printers, Ltd. Both Reprinted by permission of The Caxton Printers, Ltd.

CENTRO INTERNAZIONALE DEL LIBRO (Florence). Illustration by Adriana Saviozzi Mazza from *Fables of Leonardo da Vinci* interpreted and transcribed by Bruno Nardini. English language text copyright © 1973 by William Collins and Sons, Ltd. Reprinted by permission of Centro Internazionale del Libro.

THE CENTURY CO. Illustration by Reginald Birch from *The Enchanted Flivver* by Berton Braley. Copyright 1926 by Berton Braley. Copyright 1925, 1926 by The Century Co./ Illustration by Reginald Birch from *The Lucky Stone* by Abbie Farwell Brown. Copyright 1914 by The Century Co. Both reprinted by permission of The Century Co.

CHILDRENS PRESS. Illustration by Marjorie Burgeson from *The Christmas Magic-Wagon* by June Behrens. Copyright © 1975 by Regensteiner Publishing Enterprises. Reprinted by permission of Childrens Press.

COLLIER BOOKS. Illustration by Pauline Baynes from *The Voyage of the Dawn Treader* by C.S. Lewis. Copyright 1952 by Macmillan Publishing Co., Inc. Reprinted by permission of Collier Books, a division of Macmillan, Inc.

WILLIAM COLLINS & SONS, LTD. (Glasgow). Illustration by Adriana Saviozzi Mazza from *Fables of Leonardo da Vinci* interpreted and transcribed by Bruno Nardini. English language text copyright © 1973 by William Collins & Sons, Ltd. Reprinted by permission of William Collins & Sons, Ltd.

WILLIAM COLLINS & SONS, LTD. (London). Illustration by Pauline Baynes from "Thumbelina" in *Andersen's Fairy Tales* by Hans Christian Andersen. Reprinted by permission of William Collins & Sons, Ltd.

WILLIAM COLLINS & WORLD PUBLISHING CO., INC. Illustration by James Daugherty from *The Last of the Mohicans* by James Fenimore Cooper. Special contents copyright © 1957 by the World Publishing Co. Reprinted by permission of William Collins & World Publishing Co., Inc.

THOMAS Y. CROWELL CO., INC. Illustration by Moneta Barnett from *Me and Nessie* by Eloise Greenfield. Illustrations copyright © 1975 by Moneta Barnett./ Illustration by Paul Galdone from *Paul Revere's Ride* by Henry Wadsworth Longfellow. Illustrations copyright © 1963 by Paul Galdone./ Sidelight excerpts from *Recollections of Johanna Spyri's Childhood* by Anna Ulrich, translated by Helen B. Dole. All reprinted by permission of Thomas Y. Crowell Co., Inc.

CROWN PUBLISHERS, INC. Illustration from *Nature's Ways: How Nature Takes Care of Its Own* by Roy Chapman Andrews. Copyright 1951 by Crown Publishers, Inc. and Creative Bookmaking Guild, Inc./ Illustration by Edmund Dulac from "Blue Beard" in *The Sleeping Beauty and Other Fairy Tales* retold by Sir Arthur Quiller-Couch./ Photograph from *Gertrude Stein* by Howard Greenfeld. Photo courtesy of *Pictorial Parade.* Copyright © 1973 by Howard Greenfeld. All reprinted by permission of Crown Publishers, Inc.

DELACORTE PRESS. Jacket painting by Gary Watson from *Rumble Fish* by S.E. Hinton. Copyright © 1975 by S.E. Hinton. Reprinted by permission of Delacorte Press, a division of Dell Publishing Co., Inc.

J.M. DENT & SONS, LTD. Illustration by Joan Kiddell-Monroe from *The Song of Hiawatha* by H.W. Longfellow. Introduction and illustrations copyright © 1960 by J.M. Dent & Sons, Ltd./ Illustration by Vincent O. Cohen from *Heidi* by Johanna Spyri./ Illustration by Arthur Rackham from *Gulliver's Travels* by Jonathan Swift. All reprinted by permission of J.M. Dent & Sons, Ltd.

DODD, MEAD & CO. Illustrations by H.M. Brock and Frank T. Merrill from *The Last of the Mohicans* by James Fenimore Cooper./ Photographs from *The Pathfinder* by James Fenimore Cooper./ Illustration by F.O.C. Darley from *The Pioneers* by James Fenimore Cooper./ Drawings by F.O.C. Darley and J. Hamilton and photographs from *The Prairie* by James Fenimore Cooper./ Illustration by Jean de Bosschere from *Gulliver's Travels* by Jonathan Swift. All reprinted by permission of Dodd, Mead & Co.

DOUBLEDAY & CO., INC. Drawing by Thomas W. Voter and sidelight excerpts from *An Explorer Comes Home* by Roy Chapman Andrews. Copyright 1939, 1940, 1945, 1946, 1947 by Roy Chapman Andrews./ Illustration by Charles W. Walker from *White Water, Still Water* by J. Allan Bosworth. Copyright © 1966 by J. Allan Bosworth./ Illustration by Edmund Dulac from *Treasure Island* by Robert Louis Stevenson./ Illustration by Ib Ohlsson from *The Mysterious Bender Bones* by Susan Meyers. Copyright © 1970 by Susan Meyers./ Illustration by Roberta MacDonald from *Heidi* by Johanna Spyri. Illustrations copyright MCMLIV by Nelson Doubleday, Inc./ Illustration by John Corbino from *Gulliver's Travels* by Jonathan Swift. Copyright 1945 by Doubleday & Co. All reprinted by permission of Doubleday & Co., Inc.

ELSEVIER-DUTTON PUBLISHING CO., INC. Illustration by Jessie Willcox Smith and Harrison Cady from *Bugs and Wings and Other Things* by Annie W. Franchot. Copyright 1918 by E.P. Dutton & Co. Reprinted by permission of Elsevier-Dutton Publishing Co., Inc.

FOUR WINDS PRESS. Illustration by Tony Chen from *About Owls* by May Garelick. Text copyright © 1975 by May Garelick. Illustrations copyright © 1975 by Anthony Chen./ Illustration by Jacquie Hann from *That Man is Talking to His Toes* by Jacquie Hann. Copyright © 1976 by Jacquie Hann. Both reprinted by permission of Four Winds Press, a division of Scholastic Book Services.

GARRARD PUBLISHING CO. Illustration by June Goldsborough from *Tanya and the Geese* by Jane Werner Watson. Copyright © 1974 by Jane Werner Watson. Reprinted by permission of Garrard Publishing Co.

GOLDEN PRESS. Illustration by Gustaf Tenggren from *Little Black Sambo* by Helen Bannerman. Copyright 1948 by Simon and Schuster, Inc. and Artists and Writers Guild, Inc. Reprinted by permission of Golden Press, a division of Western Publishing Co., Inc.

GREENWILLOW BOOKS. Illustration by Douglas Florian from *Tit for Tat* by Dorothy O. Van Woerkom. Copyright © 1977 by Douglas Florian. Reprinted by permission of Greenwillow Books, a division of William Morrow & Co.

GROSSET & DUNLAP, CO. Illustration by Harrison Cady from *The Adventures of Chatterer the Red Squirrel* by Thornton W. Burgess. Copyright 1943 by Thornton W. Burgess./ Illustration by William Sharp from *Heidi* by Johanna Spyri, translated by Helen B. Dole. Copyright 1945 by Grosset and Dunlap./ Illustration by Aldren Watson from *Gulliver's Travels* by Jonathan Swift. Special contents of this edition copyright 1947 by Grosset and Dunlap, Inc. All reprinted by permission of Grosset & Dunlap, Co.

HARCOURT BRACE JOVANOVICH, INC. Illustrations by Reginald Birch from *Rainbow in the Sky* by Louis Untermeyer. Copyright 1935 by Harcourt Brace and World, Inc. Copyright © 1963 by Louis Untermeyer./ Illustration by Peter Boston from *The River at Green Knowe* by L.M. Boston. Copyright © 1959 by Lucy Maria Boston./ Illustration by Harper Johnson from *Bemba* by Andree Clair. Copyright © 1962 by Harcourt Brace and World, Inc./ Illustration by James J. Spanfeller from *A Tune Beyond Us*, edited by Myra Cohn Livingston. Copyright © 1968 by Myra Cohn Livingston. Illustrations copyright © 1968 by Harcourt Brace and World, Inc./ Illustrations by Heidrun Petrides from *Hans and Peter* by Heidrun Petrides. Copyright © 1962 by Atlantis Verlag, Zurich. English translation copyright © 1962 by Oxford University Press. All reprinted by permission of Harcourt Brace Jovanovich, Inc.

HARPER & ROW, PUBLISHERS. Sidelight excerpts from *When Children Ask* by Margueritte Harmon Bro. Copyright 1940, 1956 by Margueritte Harmon Bro./ Illustration by Frank Schoonover from *The Deerslayer or The First Warpath* by James Fenimore Cooper. Copyright 1926, 1953 by Harper & Row, Publishers, Inc./ Illustrations by A.B. Frost from *Brer Rabbit: Stories from Uncle Remus* by Joel Chandler Harris. Copyright 1941 by Harper & Bros./ Illustration by Frank Schoonover from *Heidi* by Johanna Spyri. All reprinted by permission of Harper & Row, Publishers.

HARVARD UNIVERSITY PRESS. Sidelight excerpts from *The Letters and Journals of James Fenimore Cooper*, Volumes I and II, edited by James Franklin Beard. Copyright © 1960 by the President and Fellows of Harvard College./ Sidelight excerpts from *The Letters and Journals of James Fenimore Cooper*, Volume VI, edited by James Franklin Beard. Copyright © 1968 by the President and Fellows of Harvard College. All reprinted by permission of The Belknap Press of Harvard University Press.

HARVEY HOUSE, PUBLISHERS, INC. Illustration by Beverly Dobrin Wallace from *The Secret of Bruja Mountain* by Mary Louise Sherer. Copyright © 1972 by Harvey House, Inc. Reprinted by permission of Harvey House, Publishers, Inc.

HASTINGS HOUSE, PUBLISHERS, INC. Illustration by Marian Parry from *The Zoo Conspiracy* by Betty Levin. Copyright © 1973 by Betty Levin. Reprinted by permission of Hastings House, Publishers, Inc.

HAWTHORN BOOKS, INC. Sidelight excerpts from *Adventuring with Beebe* by William Beebe. Copyright 1956 by William Beebe./ Sidelight excerpts from *Unseen Life of New York* by William Beebe. Copyright 1953 by William Beebe./ Sidelight excerpts from *High Jungle* by William Beebe. Copyright 1949, 1977 by William Beebe./ Illustration by Howard Simon from *Evangeline: A Tale of Acadie* by Henry Wadsworth Longfellow, edited by Mina Lewiton. Introductory text copyright © by Mina Lewiton. Illustrations copyright © by Howard Simon. All reprinted by permission of Hawthorn Books, Inc., division of Elsevier-Dutton Publishing Co., Inc.

WILLIAM HEINEMANN, LTD. Illustration by Rowland Hilder from *The Midnight Folk* by John Masefield. Copyright © 1957 by John Masefield./ Illustration by Jean de Bosschere from *Gulliver's Travels* by Jonathan Swift. Both reprinted by permission of William Heinemann, Ltd.

HODDER & STOUGHTON, LTD. Illustration by Edmund Dulac from *Shakespeare's Comedy of The Tempest* by William Shakespeare./ Illustrations by Edmund Dulac from *Stories from Hans Andersen.* All reprinted by permission of Hodder & Stoughton, Ltd.

HOLIDAY HOUSE, INC. Jacket illustration by Gail Owens from *My Mom, the Money Nut* by Betty Bates. Copyright © 1979 by Betty Bates./ Illustration by Dick Gackenbach from *Is Milton Missing?* by Steven Kroll. Illustrations copyright © 1975 by Dick Gackenbach. Both reprinted by permission of Holiday House, Inc.

HOLT, RINEHART & WINSTON, INC. Illustration by E. Boyd Smith from *The Last of the Mohicans: Or a Narrative of 1757* by James Fenimore Cooper. Copyright 1910 by Henry Holt & Co./ Illustration by Carlos Antonio Llerena from *Sticks, Stones* by Carlos Antonio Llerena. Copyright © 1977 by Carlos Antonio Llerena./ Illustration by Dorothy Schmiderer from *The Alphabeast Book: An Abecedarium* by Dorothy Schmiderer. Copyright © 1971 by Dorothy Schmiderer./ Illustration by Don Freeman from *Come One, Come All!* by Don Freeman. Copyright 1949 by Don Freeman. All reprinted by permission of Holt, Rinehart & Winston, Inc.

HORN BOOK, INC. Sidelight excerpts from "Reginald Birch: Gallant Gentleman and Distinguished Illustrator" by Elizabeth Bevier Hamilton, January-February, 1944 in *Horn Book* magazine. Copyright 1944 by The Horn Book, Inc./ Sidelight excerpts from *Illustrators of Children's Books, 1946-1956* by Bertha M. Miller and others, compilers. Both reprinted by permission of Horn Book, Inc.

HOUGHTON MIFFLIN CO. Illustration by Conrad and Mary Buff from *The Apple and the Arrow* by Conrad and Mary Buff. Copyright 1951 by Mary Marsh Buff and Conrad Buff./ Illustrations by A.B. Frost from *The Favorite Uncle Remus* by Joel Chandler Harris. Copyright 1948 by Houghton Mifflin Co./ Illustration by A.B. Frost from *Uncle Remus: His Songs and Sayings* by Joel Chandler Harris. Copyright 1908, 1921 by Esther La Rose Harris./ Sidelight excerpts from *The Man with the Calabash Pipe* by Oliver La Farge, edited by Winfield Townley Scott. Copyright © 1966 by Consuelo de Baca La Farge./ Illustration by Karl Larsson from *The Mother Ditch* by Oliver La Farge. Copyright 1954 by Oliver La Farge and Karl Larsson./ Sidelight excerpts from *Raw Material* by Oliver La Farge. Copyright © 1969, 1970, 1971, 1972 by Consuelo de Baca La Farge./ Illustration by N.C. Wyeth from *The Courtship of Miles Standish* by Henry Wadsworth Longfellow. Illustrations by Frank Schoonover, N.C. Wyeth, Howard Smith, and C.W. Ashley from *The Children's Own Longfellow* by Henry Wadsworth Longfellow. Copyright 1908 by Houghton Mifflin Co./ Illustration by Milo Winter from *Story-Telling Ballads* by Frances Jenkins Olcott. Copyright 1920 by Houghton Mifflin Co./ Illustration by Willy Pogany from *Bible Stories to Read and Tell,* selected and arranged by Frances Jenkins Olcott. Copyright 1916 by Frances Jenkins Olcott and Willy Pogany. All reprinted by permission of Houghton Mifflin Co.

INDIANA UNIVERSITY PRESS. Sidelight excerpts from *Indian Man: A Life of Oliver La Farge* by D'Arcy McNickle. Copyright © 1971 by Indiana University Press. Reprinted by permission of Indiana University Press.

ALFRED A. KNOPF, INC. Illustration by Jonathan David from *Dugout Mystery* by M.G. Bonner. Copyright 1953 by Alfred A. Knopf, Inc./ Photograph by Nadar from *Nadar* by Nigel Gosling. Copyright © 1976 by Nigel Gosling. Both reprinted by permission of Alfred A. Knopf, Inc.

THE LIMITED EDITIONS CLUB. Illustration by John Stewart Curry from *The Prairie* by James Fenimore Cooper. Reprinted by permission of The Limited Editions Club.

J.B. LIPPINCOTT CO. Illustrations by Helen Bannerman from *The Story of Little Black Sambo* by Helen Bannerman./ Sidelight excerpts from "L.M. Boston Writes" from *A Sense of Story: Essays on Contemporary Writers for Children* by John Rowe Townsend. Copyright © 1971 by John Rowe Townsend. All reprinted by permission of J.B. Lippincott Co.

LITTLE, BROWN & CO. Illustration by William D. Berry from *How to Understand Animal Talk* by Vinson Brown. Copyright © 1958 by Vinson Brown./ Illustration by Marvin Friedman from *Pinch* by Larry Callen. Text copyright © 1975 by Larry Callen./ Illustration by Leonard B. Lubin from *The Perfect Peach* by Stephen Schwartz. Copyright © 1977 by Stephen Schwartz and Leonard B. Lubin. All reprinted by permission of Little, Brown & Co.

MACMILLAN & CO., LTD. (London). Illustration by Arthur B. Frost from *Rhyme? and Reason?* by Lewis Carroll. Reprinted by permission of Macmillan & Co., Ltd.

MACMILLAN, INC. Illustration by Zhenya Gay from *The Major and His Camels* by Miriam E. Mason. Copyright 1953 by the Macmillan Co./ Photograph from *Jimmy Doolittle* by Carroll V. Glines. Copyright © 1972 by Carroll V. Glines./ Photograph from *Young Longfellow (1807-1843)* by Lawrance Thompson. Copyright 1938 by the Macmillan Co./ Illustration by Judith Masefield from *The Dream and Other Poems* by John Masefield. Copyright 1922 and 1923 by John Masefield./ Sidelight excerpts from *Grace Before Ploughing* by John Masefield. Copyright © 1966 by John Masefield./ Illustration by Judith Masefield from *King Cole* by John Masefield. Copyright 1921, 1949 by John Masefield./ Sidelight excerpts from *In the Mill* by John Masefield. Copyright 1941 by John Masefield; renewal copyright © 1969 by Judith Masefield./ Sidelight excerpts from *So Long to Learn* by John Masefield. Copyright 1952 by John Masefield./ Illustration by Greta Elgaard from *Heidi* by Johanna Spyri. Afterword and illustrations copyright © 1962 by the Macmillan Co./ Illustration by Willy Pogany from *Gulliver's Travels* by Jonathan Swift, retold by Padraic Colum. Copyright 1917 by the Macmillan Co., copyright renewed 1945 by Padraic Colum and Willy Pogany. All reprinted by permission of Macmillan, Inc.

McGRAW-HILL, INC. Illustration by Joyce Bee from *Spiders and Scorpions* by J.L. Cloudsley-Thompson. Text copyright © 1973 by J.L. Cloudsley-Thompson. Illustration copyright © by Joyce Bee 1973./ Illustration by Jessica Ann Levy from *She Was Nice to Mice* by Alexandra Elizabeth Sheedy. Copyright © 1975 by Alexandra Elizabeth Sheedy and Jessica Ann Levy. All reprinted by permission of McGraw-Hill, Inc.

DAVID McKAY CO., INC. Photograph from *The Railroad Book* by Anne Feldman. Copyright © 1978 by Anne Feldman. Reprinted by permission of David McKay Co., Inc.

WILLIAM MORROW & CO., INC. Illustration by Leonard Shortall from *Just-In-Time Joey* by Leonard Shortall. Copyright ©1973 by Leonard Shortall. Reprinted by permission of William Morrow & Co., Inc.

W.W. NORTON & CO., INC. Illustration by James J. Spanfeller from *Joanna and Ulysses* by May Sarton. Copyright © 1963 by May Sarton. Reprinted by permission of W. W. Norton & Co., Inc.

OXFORD UNIVERSITY PRESS, INC. Illustration by Heidrun Petrides from *Hans and Peter* by Heidrun Petrides. Copyright © 1962 by Atlantis Verlag, Zurich. English translation copyright © 1962 by Oxford University Press./ Drawing by Robin Jacques from *Gulliver's Travels* by Jonathan Swift./ Sidelight excerpts from *Satires and Personal Writings* by Jonathan Swift, edited by W.A. Eddy. All reprinted by permission of Oxford University Press, Inc.

PANTHEON BOOKS, INC. Illustration by Hilary Knight from *That Makes Me Mad* by Steven Kroll. Text copyright © 1976 by Steven Kroll. Illustrations copyright © 1976 by Hilary Knight./ Illustration by James Spanfeller from *Dorp Dead* by Julia Cunningham. Copyright © 1965 by Julia Cunningham. All reprinted by permission of Pantheon Books, Inc., a division of Random House, Inc.

PARENTS' MAGAZINE PRESS. Etchings by Barbara Garrison from *The Sultan's Perfect Tree* by Jane Yolen. Text copyright © 1977 by Jane Yolen. Illustrations copyright © 1977 by Barbara Garrison./ Illustration by Helene Nyce from *A Jolly Christmas at the Patterprints* by Vera Nyce. Copyright © 1971 by Parents' Magazine Press. Both reprinted by permission of Parents' Magazine Press.

PENGUIN BOOKS, LTD. Sidelight excerpts from "L.M. Boston Writes" from *A Sense of Story: Essays on Contemporary Writers for Children* by John Rowe Townsend. Copyright © 1971 by John Rowe Townsend. Reprinted by permission of Penguin Books, Ltd.

PRENTICE-HALL, INC. Illustration by A.B. Frost from *Uncle Remus: His Songs and Sayings* by Joel Chandler Harris. Copyright 1908, 1921 by Esther La Rose Harris. Reprinted by permission of Prentice-Hall, Inc.

PUFFIN BOOKS. Illustration by Cecil Leslie from *Heidi* by Johanna Spyri. Copyright © 1956 by Penguin Books. Reprinted by permission of Puffin Books.

G.P. PUTNAM'S SONS. Photograph from *Ends of the Earth* by Roy Chapman Andrews. Copyright 1929 by The Curtis Publishing Co. Reprinted by permission of G.P. Putnam's Sons.

RAND McNALLY & CO. Illustration by Andriana Saviozzi Mazza from *Fables of Leonardo da Vinci,* interpreted and transcribed by Bruno Nardini. English language text copyright © 1973 by William Collins & Sons, Ltd./ Illustrations by Maginel Wright Enright from *Heidi* by Johanna Spyri, translated by Philip Schuyler Allen. All reprinted by permission of Rand McNally & Co.

RANDOM HOUSE, INC. Illustration by Thomas W. Voter from *All About Whales* by Roy Chapman Andrews. Copyright 1954 by Roy Chapman Andrews./ Illustration by Reginald Marsh from *The Prairie* (in *The Leatherstocking Saga*) by James Fenimore Cooper. Copyright 1954 by Pantheon Books./ Illustration by Henry C. Pitz from *The Vikings* by Elizabeth Janeway. Copyright 1951 by Elizabeth Janeway. All reprinted by permission of Random House, Inc.

RUSSELL & RUSSELL, PUBLISHERS. Sidelight excerpts from *Fenimore Cooper Critic of His Times* by Robert E. Spiller. Copyright 1931, 1959 by Robert Ernest Spiller. Reprinted by permission of Russell & Russell, Publishers.

BENJAMIN H. SANBORN & CO. Photograph by J. Gaberell from *Jorli: The Story of a Swiss Boy* by Johanna Spyri. Copyright 1924 by Benjamin H. Sanborn & Co. Reprinted by permission of Benjamin H. Sanborn & Co.

SCARECROW PRESS, INC. Sidelight excerpts from "Portrayal of the Black in Children's Literature," in *The Black American in Books for Children: Readings in Racism* by Jessie M. Birtha, edited by Donnarae MacCann and Gloria Woodard. Reprinted by permission of Scarecrow Press, Inc.

SCHOLASTIC BOOK SERVICES. Illustration by Leonard Shortall from *Deadline at Spook Cabin* by Eugenia Miller. Copyright © 1958 by Eugenia Miller. Reprinted by permission of Scholastic Book Services.

CHARLES SCRIBNER'S SONS. Illustration by N.C.Wyeth from *The Deerslayer* by James Fenimore Cooper. Copyright 1925, 1953 by Charles Scribner's Sons./ Sidelight excerpts from *Edmund Dulac* by Colin White. Copyright © 1976 by Colin White./ Sidelight excerpts from *All In the Day's Riding* by Will James. Copyright 1933 by Charles Scribner's Sons; renewal copyright © 1961 by Auguste Dufault./ Illustration by Will James and photograph from *Big Enough* by Will James. Copyright 1931 by Charles Scribner's Sons./ Sidelight excerpts from *Cowboys North and South* by Will James. Copyright 1924 by Charles Scribner's Sons; renewal copyright 1952 by Auguste Dufault./ Illustration by Will James from *The Drifting Cowboy* by Will James. Copyright 1925 by Charles Scribner's Sons./ Sidelight excerpts from *Lone Cowboy: My Life Story* by Will James. Copyright 1930, 1952 by Charles Scribner's Sons; renewal copyright © 1958 Auguste Dufault./ Illustration by Will James from *Look-See with Uncle Bill* by Will James. Copyright 1938 by Charles Scribner's Sons; renewal copyright © 1965 by Auguste Dufault./ Illustration by Will James from *Scorpion: A Good Bad Horse* by Will James. Copyright 1936 by Charles Scribner's Sons; renewal copyright © 1964 by Auguste Dufault./ Illustration by Will James from *Smoky the Cow Horse* by Will James. Copyright 1926 Charles Scribner's Sons; renewal copyright 1954 by Auguste Dufault./ Illustration by Felix Mendelssohn from *Felix Mendelssohn* by Herbert Kupferberg. Copyright © 1972 by Herbert Kupferberg./ Sidelight excerpts from *Jonathan Swift* by A.L. Rowse. Copyright © 1975 by A.L. Rowse. All reprinted by permission of Charles Scribner's Sons.

SCROLL PRESS, INC. Illustration by Xavier Cugat from *Pepito: The Little Dancing Dog* by Mark Evans. Text and illustrations copyright © 1979 by Mark Evans and Xavier Cugat. Reprinted by permission of Scroll Press, Inc.

STUDIO VISTA. Photographs from *Edmund Dulac* by Colin White. Copyright © 1976 by Colin White. Reprinted by permission of Studio Vista, a division of Cassell & Collier Macmillan Publishing Co., London.

TRIANGLE PUBLISHING, INC. Sidelight excerpts from an article "Face to Face," October, 1967 in *Seventeen*. Reprinted by permission of Triangle Publishing, Inc.

CHARLES E. TUTTLE CO. Illustration by Herbert Meyer from *The Song of Hiawatha* by Henry Wadsworth Longfellow. Copyright (Japan) © by Charles E. Tuttle Co., Inc. Reprinted by permission of Charles E. Tuttle Co.

THE VIKING PRESS, INC. Illustration by Mary and Conrad Buff from *Big Tree* by Mary and Conrad Buff. Copyright 1946 by Mary Marsh Buff and Conrad Buff./ Illustration by Conrad Buff from *Dash & Dart* by Mary and Conrad Buff. Copyright 1942 by Mary Marsh Buff and Conrad Buff./ Copyright 1942 by Mary Marsh Buff and Conrad Buff. Both reprinted by permission of The Viking Press, Inc.

FREDERICK WARNE & CO., INC. Illustration by Clinton Arrowood from *Witch, Witch!*, edited by Richard Shaw. Copyright © 1975 by Frederick Warne and Co., Inc./ Jacket illustration by Ronald Himmler from *Four Miles to Pinecone* by Jon Hassler. Copyright © 1977 Jon Hassler. Both reprinted by permission of Frederick Warne & Co., Inc.

WATSON-GUPTILL PUBLICATIONS. Sidelight excerpts from *Forty Illustrators and How They Work* by Ernest W. Watson. Reprinted by permission of Watson-Guptill Publications.

FRANKLIN WATTS, INC. Photograph from *The First Book of the Netherlands* by Angelo Cohn. Copyright © 1962, 1971 by Franklin Watts. Reprinted by permission of Franklin Watts, Inc.

WEATHERVANE BOOKS. Illustration by Edmund Dulac from *Rubaiyat of Omar Khayyam* rendered into English verse by Edward Fitzgerald./ Illustration by Edmund Dulac from *Sindbad the Sailor and Other Stories from the Arabian Nights*. Both reprinted by permission of Weathervane Books.

WESTERN PUBLISHING CO., INC. Illustration by Leonard Shortall from *Little Toad to the Rescue* by Leonard Shortall. Copyright © 1977 by Western Publishing Co., Inc. Reprinted by permission of Western Publishing Co., Inc.

WINDMILL BOOKS, INC. Illustration by Joseph Low from *Paul Revere's Ride* by Henry Wadsworth Longfellow. Illustrations copyright © 1973 by Joseph Low. Reprinted by permission of Windmill Books, Inc.

Photograph of Henry Wadsworth Longfellow by Julia Margaret Cameron from *Victorian Photographs of Famous Men and Fair Women*, preface and notes by Tristram Powell. Copyright © 1973 by The Hogarth Press. Reprinted by permission of A & W Visual Library./ Sidelight excerpts from *Under a Lucky Star* by Roy Chapman Andrews. Reprinted by permission of the estate of Roy Chapman Andrews./ Portrait of Cooper by Carel Christiaan Anthony Last. Courtesy of Collection of American Literature, The Beinecke Rare Book and Manuscript Library, Yale University./ Painting of A.B. Frost by J.W. Alexander. Reprinted by permission of the Bettman Archive./ Poster for *Macbeth* by Dulac in 1911. Reprinted by permission of the British Museum./ Illustration by Kurt Wiese from *Su-mei's Golden Year* by Margueritte Harmon Bro. Copyright 1950 by Margueritte Harmon Bro. Reprinted by permission of Andrew Bro./ Illustration by Leonard B. Lubin from *The Perfect Peach* by Stephen Schwartz. Copyright © 1977 by Stephen Schwartz and Leonard B. Lubin. Reprinted by permission of Sheldon Fogelman./ Lithograph of Cooper by Julien Leopold Boilly. Courtesy of the Historical Society of Pennsylvania./ Sidelight excerpts from *The Man with the Calabash Pipe* by Oliver La Farge, edited by Winfield Townley Scott. Copyright © 1966 by Consuelo de Baca La Farge. Reprinted by permission of the estate of Oliver La Farge./ Sidelight excerpts from *Raw Material* by Oliver La Farge. Copyright © 1969, 1970, 1971, and 1972 by Consuelo de Baca La Farge. Reprinted by permission of the estate of Oliver La Farge./ Grant Wood's painting of "The Midnight Ride of Paul Revere." Reprinted by permission of Metropolitan Museum of Art and Visual Artists and Galleries Associated, Inc./ Sidelight excerpts from "Home to Moberly," by Jack Conroy in *Missouri Library Association Quarterly*. Copyright © 1968 by Jack Conroy. Reprinted by permission of *Missouri Library Association Quarterly*./ Photographs from *Historical Catastrophies: Snowstorms and Avalanches* by Walter R. Brown and Norman D. Anderson./ Illustrations copyright © 1976 by Addison-Wesley. Text copyright © 1976 by Walter R. Brown and Norman D. Anderson. Reprinted by permission of the National Oceanic and Atmospheric Administration and The New York Historical Society./ Photograph from *Natural Man, The Life of William Beebe* by Robert Henry Welker. Copyright © 1975 by Indiana University Press. Reprinted by permission of the New York Zoological Society./ Sidelight excerpts from *A.B. Frost Book* by Henry M. Reed. Reprinted by permission of Henry M. Reed./ Sidelight excerpts from "Comment on a Commentator," by Robert Lewis Shayon, July 11, 1953 in *Saturday Review*. Reprinted by permission of *Saturday Review*./ Illustration by Judith Masefield from *King Cole* by John Masefield. Copyright 1921, 1949 by John Masefield. Reprinted by permission of The Society of Authors and Judith Masefield./ Sidelight excerpts from *So Long to Learn* by John Masefield. Copyright 1952 by John Masefield. Reprinted by permission of The Society of Authors./ Sidelight excerpts from *In the Mill* by John Masefield. Copyright 1941 by John Masefield; renewal copyright © 1969 by Judith Masefield. Reprinted by permission of The Society of Authors./ Sidelight excerpts from *Grace Before Ploughing* by John Masefield. Copyright © 1966 by John Masefield. Reprinted by permission of The Society of Authors./ Sidelight excerpts from *Young Longfellow, (1807-1843)* by Lawrance Thompson. Copyright 1938 by the Macmillan Co. Reprinted by permission of Janet Thompson./ Engraving of Cooper by Madame Lizinska de Mirbel. Courtesy of the Yale University Library.

PHOTOGRAPH CREDITS

Roy Chapman Andrews: World Wide Photos; Pauline Baynes: P. & M. Photographic; William Beebe: (1931) N. C. Owen, (in the diving helmet) (1949) New York Public Library Picture Collection; A. B. Frost: The Bettman Archive; May Garelick: Bernard Bushkin; Barbara Garrison: Ed Lauit; Robert Hayden: C. H. Walton; Susan Meyers: Ilka Hartmann; Leonard Shortall: Lisa Bryon.

SOMETHING ABOUT THE AUTHOR

ANDREWS, Roy Chapman   1884-1960

PERSONAL: Born January 26, 1884, in Beloit, Wisconsin; died March 11, 1960; son of Charles Ezra (a wholesale druggist) and Cora May (Chapman) Andrews; married Yvette Borup, 1914 (divorced, 1930); married Wilhelmina Christmas, February 21, 1935; children: (first marriage) George Borup, Roy Kevin. *Education:* Beloit College, B.A., 1906; Columbia University, M.A., 1913. ·*Politics:* Republican. *Homes:* "Pondwood," Colebrook, Connecticut, and Tucson, Arizona.

CAREER: Explorer, naturalist, and author. Began working in the preparations department at the American Museum of Natural History, New York City, 1906, and took part in various museum expeditions; one-man whaling expedition to Vancouver Island and Alaska, 1908; special representative aboard the USS Albatross on a whale-studying voyage to the Dutch East Indies, Celebes, and Borneo, 1909-10; studied whales in Japanese and Korean waters, 1911-12; member of the Borden Expedition to Alaska, 1913; leader of the museum's Asiatic expeditions to Tibet, Southwest China, and Burma, 1916-17, Northern China and Outer Mongolia, 1919, and Central Asia, including the Gobi Desert, 1921-32; director of the museum, 1935-42, honorary director, beginning 1942. Narrator of the geography and science program, "New Horizons," on CBS' American School of the Air; widely known lecturer and speaker. *Military service:* Served in Naval Intelligence in China and Mongolia during World War I.

MEMBER: Member of numerous scientific societies both in the United States and abroad, including the National Geographic Society (fellow), American Museum of Natural History (New York City; honorary member), American Association for the Advancement of Science (fellow), American Philosophical Society of Philadelphia (fellow), New York Academy of Sciences, New York Zoological Society (fellow), Biological Society of Washington, California Academy of Sciences, Sigma Chi, Phi Beta Kappa. Also member of the Explorer's Club (president, 1931-35), Ends of the Earth Club, Angler's Club (New York City), Wilderness Club (Philadelphia), Wayfarer's Club (Chicago), Doolittle, Boone, and Crockett Club, Peking Club (Peking, China). *Awards, honors:* Elisha Kent Kane gold medal of the Philadelphia Geographic Society, 1929; Hubbard gold medal of the National Geographic Society, 1931; Explorer's Club medal, 1932; medal of Sigma Chi Fraternity, 1935; Charles P. Daly gold medal of the American Geographic Society, 1936; Vega gold medal of the Royal Swedish Anthropological and Geographic Society, 1937; Loczy medal of the Hungarian Geographic Society, 1937; Silver Buffalo award of the National Council of Boy Scouts of America, 1952; D.Sc. from Brown University, 1926, and Beloit College, 1928.

WRITINGS: Monographs of the Pacific Cetacea, [New York], 1914-16; *The Sci Whale,* [New York], 1916; *Whale Hunting With Gun and Camera,* Appleton, 1916; (with wife, Yvette Borup Andrews) *Camps and Trails in China: A Narrative of Exploration, Adventure, and Sport in Little-Known China,* Appleton, 1918; *Across Mongolian Plains: A Natu-*

ralist's Account of China's "Great Northwest", Appleton, 1921; *On the Trail of Ancient Man: A Narrative of the Field Work of the Central Asiatic Expeditions*, Putnam, 1926; *Ends of the Earth*, Putnam, 1929, reprinted, Tower Books, 1971; *The New Conquest of Central Asia*, American Museum of Natural History, 1932; *This Business of Exploring*, Putnam, 1935; *Exploring with Andrews* (selections for young readers), Putnam, 1938; *This Amazing Planet*, Putnam, 1940; *Under a Lucky Star: A Lifetime of Adventure* (autobiography), Viking, 1943; *Meet Your Ancestors: A Biography of Primitive Man*, Viking, 1945, reissued, 1967; *An Explorer Comes Home: Further Adventures of Roy Chapman Andrews* (autobiography), Doubleday, 1947; (editor) *My Favorite Stories from the Great Outdoors*, Greystone Press, 1950; *Nature's Ways: How Nature Takes Care of Its Own* (illustrated by Andre Durenceau), Crown Publishers, 1951, reissued, 1969; *Heart of Asia: True Tales of the Far East*, Duell, Sloan & Pearce, 1951; *Beyond Adventure: The Lives of Three Explorers*, Duell, Sloan & Pearce, 1954.

For children: *Quest in the Desert* (illustrated by Kurt Wiese), Viking, 1950, reissued, 1966; *All about Dinosaurs* (illustrated by Thomas W. Voter), Random House, 1953; *All about Whales* (illustrated by Voter), Random House, 1954; *Quest of the Snow Leopard* (illustrated by K. Wiese), Viking, 1955, reissued, 1969; *All about Strange Beasts of the Past* (illustrated by Matthew Kalmenoff), Random House, 1956; *In the Days of the Dinosaurs* (illustrated by Jean Zallinger), Random House, 1959.

ADAPTATIONS: "Frontiers of a Forbidden Land" (motion picture), American Museum of Natural History, 1918.

SIDELIGHTS: **January 26, 1884.** Born in Beloit, Wisconsin—the perfect environment for a budding explorer: "Beloit lay on the banks of the Rock River in a part of southern Wisconsin that was all fields and woods and rushing streams. I was like a rabbit, happy only when I could run out of doors. To stay in the house was torture to me then, and it has been ever since. Whatever the weather, in sun or rain, calm or storm, day or night, I was outside, unless my parents almost literally locked me in.

"The greatest event of my early life was when, on my ninth birthday, Father gave me a little single-barrel shotgun. Previous to this I had been allowed to shoot Grandfather's muzzle loader once or twice, but it was too much for me to negotiate with its forty-inch-long barrel.

". . . I never had any choice of a profession. I wanted to be an explorer and naturalist so passionately that anything else as a life work just never entered my mind. Of course, I didn't know *how* I was going to do it, but I never let ways and means clutter my youthful dreams. I have often said that if I had inherited ten million dollars at birth I should have lived exactly the kind of life I have lived with no inheritance at all.

". . . I began to mount [birds and animals] for others, and, since I was the only taxidermist in our neck o' the woods, I had as much as I could do during the fall shooting season. I used to have a sizable amount of money by Christmas, for every bird and deer head shot within a radius of fifty miles came to me if a sportsman wanted it mounted." [Roy Chapman Andrews, *Under a Lucky Star*, Viking, 1943.[1]]

1902. Entered Beloit College.

1905. Having nearly drowned, he watched helplessly as a friend drowned. "Although I was not physically sick after the experience, the shock and my sorrow over Monty's death played havoc with my nerves. During the next few weeks I lost forty pounds in weight and the slightest excitement would set my body to shaking and twitching painfully. All that spring and summer I spent most of the daylight hours wandering alone in the woods with field glasses and notebook studying birds and sleeping in the sun. After a year I had pretty well regained my weight and strength, but the tragedy left me with a nervous affliction from which I never recovered. Also my hair began to come out slowly and it did not stop until it was nearly gone."[1]

1906. Graduated from Beloit College." . . . The graduation exercises were in the morning and that afternoon I went into the woods alone and stayed for hours, mostly sitting on the river bank. Mentally I took myself apart and examined the pieces. I didn't like what I saw. On that June afternoon I changed from an irresponsible boy to a man just as though one suit of clothes had been taken off and another put on. . . ."[1]

July, 1906. Applied for job at American Museum of Natural History saying: "I'm not asking for a position. I just want to work here. You have to have someone to clean the floors."[1] Later, received assignment to construct a replica of a whale. "Construction details, however, were a hidden mystery to me, for I've never had the slightest interest in mechanics. My mind doesn't run that way any more than to mathematics. . . . The framework of angle iron and bass wood strips was impressive, for the whale boasted a length of seventy-six feet. But the paper wouldn't work. It buckled and cracked and sank in between the ribs. Our whale looked awful. It seemed to be in the last stages of starvation. I used to dream about it at night. . . .

"It was amazing what a well-regulated diet of papier-mâché did for the beast. He lost that pitiful, starved, lost-on-dry-land appearance, his sides filled out and became as smooth as a rubber boot; we could almost feel him roll and blow as we built him up with our new tonic. After eight months, the job was done. During thirty-five years our whale has hung in the gallery and is still as good as new. He has been stared at by millions of eyes, and is still one of the most popular exhibits in the Museum."[1]

1908. Went on whaling expedition for Victoria Pacific Whaling Company. "It was positively indecent the way I pried into the private lives of whales during those days at sea. With field glasses from the masthead, I watched the love-making of a pair of humpback whales fifty feet long. An amorous bull whale may be very amusing to us but to his lady friend he is doubtless as exciting as a matinee idol is to a debutante. In this particular case the gentleman whale executed a series of acrobatic performances evidently with the object of impressing the female. He stood on his head with the tail and fifteen feet of body out of water. The great flukes were waved slowly at first; then faster until the water was pounded into spray and the terrific slaps on the surface could be heard a mile away. This performance ended, he slid up close to the female, rolling about and stroking her with his right flipper. She lay on her side apparently enjoying his caresses. Then he backed off and dived. I thought he had left her for good but she lay quietly at the surface; she knew full well that he would not desert her—yet. He was gone for, perhaps, four minutes, then with a terrific rush he burst from the water throwing his entire fifty foot body straight up into the air. It was a magnificent effort and I was proud of him.

Sometimes the boat would touch the great whale's side.

Sailors used to call this "wood to the black skin."

(From *All About Whales* by Roy Chapman Andrews. Illustrated by Thomas W. Voter.)

Falling back in a cloud of spray he rolled over and over up to his mate, clasping her with both flippers. Both whales lay at the surface, blowing slowly, exhausted with emotion.

"I felt embarrassed to be spying on their love-making like a Peeping Tom but the Captain was made of sterner stuff. The exhibition left him cold. His materialistic mind visualized the thousands of dollars their carcasses would bring in oil and fertilizer to the exclusion of all else. From the mast head I pleaded with him to 'have a heart' but without avail. The ship slid closer and closer to the half slumbering lovers and bomb-harpoon crashed into the side of the amorous bull. Half an hour later the lady, too, was killed for she refused to leave the vicinity of her dead lord."[1]

Autumn, 1908. Returned from the expedition; wrote an account of it for *World's Work*. ". . . I realized before long that it was fun to relate my experiences but that I'd never be a great writer; that I couldn't produce literature. All I could do was to set down whatever story I had to tell as simply as possible. That is all I have tried to do ever since."[1]

1908. Entered Columbia University, studied comparative anatomy, and began lecturing.

1909-1910. Carried out a whale studying voyage in the Dutch East Indies. "Again I felt all of the sensations of wonder and joy I had known when, as a child, I had listened to my mother reading *Robinson Crusoe* to me over and over again, and I, in fantasy had lived on just such an island as this. Now here I was, with my childhood dreams come true. . . .

"We made our camp beside a huge rock and swung ship's hammocks from the branches of an overhanging tree to be well away from the land crabs. Disgusting creatures, these giant crabs, which swarm over a wounded animal, literally eating it alive, or one that is dead, if they are a little late in getting there. Half the specimens caught in my traps during the night were devoured before I could rescue them in the early morning. There was only one family of monkeys on the island and a few smaller mammals, but the place was alive with birds. Parrots flashed among the trees and beautiful cream-white pigeons with black wings and tails filled the air with soft cooings and fluttering wings.

"Each morning I was up at the first rosy flush of dawn to run the traps, explore every nook and cranny of the island, and shoot new birds. Then back to camp for a swim off the beach before settling down with the boys to skinning and preparing the day's specimens. In the afternoon we waded the tide pools, collecting fish, crabs, snails and everything that moved and was alive. The glorious weather held without a break. It was hot during the day, of course, but we wore nothing but a pair of trunks, and the nights were always cool.

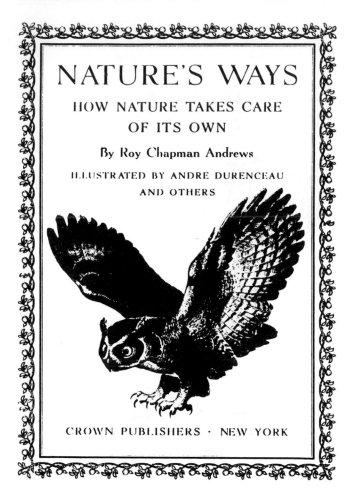

NATURE'S WAYS

HOW NATURE TAKES CARE
OF ITS OWN

By Roy Chapman Andrews

ILLUSTRATED BY ANDRE DURENCEAU
AND OTHERS

CROWN PUBLISHERS · NEW YORK

(From *Nature's Ways: How Nature Takes Care of Its Own* by Roy Chapman Andrews.)

"For five days I lived in a glow of ecstatic happiness and bemoaned the fact that the ship would return to end my island dream. . . .

"Curiosity about life has always been my dominant characteristic. I never can learn by someone else's experience; I must try it for myself. I had read about all sorts of temptations that the world had to offer. Some of them sounded exciting; some didn't. Anyway I was keen to try everything once and see what my personal reactions would be; to find out what sort of chap I really was inside. I don't think that I phrased it mentally but I did know that I was undertaking an exploration of myself. It was just as exciting as when later I stood on the top of a mountain in Central Asia looking out over a land which no white man had ever seen before and wondered what hidden secrets it contained. Thus my strictly personal adventure began."[1]

1911. Appointed assistant curator of Museum of Natural History. "The only trouble was that I never had time to 'curate.' In order to curate properly a curator must stay at home—at least some of the time. I couldn't do it. During all my years at the Museum I almost never returned from an expedition without having plans ready for another. I had found it wise to strike while the iron was hot. The enthusiasm of returning from a successful trip carried great weight in the plans for a new one. Then again, I was afraid I would get so immersed in Museum affairs that the authorities might

think I had better stay at home for a while. If the new trip had been approved, and was in the offing, it was much easier to keep my particular decks clear for action. Not that I didn't like Museum work. On the contrary, I loved it. The Museum had come to be a part of myself, and there was no phase of the activities in the great institution that did not fascinate me. But I loved wandering more. Sometimes when I walked across the park on a starlit summer night I used to look up at the drifting clouds, going with them in imagination far out to sea into strange new worlds. Then I would count the days that still remained before I could set my feet upon the unknown trails that led westward to the Orient. Seldom did I leave my office in the Museum before one o'clock in the morning. I had so much to do and so few hours in which to do it that I hated to waste any of them in sleep."[1]

1911-1912. Whaling expedition in Japanese and Korean waters. "During the next six weeks I examined more than forty gray whales; saw them hunted by men and killers; learned their clever tricks to avoid their enemies; and pieced together, bit by bit, the story of their wanderings. The days at sea were torture. Always heavy weather and deathly seasickness for me, bitter cold, sleet and ice. Standing behind the gun for hours on end, my oilskins stiff from frozen spray, I used to curse the sea. Why had I deliberately chosen a job which took me off the land? But hardly was I back on shore transcribing my wealth of new data before the suffering was forgotten and I was keen to go out again."[1]

1914. Married Yvette Borup.

March, 1916. Led expedition to hunt the "blue tiger" in South China. "I decided to go to the Salween even though we were flirting with death, for other collectors had avoided it like a plague spot and I knew that whatever mammals we obtained would be new to science. There were gloves and mosquito nets for every man, and I was prepared to give deep injections of quinine which is the only way successfully to battle the fever. So we went and remained ten days. Our reward was a fine collection of mammals and I was the only one who contracted fever. The mosquitoes bit me while I was waiting for peacocks on the river's edge, for I had lost my gloves. That night I was shot full of quinine and the next day we climbed gratefully five thousand feet out of the poison valley to the healthy ridges where we could look down upon the river winding like a thin green line below. For three days I shook with chills and burned as though there was fire in my blood, but the blessed quinine brought me through and never has the fever returned."[1]

1918. Sent to China to work for Navy intelligence during World War I.

1919. Explored deserts of Outer Mongolia. ". . . Loyal friends pledged enough money to make possible five months in the Gobi. It was to be a zoological expedition, of course, bringing to the Museum new collections of mammals and birds from an almost unknown country.

"Never, I think, have I been happier in the field than during that summer in Mongolia. There were no details or people to worry about; I could go where I pleased, enjoying every campfire and every day of brilliant sun. . . ."[1]

1921. Set out on an extensive expedition to explore the outer reaches of Mongolia, including the Gobi Desert. ". . . We should try to reconstruct the whole past history of the Central Asian plateau—its geology, fossils, past climate, and vegetation. We've got to collect its living mammals, birds, fish, reptiles, insects, and plants and map the unexplored parts of the Gobi. It must be a thorough job; the biggest land expedition ever to leave the United States.

"... In the desert, we had to create our own little world. There were no newspapers, letters, telegrams, or other diversions. Whatever we had, we had to make for ourselves. Day after day, we saw the same faces, learned every mannerism, the innermost secrets of a man's character.

"When one is at grips with crude nature, when the struggle to maintain oneself and do one's work against physical odds, is really on, the gloss of civilization quickly fades. It leaves character bare for all to see. There is little left to know about a man after one has lived with him in the field for a few weeks under primitive conditions. I had brought together a group of men who were considerate of their fellows, generous, unselfish, ready to accept the worst with the best; men so keen on their jobs that hardships were incidents; men with such steadfastness of purpose that nothing could turn them aside.

"I shall always remember the day we found the first fossils. Before we went to Mongolia, only one fragment of a 'rhinoceros' jaw had been discovered on the whole Central Asian plateau. At a promising looking exposure of yellow gravel on the edge of a great basin filled with camel sage. . . .

"Then we all laughed and shouted and shook hands and pounded one another on the back and did the things men do when they are very happy. No prospector ever examined the washings of a gold pan with greater interest than that with which we handled that little heap of fossil bones. Some we knew were rhinoceros and we were sure that others were titanotheres. That was what was so exciting, for *no titanotheres had ever before been discovered outside of America.* . . .

"The evening of August 4 was one of the high spots of the first expedition. We were camped on the shore of a lovely desert lake called by the Mongols, Chagan Nor, the 'White Lake.' Across the water, beyond a rim of fantastic sand dunes, toward the eastern Altai Mountains lay a new and enticing world, completely unexplored.

"My journal says: 'Late in the afternoon, there was a little rain and just at sunset a glorious rainbow stretched its fairy arch from the plain across the lake to the summit of Baga Bogdo. Below it the sky was ablaze with ragged tongues of flame; in the west billowy gold-margined clouds shot through with red, lay thick upon the desert. Wave after wave of light flooded the mountain across the lake—lavender, green and deepest purple—colors which blazed and faded almost before they could be named. We exclaimed breathlessly at first and then grew silent with awe. Never might we see the like again. Suddenly a black car with Granger and Shackelford in it came out of the north and slipped quietly into camp. Even Shackelford's buoyant spirit was stilled by the grandeur of what was passing in the sky. Not until the purple twilight had settled over mountain, lake, and desert, did the two men tell us why they had been so late. They had discovered parts of the skeleton of a *Baluchitherium*!'

"The 'Beast of Baluchistan' was the largest mammal ever known to have lived upon the earth. Only a neck vertebrae and foot bones had been found in India by my old friend C. Forster Cooper of Cambridge University, England, and one could only guess what sort of creature it would prove to be.

Now the mystery would be dispelled. Except for the remains of primitive man, no discovery could have been more exciting to a palaeontologist.

"My journal goes on to say:

"'The parts Granger had discovered were the end of the humerus, or upper fore-leg bone, and the whole side of the lower jaw with the teeth as large as apples, well preserved. I went to sleep very late that night, my mind full of *Baluchitherium* and had a vivid dream of finding the creature's skull in a canyon about fifteen miles from the spot where the jaw had been discovered the day before. I determined to go back to the place and make a further search.

"'With Shackelford, and a Chinese chauffeur, Wang, we returned to "Wild Ass Camp" the next afternoon. The two other men set to work in the bottom of the gully while I inspected the side, now and then sticking my pick into a bit of discolored earth. From the summit of the tiny ridge, I looked down the other side. Fragments of bone peeped out of the sand in the bottom of the wash. Its color was unmistakable. With a yell, I leaped down the steep slope. When "Shack" and Wang came around the corner on the run, I was on my knees, scratching like a terrier. Already a huge chunk of bone had been unearthed and a dozen other bits were visible in the sand. They were so hard we had no fear of breaking them. Laughing in hysterical excitement, we made the sand fly as we took out piece after piece of bone.

ROY CHAPMAN ANDREWS

"'Suddenly my fingers struck a huge block. Shack followed it down and found the other end; then he produced a tooth. My dream had come true! We had discovered the skull of a *Baluchitherium.*'

"The badlands were almost paved with white fossil bones and all represented animals unknown to any of us. Granger picked up a few bits of fossil egg shell which he thought were from some long-extinct birds. No one suspected, then, that these were the first dinosaur eggs ever to be discovered by modern man—or to be identified. Neither did we dream that the great basin with its beautiful sculptured ramparts would prove the most important locality in the world from a palaeontological standpoint. In the late afternoon sun the brilliant red sandstone seemed to shoot out tongues of fire and so we named the spot the 'Flaming Cliffs.'

"We had ... obtained complete skeletons of small dinosaurs, and parts of fifty foot dinosaurs, skulls of rhinoceros, hundreds of specimens, including skulls, jaws, and fragments, of mastodon, rodents, carnivores, horses, insectivores, deer, giant ostrich, and egg fragments. We had found wonderfully preserved Cretaceous mosquitoes, butterflies, and fish, unknown reptiles, titanotheroids, and other mammals."[1]

April 17, 1923. Set out on second Gobi expedition, making a stopover in China. He was accosted by a man with a rifle. "... Now, there were only two kinds of men who carried rifles in China—bandits and soldiers—and, at that time, the two were synonymous. Anyway, I had no mind to have him there, whoever he was. I dropped a bullet from my .38 revolver too close for comfort but didn't try to hit him. He disappeared abruptly.

"Just then my car swept over the rim of the basin and started down the slope. In the bottom two hundred yards away were four horsemen, rifles on their backs. I knew instantly they were bandits and I was in for it. The trail was narrow and rocky and I couldn't turn; also I knew that a Mongol pony never would stand against the charge of a motor car. Opening the cutout, I stepped on the accelerator and the car rushed down the hill roaring like an airplane. The ponies went mad with fright. At first the bandits tried to get the rifles off their backs, but in a moment their chief concern was to stay in their saddles. Three of the ponies rushed wildly across the valley, rearing and plunging madly. The fourth seemed too frightened to run. I was right beside him and I'll never forget the look of abject terror on the face of that Chinese brigand!

"The revolver was in my right hand and, of course, I could have killed him easily but there was no sense in doing that. But the peaked Mongol hat he wore bobbed up and down and was too great a temptation to be resisted. I fired at it four or five times, trying to knock it off his head. Finally his pony started after the others, with me right behind, yelling and shooting. When we reached the rim of the valley I let him go....."[1]

October, 1923. Returned to the U.S. from Shanghai, to a widely publicized reception of his expedition. "... The subject of radio came up and I happened to mention that I never had heard a broadcast. When I left America nearly three years before radio was in its swaddling clothes. During that brief time, the baby had grown enormously and already was almost as commonplace as an automobile. Mr. Ochs was excited. 'What! You never have heard a broadcast! Gentle-

men, this will be a rare treat. He really has been out of the world, hasn't he? ...'

"Dinosaur eggs! Dinosaur eggs! That was all I heard during eight months in America. There was no getting away from the phrase. Vainly did I try to tell of the other, vastly more important discoveries of the expedition. No one was interested. No one even listened. Eventually, I became philosophical about it. After all the situation had its bright side.

"I'm convinced the general public would help finance the expedition but they think small contributions aren't wanted. They believe this is only a rich man's show. If we could auction off one dinosaur egg as a contribution to the expedition's funds, it would be a grand publicity stunt. Every news story could explain that we've got to have money or quit work; that small contributions are more than welcome.

"... It proved to be a boomerang. Nothing else so disastrous ever happened to the expedition. Up to this time the Chinese and Mongols had taken us at face value. Now they thought we were making money out of our explorations. We had found about thirty eggs. If one was worth five thousand dollars, the whole lot must be valued at one hundred fifty thousand. They read about the other fossils—dinosaurs, titanotheres, *Baluchitherium.* Probably, those, too, were worth their weight in gold. Why should the Mongols and the Chinese let us have such priceless treasures for nothing! I had to combat this idea throughout all the remaining years of the expedition."[1]

1925. Continued desert explorations making discoveries at the "Flaming Cliffs." "... At the Flaming Cliffs we found seven skulls and parts of skeletons of these Mesozoic mammals. They were tiny creatures not larger than a rat and crawled about in the midst of dinosaurs at the close of the Age of Reptiles a hundred million years ago. After the dinosaur eggs have been forgotten these little skulls will be remembered by scientists as the crowning single discovery of our palaeontological research in Asia.

"We left the Flaming Cliffs with regret. They had given us more than we dared to hope from the entire Gobi—dinosaur eggs, a hundred skulls and skeletons of unknown dinosaurs, seven Mesozoic mammals, and the new Dune Dweller human culture. As my car climbed the steep slope to the eastern rim I stopped for a last look into the vast basin, studded with giant buttes like strange prehistoric beasts carved from sandstone. There were medieval castles with spires and turrets, colossal gateways, walls and ramparts; caverns that ran deep into the living rock, and a labyrinth of ravines and gullies. I would never see them again. 'Never' is a long word but I knew that for the last time my caravan had fought its way across the desolate reaches of the Gobi to this treasure vault of world history."[1]

1925. Dislocated his collar bone, and turned to writing while hospitalized. "... By putting together a lot of articles I had written for *Asia* magazine and dictating other chapters, the book was completed in a month. The title is *On the Trail of Ancient Man.* It isn't a very good book but not bad either, as my books go. Somewhat wooden in spots. Still, it does tell the story of those first three years well enough."[1]

1929. Lost investments in stock market crash. "Along with the other things I made a lot of money lecturing and writing. Our exposition was spot news and magazine editors paid well. I did a series of articles on the field work for the *Saturday Evening Post* and six or seven more on adventures.

These were combined in a book *Ends of the Earth* which sold like hot cakes. Always my lecture managers were pleading for more time. When I couldn't give it to them they boosted the fee. Even then I couldn't begin to fill the engagements offered. Money came easily and went just as easily. I never did have a grain of sense about my personal finances because wealth didn't interest me in the slightest. So long as I could do my job, that was all I cared about. If I had been sensible enough to put a third of my income into an annuity or a trust fund, I could have forgotten about money for the rest of my life. But, of course, I didn't. Some of my friends suggested that they could make me millions in the stock market so I let them 'invest' my money. Then . . . it dissolved like mist before the sun. It was all gone; there wasn't anything! But it didn't make me lose a single hour's sleep. I couldn't visualize a time when wealth would be necessary to my personal happiness. It never will be. My wants and needs are simple. So long as I have a gun to shoot, a good fly rod, and work to do, what can money buy in the way of happiness? Nothing, so far as I am concerned. But the gentle spur of necessity is a fine antidote to mental stagnation."[1]

1930. Divorced wife, Yvette.

1931-1932. Wrote narrative volume of the Central Asiatic expedition's final reports. "For years up to 1932 I was a regular commuter between the Orient and America. Sometimes I went by way of the trans-Siberian railway, sometimes southward through the Suez Canal. Each trip around the world seemed to reduce the globe in size. There was no more mental or physical effort involved in starting for Paris, Vienna or Moscow, Singapore, Hong Kong or Peking than in taking a train to Chicago. I had a horror of accumulating possessions or responsibilities which might anchor me in any one spot. A small army trunk and a suitcase were sufficient baggage for I had regular stopping places all over the world and deposits of clothes. The ship lanes of the seven seas and the cities of Europe or Asia were as familiar to me as the streets of New York.

"There were, of course, the usual rewards of a successful explorer; honorary degrees from universities, medals, and election to scientific societies. All of us on the expedition knew we had done a worth-while job. The results spoke for themselves. The satisfaction and excitement I had had in conceiving, organizing, and directing the expeditions were the important rewards. Don't mistake my meaning. I liked receiving medals that in half a century had been given only to seven or eight explorers such as Peary, Nansen, Scott, Shackleton, Amundsen, Byrd. It was enormously satisfying to have my name enrolled with theirs. I'd have been less than human not to have found it so. What I am trying to say is that I considered the public recognition only as a pleasant side issue of a job which in itself had given me ample reward."[1]

1935. Appointed Director of American Museum of Natural History.

February 21, 1935. Married Wilhelmina "Billie" Christmas. Went on skin diving trip to Bermuda. "Then I went down. At first I did not try to look. I was too occupied in staying on the swaying ladder. Near the end I stopped, clung with one hand and let my body float off obliquely. I was enveloped in a strange intense moonlight blue, darkening imperceptibly. Below, the same weird blue. I looked up. No water ceiling, no comforting shadow of the boat; only blue and darker blue. The absolute silence was appalling. A few feet away three

ROY CHAPMAN ANDREWS

great circular jelly fish, ghostly white, floated past. Others rose almost under my swaying body; a single color-less pulsing mass hung like a halo just above my head.

"Suddenly I was afraid. A nameless terror took possession of my bones and flesh and blood. It seemed that I had died and gone to some strange place unknown to human minds! Corpses, dead white, women with streaming hair floating past, staring at me with sightless eyes, should have been part of that ghastly world. The only touch of reality, my one tangible hold on the life I knew was the rung of that iron ladder.

"Rising to the surface was like waking from a nightmare. Yet we had not reached shore before I wanted to go down again. Analyzing, unemotionally, what had happened, I realized that I had been so completely absorbed in sensations that my brain had ceased to function. Had there been anything familiar, fish that I knew, coral, something other than that vast weird emptiness of blue and the ghostly jelly fish, I would not have been affected so profoundly. Doubtless were I to drift down again in the same place and under the same lowering sky I would not have that sensation of bodily detachment. But I am glad it happened just as it did. Otherwise I should have missed an extraordinary experience."[1]

1942. Resigned as museum director, retired to "Pondwood," his Connecticut farm, to write. "Never before had I wanted possessions; things that would anchor me to one spot. I wished only to be free to leave at a moment's notice for the ends of the earth. Billie, too, had the travel fever. Now we didn't want to go anywhere. It was, I suppose, the natural corollary to a life of continual change, like the desire of every deep sea sailor to have a farm and raise chickens.

"Though Billie and I had bought Pondwood Farm overnight, without looking at another place, we could not have found another property that would have suited us more completely had we searched for ten years. Groves of pines and hemlock, mixed forest, pond and swamp held birds of every kind. Splendid fishing and shooting were at our very doors. Again my Lucky Star had guided me, and together we had followed it blindly to happiness."[1]

"... I looked forward as much to the coming of spring at Pondwood as I did when a boy in Wisconsin. Then I wandered restlessly about our village home in the evening, filled with vague excitement and blood fever, pressing my face into the new grass, chewing the lilac buds, and straining my ears for the honk of wild geese flying to the river. The damp, sodden smell of the marshes and the *oka-ma-lee* of the redwing blackbirds perching on dead cattails were the most delightful odor and the sweetest music in the world. By a single revolution of the Wheel of Life it had all returned. There was one difference. In those days every week was a year; now every year is a week.

"... I loved the Museum, but after more than a quarter of a century of exploration I felt like an animal in the zoo which, captured late in life, could not adjust itself to crowds and people. In spite of interesting work, the longing for woods and fields, the smell of fresh grass, and the songs of birds, instead of carbon monoxide and the blare of motor horns, was an insistent call.

"Shortly after we bought the farm Billie and I started one cloudy morning to explore the more distant parts of our domain. Lord Jitters [a cat] was with us. On this particular day, I must admit, frankly, that I got lost. It is the cause of deep humiliation to me and of never-ending teasing by my wife. I would much prefer to let the distressing incident remain dead and buried, but that she will not do.

"I discovered a spot under a great beech tree, deep in the forest, where the birds twittered, the woodpeckers pecked, and I was alone. Blessed silence, except for the subdued voices of wild things. There I could write and 'list to nature's teachings.' " [Roy Chapman Andrews, *An Explorer Comes Home*, Doubleday, 1947.[2]]

"Every explorer must tell what he has done in order to maintain public interest and support. Writing was a necessary corollary of exploration.

"Suddenly the position was reversed. What had been an avocation became my vocation. Library interests were paramount and Billie's and my personal contacts changed immediately."[1]

"Heaven favors the poor workingman! In the next mail came a suggestion from a magazine that I do an article for them on dinosaurs. Would I do an article on dinosaurs! Would I! It solved my studio problem if I could satisfy the editor. Dinosaurs were right down my alley. Of course the blessed editor didn't know it, but dinosaurs were practically sitting on our

doorstep. He visualized the thousands upon thousands of miles I had traveled in quest of dinosaurs; he remembered that I had dug up some eggs, which I am never allowed to forget, in the Gobi Desert. To him I was the 'big egg man.'

"But Pondwood Farm is all things to a naturalist. Was there not a kitchen midden of extraordinary archaeological interest in our own front yard? The editor had asked for dinosaurs. Certainly. I had only to travel a few miles to be in the ancestral home of dinosaurs. Even Connecticut folklore has tales of the footprints of 'Noah's Raven.' They happen to be fossilized tracks of a birdlike dinosaur, but what is that to folklore?

"Life for me has been a series of distinctly separate episodes and violent contrasts. Each one, apparently, had no relation to the immediate past, yet in reality was a logical outgrowth of what went before. I had written eight books and dozens of magazine articles but never thought of myself as a writer. Every explorer must tell what he has done in order to maintain public interest and support of his expeditions. Writing was a necessary corollary to exploration but only an avocation. Radio, too, was an avocation which materially assisted my work. I sometimes wondered, vaguely, if I could make a living by writing. I never thought I wrote well, but believed that if I had time to devote to it exclusively I might do better. All my writing had been done under pressure—just snatching an hour here and there. I often carried the last page of a magazine article in my pocket and wrote a sentence or two while my shoes were being shined, while riding in a taxi, or waiting for a train. My books had been produced between expeditions, on ships, trains, and airplanes; often when I was too tired to care whether the stuff was good or bad—just to get what I had done down on paper. If an editor thought the field accomplishment was important enough to carry the deficiencies in expression that was the best I could hope for.

"I often thought how I would enjoy leisurely writing—when I felt like it, and only then. That happy day arrived when I retired. I now go to my study or log-cabin studio, pregnant with ideas waiting to be born into words. Sometimes the accouchement does not happen on schedule. Thoughts are elusive and defy me to express them on paper. So be it. I do not resort to a Caesarean operation. There are always trout or bass to be caught, and a rabbit to shoot or fox traps to tend in winter. I know full well that sometime that day, or the next, I will be eager to return to my desk.

"Frequently an idea comes at the most inopportune moment. Perhaps I have been mulling over a magazine article or a chapter in a new book. The facts are all there in my subconscious mind but they won't jell. Then, suddenly, I see it clearly. Sentences materialize, the picture takes shape. If I don't write it down instantly the inspiration is lost. One day Billie was in town. It was hot and I had been fishing. A magazine editor had asked me to do an article for him but I couldn't get started. So I took a cold bath and began to shave. For no reason whatever the whole article assumed concrete form. Face still lathered, I ran to my study to get the opening remarks on paper. The words just rushed—they came faster than my pencil could put them down. For four mortal hours I sat there, until the article was finished. My skin was stiff from the dried shaving soap, but I was afraid to interrupt the flow of thought. At the end I had a glow of satisfaction. Whether or not the editor would like my production seemed unimportant at the time. It was the best I could do and, in its way, had been as exciting as killing a thirty-pound salmon.

"Lord Jitters, may I present your readers?"...I forgot to say that Lord Jitters is a white Persian cat. ■ (From *An Explorer Comes Home* by Roy Chapman Andrews. Drawings by Thomas W. Voter.)

"While writing a book on human evolution called *Meet Your Ancestors,* one chapter, the story of Peking man, defeated me. It is full of the romance of a great discovery, but in spite of all I could do it remained as dead as the dodo. So, fishing rod in hand, I hied to Sandy Brook. The trout were rising avidly to a hatch of insects. I had just netted a fine fish and was drying my fly when I happened to see a stone shaped like a fist ax of Neanderthal man. While examining it, the ideas I had been trying to capture arranged themselves mentally like parts of a jigsaw puzzle falling into place.

"Trout or no trout, I dared not delay. I always carry a pencil in my pocket, but alas there was no paper. Looking wildly around, I spotted an enormous white birch tree and waded out of the stream. Stripping off a length of bark, I sat down with my back against a pine and began to write. For two hours I scribbled furiously, until the birch was denuded of bark as high as I could reach and the chapter finished. My back ached, my legs were cramped and stiff, but joy filled my heart. Packing my beautiful thoughts carefully in the creel, I wrapped the lone trout in ferns and set off happily up the hill. Billie met me in the gun room with an expectant look, for she likes trout."[2]

1943. Broke his leg. Andrews decided to write an autobiography. "... Complete isolation is no novelty to me. For months on end I have lived in the wilderness or on the desert divorced from all touch with civilization, dependent upon myself alone for the fundamentals of existence. I have always enjoyed the feeling. There is a sense of privacy in creating one's own little world where others cannot possibly intrude even by the printed or written word. Every man, woman, or child has obligations to someone else and to society from the moment he becomes of thinking age. But when one is completely isolated, physically, obligations cease to exist in one's mind. The enjoyment comes, of course, from an inborn selfishness; a natural desire to live, for a time, an absolutely individual existence. Still my separation from the world has always been self-imposed. To adjust one's mental perspective to forced isolation is quite another thing.

"... Everyone in the community knew that I was crippled because the newspapers had had a field day with headlines to the effect that: 'After thirty-five years of exploration, Andrews breaks leg at home.'

"The heat situation began to worry us a bit. Ordinarily we use the fireplaces simply for cheer. Warming the house with wood alone had made the stock in the cellar disappear like mist before the sun. So fires in the gun room and our bedroom were stopped and we continued only those in the kitchen and living room. Walter slipped and slid with his ax among the ice-covered branches on the lawn, trying to get something to eke out our meager store. But it was wet and green and gave out little heat.

"Meanwhile Billie and I were very busy. In the morning I was ensconced on the sofa in front of the fire and wrote steadily until late in the evening. Billie typed the sheets as they came from my pencil. After dark, with candles at my head, I looked very much like a corpse laid out for burial.

"*Under a Lucky Star* progressed rapidly. Billie found it interesting because, as my life story unfolded, she learned many details that were unknown to her, even though we had been married seven years. Some of them required a bit of adroit explanation. Now and then her typewriter stopped abruptly. After an interval of silence she would remark: 'Well, I never knew *that* before.'

"Almost all of it was drawn from memory. When I began to review my life from the beginning in orderly sequence, I was surprised how clearly some events stood out. They seemed to have been mental photographs, exactly as on a film, that had been filed away in my subconscious mind, and I could recall the most minute and unimportant details. It was like turning the pages of an album of snapshots."[2]

March 11, 1960. Suffered a fatal heart attack.

FOR MORE INFORMATION SEE: Stanley J. Kunitz and Howard Haycraft, editors, *Twentieth Century Authors*, H. W. Wilson, 1942, first supplement, 1955; Roy C. Andrews, *Under a Lucky Star: A Lifetime of Adventure*, Viking, 1943; Andrews, *An Explorer Comes Home: Further Adventures of Roy Chapman Andrews*, Doubleday, 1947; R. Dempewolff, "Born to Explore," *Science Illustrated*, February, 1948; Irving Stone and Richard Kennedy, editors, *We Speak for Ourselves*, Doubleday, 1950; Henry T. Schnittkind and Dana A. Schnittkind, *Living Adventures in Science*, Hanover House, 1954; R. C. Andrews, *Beyond Adventure*, Duell, Sloan & Pearce, 1954; Bernadine Bailey, *Famous Modern Explorers*, Dodd, 1963; Alonzo W. Pond, *Andrews: Gobi Explorer*, New Grosset, 1972; *From Whales to Dinosaurs*, St. Martin's, 1976.

Obituaries: *New York Times*, March 12, 1960, March 13, 1960; *Illustrated London News*, March 19, 1960; *Newsweek*, March 21, 1960; *Time*, March 21, 1960; *Publishers Weekly*, March 28, 1960; *Nature*, May 21, 1960; *Science*, July 1, 1960; *Current Biography Yearbook, 1960*; *Americana Annual, 1961*; *Britannica Book of the Year, 1961*.

ARROWOOD, (McKendrick Lee) Clinton 1939-

PERSONAL: Born October 16, 1939, in Price, Utah: son of Henry Elbert and Lila (McKendrik; a violinist) Arrowood; married Domenica Laura Vittoria Brunetta (a concert pianist), August 22, 1976; *Education:* Attended Peabody Conservatory of Music, Baltimore, Md., Vienna Academy of Music, Austria, two years; Johns Hopkins University, Baltimore, Md. *Home and office:* Garrison Forest School, Garrison, Maryland 21055.

CAREER: Illustrator; flutist. Garrison Forest School, Garrison, Md., teacher, 1968—. Gettysburg Symphony Orchestra, first flute, 1977. *Military service:* U.S. Army, played piccolo in Third U.S. Army Band, Spec. 4, Atlanta, Ga., 1965-67. *Member:* Greater Baltimore Flute Club (vice-president, 1977). *Awards, honors:* Senatorial Scholarship, Peabody Conservatory, 1960.

ILLUSTRATOR: Music for the Listener, Allyn & Bacon, 1970; Richard Shaw, *Witch, Witch! Stories of Sorcery Spells and Hocus-Pocus*, Warne, 1975; Donald Elliott, *Of Alligators and Music*, Gambit, 1976; Donald Elliott, *Frogs and Ballet*, Gambit, 1978.

SIDELIGHTS: "Music is the real joy of my life and the inspiration of my soul. Recognition and money have been strong motivations; I've received very little of either, but still I go on—perhaps then it's for other reasons.

"I never studied formally but I was largely influenced by Dr. Erwin Szilagyi, a Hungarian portrait painter and learned humanist [and also] (Dürer, Beardsley, Shepard, Rackham).

"I speak and write German and Italian."

CLINTON ARROWOOD

Dainty morsel! dainty morsel!
Little toothsome mankin come,
now let me see your thumb!
■ (From *Witch, Witch!* edited by Richard Shaw. Illustrated by Clinton Arrowood.)

HELEN BANNERMAN

BANNERMAN, Helen (Brodie Cowan Watson) 1863(?)-1946

PERSONAL: Born about 1863, in Edinburgh, Scotland; died October 13, 1946, in Edinburgh; daughter of Robert Boog Watson (an army chaplain); married William Burney Bannerman (a surgeon), 1889 (died, 1924); children: two daughters, two sons. *Education:* Educated by father, abroad, and through correspondence courses; St. Andrew's University, London, Eng., L.L.A. *Home:* India and Edinburgh, Scotland.

CAREER: Children's author.

WRITINGS—All illustrated by the author: *The Story of Little Black Sambo,* G. Richards, 1899, F. A. Stokes, 1900, reissued, Platt, 1978 [other editions include one with an introduction by L. Frank Baum, Reilly & Britton, 1905; and those illustrated by Kurt Wiese, Garden City Publishing, 1933; and Gustaf Tenggren, Simon & Schuster, 1948]; *The Story of Little Black Mingo,* J. Nisbet, 1901, reissued, Chatto, 1972; *The Story of Little Black Quibba,* F. A. Stokes, 1903, reissued, Chatto, 1960; *Little Dechie-Head: An Awful Warning to Bad Babas,* J. Nisbet, 1903, published in America as *The Story of Little Kettle-Head: An Awful Warning to Bad Babas,* F. A. Stokes, 1904; *Pat and the Spider: The Bitter Bit,* J. Nisbet, 1904, F. A. Stokes, 1905; *The Story of the Teasing Monkey,* F. A. Stokes, 1907; *The Story of Little Black Quasha,* F. A. Stokes, 1908, reissued, Chatto, 1960; *The Story of the Little Black Bobtail,* F. A. Stokes, 1909, reissued, Chatto, 1960; *Sambo and the Twins: A New Adventure of Little Black Sambo,* F. A. Stokes, 1936; *The Jumbo Sambo* (collection), F. A. Stokes, 1942; *The Story of Little White Squibba,* Chatto, 1966.

ADAPTATIONS: "Little Sambo" (filmstrip; 10 minutes, color), McGraw-Hill, 1960.

SIDELIGHTS: Chance led Helen Bannerman to write her famous children's book, *Little Black Sambo.* As a child her favorite books were "little ones" that she could hold in her hands and that was the kind of book she made for her own children.

Bannerman's father, Robert Boog Watson, was an army chaplain whose career led him to various parts of the British Empire. Until age ten, she was educated by her father and then sent to a Dame school back in Scotland. Her education continued abroad where she studied French and German. She later returned to Edinburgh and received her L.L.A. degree from St. Andrew's University through correspondence courses.

In 1889 she married William Burney Bannerman, a doctor in the British military service, and spent thirty years of her married life in India. She had four children; two sons and two daughters. The story of "Sambo" was written for her two little girls who had to be left in Scotland for their education and was written as much to comfort herself as to amuse her children.

The story of *Little Black Sambo* was so loved by her family and friends that Bannerman decided to send it to a London friend for publication. It first appeared in print in 1899. "Sambo" was followed by other little books written and illustrated by Bannerman. *The Story of the Teasing Monkey* was written for her younger son in 1906.

When William Bannerman died in 1924, his widow returned to Edinburgh to live with one of her daughters. Ten years before her death Bannerman was once again encouraged to write a sequel to "Sambo" by her publisher. At first she refused and told him, "You must remember that many years have passed. *Little Black Sambo* is a middle-aged gentleman now." [Helen Dean Fish, "The Story of Little Black Sambo," *Wilson Library Bulletin,* January, 1941.[1]]

Her grown daughter, however, persuaded her to write and illustrate *Sambo and the Twins: A New Adventure of Little Black Sambo.*

In October, 1946, the little, grey-haired Scotchwoman died at about eighty-three years of age at her daughter's home in Edinburgh. Helen Bannerman was described as a kind-faced woman with a definite "twinkle in her eyes."

Once a children's classic, *The Story of Little Black Sambo* has become a controversial book in England and America. Much of the American controversy which led to the book being banned from many children's libraries stemmed from the derogatory connotation of "Sambo" which evokes an image of a submissive and childish black. Jessie M. Birtha, in an article entitled "Portrayal of the Black in Children's Literature," suggested that the book should be placed in a special collection in the library, but not circulated. ". . . The usefulness of *Little Black Sambo* is dead. The acceptability of *Little Black Sambo* is dead. The story itself is not about an African child. It is about a child in India, and contains little in the slight plot that is objectionable, although as racial sensitivity and pride grew, the book has been dissected and all manner of symbolism attributed to its motivation, including sexual. However, a librarian will never offer this book to a black child if he stops to realize that the name Sambo has

So the Tiger got poor Little Black Sambo's beautiful little Blue Trousers, and went away saying, "Now I'm the grandest Tiger in the Jungle." ■ (From *The Story of Little Black Sambo* by Helen Bannerman.)

So he got poor Little Black Sambo's beautiful Green Umbrella, and went away saying, "Now I'm the grandest Tiger in the Jungle." ■ (From *The Story of Little Black Sambo* by Helen Bannerman. Illustrated by the author.)

been used so often to refer to a Negro in a derogatory sense. Remember that the end man in the minstrel show, the stupid one who was the butt of all the jokes, was Sambo. The ventriloquist's little black, red-lipped dummy was named Sambo. *Webster's Third New International Dictionary* defines Sambo as 'Negro, mulatto, perhaps from Kongo *nzambu,* monkey. Often capital: NEGRO—usually used disparagingly.'

"The argument has been offered, children don't know or care about the background of a name. They only listen to the story. But it has been proved—and experienced—that if a story of this type is used in an integrated story hour or classroom, there is a certain amount of discomfort and—yes, inferiority feeling—for a black child when white classmates look at him and giggle, later teasing him by calling him Sambo. No matter how entertaining a book is, one group of children should never be entertained at the expense of another group's feelings.

"... I am not saying that I advocate destroying all of the existing copies of such books. These books have been classics in children's literature and as such have value for adults in tracing the development of black children's literature. However, I feel that at this time, their existence should be relegated to the historical collection in the children's library." [Jessie M. Birtha, "Portrayal of the Black in Children's Lit-

erature," *The Black American in Books for Children: Readings in Racism,* edited by Donnarae MacCann and Gloria Woodard, Scarecrow Press, 1972.[2]]

The controversy has led to a publisher's dilemma, as Albert R. Levinthal, president of Golden Press, explained: "Golden Press has been critized from both sides. . . . Almost every time we reissue *Little Black Sambo* we receive mail deploring it. When it is not available in our Little Golden Book series, we have had letters asking why we do not keep this classic in print!"[2]

The American Library Association's Intellectual Freedom Committee, regarding *Little Black Sambo* and other racially controversial books, postulated that the parents, not librarians, were the sole arbiters in the selection of books for children. Therefore, despite concern from many Americans, Bannerman's classic story continues to remain in print eighty years after its inception.

FOR MORE INFORMATION SEE: Helen Dean Fish, "The Story of Little Black Sambo," *Wilson Library Bulletin,* January, 1941; Bertha E. Mahony and others, compilers, *Illustrators of Children's Books, 1744-1945,* Horn Book, 1947; Elizabeth R. Montgomery, *Story Behind Great Stories,* McBride, 1947; Stanley J. Kunitz and Howard Haycraft, edi-

And the Tigers all caught hold of each other's tails, as they wrangled and scrambled, and so they found themselves in a ring round the tree. ■ (From *The Story of Little Black Sambo* by Helen Bannerman. Illustrated by the author.)

Once upon a time there was a little black boy, and his name was Little Black Sambo. ■ (From *Little Black Sambo* by Helen Bannerman. Pictures by Gustaf Tenggren.)

tors, *Junior Book of Authors,* second edition revised, H. W. Wilson, 1951; Brian Doyle, *Who's Who of Children's Literature,* Schocken Books, 1968; Donnarae MacCann and Gloria Woodard, editors, *The Black American in Books for Children: Readings in Racism,* Scarecrow Press, 1972; Phyllis J. Yuill, *Little Black Sambo,* Racism & Sexism Resource Center for Educators, 1976.

Obituaries: *New York Times,* October 31, 1946; *Newsweek,* November 11, 1946; *Time,* November 11, 1946; *Publishers Weekly,* November 16, 1946; *Wilson Library Bulletin,* December, 1946; *Horn Book,* January, 1947.

(Died October 13, 1946)

BATES, Betty   1921-

PERSONAL: Born October 5, 1921, in Evanston, Ill.; daughter of Alexander Willett (a civil engineer) and Elizabeth (a teacher; maiden name, Bragdon) Moseley; married Edwin R. Bates (a lawyer), September 3, 1947; children: Thomas, Daniel, Lawrence, Sarah. *Education:* Attended National Park College, 1939-40, Beloit College, 1940-41, and Katharine Gibbs Secretarial School, 1941-42. *Home:* 5 Milburn Park, Evanston, Ill. 60201.

CAREER: Worked as a secretary, 1942-48; writer, 1963—. Past member of Evanston board of directors of Rehabilitation Institute of Chicago. *Member:* Authors Guild, Evanston Board of Rehabilitation Institute of Chicago (corresponding secretary), Children's Reading Round Table (Chicago), Planned Parenthood Association (Chicago; member of Evanston board of directors), Off-Campus Writers Workshop (Winnetka, Ill.; member of board of directors), Garden Club of Evanston (past member of board of directors), Phi Theta Kappa. *Awards, honors:* Junior Literary Guild selection for *Bugs in Your Ears,* September, 1977 and for *The Ups and Downs of Jorie Jenkins,* March, 1978.

WRITINGS—Juvenile: *Bugs in Your Ears,* Holiday House, 1977; *The Ups and Downs of Jorie Jenkins,* Holiday House, 1978; *My Mom, the Money Nut,* Holiday House, 1979; *Love is Like Peanuts,* Holiday House, 1980.

SIDELIGHTS: "To me, the family is all-important. The years when my three sons and a daughter were growing up were hectic for all six members of my family, but not for the most glamorous of outside jobs would I have given up my work as full time mother, homemaker, and counselor to my living, breathing, feeling children. Thus, I'm horrified by the continuing disintegration of the family unit, so vital to the needs of children for love and sense of worth. In my talks at schools, I've discovered that my books are giving support to the children who are victims of this breaking down by showing them their troubled feelings are shared by others.

"Although my main plots come from my imagination, the germs of ideas for books come from situations around me. *Bugs in Your Ears* grew out of the experience of a young cousin. The illness of the father in *The Ups and Downs of Jorie Jenkins* came from such a problem with another relative, and the warmth within Jorie's family corresponds with that in my own. So far, each of my books has had material on sports, derived from my boys' passion for athletics. In *My Mom, the Money Nut,* when Stuart Shanks is stung on the tongue by a bee while training for a track meet, the incident must seem far-fetched, but it actually happened to one of my sons. Like most writers, I've developed a bloodhound's skill in tracking down information I need through relatives, friends, and even strangers. When I needed help with the chapter in *My Mom, the Money Nut* in which Fritzi goes to visit her grandfather in the mountains, I formed a long-distance friendship with fellow writer May Justus, whom I've never met.

"About fifteen years ago, I joined a writers' workshop to overcome the empty nest syndrome. After trying to write for every age group, I finally discovered that authoring for pre-teens worked best for me. I was delighted to be discovered by Margery Cuyler, the editor at Holiday House, who seemed to appreciate my first-person, present-tense approach, and we have a warm working relationship.

"It's important, of course, that young people learn to read well, and that we provide bright humor, lively characterizations, and humming plots to draw them into the book-loving habit. I hope my writing is helping. At any rate, I intend to go on writing for young people for years to come."

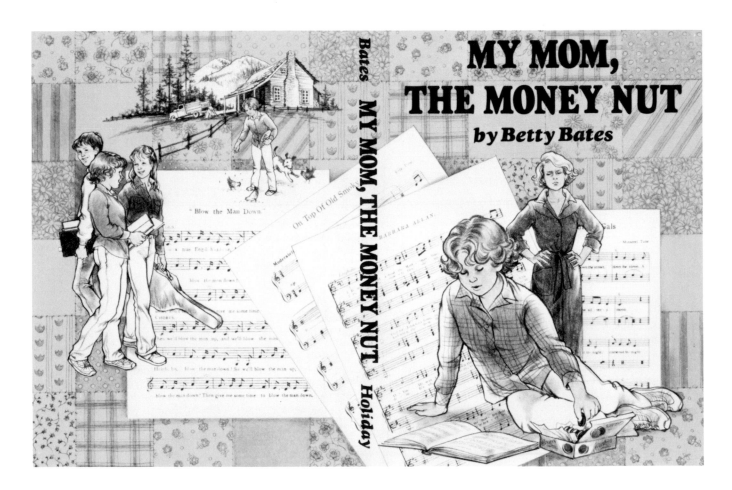

(From *My Mom, the Money Nut* by Betty Bates. Jacket illustration by Gail Owens.)

BETTY BATES

FOR MORE INFORMATION SEE: *Evanston Review*, September 15, 1977, April 13, 1978, June 7, 1979; *North Shore Monthly*, April-May, 1978.

BAYNES, Pauline (Diana)   1922-

PERSONAL: Born September 9, 1922, in Brighton, England; daughter of Frederick W. W. (an Indian civil service employee) and Jessie Harriet Maude (Cunningham) Baynes; married Fritz Otto Gasch (a garden contractor), 1961. *Education:* Attended Farnham School of Art, one year, and Slade School (London University), two terms. *Politics:* Conservative. *Religion:* Church of England. *Home:* Rock Barn Cottage, Dockenfield, Farnham, Surrey GU10 AHH England.

CAREER: Illustrator. Beaufront School, Camberley, England, art teacher. Currently teaches, once a week, a class of mentally deficient girls. *Exhibitions:* Work has been exhibited in London, Farnham and Chichester. *Military service:* Civil employee at the Army Camouflage Centre, during World War II, making demonstration models and at the Hydrographic Department of the Admiralty, drawing charts. *Member:* Women's International Art Club, Society of Industrial Artists, Association of Illustrators. *Awards, honors:* *Puffin Book of Nursery Rhymes* received the Caorle Prize, 1963; *A Dictionary of Chivalry* received the Kate Greenaway

Medal, 1968; *Snail and Caterpillar* was a runner-up for the Kate Greenaway Medal and the Carnegie Medal, 1972.

WRITINGS: (Self-illustrated) *Victoria and the Golden Bird,* Blackie, 1947.

Illustrator: J.R.R. Tolkien, *The Hobbit,* Penguin, 1937; Enid Blyton, *Land of Far Beyond,* Methuen, 1942, 1973; Victoria Stevenson, *Clover Magic,* Country Life, 1944; Victoria Stevenson, *The Magic Footstool,* Country Life, 1946; J.R.R. Tolkien, *Farmer Giles of Ham,* Allen & Unwin, 1949, Houghton, 1950.

Victoria Stevenson, *The Magic Broom,* Country Life, 1950; W. T. Bebbington, *And It Came to Pass,* Allen & Unwin, 1951; C. S. Lewis, *The Lion, the Witch and the Wardrobe* (ALA Notable Book), Macmillan, 1951, Collins, 1965; Henri Pourrat, *Treasury of French Tales,* Allen & Unwin, 1951, Houghton, 1954; C. S. Lewis, *Prince Caspian,* Macmillan, 1951; E.J.S. Lay, *Men and Manners,* Macmillan, 1952; C. S. Lewis, *The Voyage of the Dawn Treader,* Macmillan, 1952, Penguin, 1970; Marjorie Phillips, *Annabel and Bryony,* Oxford University Press, 1953; C. S. Lewis, *The Silver Chair,* Macmillan, 1953, Collins, 1969; C. S. Lewis, *The Horse and His Boy,* Macmillan, 1954, Collins, 1970; A. and L. J. Hitchcock, *Great People Thru' the Ages,* Blackie, 1954; A. and L. J. Hitchcock, *The British People,* Blackie, 1955; C. S. Lewis, *The Magician's Nephew* (ALA Notable Book), Macmillan, 1955;

Llewellyn, *China's Court and Concubines,* Allen & Unwin, 1956; C. S. Lewis, *The Last Battle* (ALA Notable Book),

PAULINE BAYNES

(From "Fastitocalon," in *The Adventures of Tom Bombadil* by J. R. R. Tolkien. Illustrated by Pauline Baynes.)

Macmillan, 1956; Emmeline Garnett, *The Tudors,* Blackie, 1956; Emmeline Garnett, *Queen Anne,* Blackie, 1956; Emmeline Garnett, *Civil War,* Blackie, 1956; Amabel Williams-Ellis, *The Arabian Nights,* S. G. Phillips, 1957, Criterion, 1958; Rhoda Power, *Fury from the Northmen,* Riverside Press, 1957; Denton, *Stars and Candles,* Benn, 1958; Monica Backway, *Hasan of Basorah,* Blackie, 1958; Joan Mary Bete, *The Curious Tale of Cloud City,* Blackie, 1958; Anne Malcolmson, *Miracle Plays,* Houghton, 1959.

Amabel Williams-Ellis, *Fairy Tales from the British Isles,* Peal Press, 1960, Warne, 1964; Loretta Burrough, *Sister Clare,* Houghton, 1960; Dorothy Ensor, *The Adventures of Hatim Tai,* Harrap, 1960, Walck, 1962; Mary C. Borer, *Don Quixote,* Longmans, 1960; Edmund Spenser, *Saint George and the Dragon,* adapted by Sandol S. Warburg, Methuen, 1961, Houghton, 1963; Gladys Hickman and E. G. Hume, *Pilgrim Way Geographies,* Volumes I, II, IV, Blackie, 1961; Lynette Muir, *The Unicorn Window,* Abelard, 1961; James Morris, *The Upstairs Donkey and Other Stolen Stories,* Pantheon, 1961; Alison Uttley, *The Little Knife Who Did All the Work,* Faber, 1962; J.R.R. Tolkien, *The Adventures of Tom Bombadil,* Allen & Unwin, 1962, Houghton, 1963; Hans Christian Andersen, *Andersen's Fairy Tales,* Collins, 1963; Iona and Peter Opie, compilers, *A Family Book of Nursery Rhymes,* Oxford University Press, 1964; Allan, *Come Into*

My Castle, Macmillan, 1964; Iona and Peter Opie, *Puffin Book of Nursery Rhymes,* Puffin, 1964; K. G. Lethbridge, *The Rout of the Ollafubs,* Faber, 1964; M. Gail, *Avignon in Flower,* Houghton, 1965; Mary C. Borer, *Famous Lives* (series), Longmans, 1965, Eichosha [Japan], 1968.

Alison Uttley, *Recipes from an Old Farmhouse,* Faber, 1966; Radost Pridham, *A Gift from the Heart: Folk Tales from Bulgaria,* Methuen, 1966, World, 1967; Abigail Homes, *Education for Uncles,* Houghton, 1966; J.R.R. Tolkien, *Smith of Wootton Major,* Allen & Unwin, 1967; Jennifer Westwood, editor, *Medieval Tales,* Hart-Davis, 1967, Coward, 1968; Grant Uden, *A Dictionary of Chivalry,* Longman Young, 1968, Crowell, 1969; Joseph W. Krutch, *The Most Wonderful Animals that Never Were,* Houghton, 1968; Lady Jekyll, *Kitchen Essays,* Collins, 1969.

Richard D. Blackmore, *Lorna Doone,* Collins, 1970; Constance Hieatt, *The Joy of the Court,* Crowell, 1970; Naomi Mitchison, *Graeme and the Dragon,* Cambridge, 1970; Jennifer Westwood, *Isle of Gramarye: An Anthology of the Poetry of Magic,* Hart-Davis, 1970; Leonard Clark, *All Along Down Along,* Longmans, 1971; Jennifer Westwood, *Tales and Legends,* Coward, 1971; Philippa Pearce, *Stories from Hans Andersen,* Collins, 1972; Helen Piers, *Snail and Cater-*

(From *Smith of Wooten Major* by J.R.R. Tolkien. Illustrated by Pauline Baynes.)

(From *The Voyage of the Dawn Treader* by C. S. Lewis. Illustrated by Pauline Baynes.)

(From "Thumbelina" in *Andersen's Fairy Tales* by Hans Christian Andersen. Illustrated by Pauline Baynes.)

pillar, American Heritage, 1972, McGraw, 1972; Katie Stewart, *The Times Cookery Book,* Collins, 1972; John Symonds, *Harold,* Dent, 1973; Claude Nicolas, *The Roe Deer,* Chambers, 1974; Claude Nicolas, *The Frog,* Chambers, 1974; Claude Nicolas, *The Butterfly,* Chambers, 1974; Claude Nicolas, *The Duck,* Chambers, 1974.

Helen Piers, *Grasshopper and Butterfly,* McGraw, 1975; Geoffrey Squire, *The Observer's Book of European Costume,* Warne, 1975; G. Markham, *The Compleat Horseman,* Houghton, 1976; Claude Nicolas, *The Bea & the Cherry Tree,* Chambers, 1976; Claude Nicolas, *The Salmon,* Chambers, 1976; Claude Nicolas, *The Dolphin,* Chambers, 1977; Eileen Hunter, *Tales from Way Beyond,* Deutsch, 1979; Richard Barber, *A Companion to World Mythology,* Kestrel, 1979.

Illustrator—covers only: William Dickinson, *Borrobil,* Penguin, 1944; J.R.R. Tolkien, *Lord of the Rings,* Allen & Unwin, 1955; Roger Lancelyn Green, *The Tale of Troy,* Penguin, 1958; George MacDonald, *The Princess & the Goblin,* Penguin, 1964; Jane Austin, *Emma,* Macmillan, 1966; George MacDonald, *The Princess & Curdie,* Penguin, 1966; Rosemary Harris, *The Moon in the Cloud,* Penguin, 1968; Richard Adams, *Watership Down,* Penguin, 1972; Rosemary Harris, *The Bright & Morning Star,* Faber, 1972; M. Halsall, *Dragon Year,* Scripture Union, 1972; Natalie Babbit, *The Search for Delicious,* Fontana Lions, 1977; J.R.R. Tolkien, *Sir Gawain & the Green Knight,* Houghton, 1978; Natalie Babbit, *Tuck Everlasting,* Fontana Lions, 1978; Walter de la Mare, *The Three Royal Monkeys,* Puffin, 1979; K. M. Briggs, *Kate Crackernuts,* Kestrel, 1979.

Illustrator of two maps in J.R.R. Tolkien's *Bilbo's Last Song* and C. S. Lewis' "Map of Narnia."

WORK IN PROGRESS: Illustrating Christopher Tower's "Oultre Jourdain"; and an Indian tale by Rosemary Harris.

SIDELIGHTS: "My only ambition as a school girl was to illustrate books, and my only ambition now is to try to illustrate better. I am really a designer and a decorator, but not very good at actually depicting. I work in gouache paint mainly now, but occasionally use pen and ink—also crayon, pastels, etc.—when it is needed.

"I was strongly influenced by practically every artist whose work appeared in books, but mainly by Rackham, Dulac, and John Austen, and by reproductions of Persian, Indian and early medieval manuscripts.

"I have a strong affiliation with Minneapolis, for whose Plymouth Congregational Church I designed an embroidery which hangs in their Guild Hall. It is the largest crewel work in the world—featured in the *Smithsonian* Journal, August, 1975. I spent a marvellous fortnight there, which could never be forgotten."

Pauline Baynes' works are included in the Kerlan Collection at the University of Minnesota, and in the Marion Wade Collection at Wheaton College in Illinois.

HOBBIES AND OTHER INTERESTS: Buying books, taking her dogs for walks.

FOR MORE INFORMATION SEE: Bertha M. Miller and others, compilers, *Illustrators of Children's Books: 1946-*

1956, Horn Book, 1958; *Childhood in Poetry,* Gale Research, 1967; Lee Kingman and others, compilers, *Illustrators of Children's Books: 1957-1966,* Horn Book, 1968; Brian Doyle, *The Who's Who of Children's Literature,* Schocken Books, 1968; Doris de Montreville and Donna Hill, editors, *Third Book of Junior Authors,* H. W. Wilson, 1972; *Horn Book,* June, 1973; *Signal,* May, 1973; *The Times,* October 17, 1973; *Illustrators of Books for Young People,* Scarecrow Press, 1975; *Smithsonian,* August, 1975.

BEEBE, (Charles) William   1877-1962

PERSONAL: Born July 29, 1877, in Brooklyn, N.Y., died June 4, 1962; son of Charles and Henrietta Marie (Younglove) Beebe; married Mary Blair (writer; divorced); married Elswyth Thane (an author), September, 1927. *Education:* Columbia University, B.S., 1898, graduate study, 1898-99. *Home:* New York City.

CAREER: Naturalist and author. Became curator of ornithology, New York Zoological Park (also known as the Bronx Zoo), 1899; later became director of the Zoological Society's department of tropical research, 1899-1962; director of the British Guiana Zoological Station. *Military service:* Served as an aviator during the First World War. *Member:* American Association for the Advancement of Science, American Ornithologists' Union, Societe d'Acclimatation de France, Zoological Society (New York and London), New York Academy of Sciences (fellow), Audubon Society, Ecological Society, Linnaean Society, Society of Mammologists. *Awards, honors:* Sc.D., Tufts College, 1928, Colgate University, 1928, Elliot Medal; John Burroughs Medal.

*WRITINGS—*Nonfiction: *Two Bird-Lovers in Mexico* (photographs by the author), Houghton, 1905; *The Bird: Its Form and Function* (photographs by the author), Holt, 1906; *The Log of the Sun: A Chronicle of Nature's Year* (illustrated by Walter King Stone), Holt, 1906; (with first wife, Mary Blair) *Our Search for a Wilderness: An Account of Two Ornithological Expeditions to Venezuela and to British Guiana* (photographs by the authors), Holt, 1910; (with G. Inness Hartley and Paul G. Howes) *Tropical Wild Life in British Guiana,* New York Zoological Society, 1917; *Jungle Peace,* Holt, 1918; *A Monograph of the Pheasants,* Witherby, 1918-22, reissued as *Pheasants: Their Lives and Homes,* Doubleday, Page, 1926; *Edge of the Jungle,* Holt, 1921, new edition, Duell, Sloan, & Pearce, 1956; *Jungle Days,* Putnam, 1923; *Galapagos: World's End* (illustrated by Isabel Cooper and John Tee-Van), Putnam, 1924; *The Arcturus Adventure: An Account of the New York Zoological Society's First Oceanographic Expedition,* Putnam, 1926; *Pheasant Jungles* (photographs by the author), Putnam, 1927; *Beneath Tropic Seas: A Record of Diving among the Coral Reefs of Haiti,* Putnam, 1928.

Exploring with Beebe: Selections for Younger Readers, Putnam, 1932; *Nonsuch: Land of Water,* Brewer, Warren, 1932; (with John Tee-Van) *Field Book of the Shore Fishes of Bermuda,* Putnam, 1933, reissued as *Field Book of the Shore Fishes of Bermuda and the West Indies,* Dover, 1970; *Half Mile Down,* Harcourt, 1934, new edition, Duell, Sloan, & Pearce, 1965; *Zaca Venture,* Harcourt, 1938; *Book of Bays,* Harcourt, 1942; (editor) *The Book of Naturalists: An Anthology of the Best Natural History,* Knopf, 1944; *High Jungle,* Duell, Sloan, & Pearce, 1949; *Unseen Life of New York* (illustrated by Donald T. Carlisle), Duell, Sloan, & Pearce, 1953; *Adventuring with Beebe,* Duell, Sloan, & Pearce, 1955. Also contributor to *Atlantic Monthly.*

WILLIAM BEEBE, 1931

SIDELIGHTS: **July 29, 1877.** Born in Brooklyn, N.Y. Son of Charles and Henrietta Marie (Younglove) Beebe.

1885. Family moved to East Orange, N.J. where Beebe attended the Ashland Grammar School. "One of my earliest and most cruel disillusionments came during a season of grammar school wrestling with geography, when I left my pink natal state of New York and, in the course of a short trip discovered to my disgust that New Jersey was not blue, nor Pennsylvania even scarlet." [Robert Henry Welker, *Natural Man: The Life of William Beebe,* Indiana University Press, 1975.[1]]

Even then, he displayed a romantic concern for the mysteries of the universe. "I wonder, if at some momentous happening in life everyone does not have the sudden recurrence of an emotion which has not been experienced since early childhood. Mere height or depth never affected me,—I could always look with pleasurable exhilaration over the edge of a precipice or down from a roof. But sometimes under the stars, when there came the realization of cosmic space, or at my first glimpse of moon mountains through a telescope or my first trip in an airplane,—then I shuddered to my soul, and my heart skipped a beat. I remember pulling in a kite with all my might, trembling with terror, for I had sensed the ghastly isolation of that bit of paper aloft in sheer space, and the tug of the string appalled me with the thought of being myself drawn up and up, away from the solid earth."[1]

September, 1891. Entered East Orange High School.

1896-1898. Studied at Columbia University, in the department of zoology.

October, 1899. Appointed curator of the bird house for the New York Zoological Society, located in the Bronx, just months after the zoo's opening.

1900-1906. Contributed articles to the *Zoological Society Bulletin,* as well as the New York *Tribune,* and the New York *Evening Post.*

August 6, 1902. Married Mary Blair in Clarkton, Virginia.

December 17, 1903. Departed, with Mary, for a major bird expedition in Mexico. There, the joy of being on their honeymoon was doubled by their closeness to nature. "How close to Nature one seems to live thus! closer to Mother Earth than did Thoreau at Walden; and yet when this framework of mud is clothed within with clean plaster, in rooms cool-tiled and with ceilings of taut linen, sleep and study and the joys of very life come in pleasantest forms."[1] And of their first night in camp by a stream near the base of Mount Colima: "The sleep that came to us that night was of the quality of sweetness known only to those whose happiest days and nights are the ones spent closest to the heart of wild Nature."[1]

1905. *Two Bird-Lovers in Mexico,* co-authored by Mary Beebe, published.

February 22, 1908. Left New York with wife, arriving in Trinidad on March 9, then on to Venezuela for animal research and bird study. "Finally we envisage ourselves, voluntary migrants from cold and sleet to tropical warmth, from the scanty winter fauna of a New York February to the swarming wild life of Venezuelan jungles. All winter we have hibernated in our reference libraries, burrowed deep into the collections of former expeditions, messed about with laboratory dissections. Daily, as we walked about our Zoo we gained inklings of habits or voices from captive reptiles, birds, and mammals in their capacious cages. All this we were now, for about the fiftieth time, to exchange for the wild living creatures themselves in the very haunts in which they had evolved through the ages.

"Both the migrant birds and ourselves got off to a flying start, but romance and beauty were wholly on the side of the feathered wings. Their owners had sense enough to start before the leaves had wholly gone, in the midst of autumnal glory. After an abundance of nutritious gnats had lined their little bodies with precious reserves of fat, they took off one evening, without fanfare or preliminary warning up, even without knowing why. They fluttered up and up into the

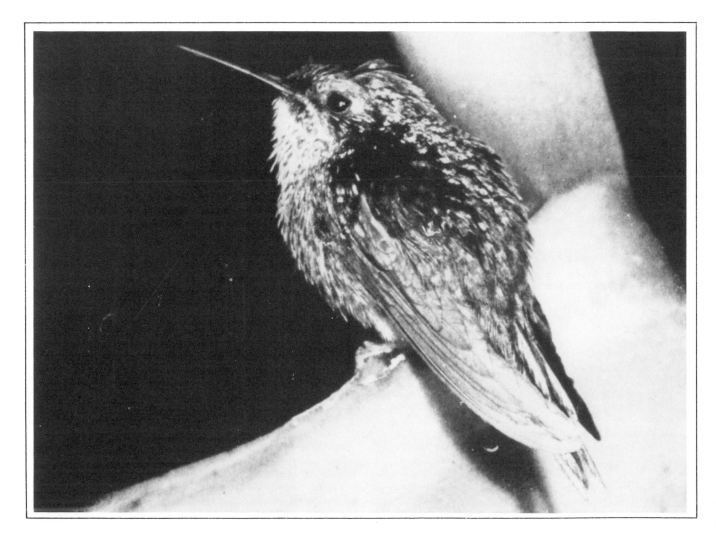

Hummingbird drinking from heliconia blossom. ■ (From *Pacific Cruise* by William Beebe.)

The bird blind at South Beach, Nonsuch, and the giant binoculars in action. ■ (From *Pacific Cruise* by William Beebe.)

night, through clouds into the cold moonshine. As far as the migrant birds are concerned we can watch them through high-power glasses, we may see them take off, later to land a quarter world away, we can photograph them in flight, shoot, and dissect them with microscopic thoroughness, and in addition we can endow them with super-visual ability, or with delicate geographic, radar, or magnetic perceptions and powers. After all this we have gained no hint of what sense organs provide compass, altimeter, orientation; what austral beam guides them so surely. We have our own secret flying instruments, jealously guarded from alien eyes, complex but mechanically reasonable. Yet in secrecy of operation the birds put us to shame. Our mental unawareness makes ignorance of their methods complete.

"In one thing bird and plane are identical; each has a limited amount of fuel, and en route, sooner or later, each must land to replenish its stock—whether gasoline or gnats is aside from the question. All differences vanish when tanks are empty or fat reserves used up. Then bird and man must recoup, or else succumb—united in the same end."[William Beebe, *High Jungle,* Duell, Sloan, 1949.[2]]

February 24, 1909. Arrived in British Guiana for further research.

December 26, 1909. Left New York for London, and from there sailed to Egypt, Ceylon, India, Sikkin, Burma, Yuman, the Malay States, Java, Borneo, China, and Japan, completing the journey on May 27, 1911 after seventeen months in search of pheasants.

February, 1913. His wife, Mary, left for Reno, Nevada to begin divorce proceedings, the decree granted her on August 29, 1913.

January, 1916. Left with party of scientists and artists to establish a research station for jungle studies, eventually settling on an estate in British Guiana, called Kalacoon. Here his narration began with the desk at which he was writing: "Many, many, many years ago, in some distant place, among trees or rocks, perhaps on the banks of a river, certainly in the warm light of the sun, one of your ancestors and mine became tired of squatting on a branch or on the ground, and sat himself—or herself—on a fallen log. If it was himself then he must soon have felt the need of a lap on which to rest things—his hands if nothing else. And from that day to this, his male descendants still feel that lack down to the last unfortunate who is handed a cup of tea or a three-legged eggshell of cocoa, a serviette and a cake with no support other than wholly inadequate knees.

"Of the first table I can relate nothing with certainty, but of the last I could gossip endlessly, limited only by writer's cramp and my supply of adjectives. For I am at this moment sitting at the last table ever made—last because it is not quite finished. I am forever tacking on a little shelf or an annex at one side, and so I feel a right to place it at the opposite end of our distant forebear's piece of bark or stiff frond or whatever it was that he balanced on his hairy, bowed knees. And yet his table and mine are much more alike than the mahogany roll-top with swinging telephone and octave of assistants' push buttons to which our more sophisticated but less happy bank presidents sit down.

"That reminds me, however, that my laboratory table is also of mahogany, because here in the jungle of British Guiana it is the cheapest material in the form of boards.

"The crab-wood top grew in this very jungle, its first, firch red-brown cells fashioned from the water and earth and sun at least a century and a half ago. It is possible to detect the double character of the rings, indicating the two annual rainy seasons—the two springs which quickened the sap and leafage, and the two periods of drought when the life of the tree slowed down. . . .

"Close to the heart of the great board is a strange ring, or rather node between rings—a wide, even space, which my reckoning places about 1776; about the time when our forefathers were fighting for freedom, whose memory we cannot toast even in wine; they had just penned a Declaration of Independence, whereas we are considering passing a law to keep monkeys in their proper place. I pause in my table talk long enough to thank heaven that we are still allowed to believe in the rotundity of the earth, that the Indians' gift of tobacco is still permitted us, and that tea is not yet thrown overboard!" [William Beebe, *Jungle Days,* Putnam, 1923.[3]]

On the beauty of jungle flora: "The living leaf—both singly and in foliage mass—has been epitaphed, eulogized, sung, praised and similed for centuries, but except for occasional references to the 'sere and yellow leaf,' dying, falling and dead leaves have been left where they lie, with only the increase of their funeral pyres woven into the haze of Indian Summer.

"I have seen an orang-utan build him a sleeping platform of leaves in less than three minutes, so it is not improbable that the first artificial home our more direct ancestors knew was a leafy nest. Leaves at least formed the sole clothing of our early parents, according to Scripture, and from nursery days we have always known that falling leaves were a shroud for the babes in the wood. More than this, botanists tell us that the leaf is the foundation of flower and fruit, so that it was really only a mass of highly specialized leaves which introduced Newton to gravitation.

"But the importance and interest of falling leaves in this world needs no brief from me. I merely want to know them better for my own pleasure, I wish to hear and see and feel them, and so I leave my laboratory after a day of intensive technical work and slip into the jungle, where millions of leaves are falling during my lifetime, and hundreds of millions fell before I was born.

"With all my desire to clothe the fallen leaf with dramatic interest and an abstract vitality, my first and last thoughts are those of sadness. Alien as I am to these tropical jungles, a mere transient injection from the North, the sere and yellow leaf means to me the end of a season, of a year—a very appreciable fraction of lifetime—and even in this evergreen land, this jungle *de le printemps éternel,* the dead leaf eddying to earth is a sad and a tragic happening."[3]

1917. Enrolled with the French Aviation Service, suffering a fall that resulted in a serious wrist injury. While recuperating, he ventured to British Guiana to acquire specimens for the Zoological Park.

1918. Recorded in *Jungle Peace* his observations on war: "In war men do all in their power to maim and kill one another, yet when wounded enemies are captured, instead of being subjected to the logical process of extermination they are taken to hospitals, cured if possible, exchanged for other cured prisoners and shot at all over again. I suppose it is the remains of the almost extinct idea of chivalry. Probably there are aviators who would hesitate at driving a sword through a woman or baby who, without demur, will drop bombs on them when disguised as 'civilian population . . .'

William Beebe in the diving helmet.

"After creeping through slime-filled holes beneath the shrieking of swift metal, after splashing one's plane through companionable clouds three miles above the little jagged, hero-filled ditches, and dodging other sudden-born clouds of nauseous fumes and blasting heart of steel; after these, one craves thoughts of comfortable hens, sweet apple orchards, or ineffable themes of opera. And when nerves have cried for a time 'enough' and an unsteady hand threatens to turn a joy stick into a sign post to Charon, the mind seeks amelioration—some symbol of worthy content and peace—and for my part, I turn with all desire to the jungles of the tropics."[1]

Wartime conditions prevented research at Kalacoon, but Beebe was given the title of Honorary Curator of the Department of Birds, and also became director of the department of tropical research.

1923. Made the naturalist's inevitable journey to the Galapagos archipelago. Here he studied closely the species discovered by Charles Darwin, and responded rather emotionally to what he discovered there. "May the little island long keep her secret from devastating mankind—a single boatload of which could exterminate the whole colony in a few hours."[1]

September 22, 1927. Married writer Elswyth Thane.

1928. Obtained permission from the British authorities to take his tropical research group to the island of Nonsuch in the Bermudas, beginning eleven years of study and sea expedition aboard the *Arcturus.* "Six days ago I made my first map of Almost Island, south of Nonsuch, and northeast of Gurnets Rock. We are accustomed to speak of air pockets and mountain chains and hanging valleys, so why cannot we have something which is almost an island? The distinction is much more accurate than that between hill and mountain, creek and river. I might, in fact, call my area Once Island, for from its configuration and our knowledge of the land hereabouts, there is no doubt that it was formerly well above water.

"I discovered it by accident three years ago when I rowed out to Gurnets, threw out the anchor at random, and went down in the helmet. I found myself in five or six fathoms on the whitest of sand, looking up at the walls of a splendid reef—great cliffs waving with sea fans and alive with fish. The minute the helmet was removed, I located the spot definitely in its relation to Gurnets Rock—two hundred yards southwest of my boat and marked by a giant angle in the center of the reef. . . .

"My island is divided almost equally into sand and reef, and these correspond to all the varied phases of dry physical geography—sand taking the place of deserts, plains, pampas and tundras, and a reef embodying mountains, canyons and jungles.

"We do not think of there being weather under water, but if we consider terrestrial weather as heat, cold, dryness, moisture, wind, rain, snow and fog, then my submerged islet has weather in abundance. I may descend in water which feels delightfully warm to my skin, but in half an hour I come shivering to the surface with teeth chattering; of dryness, we submariners know nothing, except concerning our face, and when dryness leaves the helmet, we expire or ascend; as for moisture, we have nothing else but. . . .

"The coming of night to Almost Island deserves a chapter, or if we knew even a fraction of the great changes which every evening brings, an entire volume. The setting sun gives way to blue, always blue, blackness, the movement of one's hand sets fire to a thousand luminous creatures in mid-water; many of the day-loving fish go to sleep in amazing positions; the big-eyed squirrelfish and the sinister morays come forth,

For helmet diving, Beebe's first fixed base was the schooner *Lieutenant,* anchored at Bizoton near Port-au-Prince, Haiti.

and the sharks begin to work their way in from the open sea. A sight I shall not forget is that of a dead horse which we tied to the western buoy; at sunset Almost Island was alive with sharks. There were dozens of the four-foot puppy sharks which are so common about Nonsuch, and now and then I caught a glimpse of the white belly of one much larger, as it twisted up from below to share the feast. The next morning the horse had disappeared, not a shark was in sight, and over the spot five angelfish swam lazily, their golden filaments streaming out behind—the usual peace of early morning had returned to Almost Island." [William Beebe, *Adventuring with Beebe*, Little, Brown, 1955.[4]]

December, 1928. Took his plans for the soon famous "Bathysphere" to the Watson-Stillman Hydraulic Machinery Company; this tank was designed for deep sea research.

June 10, 1930. The Bathysphere was lowered, this time with Beebe and Otis Barton, his associate, inside. They reached the depth of 1,426 feet.

September, 1932. NBC Radio arranged to broadcast a Bathysphere dive on its network with a simultaneous shortwave link to the BBC.

1942. After several years of residing in Bermuda, the Beebes found refuge in Vermont when their island retreat was converted to an airfield for war purposes. His wife's account of restoring the house and land they bought in New England was later published in a book called *Reluctant Farmer*.

1942-1948. Embarked on four major research expeditions, all to Venezuela. "In my journal I find under date of May fourteenth, that it is a red-letter day because we are at last moving up for good to Rancho Grande. On the following day the few paragraphs are rather less coherent, descriptive of a peculiar combination of a sloth, of Pedro, and of a ladder (which I strove to hold aloft) falling on me and by some miracle breaking only my leg. It confirmed the old saying that the only time it is unlucky to walk under a ladder is when you are carrying it.

"Next morning when my pleasant, Venezuelan nurse came in, I smilingly told her to her horror that I had been bothered all night by the humming of vultures. She was quieted later when it turned out that I had confused the Spanish words *zamuros* and *zancudos,* and that I had been attacked by nothing more grisly than mosquitoes. . . ."[2]

June 4, 1942. "A day came when with the aid of a pair of crutches it was possible to lever the cast and myself into the air and forward, and hobble out on the great stone verandah. I sat down on the upper step and thought about my work. To think about what a naturalist wishes, or ought to do to justify himself in the opinion of the world, or what is much more important, in his own estimation is exceedingly easy: merely a matter of observation, analysis, and synthesis. Actually to accomplish this is something else again.

"I finally mastered the technique of those excellent homemade crutches and demanded a chance to do jungle work. I was motored two hundred yards to the summit of Portachuelo Pass and thence became a most awkward quadruped, and crutched my way through tall grass, which recalled swimming through dense sargassum weed. My goal was a small flat terrace, exactly in the center of the pass, from which I looked down the most tropical of gorges, up at the cloud jungle of Pico Periquito, and around at a dense undergrowth of melastomes, palms, and treeferns. Only at an un-

forgettable placed called Ghoom, en route to Kinchenjunga in the Himalayas, between Nepal and Sikhim, have I seen moss and airplants equal, in luxuriance and abundance, to those of this pass.

"With a leg, which seemed no longer a part of me, propped up on a low, cut bough, and seated in a rookha chair bought forty years ago at Whiteaway-Laidlaw in Calcutta, I was as content as a crocked-up human can be. I looked around with little hope of doing more than amuse myself with some sentimental twaddle for the eyes of my journal alone; some mouthings on the lives of the small folk whose abode has been crashed. I imagined some such sweet maudlinity as 'Watching the Wildings,' or 'Cute Doings of My Jungle Friends.'"[2]

June 6, 1942. "I settle down in the same place close to the gorge at the summit of Portachuelo Pass.

"Just as the neblina makes visible every breeze and shift and small whirlwind of the otherwise invisible ether, so at this moment I am certain that the air before me is filled with myriad insects. They are wholly invisible both to my eyes and binoculars, but are revealed by twenty-six blue-and-white swallows hawking and diving or swooping up to a stop like the apogee of a lobbed tennis ball. On the single jungle telephone wire which stretches down and down the dark trail are perched sixteen young swallows, their exact juvenile age revealed by the less or greater extent of tail feathers, in addition to which all those with short, stubby tails have much more baby yellow at the gape. In the sunlight this bright color is as useless as a rainbow. Five days ago in the dim recesses of a nesting hole in the castle wall of Rancho Grande this spot of pigment made all the difference between meals and no meals. It played the part of an effective colored beacon in the semi-darkness to guide the bugfilled beaks of the parents to their goal. Swallows cannot count, and an unfortunate nestling without this jaundiced reflection might well be passed by in favor of his two sisters with heliographic lips of saffron.

"The present, wire-perched wights with ridiculously abbreviated tails and excess of oral gamboge all, as in a trained chorus, raise their heads, open their beaks, and flutter their wings as first one, then another adult swallow swoops close. I see only a single flutter among the older young. To my scientific mind, it is a perfect example of the delicately graduated weakening of an instinct whose usefulness is passing."[2]

February 26, 1943. "Today . . . I climbed an Ande. Elsewhere I might have seen a play, or caught a fish, or by the accident of time and space have won or lost a tennis match, or read a good book. Simple statements of such experiences are to be distinguished by only slightly differing words, and these in English. Suppose I put it thus: '*Dnes jsem prelezl horu Ande.*' When I realize that to millions upon millions of human beings that is clear as A-B-C, and that my words, to them, are meaningless gibberish, I have less fear that we shall never be able to understand the fluent and significant utterances of my capuchin monkey, or comprehend a reason for the notes of the whippoorwill wren at this moment singing close above me. To return, I insist that today I have climbed an Ande.

"The slope selected for the climb was just opposite the pass. By the well-meant over-zealousness of road menders the lower few meters were shaved down to nubbins of former shrubs and grass tufts, now ill-fixed in the loose soil. A rough estimate with a protractor the following day showed the angle to be fifty out of ninty degrees. If I had realized this at the time I doubt whether this exact spot would have been chosen. But with the assurance of ignorance I aimed at the stump of a two-inch trunk about twenty feet up and, with a flying start from across the road, sought to reach this first goal with the minimum of effort. I missed it by inches, turned on my back, and slid down faster than I had mounted. I sat comfortably in the road-side ditch for a few minutes and pondered on the omnipresence of gravity. How helpfully this invisible force kept my feet on the planet as I walked along the road; how it dragged on every muscle as I rushed up into space from the road level; how exultingly it pulled me back again to flat, hard ground, as near as possible to the center of the earth.

"In the world of man and business when a man is down, he is frequently out; at least he is considered to be in an unenviable position. In the world of nature, of the naturalist, to lie supine, even to have slid violently into that posture, is merely to be presented with a fresh, new view of the world.''[2]

1949. Purchased an estate, called Simla, in Trinidad, which became his own personal tropical research station.

July 29, 1952. Retired from post of director of department of tropical research, at age 75.

1953. Published *Unseen Life of New York,* which explored the animal and plant life in and around New York City usually left unobserved by man. "It is sometimes worth while to stop and look about us in New York City and try to understand it as it really is. Ninety-two million, nine hundred thousand miles south (or north, east or west) of the sun, there floats loose in space a lonely pinprick of a planet, which is only one and one third millionth the volume of the sun. On a certain spot on this planet earth is, astronomically speaking, a fraction of a grain of sand which is known as New York City. The equator is 2450 miles to the south, the North Pole about 2000 miles to the north (although there are times when both these spots seem to have shifted to our very doorstep). If we travel to the point exactly opposite New York, we find ourselves among the waves of the South Pacific, southwest of Australia. . . .

"No Noah's Ark or zoo ever equalled the parade of life which has called New York's city 'home.' From anomalous creatures which were half plants, half animals, we skip through eons of lowly water and land creatures, ancient fish, reptiles, birds, mammoths and saber-toothed tigers to early cave men, and, in an infinitely shorter jump, to city folk of 1953. Today, we have our bogies, but imagine one of your and of my ancestors with a stone or a club, facing an angry saber-tooth! If our nth gran'ther got away with it, who are we to worry!

"From cave men we pass on to Red Indians, Dutch, British, Colonials, and now the hodgepodge of races which we call Americans.

"Shelters and buildings run the same gamut. First, caves, sometimes with wild beasts, sometimes with early humans as tenants. The first mortgage foreclosure was when a family of great cave bears ousted skin-clad near-humans from their air-conditioned cavern. There followed shelters, lean-tos, huts, wigwams and log cabins, succeeded by real houses and the first skyscrapers. These are in turn pulled down to give way to groups of gigantic modern cave-warrens concealed under the name of housing projects. Wild animal commen-

Crusoe-like in his hunting gear, and with his wrist still bound from a flight training accident, Beebe sets out to collect specimens in Guiana in 1917.

sals are now confined to cockroaches and other unmentionables, mice and pigeons.

"We speak of New Yorkers, but this assemblage is a flowing stream, forever going and coming, appearing and disappearing. Since the founding of the city, more than half a hundred generations have been conceived and born, have lived, and, as certain as the precession of the equinoxes, have died and been buried or their ashes scattered to make room for the next generation. . . .

"Years ago I remember following a circus parade up Broadway. A half-dozen elephants swung slowly along in their preoccupied, aloof manner, forever immersed in some proboscidian reverie. They passed the many blocks solidly built up with houses, and on uptown plodded by the vacant spaces of high, rounded glacier-worn rock. One elephant seemed to me immense—it must have been full eight feet in height. All had been brought from India and with dignity and gentleness submitted their lives to be dictated by their human masters.

"Thousands of years before, on this very spot, all that was recognizable of my circus parade was the sunlight, sky and air, and the same glacier-scoured rock. Yet about this time (years and months and days not having been invented) another elephant had wandered up this way, along some pre-Broadway trail—a strange elephant, which we now call a mastodon.

"On this particular day he stepped to one side, perhaps to pluck at a branch of hemlock. He suddenly felt himself sinking into a bog. The more he struggled, the more he sank. And there he died. A few years ago when the Harlem ship canal was being cut, a workman found one of his ivory tusks. It lay beneath four feet of sod roots and twelve feet down at the bottom of the selfsame peat bog.

"Many years ago (forty-nine to be exact, in 1904) I had a memorable experience watching birds on migration, high in the air, within the limits of Greater New York. In company with Madison Grant, Secretary of the Zoological Society, I obtained permission from the city authorities to spend a night in the top of the Statue of Liberty. This was about mid-May, a time when migration ought to be at its height. We caught the last boat to Bedloe's Island, and on its return trip it carried away the final sight-seer, reducing the population to the superintendent, his assistant, Mr. Grant and myself.

"My first activity was rather comparable to mountain climbing. It was not the actual mounting of one hundred and sixty-eight steps from the base to the summit, but the difficulty of toting a blanket, lantern, food and binoculars up the narrow convolutions of the circular stairway. I finally had to make two trips, and unloaded in the crown of the noble goddess. As if I were planning an assault on Mount Everest, I made my base camp in the crown and my advance perch, or roost, in the torch.

"In early evening, a downward look toward the water of the bay, three hundred feet below, showed the wakes of tugs and steamers, stretching out in long, well-defined lines, intersecting one another like the strands of a gigantic, waving cobweb.

"The day had been clear, but as the sun sank lower, clouds collected, and soon there began that most wonderful of earthly sights—an ever familiar, ever new sunset. The sun became obscured, but I knew when it sank below the hidden horizon by the sunset guns echoing from fort to fort.

"Half an hour later the whole outlook had changed. After the beacon of the statue had been turned on, a feeling of complete isolation became very real, and the distant glimmering lights of the city made this sensation more intense. One felt suspended in mid-air with no apparent contact with sea or land.

"I climbed the vertical ladder on to the narrow duckwalk around the torch itself and prepared to take a short nap before beginning my migration vigil. Hardly had I closed my eyes when a new characteristic of the copper giantess became apparent—she swayed. I was told this oscillation was through a twenty-four inch arch, back and forth, and that it had something to do with the safety stresses of the whole structure. As long as I remained conscious, the movement was soothing, somewhat like the swinging of a hammock. When sleep closed down, the mobility changed from oscillation to acceleration, and several times I awoke and sat up terrified, certain that the massive figure was hurtling to the ground. I have had a similar sensation three other times, in the midst of the sickening waves of a violent earthquake.

"The night had suddenly turned cold, a breeze arose, and I changed my pallet to the wooden platform at the head of the stairway. With the rising wind the hollow statue came to life. During the day, with many people passing up and down, the echoes would be confused and not particularly noticeable. With the absence of humanity and the presence of a wind, the sounds become weird and awesome. I dropped a loose bolt which I had picked up, and the reverberations increased

by echoes and distance, until from far down they sounded like thunder on distant mountains. The scratching of a pin was taken up and magnified until the screekings died out in uttermost coppery hollows. When I laughed and shouted aloud, there resulted a pandemonium of tortured devils yelling back at me. Long after all seemed quiet, a faint squeak, squeak, came softly to the ear, perhaps a mouse feeding on crumbs dropped by some sight-seer.

"At eleven o'clock I mounted again to the torch. The wind had quieted down, but haze was drifting up the bay and down from the sky. Every few seconds the sound of bird voices came from overhead; the peet-sweet of a sandpiper, the croak of perhaps a green heron, the thin notes of warblers, and the more palpable chirps of sparrows. The haze changed to fog, and now, to the chorus of bird voices, there was added the occasional, distant, sonorous bass of a foghorn. Several times birds called from below my level, and then, without warning, something hurtled past my head, struck, and fell at my feet—a warm, palpitating but dying magnolia warbler.

"The most surprising event of the entire night was a burst of song from two birds, heard a half hour apart. The first, I am certain, was a red-eyed vireo. Five of the brief, thrushlike phrases came to my ear. The first was dim in the distance, three others were hurried and close, one as the bird actually passed almost within sight. The fifth was half lost in a foghorn. The second song was the ummistakable four-syllabled utterance of a goldfinch. A single phrase come out of the fog, then the beginning of a second, apparently given as the bird passed, for the call rose into an indeterminate screech as it receded into the distance. I wondered at the emotion—a perfect example of displacement behavior—which prompted such an utterance under such inappropriate conditions.

"As the fog increased and condensed in the warmth to almost rain, birds began to pass through the periphery of illumination, then to strike intermittently against railing and glass. I crouched low behind what protection I could find, to avoid being hit. One warbler flew against my coat and sank down panting. They came in waves, a few scattered birds, then a mob, swift and dense as a swarm of golden bees. All appeared bright and shining as they passed. Occasionally a dozen or more would seem to come in obliquely to the general line of flight, and at slower speed. In this case they would all keep on to the light, but put their feather brakes on in time, so that I would have five or six sparrows clinging to me at one time, unharmed, wings spread, heads back, panting.

"For the period of a few hours I was permitted to share the feelings and activities of birds and migration, sensing altitude, isolation, darkness, wind, speed, and the awful confusion and dangers of light-in-fog.

"At three o'clock in the morning the fog had lifted, and there was neither sight nor sound of the birds. They had flown down somewhere to a precarious landing in the thinning fog, or had reascended to migration levels. I climbed again into the torch and watched for the first hint of dawn and life. The first came almost imperceptibly as a pale line of gradually brightening light; the latter was startling. A herring gull, all gray and white, swung swiftly toward me from the direction of the sea, shrieked when it saw my muffled figure and passed up river. The gull presented a double surprise for at this time of year it must have been a maverick of sorts, and should have been with its fellows on some distant breeding grounds. Prosaic tugs appeared and smoke arose from a

WILLIAM BEEBE, 1949

hundred chimneys: a new day had begun over New York City." [William Beebe, *Unseen Life of New York*, Duell, Sloan & Pearce, 1953.[5]]

June 4, 1962. Died at Simla. The creed by which he tried to live was the following: "To sum up, I present an *ideal* equipment for a naturalist writer of literary natural history: Supreme enthusiasm, tempered with an infinite patience and a complete devotion to truth; the broadest possible education; keen eyes, ears, and nose, the finest instruments; opportunity for observation; thorough training in laboratory techniques; comprehension of known facts and theories, and the habit of giving full credit for these in the proper place; awareness of what is not known; ability to put oneself in the subject's place; interpretation and integration of observations; a sense of humor; facility in writing; an eternal sense of humbleness and wonder."[1]

FOR MORE INFORMATION SEE: Current Biography Yearbook 1941; Frederick Wagner, *Famous Underwater Adventurers,* Dodd, 1962; Bernadine (Freeman) Bailey, *Famous Modern Explorers,* Dodd, 1963; F. Osborn, "My Most Unforgettable Character," *Reader's Digest,* July, 1968; Robert Henry Welker, *Natural Man: The Life of William Beebe,* Indiana University Press, 1975.

Obituaries: *New York Times,* June 6, 1962; *Illustrated London News,* June 16, 1962; *Newsweek,* June 18, 1962; *Publishers Weekly,* June 18, 1962; *Current Biography Yearbook 1962; American Annual 1963; Britannica Book of the Year 1963.*

(Died June 4, 1962)

JUNE BEHRENS

BEHRENS, June York   1925-

PERSONAL: Born April 25, 1925, in Maricopa, Calif.; daughter of Mark Hanna and Aline (Stafford) York; married Henry W. Behrens (a school principal), August 23, 1947; children: Terry Lynne, Denise. *Education:* University of California, Santa Barbara, B.A., 1947; University of Maryland (Overseas Program), Munich, Germany, graduate study, 1955; University of Southern California, M.A., 1961; graduate study, University of California, Los Angeles, and University of London. *Religion:* Protestant. *Home:* 2732 San Ramon Dr., Rancho Palos Verdes, Ca. 90274.

CAREER: Elementary teacher in California, 1947-54, 1956-63, in overseas schools, 1954-56; vice-principal in Los Angeles, 1966; reading specialist in Los Angeles City Schools, 1966—. *Member:* National Education Association, American Association of University Women, California Teachers' Association, Authors Guild, International Reading Association, Delta Kappa Gamma, National Association for Education of Young Children, California Writers Guild, Southern California Council on Literature for Children and Young People, Reading Specialists of California. *Awards, honors:* Distinguished Achievement Award in Education, 1979, University of California, Santa Barbara.

WRITINGS—Juvenile books, all published by Elk Grove Press, except as indicated: *Soo Ling Finds a Way* (Junior Literary Guild selection), Golden Gate, 1965; *A Walk in the Neighborhood,* 1968; *Who Am I?,* 1968; *Where Am I?,* 1969; *Look at the Zoo Animals,* 1970; *Earth is Home: The Pollu-*

tion Story, 1971; *Look at the Farm Animals,* 1971; *How I Feel,* 1973; *Look at the Desert Animals,* 1973; *Look at the Forest Animals,* 1974; *True Book of Metric Measurement,* 1975; *Look at the Sea Animals,* 1975; *Together,* 1975; (with Pauline Brower) *Colonial Farm,* Golden Gate, 1976; *Can You Walk the Plank?,* Childrens Press, 1976; *What Do I Hear?,* Childrens Press, 1976; *Twisters,* Childrens Press, 1977; (with Pauline Bower) *Algonquin Indians: At Summer Camp,* Childrens Press, 1977; (with Pauline Bower) *Pilgrims Plantation,* Childrens Press, 1977; (with Pauline Bower) *Canal Boats West,* Childrens Press, 1978; *My Name is Jimmy Carter,* Childrens Press, 1978; *Fiesta,* Childrens Press, 1978.

"Fine Art" Series—All published by Childrens Press: *Looking at Horses,* 1976, *Looking at Children,* 1977, *Looking at Beasties,* 1978.

"Childhood Awareness" Series—All published by Alden: *My Brown Bag Book,* 1974, *My Favorite Thing,* 1975, *What Is a Seal?,* 1975.

"Economic, Transportation and Trade" Series—All published by Elk Grove Press: *Air Cargo,* 1970, *Truck Cargo,* 1970, *Ship Cargo,* 1971, *Train Cargo,* 1974.

Plays—All published by Childrens Press: *Feast of Thanksgiving: The First American Holiday,* 1975, *A New Flag for a New Country,* 1975, *The Christmas Magic-Wagon,* 1975, *Martin Luther King,* 1979.

Films: "Children of the World," media series produced by Barr Films, 1978; "The Mediterranean" (four filmstrips), 1978; "Northern Africa" (four filmstrips), 1978; "Asia" (four filmstrips), 1978.

SIDELIGHTS: "My need to write started in elementary school. Our fifth grade teacher Mrs. Otis was in love with books. That love spilled over into the classroom and touched those of us who adored her. I wrote my first book for Mrs. Otis. She said it was one of her favorite stories. The book was about horses, illustrated with cut-outs from magazines. Many years later I did another book *Looking at Horses.* I thought about Mrs. Otis when the book came back from the printer.

"In high school I was a regular contributor to our school poetry anthology. I worked on the newspaper and edited the yearbook. My interest in writing took second place to career goals in college. I did take time to serve as editor of the University of California yearbook.

"As a new teacher I hoped to instill the same love for writing in my students as Mrs. Otis had inspired in me. Many of my younger students learned to read by writing books they had dictated to me. We'd write about ourselves, our families, our ideas and thoughts and feelings. It was an exciting part of our school day.

"Once, when we were studying about an obscure California Indian tribe, I could find no materials suitable for child reference. I researched available adult texts and wrote a book my class could read. It was a very satisfying project and one that eventually led to another career.

"As a teacher I often looked for books on a given subject only to find that a book hadn't been written yet. That was my cue. I am still finding needs and filling them as best I can.

If Joe Smith didn't have time enough to fix that wheel, there's no way to get out to Gibson Road tonight. ■ (From *The Christmas Magic-Wagon* by June Behrens. Illustrated by Marjorie Burgeson.)

"Writing plays for young children is an exciting new adventure for me. What a thrill to see children become the characters and change into completely different personalities!

"My love for travel has found its way into writing. Through filmstrip scripts and media programs I have been able to introduce children to other people and other places in the world. I am most pleased with my 'Children of the World' media series produced by Barr Films.

"Whatever the form of written expression—manuscripts, plays or scripting for filmstrips, my greatest joy comes from learning that the work has provided entertainment and learning experiences for young children."

Behrens and her husband have traveled on all continents. On April 20, 1979 the University of California, Santa Barbara, presented Behrens with a Distinguished Achievement Award for outstanding achievement as an educator.

BIRCH, Reginald B(athurst) 1856-1943

PERSONAL: Born May 2, 1856, in London, England; emigrated to the U.S. during his teens; died June 17, 1943; son of William Alexander (an army officer) and Isabella (Hoggins) Birch; married twice; children: one son, one daughter. *Education:* Studied art in Paris, Antwerp, Rome, and Munich. *Home:* New York City.

CAREER: Artist; prolific illustrator for books, magazines, and newspapers. His early drawings were published in *St. Nicholas* magazine; he later gained fame with his illustrations for Frances Hodgson Burnett's *Little Lord Fauntleroy.*

ILLUSTRATOR: James Baldwin, *Story of Roland,* Scribner, 1883; Frank Richard Stockton, *Story of Viteau,* Scribner, 1884; Frances Hodgson Burnett, *Little Lord Fauntleroy,* Scribner, 1886, reissued, 1955; F. H. Burnett, *Sara Crewe,* Scribner, 1888; Cecilla Viets Jamison, *Lady Jane,* Century,

REGINALD BIRCH

1891; Charles Edward Carryl, *Admiral's Caravan*, Century, 1892; C. V. Jamison, *Toinette's Philip*, Century, 1894; Albert Stearns, *Sinbad, Smith & Co.*, Century, 1896; John Bennett, *Master Skylark*, Century, 1897; Virginia Woodward Cloud, *Down Durley Lane, and Other Ballads*, Century, 1898; Virna Sheard, *Trevelyan's Little Daughters*, W. Briggs, 1898; Beulah M. Dix, *Soldier Rigdale*, Macmillan, 1899; George Eliot (pseudonym of Marian Evans), *Silas Marner, the Weaver of Raveloe*, W. Blackwood, 1899.

Louisa May Alcott, *Little Men*, Little, Brown, 1901; Abbie Farwell Brown, *Lucky Stone*, Century, 1914; William Alvin Bowen, *Old Tobacco Shop*, Macmillan, 1921; Louis Untermeyer, *Last Pirate*, Harcourt, 1934; L. Untermeyer, editor, *Rainbow in the Sky*, Harcourt, 1935; Ogden Nash, *Bad Parents' Garden of Verse*, Simon & Schuster, 1936; F. R. Stockton, *Reformed Pirate*, Scribner, 1936; Hallie Erminie Rives, *Tales from Dickens*, Macmillan, 1937; Constance Savery, *Moonshine in Candle Street*, Longmans, Green, 1937; Clement Clarke Moore, *Night Before Christmas*, Harcourt, 1937; Laura Elizabeth Richards, *Harry in England*, Appleton, 1937; F. H. Burnett, *Little Princess*, Scribner, 1938; L. E. Richards, *I Have a Song to Sing You*, Appleton, 1938; Thomas Burns, *Terrence O'Hara*, Harcourt, 1939; Charles

Dickens, *Five Christmas Novels*, Heritage Press, 1939; Elisabeth B. Hamilton, editor, *Reginald Birch—His Book: A Selection of Stories and Poems*, Harcourt, 1939. Has been credited with illustrating almost 200 books.

Contributor of illustrations to numerous newspapers and magazines, including *St. Nicholas, Youth's Companion, Harper, Century*, and the old *Life*.

SIDELIGHTS: **May 2, 1856.** Born in London, Birch's first ambition was to become a sailor or an actor. He spent a great deal of his earliest years with his grandfather, a former surgeon general in the British Navy.

1871. First trip to the United States with his parents. "Books had a great deal to do with my coming to America . . . for at that time I was given my choice of going to San Francisco with my father and mother or of staying in England and entering Rugby. I had been reading avidly, two very different stories. One was *Tom Brown's School Days* and the other was Captain Mayne Reid's impossible tales of adventures with American Indians. I loved them both but I weighed one against the other in my mind and the Redskins won!" [Reginald Birch, "Some Books I've Illustrated," *Publishers Weekly*, October 19, 1935.[1]]

1873. Studied painting at the Royal Academy in Munich.

1881. "It was ten years later . . . when I made my second visit to the States that I had my first introduction to the *St. Nicholas* magazine and its editor, Mary Mapes Dodge. Long before, when a boy in school, I got a prize (the only one I ever received) and it was her story *Hans Brinker*, but at that time I hadn't the faintest idea of ever seeing America or Mrs. Dodge.

"Her point of view in regard to my work was refreshing in contrast to that of Frederick Dielman who had been a great chum of mine in Munich. He was the same who later became President of the National Academy. One day in looking over some sketch books of mine (those were the days when we all carried sketch books. Alas, the camera has now replaced them) he remarked that the drawings were damned clever but that he didn't believe that I could draw a respectable woman if I tried. When I started making illustrations for *St. Nicholas*, Mrs. Dodge said to me one day, 'Mr. Birch, the thing we love about your work is that you draw such perfect ladies!'

"When I commenced at *St. Nicholas* they gave me as a tryout a little jingle which was to be more or less a test because I was told afterwards that they had given it to nine different men to illustrate and they had made nothing of it. It ran like this:

> 'Oh, carry me to college, sir
> To get a high degree
> A very learned doctor
> In college I would be
> They sent me home from college
> With never a degree
> And told me for to go and learn
> My A B C.'

"I can remember my illustration for this now. I put the portrait of a very learned doctor in the large initial at the beginning, then a youth carried in a sedan chair followed by a small 'Buttons' with arms full of books, some of them falling to the ground. At the end of the verse I made the same student tearing his hair and being regarded by a grinning bust of Minerva. My drawing was accepted and this was my introduction to the Century Company and *St. Nicholas* Magazine."[1]

1886. Gained fame with his illustrations of Francis Hodgson Burnett's *Little Lord Fauntleroy*. The author purportedly made over one third of a million dollars while the illustrator received four hundred dollars for his drawings. "... I was surprised by a request to illustrate a full length story to be printed serially and later published in book form. It was called *Little Lord Fauntleroy*. I don't like to look at these drawings now. They seem to me crude and unworthy, but it is one book that I haven't been able to lose or forget. It has followed me all of my life and all of my work of better quality has been pushed in the background. I am doomed to be known as the creator of *Little Lord Fauntleroy*. I have tried to accept this punishment in a contrite spirit as penance for the suffering my pictures have inflicted upon innumerable small boys forced to go through their early trousered years in long-curled; velvet-suited and lace-collared misery, the victims of their mothers' adoration for Mrs. Frances Hodgson Burnett's hero. Many men have told me that they had to go through the 'misery' of wearing that 'Damned suit' that I invented—with one illustrious exception—no less than the famous author and critic, Alexander Woollcott, who told me that he not only wore it but liked it.

"It is possible that I was better equipped to make the illustrations of this book than most men because I had met a great many people who resembled the characters in my boyhood days on the Isle of Jersey; such as half-pay officers, retired admirals and generals and some few titled people who had gone there because it was cheap and charming. They were conservative and narrow minded but distinctly of the better class of English society. . . .

"The picture of the Earl that I drew (the grandfather of Little Lord Fauntleroy) was founded on my own grandfather whom I remembered as a distinguished looking old gentleman who had entered the British Navy as a Middie of 13 years of age about two years after the Declaration of Independence in this country. Mrs. Burnett had two boys whom she dressed somewhat like the costume I finally made for Fauntleroy himself, though I modified it. . . . It was an essentially Victorian story and a life with which I was very familiar.

"Are you the earl?" said Cedric; "I'm your grandson. I'm Lord Fauntleroy." ■ (From *Little Lord Fauntleroy* by Frances Hodgson Burnett. Illustrated by Reginald B. Birch.)

"It's a magic flivver of course," Trouchee responded.
■ (From *The Enchanted Flivver* by Berton Braley.
Illustrated by Reginald Birch.)

"Mrs. Burnett was a well-known author at that time, one of
her best books being *Lass O'Lowrie* and the publishers considered it a feather in their caps to get Fauntleroy. The
amount I was paid for the illustration was absurdly small, but
I suppose I should have felt amply compensated, for after it
was put on the stage, I received two free tickets to the opening performance. There was a much finer compensation,
however, in the pleasure I had in meeting that delightful little
actress, Elsie Leslie and her beautiful sister. She originated
the part of Fauntleroy on the stage and was always to me the
best of the lot of them who came afterward.

"When I met her, I made her a present of a little drawing of
Little Lord Fauntleroy bowing to her. She said, 'Why do you
make his legs so long?' 'Naturally,' I replied, 'so he can get
to you as quickly as possible.'

"In those days we used to send our drawings to the publisher
by a messenger boy whom we called directly from our studios by a switch. We used to pay Western Union at the end
of the month. So far reaching was this service that women
often took these boys to the theater as chaperones. I deplore
this is no longer possible. One day during the time I was illustrating Lord Fauntleroy—I was living at the Benedict in
Washington Square and Century Company had just moved
up to Union Square—I called a messenger to send one of my
final drawings to the publisher. I noticed that he was a sort of

frivolous type and the drawing was quite large, so I was disturbed after he left with it. I hastily put on my things and followed him, overtaking him as he got to Union Square. It was
raining and there was a very high wind. He was amusing
himself by tossing my drawing up in the air. It would float for
awhile and then drop in the mud. We arrived at Century Co.
with the boy in my custody, and rather crestfallen.

"After the success of Little Lord Fauntleroy, Mrs. Burnett
wrote many other juvenile stories and expressing herself
pleased with my illustrations, requested that I make the
drawings for them. There was a series of books which I remember *Editha's Burglar, Sara Crewe, Giovanni, Two Little
Pilgrims* and later, *The One I Knew Best of All*, being a story
about herself. By this time I was virtually on the staff of *St.
Nicholas* and did an immense amount of work, many ballads
and stories."[1]

1888-1921. Birch's illustrations appeared regularly in such
periodicals as *Life, Century, St. Nicholas* and *Youth's Companion*, and were in great demand by publishers and editors.
"Although I have illustrated well over one hundred books in
my day, I can really remember only a few because I have
always been so dissatisfied with them after a week or two
that I have not even kept them. So they are forgotten. . . .

**Little Bo-Peep has lost her sheep,
And can't tell where to find them.**
■ (From *Rainbow in the Sky* by Louis Untermeyer.
Illlustrated by Reginald Birch.)

''The book which particularly appealed to me though, was one called *Master Skylark* by John Bennett. It was also a child's book and a delight to illustrate. I knew the author well, in fact we became very good friends and I have two letters of appreciation from him which I prize more than anything in the world. In one of these he writes me—'the setting is just full of the touch and essence of romance which you possess more than any other draftsman I know.' I am afraid the romance was in his story and had to crop out in the illustrations.

''After this along came many other books to illustrate. There was a drawing for a story of Kentucky mountaineers—*Red Head* it was called—by John Uri Lloyd which had a certain amount of value. Dodd, Mead published this. Another book, *The Admiral's Caravan* by Caryl was clever and amusing. At one time I did *Silas Marner* for Blackwood, the Edinburgh people, and *Little Men* for a Boston publisher. There were always the Children's Magazines and I may be pardoned if I quote a phrase from a letter written me by Pringle Barret, Editor of *The Youth's Companion*—'How pleasant it is to receive drawings that do not stop where the text stops! It is as if they said, ''Hurry and read the verse, then look at us; we have more to say.'' ''[1]

''Do not hurt these children. Be good to them, do you hear?'' The dog seemed to understand. ■ (From *The Lucky Stone* by Abbie Farwell Brown. Illustrated by Reginald Birch.)

Then a grating sound was heard, with the clank of an iron door, and a large brown bear appeared in the arena. The crouching African fixed her eyes upon him, but did not move. ■ (From *The Vizier of the Two-Horned Alexander* by Frank R. Stockton. Illustrated by Reginald B. Birch.)

1925-1933. Spent very little time illustrating—suffered financial trouble.

1933-1941. Illustrated Louis Untermeyer's book of stories from the Gilbert and Sullivan's operas, *The Last Pirate*. This commission resulted in a resurge of his popularity—in the next eight years Birch illustrated more than twenty books. ''It is delightful to draw for children and I never had a criticism from a child that hadn't got some vital reason and good sound sense. I think that they like simple illustrations, straight-forward and dramatic, pathetic or humorous; but they must always be more or less full of action or healthy sentiment. And, also they must be authentic. I have letters from these child readers long since grown up telling me of some long forgotten work that had clung in their memories through all the years. One of these came only a year or two ago from Leicester B. Holland, Chief of the Division of Fine Arts of the Library of Congress. He says, 'You and Howard Pyle were the first artists whose work I hailed by name. . . . I don't suppose you remember Oliver Herford's

Miss Smith sailed up to an old secretary which stood in the room, threw back the lid of the writing-desk, and sitting down before it, accompanied herself with a vigor which made the old desk rattle....
■ (From *Little Men* by Louisa M. Alcott. Illustrated by Reginald Birch.)

"Sir Rojer de Romily Rose
Had at least sixty-five suits of clothes.
   His cravats of all styles
    Measured miles upon miles,
While his ruffles and frills—goodness knows!"

"'There was a tiny drawing by you of a laundress throwing up her hands in dismay, that was a gem. The impression it made on my childish mind has never grown dim.' Such a tribute makes life worth living.

"As to the child critics, I was once told by one that a camel didn't walk the way I had drawn it. It was true, because I had made it trotting and a camel is a pacer.

"One rarely receives an unconscious compliment, so I was very flattered by the actions of a little boy who got on the same elevated with me one day. He had a copy of *St. Nicholas* in his hand. Turning the pages, he came to some illustrations I had made. He looked at them carefully, then went on and looked at others. Finally he turned back to my illustrations and began to read the story.

"But perhaps the highest praise I ever had from a child was written me by John Bennett. In speaking of the characters in *Master Skylark* and my depicting of them, he goes on, 'Carew's face in the prison-scene is as strong and sympathetic a piece of work as I can remember: a little Kansas City girl here cried over it, although she assured me she did not like Gaston Carew a bit.'

"Illustrations for children are difficult because the stories invariably introduce so many different things—animals, flowers, birds—and you have to get them right; to say nothing of the exercise of imagination necessary to picture gnomes, fairies and other fanciful creatures."[1]

1941-1943. Failing eyesight and health forced Birch to give up his work. He remarked to a friend: "I don't in the least object to the idea of dying, but I always wanted to die in harness. Now if my pen falls on the floor it takes me half an hour to find it and that I don't enjoy." [Elizabeth Bevier Hamilton, "Reginald Birch," *Horn Book,* January, 1944.[2]]

Birch was described as a gallant gentleman who had become a distinguished and almost legendary figure in his beloved New York. He was interviewed by the press annually on his birthday.

June 17, 1943. Died at the age of eighty-seven. Two days before his death he remarked: "There's still so much work I want to do. But if I'm not going to be well enough to do it, I'd much rather not wait around any longer."[2]

Reginald Birch's works are included in the Kerlan Collection at the University of Minnesota.

FOR MORE INFORMATION SEE: Publishers Weekly, October 19, 1935; *Horn Book,* May, 1941, January, 1944; Bertha E. Mahoney and others, compilers, *Illustrators of Children's Books: 1744-1945,* Horn Book, 1947; Stanley J. Kunitz, editor, *Junior Book of Authors,* revised edition, H. W. Wilson, 1951; Loring Holmes Dodd, *Generation of Illustrators and Etchers,* Chapman & Grimes, 1960; (obituary) *New York Times,* June 18, 1943.

(Died June 17, 1943)

(From "Jingles Old and New" in *Rainbow in the Sky* edited by Louis Untermeyer. Illustrated by Reginald Birch.)

BONNER, Mary Graham 1890-1974

PERSONAL: Born September 5, 1890 (or 1895, according to some sources), in Cooperstown, New York; died February 12, 1974, in New York City; dual citizen of the United States and Canada; daughter of George William Graham (a bank manager) and Margaret Cary (Worthington) Bonner. *Education:* Attended Halifax Ladies' College and Halifax Conservatory of Music in Nova Scotia. *Home:* New York City.

CAREER: Author of books, magazine articles, stories, and reviews. *Awards, honors:* Constance Lindsay Skinner award from the Women's National Book Association, 1943, for *Canada and Her Story.*

WRITINGS: Daddy's Bedtime Animal Stories (illustrated by Florence Choate and Elizabeth Curtis), F. A. Stokes, 1916; *Daddy's Bedtime Fairy Stories* (illustrated by Choate and Curtis), F. A. Stokes, 1916; *Daddy's Bedtime Bird Stories* (illustrated by Choate and Curtis), F. A. Stokes, 1917; *365 Bedtime Stories* (illustrated by Choate and Curtis), F. A. Stokes, 1923; *A Parent's Guide to Children's Reading,* Funk, 1926; *The Magic Map* (illustrated by Luxor Price), Macaulay, 1927; *Mrs. Cucumber Green* (illustrated by Janet L. Scott), Milton Bradley, 1927; *Magic Journeys* (illustrated by Luxor Price), Macaulay, 1928; *Miss Angeline Adorable* (illustrated by Janet L. Scott), Milton Bradley, 1928; *Madam Red Apple* (illustrated by Scott), Milton Bradley, 1929; *The Magic Music Shop* (illustrated by Luxor Price; with music by Harry Meyer), Macaulay, 1929.

Etiquette for Boys and Girls: A Handbook for Use by Mothers, Governesses and Teachers, McLoughlin, 1930; *A Hundred Trips to Storyland* (illustrated by Hildegard Lupprian), Macaulay, 1930; *The Magic Universe* (illustrated by Luxor Price), Macaulay, 1930; *The Big Baseball Book for Boys* (edited by Alan Gould; introduction by Ty Cobb), McLoughlin, 1931; *The Magic Clock* (illustrated by Luxor Price), Macaulay, 1931; *The Animal Map of the World* (illustrated by Price), Macaulay, 1932; *Adventures in Puddle Muddle* (illustrated by William A. Kolliker), Dutton, 1935; *Rainbow at Night,* L. Furman, 1936; *A World of Our Own* (illustrated by William A. Kolliker), Dutton, 1936; (editor) *Every Child's Story Book,* McLoughlin, 1938; (editor) *The Open Door to Storyland,* McLoughlin, 1938; *A Story Teller's Holiday* (illustrated by Janet L. Scott), McLoughlin, 1938; (editor) *A.B.C. Nursery Rhyme Book,* McLoughlin, 1939.

Sir Noble, the Police Horse, Knopf, 1940; *Danger on the Coast: A Story of Nova Scotia,* Knopf, 1941; *Canada and Her Story,* Knopf, 1942, 2nd edition, revised, 1950; *Made in Canada,* Knopf, 1943; *Couriers of the Sky: The Story of Pigeons,* Knopf, 1944, 2nd edition, revised, published as *Couriers of the Sky: Pigeons and Their Care,* 1952; *The Surprise Place* (illustrated by Lois Lenski), Knopf, 1945; *Something Always Happens* (illustrated by Avery Johnson), Knopf, 1946; *Out to Win: A Baseball Story* (illustrated by Howard Butler), Knopf, 1947, reprinted, 1965; *Hidden Village Mystery* (illustrated by Bob Meyers), Knopf, 1948; *The Mysterious Caboose,* Knopf, 1949.

The Haunted Hut: A Winter Mystery (illustrated by Bob Meyers), Knopf, 1950, published as *Mystery of the Haunted Hut* (illustrated by Norman Baer), Scholastic Books, 1969; *Winning Dive: A Camp Story* (illustrated by Bob Meyers), Knopf, 1950; *The Base-Stealer* (illustrated by Meyers), Knopf, 1951; *Wait and See* (illustrated by John N. Barron), Knopf, 1952; *Dugout Mystery* (illustrated by Jonathan Dav-

Joe Dingle lifted a long fly to right, and after the catch, Hawk tore down to third, sliding in ahead of the throw. ■ (From *Dugout Mystery* by M. G. Bonner. Illustrated by Jonathan David.)

id), Knopf, 1953; *Baseball Rookies Who Made Good,* Knopf, 1954; *How to Play Baseball* (illustrated by Bernard Krigstein), Knopf, 1955; (editor) Rebecca McCann, *Complete Cheerful Cherub,* Crown, 1956 (Bonner was not associated with earlier edition); *The Real Book about Crime Detection* (illustrated by Vincent Fodera), Garden City Books, 1957; *Wonders Around the Sun,* Lantern Press, 1957; *The Real Book about Sports* (illustrated by Albert Orbaan), Garden City Books, 1958; *Two-Way Pitcher* (illustrated by Victor Prezio), Lantern Press, 1958; *Spray Hitter* (illustrated by Prezio), Lantern Press, 1959.

The Real Book about Journalism (illustrated by Albert Orbaan), Garden City Books, 1960; *Wonders of Inventions* (illustrated by Carol Cobbledick), Lantern Press, 1961; *Mystery at Lake Ashburn,* Lantern Press, 1962; *Wonders of Musical Instruments* (illustrated by Carol Cobbledick), Lantern Press, 1963.

Author of over 3,000 "Sundown Stories" syndicated daily by the Associated Press during a ten-year period.

SIDELIGHTS: Athletics came early to Mary Bonner. In school in Halifax, Nova Scotia (where her father was a bank manager) she played basketball, hockey and rounders (British baseball). She won several awards for swimming and high diving and was an expert at skating and ice boating as well.

Bonner's earliest ambition was to become a pianist. She studied at the Halifax Conservatory of Music, but writing became her chosen profession. She had the unusual experience of having all of her earliest writings accepted. Most of Bonner's earliest books were written for the very young, although she later became famous for her books on baseball which she signed, "M. G. Bonner."

Bonner held dual citizenship from the United States and Canada. Born in the town which claims baseball as its birthplace, Cooperstown, New York, Bonner left the United States while an infant when her family settled in Nova Scotia. New York City became her residence as an adult. Her purpose in writing for children was to "... give the youngsters an idea of democracy with a small 'd.' None of the blatant kind of propaganda ... but the real feeling of understanding." [Nina Brown Baker, "Mary Graham Bonner," *Wilson Library Bulletin*, May, 1950.[1]]

For many years Bonner was on the staff of the Feature Service of the Associated Press, which syndicated her stories for children. The prolific children's author died on February 12, 1974 in New York City. She was in her early eighties.

Among her baseball books is *How to Play Baseball*—a guide for beginning players. A San Francisco *Chronicle* critic wrote that the book "... is an excellent guide to rules and regulations and full of tips and suggestions for improving play. The text is illustrated with clear, diagrammatic drawings...." *Real Book about Sports* commented briefly on some thrilling moments in sports history. *Booklist* called it "uneven in treatment, but filled with much biographical and historical information which will fascinate the sports fan." A *Kirkus* reviewer described it as a "well-paced, journalistically written text. Of obvious interest to the fan, ... [it] will, on the basis of its human interest, also appeal to the non-partisan."

The scope of Bonner's work covered many other subjects as well. *Real Book about Crime* was reviewed by a *Kirkus* critic who said, "Sanity prevails in presentation for the text emphasizes that protection of the innocent is as important as prosecution of the guilty, and there are examples of alert youngsters who have helped in the apprehension of criminals."

HOBBIES AND OTHER INTERESTS: Playing basketball, hockey, and rounders (British baseball), swimming, high diving, skating, ice boating, and camping.

FOR MORE INFORMATION SEE: N. B. Baker, "Mary Graham Bonner," *Wilson Library Bulletin*, May, 1950. Obituaries—*New York Times*, February 13, 1974; *Publishers Weekly*, March 4, 1974.

(Died February 12, 1974)

LUCY BOSTON, 1937

BOSTON, Lucy Maria (Wood)   1892-

PERSONAL: Born 1892, in Southport, Lancashire, England; daughter of James (an engineer) and Mary (Garrett) Wood; married an officer in the Royal Flying Corps., 1917 (marriage dissolved, 1935); children: Peter. *Education:* Attended Somerville College, Oxford. *Home:* Hemingford Grey, Huntingdonshire, England.

CAREER: Author of children's books. Briefly trained as a nurse before going to France to treat the wounded during the first World War; indulged herself in the cultural arts while traveling through Europe, 1935-39; began a personal restoration project of a manor house at Hemingford Grey, which later served as a background for her books; started her literary career at the age of sixty-two. *Awards, honors:* Carnegie Medal, 1961, for *A Stranger at Green Knowe;* Lewis Carroll Shelf Award, 1969, for *The Children of Green Knowe.*

WRITINGS—Fiction, except as noted: *The Children of Green Knowe* (ALA Notable Book; illustrated by son, Peter Boston), Faber, 1954, Harcourt, 1955; *Yew Hall*, Faber, 1954; *Treasure of Green Knowe* (illustrated by P. Boston), Harcourt, 1958 (published in England as *The Chimneys of Green Knowe*, Faber, 1958); *The River at Green Knowe* (ALA Notable Book; illustrated by P. Boston), Harcourt, 1959; *A Stranger at Green Knowe* (ALA Notable Book; illustrated by P. Boston), Harcourt, 1961; *An Enemy at Green Knowe* (illustrated by P. Boston), Harcourt, 1964; *The Castle of Yew* (illustrated by Margery Gill), Harcourt, 1965; *The Sea Egg* (illustrated by P. Boston), Harcourt, 1967; (contributor) Kathleen Lines, editor, *The House of the Nightmare and Other Eerie Tales*, Bodly Head, 1967, Farrar, Straus,

1968; *The House that Grew* (illustrated by Caroline Hemming), Faber, 1969; *Strongholds,* Harcourt, 1969 (published in England as *Persephone,* Collins, 1969).

The Horned Man; or, Whom Will You Send to Fetch Her Away? (play), Faber, 1970; (contributor) *Young Winter's Tales, I* (edited by M. R. Hodgkin), Macmillan, 1970; *Nothing Said* (illustrated by P. Boston), Harcourt, 1971; *Memory in a House* (nonfiction), Bodley Head, 1973, Macmillan, 1974; *The Guardians of the House* (illustrated by P. Boston), Bodley Head, 1974, Atheneum, 1975; *The Fossil Snake* (illustrated by P. Boston), Atheneum, 1975; *The Stones of Green Knowe* (illustrated by P. Boston), Atheneum, 1976; *Perverse and Foolish* (nonfiction), Bodley Head, 1979.

SIDELIGHTS: **1892.** Born in Lancashire, England; one of six children, in an intensely evangelical family. Her father died when she was six years old. "I was born in 1892, and even for that faraway date my parents were old-fashioned and so unlikely that I can hardly believe my memories are of real people. The family was rigidly, rabidly puritanical. Music, art, drama, dancing, and pleasure were all wicked. My mother thought even good food unnecessary to salvation, and therefore wrong. The most important parental influence over my life was by being specifically taught that I was born and bred to be a martyr, by burning at the stake; it was my destiny and my duty. This I have never felt up to, and have laboured all my life under a sense of absolute spiritual failure.

"We lived in a featureless, new, uninspiring town full of wealth and churches, and my memories would show a starvation of everything but hymns and sermons, if we had not moved into the country for my mother's health. This was when I was eleven, and from that moment, life was as different as for a butterfly getting out of its chrysalis, became then like the children in my books: all eyes, ears, and finger tips in a world too beautiful to take in. Every moment of day and night was bliss, and had to be prolonged with solitary rambles in the early dawn, of which my elders had certainly no idea. There was no keeping me in, day or night, wet or fine. This, I suppose, is why my book-children are early rovers.

"We lived in the north, and my sister and I were sent away to boarding school as far south as possible, to correct our north-country accent. We were, of course, great oddities and were unmercifully ragged and very unhappy. But we learnt to ride and had wild gallops on an old racecourse on the Downs. I went to a finishing school in Paris, thence to Oxford to read English, which I cut short for service in a French hospital in World War I. France became my country of adoption." [John Rowe Townsend, *A Sense of Story,* Lippincott, 1971.[1]]

1917. ". . . I married an English officer in the Flying Corps, as that romantic pioneering body was called. I have one son, the original Tolly—well qualified to draw his own dog, his own toys, his own toy box. I am not a traveller, but have wandered in France, Italy, Austria and Hungary, and studied painting in Vienna. I believe that one place closely explored will yield more than continents passed through."[1]

The garden in 1943.

The manor today.

Her marriage lasted from 1917 to the middle of the 1930's. One son, Peter. "My married home was in the industrial North, in a pocket of country depreciating rapidly under air pollution from Widnes. Its former hilly beauty showed ghostlike through, enough to feed imagination and melancholy in equal proportion.

"The break-up of my marriage caused me to move to Italy and Austria to learn to paint. Mussolini pushed me out of Italy and Hitler out of Austria, but by that time I was launched on a new career and did not contemplate ever doing anything but paint, all day and every day, with passion." [L. M. Boston, *Memory in a House,* Bodley Head, 1973.[2]]

1939. Settled at the Manor House, Hemingford, Grey, near Cambridge. The locale of most of her books. "I landed up here when I had nowhere to be. My marriage had broken up and I was in a flat in Cambridge, and then I found this; and it was a completely new life, and I have never wanted to be anywhere else. I can hardly leave it for a day!" [Justin Wintle and Emma Fisher, *The Pied Pipers,* Paddington Press, 1975.[3]]

"They gave me the date of the building, 1120, as an established fact, which I received with willing credulity. I did not at once ask for proof and have found none since, but the builder, Payne Osmundsen, died in 1154.

"Looking back now, it is hard to know why I acted with such certainty and passion. It was like falling in love. Faults were brushed away as having no valid reality, common sense or waiting-till-you-are-sure were not to be considered. I was going where it took me. I was in my late forties, I knew not a soul in the district and was going to live alone in this overwhelming atmosphere. Furthermore, to a practical mind the house was simply not fit for rational habitation. It had no adequate drains and all water was drawn from the well by hand pump; but this was real country living, almost romantic. Worse than that, it was ramshackle madness from top to bottom. For example, the servant's attic bedroom under the south gable was reached off a corkscrew staircase through a two-foot square hole at floor level, underneath a tie-beam, and could only be entered on one's knees.

"The restoration of the house took two years, which were by far the happiest in my life, even in spite of the war which broke out as soon as the builders began. I propose to describe as accurately as I can what was done, because I think it should be put on record. The antiquarian societies that visited my predecessors continue to visit me, no doubt writing articles on the house and adding particulars to their lectures. The standard approach is for one leading member to say to another 'What do you make of that?' pointing to some restored feature. An argument then begins, exploring possibilities, drawing false conclusions. If I then interrupt, explaining that the restoration was done under my orders, that I know and can tell them, they do not want to know. I am spoiling their game.

"Quite apart from what I know has been done, I have lived in the house throughout and it has seemed as if in a sense walls did speak. I lived in it when it was so stripped down that it had neither roof, windows nor doors, and the walls gaped in section from rafter to ground. It has a very strong personality, to which I submitted once and for all. I forced nothing, and faked nothing. I explored lovingly and yet seemed to know what would eventually come of it. Now after . . . years of living in it, it begins to be taken for my work of art, and in the sense that it lives in this century there

must be some truth in that. Shamefacedly I remember Michelangelo who said his statues were already in the stone and he only had to uncover them. Did I then only find what I had invented in imagination rebuilding it to my dreams without realising I was doing so? The answer is No, and with all my conviction No. But it is a love affair, and like all old lovers the house and I have grown alike.

"My architect was Hugh Hughes of Cambridge. He is an authority on Norman building and no doubt this interesting job was one on which he would have strong feelings. Owing to the war, petrol was scarce, so that he only came at intervals. On these occasions there was a ritual constantly disrupted by my failure to conform. Those who for the first time employ an architect often have the shock of discovering that their wishes are of no interest to anyone but themselves. On the other hand, I know one architect who left the profession because he foresaw he might come before long to murder some female client. I had found a house that, from that moment and for the rest of my life, was opening up for me emotions and interests of a range and depth I had never imagined. I knew what I wanted and I was going to have it.

"The architect brought his assistant and the builder brought his son, and below him came the foreman. This was the hierarchy of the procession that went round the house. The architect would courteously request his assistant to draw in detail some plan he had outlined. The assistant would ask the builder if he understood. The builder would ask his son if he felt able to carry it out. The son asked the old foreman simply 'Can you do it?' The foreman said 'Yes' to the son, the son said 'Yes' to his father, etc., as in a nursery rhyme, back to the architect. At this point from the bottom of the social scale, too low even to have been credited with presence, let alone an opinion, I was usually obliged to say 'No.' It seemed to cause as much shock as if I had said it in church instead of now and forever after holding my peace. For the very reason that the house meant so much to me, the fight to preserve it left me shaking and exhausted.

"The foreman was 'Old Childs.' He was a small wizened man, soured with too much bitter cold in exposed places, very deaf and grim-looking. Nevertheless I recognised him as my real collaborator. For two years I spent most of my days with him in great amity and mutual respect. He revered the house and took pride in all that he did, and from the start showed that his first loyalty was to me. Between us everything that I wanted got done, often against the architect's orders."[2]

During the Second World War—"On answering the bell one day I found the Chief Constable on the step. He introduced himself with these surprising words—'Mrs. Boston? How do you do. When somebody is reported as a spy by every other person in their village, I think it is time the Chief Constable got to know her. May I come in?'

"We had an amiable enough tea-party together. I confirmed that I had a son in the Royal Engineers, otherwise no questions were asked and only small talk passed. My impression was that he dismissed the village gossip, but there was a follow-up sometime later not altogether pleasing.

"A rather girlish middle-aged woman, a little over-dressed as if anxious not to be thought dowdy, with the falsely hearty manners of a commercial traveller, arrived without warning, saying she had been asked by the Chief Constable to call on us.

Tom Morgan was fishing in his usual place, as far away as he could get from the noise of traffic. ■ (From *The Guardians of the House* by L. M. Boston. Illustrated by Peter Boston.)

"'I am told you are very good to our boys in the RAF.'

"There was something slightly 'off' in the way she said it, but I did not get the significance. We brought her in and showed her the whole place, as I always did, but she seemed, for all her peeping, dissatisfied. Her conversation seemed to us inept to the verge of lunacy. She began by telling us how very easy she knew it was to get drunk. It even happened to her sometimes. 'You can't really blame a girl for that.'

"All-girls-together is a manner I greatly dislike. . . . She seemed to be working to put us at our ease while feeling very much out of order herself, like someone whose gears won't engage.

"She picked up the book I had been reading to look at the title, and dropped it as if it had bitten her. It happened to be the *Confessions of St. Augustine*. She hopped up and down ejaculating jollities, and finally found herself looking down through the interior Norman window in the music room that gives onto the spare room. There she saw a double bed glittering under . . . sequin-covered muslin bedspreads.

"'O!' she let out like a pop-gun. 'A fairies' room!!'

"Now what could she have meant by that? At long last she went, saying at the door that she would be coming again, probably every month.

"We were staggered, and rang up a friend who knew the district better than we did, to ask if she had ever heard of such a person. 'Oh yes, of course. She's the Welfare visitor, she keeps an eye on all the prostitutes.'

"However she also must have decided that we weren't somehow quite the type, for she never came again.

"I was still amused, far from taking in that I was a real concern to Intelligence. Meanwhile the house continued its own mysterious life and from time to time sent feelers out from its darker corners, such as slight poltergeistic displacements, footsteps up the wooden stairs, wandering lights, voices, etc., but so much immediate and dramatic human life filled the place that irrational trifles did not get much attention. If [we] . . . were alone, there were urgent hammerings at night on a side door never used. The first time it happened I took the dogs and went to open, thinking some accident must have taken place and help was needed. No one was there, nor did the dogs bark or go chasing off after an intruder. They kept well behind me. After a few recurrences we ceased to take any notice. Then one night it was very persistent, leaving one door to go round and hammer on another.

Presently the sun came out and beautifully warmed them in the shell of the canoe, and with the sun appeared another host of living things: butterflies, dragonflies, water boatmen, brightly colored beetles and lizards, and high up in the sky a weaving of swallows. ■ (From *The River at Green Knowe* by L. M. Boston. Illustrated by Peter Boston.)

We shrugged it off and continued knitting. Eventually, because of his importunity, I went to the door, and found there a policeman, displeased by his long wait. He had come about a crack of light showing. 'And I have been knocking a long time.'

"'Oh yes, we heard you, but we just thought it was our ghost. We get a lot of that.' As I said it, I realised the perfect idiocy of this when said to the police. I did not realise the insolence of it when said by a spy to cover comings and goings. Fortunately he was a junior and had not been given an official line on such an excuse.

"Some, but not all, of our hauntings were traced much later to a local maniac given to midnight wandering. For choice, I would prefer the tics of an old house.

"The only things that bothered me in what I otherwise considered a farce, were, first the insufferable insolence that the detective inspector who twice visited me contrived to put into the words 'Well, Mrs. Boston, *and how are you getting on?*' I was nauseated by Intelligence's implied belief, when I reported that I had found German ration cards in the garden, that I had picked an officer's pocket. I most minded the blushing misery of a WAAF officer for whom I had an affectionate respect, when she faced me for the first time after receiving her warning. Clearly the thought was there that it was not absolutely impossible that I should be a traitor."[2]

1954. Started her literary career at the age of sixty-two. Her son, Peter, illustrated most of her books. "Most of my books are an immediate reaction to something personally felt. The idea of *The Sea Egg* was triggered off by an egg of Cornish Serpentine sent me by Caroline Hemming in memory of Kynance Cove where she and I had revelled in the sea. Peter and I went down to Cornwall for a holiday to think it out. Daily we absorbed the waves, the seals, the rocks and the cliffs. I particularly wanted to show Peter a cove half way between Land's End and Nangisel. It was a wide semicircle, high and sheer, sea-sculpted all over with meaningful but mysterious figures crowded together as on the front of a cathedral. I had previously spent hours marveling at the carvings and trying to give dramatic interpretation to a staggering natural monument. When we got there, the whole cliff face had fallen into the sea since my last visit. There was nothing left.

"I was prevented from writing for a long time after this by having to nurse an old friend with a nervous breakdown. As everybody knows who has had to do this without help in their own house, the exhaustion and despair of the patient eventually reduces the nurse to a like state. At last, after eighteen months, my friend was well enough to leave. At once I sat down to write, and all the normal joy that had been blotted out for so long burst out and bubbled up. It is a short book, written straight off in about three weeks, but wholly happy, thinking only of the sea. Just as it was published, the *Torrey Canyon* blotted out Kynance under black oil.

"A photo in *The Times* of Guy, the gorilla in the London Zoo, triggered off *A Stranger at Green Knowe*. I spent many hours in front of his cage and was given the greatest help by his keeper and only friend, Laurie Smith, both in formal introduction to the magnificent creature from the Keeper's inner passage and in the supply of information, addresses and books. During Laurie's three weeks' holiday I saw Guy's despair, and actually witnessed, awe-struck, the tragic dance, like Samson praying for strength to pull the place down, of which I wrote in the book. I described this to

Lucy Boston, age two and a half.

Laurie on his return. He told me gorillas had been reported as doing this but that he had never seen it, and if I had, I could think myself extraordinarily privileged.

"I wished to dedicate *A Stranger* to Laurie Smith, but the Zoo authorities refused their permission on the grounds that my book was 'entirely against their principles.' Odd that the useful supposition that animals actually prefer captivity can be elevated to a principle.

"The subject to me was a big one. It had to contain the whole force of my belief that all life, not merely human, must have respect, that a man-centred conception of it was false and crippling, that these other lives are the great riches of ours. In particular I wanted to make clear my immense admiration for this creature so vulgarly shuddered at, and that there was no cosy answer to the wickedness that had been done to him.

"This book was awarded the Carnegie Medal. I was not very excited by this, because it seemed to me unlikely that a really wonderful book for children would be written every year, and as the same writer could then never receive it twice, that left one as the best in a period of twelve months after all the notable writers have already been excluded. It did not strike me as a dizzy peak. However my publishers wrote ardent congratulations, and letters from the awarding body of librarians wrote awesomely of the 'supreme award.' I was gradually coaxed away by such professional shibboleths from my common sense. I began to feel perhaps I had done something good, and that it was arrogant to depreciate an award. And not only one's vanity but one's proper pride as an artist longs to believe in recognition.

L. M. BOSTON

"I am now a grandmother and the house is filled with children every Saturday. My daughter-in-law Di already had two little boys when she married Peter, and now has two girls, of whom the eldest, Kate aged three and a half, seems to me myself reborn.

"After so long in undivided control in it, I had come to think of the house as a kind of museum for children. For years I had been adding to it things mentioned in my children's books as being here, which, till I chance to find them, had been imaginary. Friends also continually send me missing items made or·found—the wicker birdcage, the picture of 'The Frigate Woodpecker in a Storm,' a racehorse shoe, the name board for Feste's stall, a flute, a box of sea-treasures, ivory dominoes, etc., so that visiting schools could see the books come true. I have not yet succeeded in getting a harvest-mouse's nest, badly needed for my collection of nests. Very recently an enterprising schoolboy, Philip Foale, has undertaken to make a doll's house replica of the Manor.

"Each item had formerly a fixed place, and the loss of any of them I would have felt as a calamity. All this static museum stuff has now been swept away. The objects are desirable toys, strewn all over the house and lost or broken one by one in a torrent of irresponsible life. I do my best, but the epoch of possessions has gone. They are the least destructive of children, but for the young everything is kaleidoscopic, it must be broken apart and reformed every minute. Also they don't enjoy anything they have to take care of. They do not have to take care of their imagination, the vital element of

which toys are only the used and discarded tools. They are now old enough to have Green Knowe books read to them and to fill out the characters with all the power of their own feeling and fantasy. I am amused to find that Green Noah has left the page and truly prowls the garden, that Terak the giant has been *seen* lying by the river. They are enchanting in themselves, they love the house and everything in it and round about it, and every little enjoyment or game is ritually repeated every week.

"Ivy Violet [my 'cleaning lady'] touchingly adored children but had never had any of her own. Her deafness cut her off from my grandchildren, while her toothlessness and bristly white beard gave her a goblin look, straight out of the pictures in a fairy tale—the sort of face that might peer round a mushroom. The children were wary when she tried to coax them. It was sad that she got so little response.

"As she aged, she became an obsessive worker. She could not stop, except when she sat down and fell asleep, when she might sleep for a day and a night. Then she would not know what day it was, nor whether it was dawn or dusk. She would come pedalling madly along on her high bicycle and I would hear her little goat's feet running along the entrance hall. All out of breath, she would hang her red coat, that looked as if it had seen years of dirty warfare, on the tin-opener fixed to the wall, and begin work all in one movement. Every day, year after year, I took the coat off the tin-opener and hung it on the hook provided for it. She would watch me sideways round the broom handle and say, 'If I had to give you six-pence every time I hung it in the wrong place, you'd have been rich by now.'

"Often I would urge her to take it easy, not to get so out of breath. 'I don't believe in wasting time,' she said, going off at a run carrying the heavy Hoover. Her legs were like matchsticks.

"Watson the gardener told me that once, when I was away, he locked up the house long after Ivy Violet had finished work and was on his way home when he thought he had better make sure all the lights were turned off. He went back into the dining room and there in the dusk something caught his eye. It was Ivy curled up like a cat asleep in the armchair, having been overtaken by one of her twenty-four hours naps. She will certainly share with me the privilege of being one of the Manor ghosts.

"Indeed one day she never came. We did not worry, but just laughed and said she'd fallen asleep. The next morning also she was absent so I sent Watson round to her cottage—he always treated her with the greatest courtesy and helped her by sweeping her chimney or heaving coal as if he were a nephew—to see if she was ill. He found her bicycle propped against an open door, the wireless on, and Ivy lying on the sofa, dead. Her last ride standing on the pedals had been too much for her, her last sleep endless.

"For several days afterwards the house seemed to be full of her pattering steps and all the little mouselike scratching noises associated with her (she had always done a great deal of her cleaning with a *penknife!*). . . .'"[2]

"Now I have found the place I need, and though postcards from abroad excite me to fever point, this is where I stay, getting deeper in it every moment and always surprised. This is the house that all the books describe. If I were a historian, a lifetime could be spent researching into it. But I just sit and talk to it. I live in it alone and find it good company."[1]

1970—. Continues to write books while in her eighties. "Is there a conscious difference in the way I write for grownups and children? No, there is no difference of approach, style, vocabulary or standard. I could pick out passages from any of the books and you would not be able to tell what age it was aimed at. There is a difference in the range of experiences evoked. . . .

"My approach has always been to explore reality as it appears, and from within to see how far imagination can properly expand it. Reality, after all, has no outside edge. I never start with a fantasy and look for a peg to hang it on. As far as I deliberately try to do anything other than write a book that pleases me, I would like to remind adults of joy, now considered obsolete—and would like to encourage children to use and trust their senses for themselves at first hand—their ears, eyes and noses, their fingers and the soles of their feet, their skins and their breathing, their muscular joy and rhythms and heartbeats, their instinctive loves and pity and their awe of the unknown. This, not the telly, is the primary material of thought. It is from direct sense stimulus that imagination is born. . . ."[1]

FOR MORE INFORMATION SEE: Jasper A. Rose, *Lucy Boston,* Bodley Head, 1965; Brian Doyle, *The Who's Who of Children's Literature,* Schocken Books, 1968; Eleanor Cameron, *The Green and Burning Tree,* Atlantic-Little, Brown, 1969; *Horn Book,* October 1969, June, 1971, August, 1974, June, 1975, June and December, 1976; John Rowe Townsend, *A Sense of Story,* Lippincott, 1971; Doris de Montreville, editor, *Third Book of Junior Authors,* H. W. Wilson, 1972; Lucy M. Boston, *Memory in a House,* Bodley Head, 1973, Macmillan, 1974; Justin Wintle, *The Pied Pipers,* Paddington, 1975; *The London Times,* May 7, 1976; *The Observer* (London), May 16, 1976.

J. ALLAN BOSWORTH

All at once the fish was there, and moving slowly by, and the boy did not have time to do anything but aim and plunge his spear into the water. ■ (From *White Water, Still Water* by J. Allan Bosworth. Illustrated by Charles W. Walker.)

BOSWORTH, J. Allan 1925-

PERSONAL: Born in 1925, in California.

CAREER: Author. Has worked as a member of the staff of the *San Francisco Chronicle. Military service:* Served as a naval officer aboard the USS Missouri during World War II.

WRITINGS: A Bird for Peter (illustrated by Howard Simon), Criterion Books, 1963; *Voices in the Meadow* (Junior Literary Guild selection; illustrated by Joseph Schindelman), Doubleday, 1964; *White Water, Still Water* (illustrated by Charles W. Walker), Doubleday, 1966; *All the Dark Places,* Doubleday, 1968; *A Wind Named Anne,* Doubleday, 1970; *A Darkness of Giants,* Doubleday, 1972; *Among Lions,* Doubleday, 1973.

SIDELIGHTS: The reviews of Bosworth's *Voices in the Meadow* ranged from the *Atlantic Monthly* assessment, "A pleasant nature story with fine touches of humor and suspense," to the *New York Times* commentary: "There is a certain excitement in the story. . . . Unfortunately, the suspense is strung out by minor adventures and tedious consultations among the animals. Too many characters crowd the scene, and the dialogue becomes mostly wisecracks. In the end, Beaver and friends find themselves in a wondrous wood. This somehow convinces Beaver that he has a soul, but such a pat solution is disappointing."

GEORGE A. BOYCE

BOYCE, George A(rthur)   1898-

PERSONAL: Born January 20, 1898, in Scranton, Pa.; son of Arthur Jay (a printer) and Marietta (Royce) Boyce; married Elizabeth A. Coleman, May 20, 1933 (died January 22, 1962); married Oleta Merry (a home economist), January 31, 1964; children: (first marriage) George A., Jr., Robert A. *Education:* Trinity College, Hartford, Conn., B.S., 1921; Cornell University, M.A., 1926; Columbia University, Ed.D., 1941. *Religion:* Protestant. *Home:* 1203 Calle Luna, Santa Fe, N.M. 87501. *Agent:* Jody Ellis, P.O. Box 2321, Santa Fe, N.M. 87501.

CAREER: Science and mathematics teacher in schools in Concord, N.H., 1921, Lake Placid, N.Y., 1921-23, Philadelphia, Pa., 1923-27 (head of science department and dean, 1923-27), Hudson, Ohio, 1927-31, and Bronxville, N.Y., 1931-38; U.S. Bureau of Indian Affairs, Washington, D.C., curriculum specialist, 1938-66. Director of Navajo schools; superintendent of Intermountain Indian School; member of board of directors of Verde Valley School. Chairman of long-range social-economic planning on Navajo Reservation, for U.S. Navajo Service, 1944; developed and served as superintendent of a program for Institute of American Indian Arts, 1961. *Military service:* U.S. Naval Reserve, 1918.

MEMBER: Santa Fe Westerners (vice-president), Santa Fe Council on International Relations (president). *Awards, honors:* Distinguished service gold medal from U.S. Secretary of the Interior, 1952, for social-economic survey and for

Intermountain Indian School; certificate of appreciation from Navajo Tribe, 1966; certificate of appreciation from Indian Arts and Crafts Board of U.S. Department of the Interior, 1967; D.H.L. from Trinity College (Hartford, Conn.), 1968.

WRITINGS: (With Willard W. Beatty) *Mathematics of Everyday Life,* five volumes, I.N.O.R. (New York), 1936; *When Navajoes Had Too Many Sheep,* Indian Historian Press, 1974; *Some People Are Indians,* Vanguard, 1974. Editor of pamphlets for U.S. Bureau of Indian Affairs, including "Dormitory Life: Is It Living?" and "Alcohol and American Indian Students."

WORK IN PROGRESS: Neither Red Nor White.

SIDELIGHTS: "Cultural differences are 'good.' To form a democratic, multi-cultural nation calls for nurturing rather than destroying cultural differences. The 'cement' is the common denominator of all sharing problems requiring mutual assistance. But cultural differences require different education insights and techniques."

"I write particularly for young people. My Indian short stories are culturally authentic—based upon working for many years with many numerous Indian tribes as an educator. The 'message' involves universal human problems, illustrated by today's Indian people."

BRO, Margueritte (Harmon)   1894-

PERSONAL: Born August 5, 1894, in David City, Neb.; daughter of Andrew Davison (a preacher) and Alice (Gadd) Harmon; married Albin Carl Bro (a teaching missionary), May, 1918; children: Harmon (a minister and author), Kenneth, Alice, Andrew. *Education:* Cotner College, B.A., 1917; graduate study at Butler University, the University of Chicago, and the University of Nanking.

CAREER: Has worked as a teacher, pastor's assistant, editor for *Harper's,* book reviewer, and ghost writer; author.

WRITINGS—For young people: *Why Church?* (missionary stories; illustrated by Ursula H. Bostwick), Friendship Press, 1947; *Sarah,* (novel), Doubleday, 1949, reprinted, Grosset, 1965; *Su-mei's Golden Year* (illustrated by Kurt Wiese), Doubleday, 1950; *Stub: A College Romance,* Doubleday, 1952; *Indonesia: Land of Challenge,* Harper, 1954, reprinted, 1962; *Three, and Domingo* (illustrated by Leonard Weisgard), Doubleday, 1953; *The Animal Friends of Peng-U* (illustrated by Seong Moy), Doubleday, 1965; *How the Mouse Deer Became King* (illustrated by Joseph Low), Doubleday, 1966.

Other: *Al's Technique* (one-act farce), Eldridge Entertainment House, 1931; (with Frank H. O'Hara) *A Handbook of Drama,* Willett, 1938, revised and enlarged edition published as *Invitation to the Theater,* Harper, 1951, reprinted, Greenwood Press, 1970; *Urban Scene,* Friendship Press, 1938; *When Children Ask,* Willett, 1940, revised edition, Harper, 1956; *Thursday at Ten,* Willett, 1942; *Every Day a Prayer* (devotional exercises), Willett, 1943; *Let's Talk about You,* Doubleday, Doran, 1945; *More Than We Are* (prayer), Harper, 1948, revised and enlarged edition, Harper, 1965; (with Harrie V. Rhodes) *In the One Spirit: The Autobiography of Harrie Vernette Rhodes,* Harper, 1951; (with Arthur A. Ford) *Nothing So Strange: Autobiography,* Harper, 1958, reissued, Paperback Library, 1971; (with Myrtle R. Walgreen) *Never a Dull Day: An Autobiography by Myrtle R. Walgreen*, Regnery, 1963; *Today Makes a Difference! An Everyday Book of Prayer*, Thomas Nelson, 1970; *The Book You Always Meant to Read: The Old Testament*, Doubleday, 1974.

SIDELIGHTS: As the daughter of a preacher and the wife of a teaching missionary, Margueritte Bro has travelled extensively and lived in China, Indonesia, and Korea, as well as in Mount Carroll, Illinois, where her husband was president of Shimer College. She has been a ghost writer and the author of many different types of books, including novels, books on the theatre, and inspirational books.

"In 1938 when an opportunity came my way to go to Argentina to visit an old uncle, I found myself quartered for two and a half months on a small Swedish freighter with only one other passenger, a disconcerting amount of quiet, and an absence of useful activity positively upsetting to the mother of four energetic children. Soon exhausting the ship's resources, I took to standing for hours at the prow and was finally reduced to thinking. Those were revealing thoughts and what they first revealed was an astounding number of occasions when I wished we had done differently in meeting our own children's needs, but also enough satisfactory occasions so that one might continue fresh-hearted in the task of being a parent. Then I considered our friends who were trying to meet like needs in their children. And finally I decided to write a book about the different ways in which parents deal with the same questions.

"At that time our children were spread from second grade to first-year college. Now two of our sons, our daughter, and a near-daughter who lived with us for some years, are married. And there are thirteen grandchildren. The family is wiser by seventeen members and a kind of geometrical increase in mistakes and achievements. Also during the intervening years our lives have been bound in, one way and another, with the problems of other people's boys and girls. Ten years on a college campus brought to the fore the acute considerations of adolescents in regard to dating, premarital standards, marriage, and often the psychological uncertainties growing out of the divorce of parents.

"At the same time the young were raising new questions rooted in the demands of new experience precipitated by the Second World War and the ensuing compulsory military training. Also questions derived from developments in mathematics and physics, including the atom bomb; the development of television; the expansion of air travel and the shrinkage of space; likewise questions about competing ideologies.

"Two years spent in Southeast Asia, some acquaintance with the problems of the young in Korea and Japan, observation in other parts of Asia and Europe, have pointed up a common denominator in the religious questions young people are asking everywhere. To attempt definitive answers would be presumptuous. Indeed, to deal with the questions at all one needs to have, with Confucious, no foregone conclusions; with Lao-tze, a capacity for understanding while remaining unnoticed; with Buddha, a passion to *be* before teaching; with Jesus, a sense of retaining the child's approach to life. The last is the hardest and perhaps includes the others, for a child comes freshly at a situation, gives his whole interest to the object of his attention without self-consciousness, and has a natural joyousness which one suspects

She was bringing the four geese back from the pond, her feet dragging heavily, until she heard the sound of Ko-ko's voice....■ (From *Su-mei's Golden Year* by Margueritte Harmon Bro. Illustrated by Kurt Wiese.)

is the climate of insight. These qualities of a good answerer my husband has to a far greater degree than I shall ever have, but by the time we are great-grandparents . . . perhaps some of these qualifications may have brushed off on me." [Margueritte Harmon Bro, *When Children Ask*, Harper, 1956.[1]]

One of Bro's earliest attempts at writing was a collaborative effort with Frank H. O'Hara called *A Handbook of Drama*. A *Christian Century* reviewer wrote, "It is perhaps unfair to say at the outset that this is a highly entertaining volume. It was written to give instruction, not amusement. But diverting and delightful it certainly is, for no other reason than that O'Hara and Bro are just naturally that way. They do not, therefore, sacrifice substance for charm. This is a practical handbook for students and teachers of drama, prepared by a very experienced teacher and director and a successful playwright. . . ."

More Than We Are, inspirational essays on prayer, drew this reaction from a *Christian Century* reviewer: "Among books telling why and how to pray, this deserves a place of preeminence. Its excellence lies partly in its simplicity and directness, in the fact that its language is completely understandable and colloquial without being odiously intimate or flippant, and in the avoidance of conventionally pietistic phraseology."

Bro's first novel was *Sarah*. The *New York Times* called it, "Substantial, richly detailed, this is not only the story of an artist's development. It is also a family story which recreates an era. . . ." *Saturday Review of Literature* described it as, "A thoughtful book in which a philosophy of life is analyzed by interesting, convincing people."

After living in Indonesia for a few years, Bro compiled *Indonesia: Land of Challenge*. A review appearing in *Pacific Affairs* included, "This is an attractive, personal, and warmhearted book which contains a great deal more solid information than its apparently carefree mode of presentation indicates at first glance. What might be taken as an artless mixture of anecdote, reminiscence, and serious factual material is in fact presumably an artful device for spreading news of Indonesia to circles which might otherwise not be reached."

FOR MORE INFORMATION SEE: Christian Century, January 4, 1939, August 4, 1948; *New York Times,* October 16, 1949; *Saturday Review of Literature,* November 12, 1949; *Wilson Library Bulletin,* September, 1952; *Pacific Affairs,* June, 1955; Muriel Fuller, editor, *More Junior Authors,* H. W. Wilson, 1963.

BROWN, Vinson   1912-

PERSONAL: Born December 7, 1912, in Reno, Nev.; son of Henry Alexander and Bertha (Bender) Brown; married Barbara Black, June 18, 1950; children: Kirby W., Jerrold V., Tamara L., Roxana L., Keven A. *Education:* University of California, Berkeley, B.A., 1939; Stanford University, M.A., 1947. *Religion:* Baha'i World Faith. *Home:* Nine Springs Ranch, P.O. Box 1045, Happy Camp, Calif. 96039. *Office:* Naturegraph Co., 8339 West Dry Creek Rd., Healdsburg, Calif.

CAREER: Boy Naturalists' Club, Berkeley, Calif., director, 1936-41; Westinghouse Electric Co., Emeryville, Calif.,

I approached the crying mother and set the tiny kill-deers free. ▪ (From *How to Understand Animal Talk* by Vinson Brown. Illustrated by William D. Berry.)

VINSON BROWN

electrician, 1942-43; Office of War Information, San Francisco, Calif., writer, 1943-44; National School Assemblies, Los Angeles, Calif., 1949-50; Naturegraph Co. (publishers), Los Altos, San Martin, Healdsburg, Calif., owner, 1946—. Produced records on nature for San Mateo County Schools, Calif., 1951; Stanford University Press, Stanford, Calif., editorial work, 1952; *Gilroy Dispatch,* columnist, 1954-59; for four local [California] newspapers, column entitled "Exploring Sonoma County," columnist, 1960—. *Military service:* U.S. Army, 1945-46, became technical sergeant. *Member:* American Association of Icthyologists and Herpetologists.

WRITINGS: The Amateur Naturalist's Handbook, Little, 1946; *John Paul Jones,* Wheeler, 1949; *Black Treasure,* Little, 1951; (editor and rewriter) *Education in California,* Stanford University Press, 1952; *California Wildlife Region,* Naturegraph, 1953; *How to Make a Home Nature Museum,* Little, 1954; *It All Happened Right Here,* Stanford University Press, 1954; *The Sierra Nevada Wildlife Region,* Naturegraph, 1954, revised edition (with Robert Livezey), Naturegraph, 1961; (with David Allan III) *Rocks and Minerals of California,* Naturegraph, 1955; *How to Make a Miniature Zoo,* Little, 1956; *How to Understand Animal Talk,* Little, 1958; (with Charles Yocum and Aldine Starbuck) *Wildlife of the Intermountain West,* Naturegraph, 1958; (editor) *An Illustrated Guide to Fossil Collecting,* Naturegraph, 1959.

(With Henry G. Weston, Jr.) *Handbook of California Birds,* Naturegraph, 1961; *How to Explore the Secret Worlds of Nature,* Little, 1962; *Explorations in Ancient Life,* Science Materials Center, 1962; (with William Willoya) *Warriors of the Rainbow,* Naturegraph, 1962; *Backyard Wild Birds of California and the Pacific Northwest,* T.H.F. Publications,

1965; *Backyard Wild Birds of the East and Midwest,* T.H.F. Publications, 1965; *How to Follow and Map the Adventures of Insects,* Little, 1968; *Pomo Indians of California and Their Neighbors,* Naturegraph, 1969; *Reading the Woods,* Stackpole, 1969.

(With Charles Yocum) *Wildlife and Plants of the Cascades,* Naturegraph, 1971; *Knowing the Outdoors in the Dark,* Stackpole, 1973; *Reptiles and Amphibians of the West,* Naturegraph, 1974; *Voices of Earth and Sky,* Stackpole, 1974; *Great Upon the Mountain: The Story of Crazy Horse Legendary Mystic and Warrior,* Macmillan, 1975; *Sea Mammals and Reptiles of the Pacific Coast,* Macmillan, 1976; *The Explorer Naturalist,* Stackpole, 1977; *Peoples of the Sea Wind: Native Americans of the Pacific Coast,* Macmillan, 1977; *The Return of the Indian Spirit* (juvenile), Grosvenor Press, in press.

WORK IN PROGRESS: A revision of *The Amateur Naturalist's Handbook,* for Prentice-Hall.

SIDELIGHTS: "My three years as a young man in 1931, 1934 and 1935, in the jungles of Panama and Costa Rica probably shaped my writing experience more than anything else, as I roamed the jungles and the coasts at a time when they were still very primitive and full of life (unfortunately almost destroyed by now). This was a most glorious and exciting experience, on which I am basing a new novel about the last bit of wild jungle and a lost tribe and the efforts to try to save this place before it too is destroyed, interwoven with a romance about a young man and a remarkable girl, who imitates perfectly the sounds and songs of the wilderness.

"I am living on a most beautiful wilderness ranch now, with nine springs and a beautiful creek, horses, goats, sheep, turkeys, goose, ducks, and a big German Shepherd dog, Buck, who guards the place loyally. My wife is an ardent horse woman and outdoor person, as she was raised on a 4000 acre wilderness ranch in Colorado, and we both love nature and animals. Barbara has been a most wonderful wife and mother, but now four of our five children are gone, two to the South Seas, Samoa and Guam. Our oldest and youngest sons have both lived in jungles."

Brown has been on several natural history expeditions to Panama and Costa Rica jungles and in the northwest United States, Canada and Alaska.

FOR MORE INFORMATION SEE: San Francisco Chronicle, August, 1961; *Horn Book,* October, 1975.

New York City starting to shovel out after the Blizzard of 1888. ■ (From *Historical Catastrophes: Snowstorms and Avalanches* by Walter R. Brown and Norman D. Anderson. Photo courtesy of New York Historical Society.)

Many tons of ice bend and break telephone wires and trees throughout New England after an ice storm. ■ (From *Historical Catastrophes: Snowstorms and Avalanches* by Walter R. Brown and Norman D. Anderson. Photo courtesy of the National Oceanic and Atmospheric Administration.)

BROWN, Walter R(eed)   1929-

PERSONAL: Born August 25, 1929, in Oklahoma City, Okla.; son of Howard E. (an educator and writer) and Ellen (McCormack) Brown; married Billye Walker, September 2, 1949 (divorced, 1972); married E. Jane Ramsey (a teacher), June 24, 1973; children: (first marriage) Susan, Elizabeth, Cynthia. *Education:* University of Oklahoma, B.S., 1952, Ed.M., 1955; Ohio State University, Ph.D., 1964. *Home:* 797 Pine Lake Drive, Virginia Beach, Va. 23462.

CAREER: High school teacher in Rolla, Mo., 1952-53; and Oklahoma City, Okla, 1953-57; Florida State University, Tallahassee, assistant professor of education, 1958-60, 1961-62; Ohio State University, Columbus, instructor in education, 1960-61; director of youth activities for National Science Teachers Association, Washington, D.C., 1962-64; supervisor of science for Charlottesville, Va., public schools, 1964-66; consultant to Ohio State University-Agency for International Development Education Team in India, 1966-68; free-lance writer, 1968-69, 1979—; science

teacher and coordinator of science and mathematics in Albemarie County, Va., public schools, 1969-71; Virginia Beach Public Schools, Virginia Beach, Va., teacher, 1971-79. *Member:* National Science Teachers Association.

WRITINGS: (Contributor) George C. Paffenbarger and Sholom Pearlman, editors, *Frontiers of Dental Science*, Scholastic Book Services, 1962; *Science Teaching and the Law*, National Science Teachers Association, 1969; *Historical Catastrophes: Volcanoes*, Addison-Wesley, 1970; *Life Science: A Search for Understanding*, Lippincott, 1971, 1977; *Physical Science: A Search for Understanding*, Lippincott, 1972, 1977; *Historical Catastrophes: Hurricanes and Tornadoes*, Addison-Wesley, 1972; *Earth Science: A Search for Understanding*, Lippincott, 1973, 1977; *Historical Catastrophes: Earthquakes*, Addison-Wesley, 1974; (with Billye Brown) *Historical Catastrophes: Floods*, Addison-Wesley, 1975; *Historical Catastrophes: Fires*, Addison-Wesley, 1976; (with Norman D. Anderson) *Historical Catastrophes: Famines*, Addison-Wesley, 1976; *Historical Catastrophes: Snowstorms and Avalanches*, Addison-Wesley, 1976.

BUFF, Conrad 1886-1975

PERSONAL: Born January 15, 1886, in Speicher, Switzerland; died, 1975; came to the United States in 1904, naturalized in 1933; son of Conrad (an Alpine farmer) and Anna (Bruderer) Buff; married Mary Marsh (a children's author), July 7, 1922 (died November 1970); children: Conrad, David Marsh. *Education:* School of Arts and Crafts, St. Gallen, Switzerland, 1900-1903; private art school, Munich, Germany, 1903.

CAREER: Author and illustrator of books for children, artist. Began by designing laces and embroideries in Switzerland, 1900-1903; came to the United States, 1904, and held a variety of odd jobs, including sheepherder and house painter; with wife as collaborator, wrote numerous children's books between 1937 and 1968, for which he also did the illustrations. Artist, with paintings or lithographs included in the permanent collections of such museums as the British Museum, the Metropolitan Museum, the National Gallery, and the Chicago Art Institute; has done murals, including ones in the Edison Company Building in Los Angeles and the First National Bank of Phoenix. *Member:* American Artists Group. *Awards, honors:* First prize, California State Fair, 1924; Huntington Prize, 1925; fine arts prize, San Diego Museum, 1925; first museum prize, Los Angeles Museum, 1937; runner-up for the Caldecott Medal, 1943, for *Dash and Dart;* Purchase Award, Santa Paula, 1944; runner-up for the Newbery Medal, 1947, for *Big Tree;* second award, Los Angeles Municipal Exhibition, 1948; runner-up for the Newbery Medal, 1952, for *The Apple and the Arrow;* runner-up for the Newbery Medal, 1954, for *Magic Maize.*

WRITINGS—All for children; all with Mary Marsh Buff: *Dancing Cloud, the Navajo Boy* (lithographs by Conrad Buff), Viking, 1937, revised edition (with new illustrations by C. Buff), 1957; *Kobi, a Boy of Switzerland* (lithographs by C. Buff), Viking, 1939; *Dash and Dart,* Viking, 1942; *Big Tree* (ALA Notable Book), Viking, 1946; *Peter's Pinto, A Story of Utah,* Viking, 1949, reissued, Ritchie, 1965; *The Apple and the Arrow,* Houghton, 1951, reissued, E. M. Hale, 1965; *Magic Maize,* Houghton, 1953; *Hurry, Skurry, and Flurry,* Viking, 1954; *Hah-Nee of the Cliff Dwellers* (ALA Notable Book), Houghton, 1956; *Elf Owl* (ALA Notable Book; Junior Literary Guild selection), Viking, 1958; *Trix and Vix,* Houghton, 1960; *Forest Folk,* Viking, 1962; *Kemi, an Indian Boy Before the White Man Came,* Ritchie, 1966; *The Colorado, River of Mystery,* Ritchie, 1968.

SIDELIGHTS: Buff arrived in the United States in 1904 "by way of the uncomfortable steerage," and found his way to the still wild state of Wyoming. "The vast stretches of country, the freedom of the people, the lack of man-made restrictions made Wyoming the heaven I had always dreamed of. I felt this country was more my real home than the land of my birth."

After holding odd jobs, and eventually drifting to California, he began a cycle of working for a time, then quitting to paint until every penny was gone. Gradually, his work became accepted in exhibitions, gathering at the same time some awards of merit. With his marriage to Mary Marsh and the birth of their two sons, they "began to see life through their eyes. Because of them came the idea of writing books for children," with Buff also illustrating them.

Of their first book, *Dancing Cloud, the Navajo Boy,* a critic from the *New York Herald Tribune Book Review* has writ-

CONRAD BUFF

ten, "The book has color and a haunting sense of power possessed by these people, so close to earth, so tuned to nature. This sense is conveyed not so much by what is told as by the method of its telling; not so much by the subject matter of the pictures as by the manner of their making." *Big Tree,* the biography of the giant redwood Wawona, is considered by many to be one of the best efforts of this writing and illustrating team. A *Horn Book* reviewer has said about it, "A moving and dramatic interpretation of five thousand years of earth history.... Most impressive are the beautiful illustrations, bringing out in the pattern of the forest the semblance of a mighty cathedral." *Elf Owl,* the story of a cactus and the desert surrounding it, is one of their later books and has been written about this way in the *Bulletin from Virginia Kirkus' Book Shop Service,* "Though the sketches are all in conte crayon, the work is so skillful that many colors are suggested. One envisions many hues in their depiction of the plants which blossom in the thirsty desert. A beautiful book, conveying an idea of the many kinds of life supported there."

Buff has said of living the life of the artist, illustrator and author, "I believe the creative artist, if he can earn enough to live simply, has the richest of all lives. He is never bored. Life is never routine. He may not be wealthy in this world's goods, but he is wealthy in appreciation, interest, and a deep enjoyment of the visual world."

In 1975 Buff died at the age of eighty-nine after suffering a massive heart attack while painting in his studio. His son recalled that his last words, characteristically, to the young nurse wheeling him into the intensive care unit at the hospital were, "you're so pretty I could paint you from memory." Buff's works are included in the Kerlan Collection at the University of Minnesota.

"Sleep well, Son, may you not dream of evil things." ■ (From *The Apple and the Arrow* by Conrad and Mary Buff. Illustrated by the authors.)

In that distant time a handsome old buck, with great antlers, ruled the herd of does that grazed in Fallen Log Meadow. ■ (From *Big Tree* by Mary and Conrad Buff. Illustrated by the authors.)

FOR MORE INFORMATION SEE: New York Herald Tribune Book Review, April 11, 1937; *Horn Book,* November, 1946, January-December, 1947; Bertha E. Mahony and others, compilers, *Illustrators of Children's Books, 1744-1945,* Horn Book, 1947; Stanley J. Kunitz and Howard Haycraft, editors, *Junior Book of Authors,* second edition revised, H. W. Wilson, 1951; Bertha Mahony Miller and others, compilers, *Illustrators of Children's Books, 1946-1956,* Horn Book, 1958; *Bulletin from Virginia Kirkus' Book Shop Service,* February 15, 1958; Edward M. Ainsworth, "Painters of the Desert," *Desert Magazine,* 1960; Martha E. Ward and D. A. Marquardt, *Authors of Books for Young People,* Scarecrow, 1964; Jean Poindexter Colby, *Writing, Illustrating and Editing Children's Books,* Hastings House, 1967; Lee Kingman and others, compilers, *Illustrators of Children's Books: 1957-1966,* Horn Book, 1968.

(Died 1975)

**The something in the fern bed
Is a baby,
A baby deer...**

■ (From *Dash & Dart* by Mary and Conrad Buff. Illustrated by Conrad Buff.)

BUFF, Mary Marsh 1890-1970

PERSONAL: Born April 10, 1890, in Cincinnati, Ohio; died in November, 1970; married Conrad Buff (an artist and illustrator), July 7, 1922; children: Conrad, David Marsh. *Education:* University of Oklahoma, student; Bethany College, Lindsborg, Kansas, B.A.; studied painting in Chicago and Cincinnati.

CAREER: Author of children's books, teacher. Taught in an elementary school, Lewistown, Montana, for three years; taught in a teacher's college in Idaho for three years; Assistant Art Curator, Los Angeles Museum of History, Science and Art, 1920-1922; taught art in a private school in Hollywood; began writing children's books with her husband, 1937, a collaboration which produced fourteen books over the next thirty-one years. *Awards, honors:* Runner-up for the Caldecott Medal, 1943, for *Dash and Dart;* runner-up for the Newbery Medal, 1947, for *Big Tree,* 1952, for *The Apple and the Arrow,* and 1954, for *Magic Maize.*

WRITINGS—All for children; all with Conrad Buff: *Dancing Cloud, the Navajo Boy* (lithographs by Conrad Buff), Viking, 1937, revised edition (with new illustrations by C. Buff), 1957; *Kobi, a Boy of Switzerland* (lithographs by C. Buff), Viking, 1939; *Dash and Dart,* Viking, 1942; *Big Tree* (ALA Notable Book), Viking, 1946; *Peter's Pinto, a Story of Utah,* Viking, 1949, reissued, Ritchie, 1965; *The Apple and the Arrow,* Houghton, 1951, reissued, E. M. Hale, 1965; *Magic Maize,* Houghton, 1953; *Hurry, Skurry, and Flurry,* Viking, 1954; *Hah-Nee of the Cliff Dwellers* (ALA Notable Book), Houghton, 1956; *Elf Owl* (ALA Notable Book; Junior Literary Guild selection), Viking, 1958; *Trix and Vix,* Houghton, 1960; *Forest Folk,* Viking, 1962; *Kemi, an Indian Boy Before the White Man Came,* Ritchie, 1966; *The Colorado, River of Mystery,* Ritchie, 1968.

SIDELIGHTS: "One of the earliest memories of my childhood in Ohio centers around painting. On rainy days my twin sister and I would lie outstretched on the floor of the living room, painting in watercolor.... When not painting or playing over the large grounds of our suburban home, we read.... I remember mostly the books of poetry. Since I loved poetry, it became natural for me to memorize many poems and I acquired a feeling for the rhythm of words." So from this eye for art and painting and this feeling for words came the series of books Mary Marsh Buff wrote in collaboration with her husband, Conrad Buff.

Buff explained how the collaborative effort of *Kobi* came to be written. "After living thirty years in America, my husband, Conrad wished to return to Switzerland to see his aging parents. With our twelve-year-old son we left in March, 1938. After touring France, Italy, and Switzerland, we settled in the old village where Conrad was born and where he spent most of his boyhood—Speicher, near Lake Constance. We lived in an old farmhouse, exactly like the one pictured on page thirteen in *Kobi.* Soon the memories of my husband's boyhood came flooding back in stories of the boy who wanted to yodel and of Wolfram's Castle he had known and loved when he was a boy in Switzerland.

"Living with the simple country people, we soon entered into the daily routine of their life. We visited the villages, the market places, the Alpine meadows, and the herders' huts; we watched the men making cheese; and we stood in the village streets to see the Alp Processions go by on their way to the mountains.

"The episode of the Silly Goat was drawn from a similar experience in my husband's boyhood. The Chimney Sweep is a real person who was loved and feared by all the children, a vivid memory of Conrad's youth. The story of the trip that Kobi and his Uncle Jacob took to the beautiful Rhine Valley is partly a memory of my husband's childhood, partly our own experience when we went down to the spring market in a Rhineland village. We were amazed, just as Kobi was, at how different the country looked when we descended from the chilly austere land of Appenzell.

"Conrad was not a herdboy. He was a village boy. But he envied the country boys with a consuming envy. He often stood in the village square, just as Kobi did, watching the boys in their fine herders' costumes leading their goats at the head of the Alp Processions, and yearned to be in those herdboys' shoes.

"The life on the Alp is the same in *Kobi* as we saw it during the summer of 1938. Still, during storms, cows are lost over cliffs. Sometimes they are rescued, but more often they are lost. And the story about the farmer who lost all his cows during a severe storm was told to us by a herder whose Alp lay below the one that belonged to the unfortunate man.

"Throughout the book, then, Conrad and I have drawn largely upon his memories of boyhood, but added to them little incidents that occurred to us while we were there. Leading the Alp journey, which is the most beautiful experience that a boy can ever have in Switzerland, is just as Conrad always dreamed that it might have been, if only he had been a farm boy. Throughout the book we have tried to remain true to the typical life as it is lived in the Alps of Switzerland today."

A *New York Times* reviewer has said about their first effort, *Dancing Cloud, the Navajo Boy,* "Less inclusive in its material than some of its predecessors in this field, it achieves, perhaps because it tells only the essentials, a clarity of impression." The reviewer goes on to talk about the illustrations, "Fully adult in their conception, they have, nevertheless, a simplicity which should make them understandable as well as impressive for children."

Dash and Dart, the story of the lives of two fawns, was a runner-up for the Caldecott Medal in 1943. A review in the *New York Times* stated that, Buff has told the story of these two young creatures with beautiful simplicity in a rhythmic prose. Little children are charmed by baby animals, and they will follow the fortunes of Dash and Dart with delight and satisfaction."

Big Tree, the biography of the giant redwood Wawona, is considered by many to be the high point of the Buff's writing-illustrating collaboration. An *Atlantic Monthly* reviewer writes this critique, "Without undue personalization the Buffs have made their account of a giant sequoia and its centuries of life not only interesting, but very dramatic. The illustrations are beautiful." And, writes the *Library Journal,* "The authors-illustrators of this beautifully designed book communicate to the reader a sense of wonder at the grandeur and antiquity of the Sequoias and a deep need to preserve them for all time."

Harkening back to a tale of Mr. Buff's native Switzerland produced *The Apple and the Arrow,* which evoked these comments from the *New York Times,* "It was a happy idea to portray William Tell as seen through the eyes of his son

MARY BUFF

Walter, who played his own steadfast part in the legend. This device helps the young reader to grasp the implications of this old story of revolt against tyranny in his own terms."

The Buffs' last book, *The Colorado, River of Mystery,* an historical look at the river, is a diversion from their previous format of fiction, and for a reviewer for the *Library Journal,* the result is not altogether satisfactory. "Beginning with a quick look at the desert, the authors present a mediocre geographical history of the Colorado River.... The sepia-tone sketches are less informative than decorative."

Buff has written about the process of writing these books, "Our books have grown out of our own experiences. My husband has always been most cooperative in our joint work. We are very happy when working on a book together. As the text begins to take color and form in his illustrations, we both get a great thrill. We have come to believe the creative life is the happiest of lives."

FOR MORE INFORMATION SEE: New York Times, April 11, 1937; *New York Times,* December 6, 1942; *Atlantic Monthly,* December, 1946; *Library Journal,* December 1, 1946, April 15, 1969; *Horn Book,* January-December, 1947, January-December, 1948; Stanley J. Kunitz and Howard Haycraft, editors, *Junior Book of Authors,* second edition revised, H. W. Wilson, 1951; *New York Times,* September 2, 1951; Martha E. Ward and D. A. Marquardt, *Authors of Books for Young People,* Scarecrow, 1964.

(Died November, 1970)

HARRISON CADY

CADY, (Walter) Harrison   1877-1970

PERSONAL: Born July, 1877 (or 1879, according to some sources), in Gardner, Mass.; son of Edward Harrison and Eleanora (Fuller) Cady; married Melinna Eldredge, July 21, 1915. *Education:* Attended public schools; self-taught in art. *Residence:* Brooklyn, N.Y. and Rockport, Mass.

CAREER: Author and illustrator of books for children. Also worked as an artist on the *Brooklyn Eagle* and for *Life* magazine. *Member:* Authors League of America, Architectural League, Society of Illustrators, American Water Color Society (New York), New York Water Color Society, Ship Model Society, Salmagundi Club, Dutch Treat Club.

WRITINGS—All self-illustrated: *Caleb Cottontail: His Adventures in Search of the Cotton Plant,* Houghton, 1921, new edition, 1936; *Animal Alphabet,* Houghton, 1927; *Johnny Funny-Bunny's Picnic Party,* Stoll & Edwards, 1928; *Spring Moving Day: Johnny Funny-Bunny Helps His Friends,* Stoll & Edwards, 1928; *Time to Wake Up: Johnny Funny-Bunny Helps to Awaken His Friends,* Stoll & Edwards, 1928. Author of cartoons which appeared in such periodicals as *Life, Saturday Evening Post,* and *Sunday Herald Tribune.*

Illustrator; all written by Thornton W. Burgess, except as noted: Frances Hodgson Burnett, *Troubles of Queen Silver-Bell,* Century, 1906; F. H. Burnett, *The Cozy Lion, as Told by Queen Crosspatch,* Century, 1907; F. H. Burnett, *The Spring Cleaning as Told by Queen Crosspatch,* Century,

1908; *Adventures of Johnny Chuck,* Little, Brown, 1913, reissued, Grosset, 1952; *Adventures of Ready Fox,* Little, Brown, 1913, reissued, Grosset, 1950; *Adventures of Mr. Mucker,* Little, Brown, 1914; *Adventures of Peter Cottontail,* Little, Brown, 1914, reissued, Grosset, 1950, 1970; *Adventures of Jerry Muskrat,* Little, Brown, 1914, reissued, Grosset, 1951, 1962; *Adventures of Unc' Billy Possum,* Little, Brown, 1914, reissued, Grosset, 1951; F. H. Burnett, *Racketty-Packetty House,* Century, 1914, reissued, Dodd, 1961.

Tommy and the Wishing Stone, Century, 1915, reissued, Grosset, 1959; *Adventures of Sammy Jay,* Little, Brown, 1915, reissued, Grosset, 1949, 1962; *Mother West Wind "Why" Stories,* Little, Brown, 1915, reissued, Grosset, 1941; *Adventures of Chatterer the Squirrel,* Little, Brown, 1915, reissued, Grosset, 1949; *Adventures of Danny Meadow Mouse,* Little, Brown, 1915, reissued, Grosset, 1950; *Adventures of Grandfather Frog,* Little, Brown, 1915, reissued, Grosset, 1952; *Mother West Wind "When" Stories,* Little, Brown, 1916, reissued, Grosset, 1941; *Adventures of Old Mr. Toad,* Little, Brown, 1916, reissued, Grosset, 1949; *Mother West Wind "How" Stories,* Little, Brown, 1916, reissued, Grosset, 1941; *Adventures of Buster Bear,* Little, Brown, 1916, reissued, Grosset, 1950; *Adventures of Prickly Porky,* Little, Brown, 1916, reissued, Grosset, 1949; *Adventures of Old Man Coyote,* Little, Brown, 1916, reissued, Grosset, 1952; *Adventures of Paddy the Beaver,* Little, Brown, 1917; *Adventures of Poor Mrs. Quack,* Little, Brown, 1917, reissued Grosset, 1953, 1962; *Adventures of Jimmy Skunk,* Little, Brown, 1918, reissued, Grosset, 1954; *Adventures of Bobby Coon,* Little, Brown, 1918, reissued, Grosset, 1954; *Mother West Wind "Where" Stories,* Little, Brown, 1918; *Happy Jack,* Little, Brown, 1918; *Adventures of Ol' Mistah Buzzard,* Little, Brown, 1919, reissued, Grosset, 1957; *Adventures of Bob White,* Little, Brown, 1919, reissued, Grosset, 1956; *Mrs. Peter Rabbit,* Little, Brown, 1919.

Bowser the Hound, Little, Brown, 1920; *Old Granny Fox,* Little, Brown, 1920, reissued, Grosset, 1943; *Tommy's Wishes Come True,* Little, Brown, 1921, reissued, Grosset, 1959; *Lightfoot the Deer,* Little, Brown, 1921; *Tommy's Change of Heart,* Little, Brown, 1921, reissued, Grosset, 1959; *Whitefoot the Wood Mouse,* Little, Brown, 1922, reissued, Grosset, 1944, 1962; *Blacky the Crow,* Little, Brown, 1922; *Buster Bear's Twins,* Little, Brown, 1923, reissued, Grosset, 1970; *Billy Mink,* Little, Brown, 1924; *Little Joe Otter,* Little, Brown, 1925; *Jerry Muskrat at Home,* Little, Brown, 1926, reissued, Grosset, 1962; *Longlegs the Heron,* Little, Brown, 1927; *Happy Jack Squirrel Helps Unc' Billy,* Stoll & Edwards, 1928; *Baby Possum's Queer Voyage,* Stoll & Edwards, 1928; *The Neatness of Bobby Coon,* Stoll & Edwards, 1928; *A Great Joke on Jimmy Skunk,* Stoll & Edwards, 1928; *Grandfather Frog Gets a Ride,* Stoll & Edwards, 1928; *Digger the Badger Decides to Stay,* Stoll & Edwards, 1928.

Winthrop B. Palmer, editor, *American Songs for Children,* Macmillan, 1931; *The Burgess Big Book of Green Meadow Stories,* Little, Brown, 1932; *The Wishing-Stone Stories,* Little, Brown, 1935; *Mother West Wind's Animal Friends,* Grosset, 1940; *Old Mother West Wind,* Grosset, 1940, Little, Brown, 1960; *Mother West Wind's Children,* Grosset, 1940, Little, Brown, 1962; *Mother West Wind's Neighbors,* Grosset, 1940, Little, Brown, 1968; *Little Pete's Adventure,* McLoughlin, 1941; *Little Red's Adventure,* McLoughlin, 1942; *Animal Stories,* Platt & Munk, 1942, reissued as *The*

"I am the Great Dragon Fly." ■ (From *Bugs and Wings and Other Things* by Annie W. Franchot. Illustrated by Jessie Willcox Smith and Harrison Cady.)

Chatterer was sitting just where Peter had left him.
■ (From *The Adventures of Chatterer the Red Squirrel* by Thornton W. Burgess. Illustrated by Harrison Cady.)

Animal World of Thornton Burgess, 1961; *Little Chuck's Adventure,* McLoughlin, 1942; *On the Green Meadows: A Book of Nature Stories,* Little, Brown, 1944; *At the Smiling Pool: A Book of Nature Stories,* Little, Brown, 1945; *The Crooked Little Path: A Book of Nature Stories,* Little, Brown, 1946; *The Dear Old Briar-Patch: A Book of Nature Stories,* Little, Brown, 1947; *Along Laughing Brook: A Book of Nature Stories,* Little, Brown, 1949; *At Paddy the Beaver's Pond: A Book of Nature Stories,* Little, Brown, 1950; (with George Carlson) Thornton W. Burgess and Howard R. Garis, *Animal Story Library,* Platt & Munk, 1952; *50 Favorite Burgess Stories: On the Green Meadows [and] The Crooked Little Path,* Grosset, 1956; *The Million Little Sunbeams,* Six Oaks Press, 1963.

Contributor of drawings to periodicals, including *American Boy, Country Gentleman, Good Housekeeping, Ladies' Home Journal, People's Home Journal, Saturday Evening Post,* and *St. Nicholas.*

SIDELIGHTS: **1877** (or 1879, according to some sources). Born in Gardner, Mass. where he lived throughout his boyhood and adolescent years. Attended grammar school, but the bulk of his early education was aptly handled by his father, an ardent naturalist and lover of books. His father's general store housed a library of over 1,500 volumes and, here, young Cady was introduced to the heroes of history and literature. Reading grew into an enduring passion.

1895. Arrived in New York with thirteen dollars in his pocket and ambition for launching an art career. "When as a lad I arrived in New York, I was at once impressed by the pleasures and opportunities that were to be had on an empty purse in the great city. There were the wonderful museums filled with the wealth of the world; there were the art galleries and the fine shops. In the auction rooms one could sit without a dollar in pocket while pictures, sculpture, objects of art—many and sundry products of men's genius—were exhibited for everyone's inspection. And in New York with its cosmopolitan population one could watch the world go by. The poorest boy could stroll in Central Park and gaze at the fine turnouts—prancing horses, grand ladies, liveried coachmen with highbred dogs running behind. Yes, New York was, for me, the land of heart's desire, an inexhaustible treasure house to be explored and possessed. And most of it to be had for the asking." [Ernest W. Watson, *Forty Illustrators and How They Work,* Watson-Guptill, 1946.[1]]

Sold his first work for sixty dollars to *Truth Magazine* (a competitor of *Life*) who had commissioned him to design a set of decorative initial letters.

Financial situation improved when McLoughlin Brothers hired him to illustrate a "Mother Goose" book. Saved five-hundred dollars and moved to a Greenwich Village apartment with his newly widowed mother.

1907. Association with McLoughlin ended. Secured a job as a newspaper artist for the *Brooklyn Daily Eagle,* receiving twenty dollars weekly and a first hand education in draftsmanship.

1911. Submitted a series of pen sketches to *Life,* three of which were bought for ninety dollars. For the next five months *Life* accepted more of his work and finally asked Cady to join their magazine staff. He accepted and stayed with *Life* for twenty-three years. A critic commented about this association: "Cady's contributions to *Life* were by no means limited to the comical antics of bugs and rabbits. He has been crusader as well as comedian. His pictorial commentaries upon serious problems of the day were frequent full-page, sometimes double-page features. During the first World War he enlisted his pen against the Kaiser in a series of powerful cartoons. Many drawings of this period also reveal his alarm at the despoiling of the countryside by billboards and hot-dog stands that, with the advent of the automobile, were springing up along the highways.

"But Cady is, fundamentally, a humorist. He is at his illustrative best when there is a twinkle in his eye and nonsensical fantasies are taking shape on his board. It was his zoological extravaganzas that brought him fame."[1]

1913. Began illustrations for Thornton Burgess' *Bedtime Stories of Peter Rabbit.*

1915. Married Melinna Eldredge of Brooklyn where they settled for the next twenty-four years.

1920. Bought the "Headland House" in Rockport, Massachusetts. Built in 1781, this was his summer home and "for-

HARRISON CADY

tress, a safe refuge to which we could always retreat, come what may.

"Poverty was my legacy and I have ever been grateful for it. Poverty teaches great lessons so many fail to learn. To an eager mind it reveals that most of the best things in life have no price tags on them."[1]

1921. First book published.

1922. Began "Peter Rabbit" series for the New York *Herald Tribune*'s syndicated Sunday comic section.

1933. One man show of his paintings and etchings in New York City.

1945. Won the Edwin Palmer Memorial Prize at the National Academy Annual Show for his art work. Frequently exhibited and won prizes in national shows for his etchings, watercolors and oil paintings.

Trips in the United States and abroad gave Cady the opportunity to collect a "polygenetic assortment of art objects." Asked what he valued most among his collection, however, he answered quickly "my friends."

December 9, 1970. Died at his home in New York City at the age of ninety-three after a long illness. Cady's etchings are in many noted collections, including the Metropolitan Museum of Art, Library of Congress, and the New York Public Library.

FOR MORE INFORMATION SEE: "Comics—And Their Creators," *Literary Digest*, December 1, 1934; Ernest W. Watson, *Forty Illustrators and How They Work*, Watson-Guptill, 1946; Bertha E. Mahony and others, compilers, *Illustrators of Children's Books, 1744-1945*, Horn Book, 1947. Obituaries—*New York Times*, December 11, 1970; *Time*, December 21, 1970.

(Died December 9, 1970)

CALLEN, Lawrence Willard, Jr. 1927-
(Larry Callen)

PERSONAL: Born April 3, 1927, in New Orleans, La.; son of Lawrence Willard and Emily (Barrouquere) Callen; married Willa Carmouche (a learning disabilities diagnostician), December 6, 1958; children: Erin Andree, Alex David, Dashiel Noel, Holly Willa. *Education:* Attended Tulane University, 1944-45, 1953-54, and Loyola University, New Orleans, La., 1950-52; Florida State University, B.S., 1957; Louisiana State University, graduate study, 1960-63. *Home:* 1117 Tiffany Rd., Silver Spring, Md. 20904.

CAREER: Jefferson Herald, New Orleans, La., associate editor, 1952-55; H. L. Peace Publications, New Orleans, associate editor of a fishing industry magazine, 1958-59; Louisiana Department of Employment Security, Baton Rouge, in unemployment insurance and employment services, 1959-63; U.S. Department of Labor, Washington, D.C., in unemployment insurance, 1963-79; freelance writer, 1979—. *Military service:* U.S. Navy, 1945-46. U.S. Air Force, 1955-58. *Awards, honors:* School Library Journal named *The Deadly Mandrake* one of the best books for 1978.

WRITINGS—Under name Larry Callen: *Pinch* (juvenile novel), Little, Brown, 1976; *Deadly Mandrake* (juvenile novel), Little, Brown, 1978; *Sorrow's Song* (juvenile novel), Little, Brown, 1979.

WORK IN PROGRESS—Under name Larry Callen: "a fourth book about people in Four Corners"; "a mystery

(From *Pinch* by Larry Callen. Illustrated by Marvin Friedman.)

LARRY CALLEN

novel for grownups"; *Dashiel and the Night* (tentative title), for Dutton; *The Muskrat War.*

SIDELIGHTS: "There is a rather delicate middle ground between stories for children and stories for grownups. It's an elusive target. Story tellers who find it entertain both groups. I'm trying to find it.

"I am also totally sold on the value of the family in the mental, moral and emotional growth of the individual. I've indicated that in the three books published so far.

"I'll tell you how *Pinch, The Deadly Mandrake,* and *Sorrow's Song* came to be written. My children were approaching reading age. My wife and I decided to enroll in an adult education class in children's literature. Children's book author Mary Jo Borreson, taught the class. She assigned a story to be *written* the very first class. I hadn't expected that. I had been writing stories since a teenager, but never a children's story. It got a good reception.

"I started cranking stories out like my life depended upon it. All of the stories had the same characters, Pinch and his friends in Four Corners. I wrote on the way to and from work on a Trailway bus. I wrote when I got home from work each night. I tried peddling the short stories and got encouraging rejection slips, which, when the final word is in, are still rejection slips. I lightly wove them together into a picaresque novel and continued to get polite letters.

"I distilled my three or four hundred pages of material into three plus piles. One pile became *Pinch.* One became *The*

Deadly Mandrake. One became *Sorrow's Song.* The remainder became *The Muskrat War* and is at the publishers now. I have temporarily shifted to more contemporary material. But I will return to Four Corners because I've barely touched the surface of the ten or so characters I've worked with. The additional levels and the permutations are endless. That's so, even working in a rural setting with people who are what they seem to be.

"I've got many hobbies. More than I can handle. I enjoy watching my kids grow up. We have four. The youngest is eight and it saddens me to know that I'm seeing one of my children go through the 'mommy and daddy are the salt of the earth' stage for the last time. I also raise tropical fish and collect cowrie shells (cowries are salt water snails and both interesting and beautiful). I have an interest in geneaology, mainly in tracing my own Scot-Irish ancestry from Louisiana back to Georgia, North Carolina, wherever. There's a Callensburg in Pennsylvania (which we've visited and I'd very much like to find out if one of my own bearded ancestors planted that flag).

"My wife has several vocations. She works with children to determine learning disabilities and she diagnoses ways to overcome those disabilities. Someday we might decide to treat this subject in fiction. The need is there. She is also active in real estate sales and may make a million there. I hope. She also has great talent with a pen and a brush and we hope to do a book together some day soon."

FOR MORE INFORMATION SEE: School Library Journal, April and May, 1976, April, May and December, 1978, May, 1979; *Booklist,* May, 1976, March, 1978, June, 1979; *Horn Book,* August, 1976, August, 1978, August, 1979; *New York Times Book Review,* April 30, 1978; *Publishers Weekly,* May 8, 1978.

ANDRÉE CLAIR

He thrust out into the tangled mass of growth. He managed to push ahead a few feet, collecting dozens of scratches and thorns as he went. ∎ (From *Bemba* by Andrée Clair. Illustrated by Harper Johnson.)

CLAIR, Andrée

EDUCATION: University of Paris, License-es-lettres, 1948; Education Nationale, Paris, certificat d'aptitude pedagogique and certificat d'aptitude a l'enseignement des enfants arrieres (C.A.E.A.). *Residence:* Paris, France.

CAREER: School teacher and professor in Paris, France; professor in Chad; Institut d'Etudes Centrafricaine de Brazzaville, Republic of the Congo, staff ethnologist, 1945-46; cultural counsellor, Presidency, Republic of Niger, 1961—.

WRITINGS—Juveniles: *Moudaina; ou Deux enfants au coeur de l'Afrique* (novel), Bourrelier, 1952 (translation by James Cleugh published in England as *Moudaina*, Muller, 1957); *Le Mur gris de toutes les couleurs* (novel), Bourrelier, 1955; *Bemba* (novel), illustrations by Clair, La Farandole, 1957 (translation by Marie Ponsot published in America as *Bemba: An African Adventure*, Harcourt, 1962); *Eau ficelee et ficelle de fumee* (picture book), La Farandole, 1957; *Aminatou* (picture book), La Farandole, 1959; *Tchinda, la petite*

soeur de Moudaina (novel), Bourrelier, 1959; *Le Fabuleux Empire du Mali* (history of Mali, 10th through 17th centuries) Presence Africaine, 1959.

Bakari, enfant du Mali, Presence Africaine, 1960; *Rejoignons Moudaina!* (novel), Bourrelier, 1961; *Dije* (picture book), La Farandole, 1961; *Le Voyage d'Oumarou* (elementary school textbook), illustrations, photos, and letters by Clair, Bourrelier, 1963; *Les Decouvertes d'Alkassoum* (picture book), La Farandole, 1964; *Un, deux, trois* (picture book), La Farandole, 1966; *Le Babiroussa . . . et les autres* (poems), Istra, 1966; *Nicole au quinzieme etage* (picture book), La Farandole, 1968; *Nicole et l'ascenseur,* La Farandole, 1971; (with Boubou Hama) *Le Baobab merveilleux* (picture book), La Farandole, 1971.

Adult books: *Le Niger, pays a decouvrir,* Hachette, 1965; *Le Niger independent,* Istra, 1966.

Contributor of articles, stories, and poems to adult and children's journals and periodicals; children's book critic and reader of manuscripts on Africa for publishers. Stories, extracts from books, and poems anthologized in several collections, including *Et l'on raconte encore . . .* , edited by Mathilde Leriche, Bourrelier, 1969.

WORK IN PROGRESS: Several books on Africa for both children and adults.

SIDELIGHTS: Clair calls herself an "Africaniste ou antiraciste." She has traveled throughout Europe and in ten African nations, and believes it is necessary to become acquainted with other peoples and life-styles in order to combat prejudice and racism.

FOR MORE INFORMATION SEE: Marc Soriano, editor, *Guide de la litterature enfantine,* Flammarion, 1959; Natha Caputo, editor, *De quatre a quinze ans: Guide de lecture,* l'Ecole et la Nation, 1968; *Dictionnaire des Ecrivains pour la jeunesse, ausers de langue Francaise,* Seghers.

CLOUDSLEY-THOMPSON, J(ohn) L(eonard) 1921-

PERSONAL: Born May 23, 1921, in Murree, India; son of A. G. G. (a medical doctor) and M. E. (Griffiths) Thompson; married J. Anne Cloudsley (a physiotherapist and artist), 1944; children: John Hugh, Timothy, Peter Leslie. *Education:* Pembroke College, Cambridge, B.A., 1946, M.A., 1948, Ph.D., 1950. *Religion:* Church of England. *Home:* 4 Craven Hill, London W2 3DS, England. *Office:* Department of Zoology, Birkbeck College, University of London, Malet St., London WC1E 7HX, England.

CAREER: King's College, University of London, London, England, lecturer in zoology, 1950-60; University of Khartoum, Khartoum, Sudan, professor of zoology and keeper of Sudan Natural History Museum, 1960-71. Member of expeditions to Iceland, 1947, southern Tunisia, 1954, and various parts of central Africa, 1960-73. Delegate to twelve international congresses on entomology, zoology, biological rhythm, deserts, and bioclimatology; National Science Foundation senior visiting scientist-fellow, University of New Mexico, 1969; University Kuwait, visiting professor, 1978. Honorary captain, Freeman of the City of London; liveryman, Worshipful Company of Skinners. *Military service:* British Army, 1940-44; wounded in Libya, 1942, but rejoined

Female tropical scorpion (Palamnaeus fulvipes). Her swollen abdomen shows that she is pregnant. ■ (From *Spiders and Scorpions* by J. L. Cloudsley-Thompson. Illustrated by Joyce Bee.)

regiment for D-Day offensive in Normandy; became captain. *Member:* World Academy of Art and Science (fellow), Institute of Biology (fellow), Linnaean Society (fellow), Royal Entomological Society (London; fellow), Zoological Society (London; fellow). *Awards, honors:* D.Sc., University of London, 1960; Royal African Society Medal, 1969.

WRITINGS: (Editor) *Biology of Deserts,* Institute of Biology, 1954; *Spiders, Scorpions, Centipedes, and Mites,* Pergamon Press, 1958.

Animal Behaviour, Oliver & Boyd, 1960, Macmillan, 1961; (with John Sankey) *Land Invertebrates,* Methuen, 1961; *Rhythmic Activity in Animal Physiology and Behaviour,* Academic Press, 1961; (with M. J. Chadwick) *Life in Deserts,* Dufour, 1964; *Animal Conflict and Adaptation,* Dufour, 1965; *Desert Life,* Pergamon, 1965; *Animal Twilight: Man and Game in Eastern Africa,* Dufour, 1967; *Microecology,* St. Martin's, 1967; *The Zoology of Tropical Africa,* Norton, 1969; *Animals of the Desert,* Bodley Head, 1969, McGraw, 1971.

(With F. T. Abushama) *A Guide to the Physiology of Terrestrial Arthropoda,* Khartoum University Press, 1970; *The Temperature and Water Relations of Reptiles,* Morrow, 1971; *Spider and Scorpions,* Bodley Head, 1973, McGraw, 1974; *Desert Life,* Aldus, 1974, Danbury, 1974; *Bees and Wasps,* Bodley Head, 1974, McGraw, 1976; *Crocodiles and Alligators,* Bodley Head, 1975, McGraw, 1977; *Terrestrial Environments,* Croom Helm, 1975, Halsted Press, 1975; *Insects and History,* Weidenfeld & Nicolson, 1975, St. Martin's, 1976; *Tortoises and Turtles,* Bodley Head, 1976; (joint editor) *Environmental Physiology of Animals,* Blackwell, 1976; *Evolutionary Trends in the Mating of Arthropoda,* Meadowfield, 1976; *Man and the Biology of Arid Zones,* E. Arnold, 1977; *The Desert,* Orbis, 1977; *The Water and Temperature Relations of Woodlice,* Meadowfield, 1977; *Animal Migration,* Orbis, 1978; *Why the Dinosaurs became Extinct,* Meadowfield, 1978.

Also author of monographs and children's books. Contributor to science journals, *Encyclopedia Britannica, Encyclopedia Americana* and others. Editor of *Journal of Arid Environments.* Former member of editorial board, Royal Entomological Society and *Entomologist;* present member of editorial boards of *Environmental Research, Journal of Herpetology, Journal of Interdisciplinary Cycle Research, Comparative Physiology and Ecology,* and *International Journal of Biometeorology;* member of publications committee, Zoological Society of London and councils of the Linnean Society of London and British Arachnological Society; chairman of British Naturalists' Association and of the Biological Council.

WORK IN PROGRESS: Ecology, Adaptation, and Biological Rhythm; Animal Defence Mechanisms, publication by Dent; research on the ecology and physiology of desert animals, thermal physiology, and rhythms.

SIDELIGHTS: "I have always felt that ideas are more important than facts or even, unless they are friends, than the people who have engendered them. The music of *Nabucco* or *Aida* seems to me far more important than the life of Guiseppe Verdi, although he is my favourite composer. For this reason, in all my books, whether for children or adults, I have always tried to concentrate on ideas, and to explain them by reference to unusual or lesser known facts. My wife Anne and I find it exciting to travel off the beaten track, and

J. L. CLOUDSLEY-THOMPSON

to meet people from other countries: many of our best friends are Africans. In 1967 we crossed the Sahara in midsummer, and we have travelled together in many parts of Europe, Asia, Africa and America. Anne has provided several illustrations for my books, especially of the furry animals which I find much more difficult to draw than spiders and insects."

HOBBIES AND OTHER INTERESTS: Music, particularly opera; travel, and photography.

FOR MORE INFORMATION SEE: The Voices of Time, Braziller, 1966.

COHN, Angelo 1914-

PERSONAL: Born September 21, 1914, in Bucharest, Romania; son of Lazar and Tzipa (Silberman) Cohn; married Miriam Bonna Rosenbloom (professor, School of Social Work, University of Minnesota), December 18, 1949; children: Anna Rebecca, Charlotte Wila, James Avram. *Education:* University of Minnesota, B.A., 1936, graduate seminars, 1941-43. *Home:* 2008 Humboldt Ave., S., Minneapolis, Minn. 55405. *Agent:* Bertha Klausner, 71 Park Ave., New York, N.Y. 10016.

CAREER: Minneapolis Star, Minneapolis, Minn., chief of copy desk, 1939-46, assistant news editor, 1946-49, assistant city editor, 1949-58; *Minneapolis Star* and *Chicago Daily News,* foreign correspondent in Netherlands, 1958-59; Radio Nederland Wereldomroep, Hilversum, Holland, American broadcaster, 1958-59; *Minneapolis Star,* reporter, 1960-63; University of Minnesota, Minneapolis, editor of Minnesota National Laboratory *News Bulletin* and Minnemath Center *Reports,* 1963-69; University of Minnesota, editor of *Science*

Traffic aides help Dutch school children cross the road safely. In crowded Dutch cities, many schools have no playground space. The roadway and a narrow sidewalk are alongside the walls of this school. ■ (From *The First Book of the Netherlands* by Angelo Cohn. Photo courtesy of Netherlands Information Services.)

and Technology, 1969-75; editor of *Journal, Minnesota Academy of Science,* 1968—. Member of Minneapolis mayor's commission on human relations, 1954-59, board of Minneapolis Jewish Family and Children's Service, 1955-58. *Member:* Newspaper Guild of the Twin Cities (board member, eleven years; president, 1961-62), Aviation Writers Association, Minnesota Press Club, Authors Guild, 1965—. *Awards, honors:* National Conference of Christians and Jews Brotherhood Week citation for integration news project, 1955; Fairchild Aviation writing citation, 1960; Newspaper Guild Page One Awards on aviation and schools, 1961.

WRITINGS: (Editor) Cedric Adams, *Poor Cedric's Almanac,* Doubleday, 1952; *First Book of the Netherlands,* Watts, 1962; *Careers With Foreign Languages,* Walck, 1963; (editor of English edition) Meyer Sluyser, *Before I Forget,* A. S. Barnes, 1963; Norman B. Mears, *The Man Behind the Shadow Mask,* Denison, 1965; *Careers in Public Planning and Administration,* Walck, 1966; *The Wonderful World of Paper,* Abelard-Schuman, 1967; (editor) Agnes Geelan, *The Dakota Maverick,* Mays, 1975. Contributor of articles to

Nieman Reports, Rotarian, Mainliner, Sales Management, Professional Pilot, Corporate Reports, Sky, Eastern Fine Papers, New York Times, and others. Editor of catalogue for Van Gogh Exhibition, 1959.

WORK IN PROGRESS: "Two books—one as author and the other as editor."

SIDELIGHTS: "I like to say that 'I landed in America the same day as Columbus.' That's the truth to the extent that October 12 is the accepted anniversary of the landing of Columbus in the Western Hemisphere back in 1492; and October 12 is the date stamped on the official papers of our family's arrival in this country from Romania in 1920.

"There is, perhaps, a more significant coincidence which links me to Columbus. Neither he nor I knew a word of the language being used by the 'natives' of this new world into which we had come. We both began communicating with the folks already here through simple sounds or gestures.

"For me there were barely ten weeks of listening and trying to speak with a few relatives before being placed in the kindergarten of a nearby public school in Minneapolis. The language part of the educational process must have interested me more than other subject areas, for when I think back and try to assign value to the school years and follow-through, I realize that practically all my career has involved working with words and language.

"Somewhere about the sixth grade a classmate and I began to write and 'publish' our own little newspaper—two sheets covered on both sides with tales out of school and in school, that we distributed to our little friends. I also began to write for the school paper as soon as one was introduced in Phillips Junior High; continued writing and editing through high school and at the University of Minnesota, where I was a desk editor, writer, and cartoonist for several publications.

"While still in high school, I designed a recreation room with a ship theme and sold an article about it to a national magazine; and I continued to write articles for several magazines through the student years and while I was regularly employed at the *Minneapolis Star*, a rapidly-growing newspaper at the time.

"Although employed in a word and language industry, I really consider myself an 'editor' rather than a 'writer.' I believe the editing function can be every bit as creative as original writing, and that a fine touch can be applied in arranging written material, changing a word here and there, organizing sentences in a way that helps the writer to say more of what he means and mean more in what he says. Certainly the writing of interesting, meaningful and grammatically correct headlines in a newspaper, an editing responsibility, can be as demanding on one's skill with words as the writing of poetry, and poetry is recognized as perhaps the ultimate refinement of word usage.

"Writing and editing are far more than word skills, however. I believe effective writing has to be anchored in experience or observation springing from curiosity and treated with imagination.

"My first regular book was produced by editing, working in collaboration with another newspaper staff member. My task was to assemble, organize, revise and otherwise tie together material that had appeared in newspaper columns over a span of more than twenty years. Two more of my books involved editing the work of other writers; but I also have written five books of my own and I am assembling material for several others, more than I can count.

"A long-nurtured curiosity about almost everything compels me to keep notes, jot down ideas, and search for information everywhere. There has hardly been a day of my life when I have not used a library type of resource, some kind of reference book or material, in an effort to learn something that could eventually be useful in writing.

"Writing, of course, should not be separated from reading, nor should listening be separated from speaking. All are parts of the same process. The interrelationship between the senses, as I see it, is most clearly established in the minds and lives of children, for they are usually more logical than adults and use all their human resources to the limit. This, perhaps, is what has made it challenging for me to write for younger readers. They, like Columbus and I, begin to discover the world by personal effort."

ANGELO COHN

Cohn's works are included in the Kerlan Collection at the University of Minnesota.

CONROY, Jack (Wesley) 1899-
(John Conroy; pseudonyms: Tim Brennan, John Norcross)

PERSONAL: Born December 5, 1899, in a coal mining camp near Moberly, Mo.; son of Thomas Edward (one-time Catholic priest in Canada who later organized and led a miners union) and Eliza Jane (McCollough) Conroy; married Elizabeth Gladys Kelly, June 30, 1922; children: Margaret Jean (deceased), Thomas Vernon (deceased), John Wesley, Jr. *Education:* University of Missouri, student, 1920-21. *Politics:* Democrat. *Religion:* Methodist. *Home:* 701 Fisk Ave., Moberly, Mo. 65270. *Agent:* Porter, Gould & Dierks, 235 West Ohio St., Chicago, Ill. 60610.

CAREER: Toured United States, mostly by boxcar, as migratory worker in 1920's; editor of *Rebel Poet*, 1931-32, *Anvil*, 1933-37, *New Anvil*, 1939-41; associate editor of *Nelson's Encyclopedia* and *Universal World Reference Encyclopedia*, 1943-47; Standard Education Society, Chicago, Ill., senior associate editor of *New Standard Encyclopedia*, 1947-66, director of Standard Information Service, 1949-55. Columbia College, Chicago, Ill., creative writing instructor, 1962-66; lecturer on folklore at University of Chicago, University of Illinois, Northwestern University, University of Washington, University of Oregon. *Member:* International Platform Association, Society of Midland Authors. *Awards, honors:* Guggenheim fellowship for creative writing, 1935; joint recipient of James L. Dow Award of the Society of Midland Authors, 1967, for *Anyplace But Here;* L.H.D., University of Missouri, 1975; National Endowment for the Arts grant, 1977.

WRITINGS: (Editor with Edward R. Cheyney) *Unrest, 1929* (verse anthology), Stockwell, 1929; (editor with Cheyney) *Unrest, 1930,* Studies Publications, 1930; (editor with Cheyney) *Unrest, 1931,* Henry Harrison, 1931; *The Disinherited,* Covici, Friede, 1933, 2nd edition, with introduction by Daniel Aaron, Hill & Wang, 1963; *A World to Win,* Covici, Friede, 1935; (with Arna Bontemps) *The Fast Sooner Hound* (juvenile), Houghton, 1942; *They Seek a City: A Study of Negro Migration,* Doubleday, 1945; (with Bontemps) *Slappy Hooper, the Wonderful Sign Painter* (juvenile), Houghton, 1946; (editor) *Midland Humor,* Wyn, 1947; (with Bontemps) *Sam Patch, the High, Wide and Handsome Jumper* (juvenile), Houghton, 1951; (contributor) *Missouri Reader,* edited by Frank Luther Mott, University of Missouri Press, 1964; (with Bontemps) *Anyplace But Here,* Hill & Wang, 1966; (contributor) *American Writers and the Great Depression,* edited by Harvey Swados, Bobbs, 1966; (editor with Curt Johanson) *Writers in Revolt: An Anvil Anthology, 1933-1940,* Lawrence Hill & Co., 1973; *The Jack Conroy Reader,* edited by Jack Salzman and David Ray, Burt Franklin & Co., 1979. Six stories anthologized in B. A. Botkin, *A Treasure of American Folklore.*

Literary editor of *Chicago Defender,* 1946-47, and *Chicago Globe,* 1949. Regular book reviewer for *K.C. Star Sun-Times* and *Chicago Tribune;* former reviewer for *Chicago Daily News, St. Louis Post-Dispatch.* Contributor to *American Mercury, Esquire, New Republic.*

WORK IN PROGRESS: A book on oral folklore of the Ozarks; a collection of sentimental songs and poems, 1865-1910, titled *The Rosewood Casket: A Garland of Rue and Lavender;* research for autobiography.

SIDELIGHTS: **December 5, 1899.** Born in Monkey Nest coal camp near Moberly, Missouri. "My father was a man of some education and literary taste. We had a small but well-chosen library. My mother, too, though she lacked formal schooling, had an inquisitive and intelligent mind. She aspired to be a writer, and somewhere among my papers are some yellowed sheets bearing starts she made on short stories. Mother always took a keen interest in my writing, but died shortly before *The Disinherited* [1933] was published." [Jack Conroy, "Home to Moberly," *Missouri Library Association Quarterly,* March, 1968.[1]]

1920-1921. Attended the University of Missouri. "My short tenure at the University of Missouri opened many doors to a wide and exciting world I wanted to know about more and more. And I thought it ought to be seen at firsthand. For various reasons, my stay was brief, but it moved and shook me in so many ways that I have often regretted that I didn't try harder to stay on. Just to walk about the campus still revitalizes me."[1]

1920's. Toured the United States as a migratory worker. "I had begun to write some verse and have some of it published before I moved to Hannibal [Missouri] to work in a rubber heel plant there. (H. L. Mencken published in *The American Mercury* many years afterward a story based on this experience, called, appropriately enough, 'Rubber Heels.') Later, in Toledo [Ohio], what you might call my literary career really began. Working by day in the Overland automobile plant, I wrote verse and stories at night. Much of it was published, but little of it was paid for. 'The little magazines that died to make verse free' rarely can pay the printer, let alone contributors. David Webb of Chillicothe, Ohio, (another old friend now gone to that great writers' conference in the sky) asked me to join him in publishing a magazine aimed at college students called, for some reason, *The Spider.* Either our aim was bad or the college students unresponsive, for *The Spider* soon expired of malnutrition. At about the same time, I fell in with Emerson Field Price, a bank clerk in Columbus [Ohio]. Emie later wrote for *The American Mercury* and had published by Caxton Printers one of the great but neglected American novels, *Inn of That Journey.* (I ought to know, for I wrote the introduction!) Emie . . . was the workhorse of Rebel Poets, serving as secretary and sweating over its monthly bulletin—the ancestor of my first magazine, *The Rebel Poet.*"[1]

1929. "The 1929 financial earthquake drove me back to Moberly, where I had reason to believe that relatives would not see me starve. In the stricken cities there was actual fear of starvation. I felt it, as did most of the men I had worked with at the Overland automobile plant, then operating with a skeleton crew one or two days a week.

1931-1932. Editor of *The Rebel Poet.* "The midwife who brought *The Rebel Poet* into actual being was Ben Hagglund, a printer and poet of Swedish ancestry, who lived up in Holt, Minnesota, a hamlet in the wild muskeg country. Ben had a venerable hand press which had been thrown away as unusable, legend had it, by a self-respecting printer during the Boer war. Ben had been printing, editing (and writing to some extent) a poetry magazine called *The Northern Light.* I would edit a magazine called *The Rebel Poet,* and Ben would print and publish it. Fastening his press together with baling wire (the indispensable friend of the repairing farmer in those days), Ben got out a first issue. There was no money for paper, ink, or postage, so he would go out and work on the railway section or on a threshing crew until he accumulated enough do-re-mi for another issue. Hagglund later was to print many 'little' magazines in various sections of the country, traveling 'from pine to palm,' as he put it. Ben lived in East Palo Alto, Calif. for several years, printing and publishing *Caravel.* Then he had a hankering to return to Holt, his ancestral village. It no longer existed, so he settled in nearby Thief River Falls, still printing when death overtook him on December 18, 1975.

"With Ben in Holt and me in Moberly, the inconveniences other than financial were also numerous. Proofreading by mail, for instance, was a nuisance. But the magazine got around, and attracted quite a few of the rebellious poets for whom it was named. One of these was [the late] Kenneth Patchen, [who became] a highly-respected 'poet's poet.'

"*The Anvil,* which succeeded *The Rebel Poet,* was somewhat more ambitious in that it published both fiction and verse, emphasizing 'stories from the mines, mills, factories and offices of America.' Another unusual feature was that it published no criticism, thus keeping free of the ideological disputes then raging. The motto of *The Anvil* was 'We prefer crude vigor to polished banality.' Ideology? All I can answer is, 'I dunno.' It seems to me that the story too often is concealed among the ideological trees."[1]

1933. First novel, *The Disinherited,* published. "I never did consciously think of myself as a novelist. In *The Disinherited* I wanted to be a witness to the times, to set down as truthfully as I could the things I had seen. In Whitman's phrase, I was trying to 'vivify the contemporary fact' as best I could.

"What is proletarian literature? This was a subject for hot dispute in the Thirties. Some contended that only a genuine proletarian, one who had worked with the hands and thus had a worm's eye view of the class struggle, could write it.

But where do we find working stiffs with the ability, training, and will to write about themselves? Could a middle class writer turn out a proletarian novel if he took a sympathetic attitude toward the workers' struggles? Is my *The Disinherited* a proletarian novel? Well, I certainly have a proletarian background and my sympathies have never been questioned. Nevertheless, the book was not sufficiently Marxist for the leading revolutionary theoreticians in the literary department. Granville Hicks, the doyen of the *New Masses* critics, rebuked me for my lack of Marxist knowledge. Michael Gold detected dangerous Bohemian tendencies in Larry Donovan, my protagonist, (such as quoting romantic poetry to a girl he wanted to impress), and feared that I might take the easy road to success traveled by Jack London. As it turned out, his fears were unjustified. Daniel Aaron points out in his introduction to the Hill and Wang American Century edition of *The Disinherited* (reissued in 1963 more than thirty years after its first publication) that the book's tone, 'bemused and wondering rather than protesting and declamatory,' is not at all characteristic of the so-called proletarian school.''[1]

1935. Received a Guggenheim fellowship to write about Southern migrations. Wrote his second novel. "*A World to Win,* my second novel, didn't make much of a splash either with critics or book-buyers—partly, I am sure, because of the Horatio Algerish title which was not mine (mine was *Little Stranger*) but borrowed from Karl Marx. Beleaguered by winter in Moberly and desperately needing the small remainder of the advance due me, I at last yielded to the demand of the Covici-Friede on the title question. As to the novel's merits or demerits, it is more orderly in a structural sense but it lacks the strong material used in the first. Again I was chided by some of the Marxist critics, this time for representing a white collar intellectual as the revolutionary while his working-class half-brother was what the Wobblies used to call a scissors-bill—one servilely eager to please the boss at all cost.''[1]

1938. Moved to Chicago from Moberly. "When I first went to Chicago from Moberly, Missouri . . . I hardly believed that I would tarry there for 28 years. But so it turned out. My immediate object was to establish . . . a magazine to carry on the traditions of my magazine *The Anvil,* which had been swallowed up and completely effaced in an ill-advised merger with *Partisan Review.* We did manage to get *The New Anvil* going, with considerable difficulty after a round of fund-raising parties, lectures, and other events.

"In the meantime, I succeeded in qualifying for a job with the branch of the Federal Writers' Project, which had its headquarters in Chicago in a loft on East Erie Street near the office of *Poetry: A Magazine of Verse.*

"Next I found myself ensconced with Arna [Bontemps] in the former Rosenwald mansion on the South Side as his co-supervisor on a project slated to produce a volume to be called *The Negro in Illinois.* . . . The Rosenwald Foundation was sponsoring *The Negro in Illinois* venture and had donated space in the mansion once occupied by philanthropist Julius Rosenwald.

"Arna and I each had an upstairs office, formerly a bedroom. The offices were separated by a hall, down which our field-workers came to report and to deposit the fruits of their labors. Some were conducting interviews, while others searched the files of newspapers and other periodicals. A few of the workers had writing experience, but most of them had not. Their most valuable gleanings were from the files of old newspapers and magazines. They had been instructed to

JACK CONROY

copy any item relating to Negroes, and, while many of these were trivial or frivolous, there were so many and they were so varied in content and tone that in sum they aggregated a rather comprehensive social history of the colored citizen and his conditions and also yielded significant evidence of prevailing white attitudes toward him.

"Our inside information was never used in *The Negro in Illinois,* for which it was intended, because the project ended before the book was ready for the press, but Arna and I were able to take advantage of much of it in our history of Negro migration, *They Seek a City,* published in 1945." [Jack Conroy, "Memories of Arna Bontemps," *American Libraries,* December, 1974.[2]]

1942. First juvenile published. "My own experience as a juvenile writer stems from my association with Arna Bontemps. Arna and I were in charge of a survey for the Rosenwald Fund and the Illinois Federal Writers' Project when I submitted a group of industrial folk tales (these are stories they tell around factories, etc.) to Houghton Mifflin as an adult book. They couldn't see them for that, but Hardwick Moseley, then one of their salesmen, suggested that one, 'The Boomer Fireman's Fast Sooner Hound,' would make a fine juvenile. I told Arna, who had written a couple, of this and he said: 'Why not collaborate?' So we did, and *The Fast Sooner Hound,* published by Houghton Mifflin in 1942, was the result. It has been the most successful of all my books, . . . still going strong. Many school readers, anthologies, etc. have published excerpts or adaptations not only of the collaboration but my original version which may be found, with a group of others, in B. A. Botkin's *A Treasury of American Folklore.* These are tall tales in the frontier tradition of exaggeration. The stories of the Sooner Hound and Slappy

Hooper are based on a single anecdote I learned while working in the Wabash Railway shops in Moberly. I added similar incidents from my imagination. In the anecdote I heard, it was merely a fast dog and Slappy Hooper was a name I gave a painter too good for his own good—about which I had heard a single incident. So it goes. In Maria Leach's two-volume *Funk and Wagnalls Standard Dictionary of Folklore, Mythology and Legend* (Funk and Wagnalls, 1950) there is an entry for 'Slappy Hooper . . . legendary hero of old-time billboard craftsmen.' That's how legends are born!''

1947-1966. Senior editor for *The New Standard Encyclopedia* in Chicago.

1966. Returned to Moberly. "I returned to Moberly in November after twenty-eight years of standing in tears amid the alien corn of Chicago, often with a sad heart sick for home. Still I wouldn't want to badmouth Chicago, for I made a great many lasting friends while there. Book editors were always hospitable and helpful. I often said that as a reviewer I wore out five or six book editors on the *Sun* and *Sun-Times*. . . .''[1]

After his return to Moberly, Conroy began writing his autobiography. Conroy has been a lecturer of folklore at several universities and six of his stories are anthologized in B. A. Botkin's, *A Treasury of American Folklore.* "Well, where do I go from here? The answer is, 'no place for very long.' I still think that writers frequently resemble the ancient Greek wrestler Antaeus. He could be thrown to the ground, but the minute he touched Mother Earth his strength was renewed. Hercules bested him by lifting him into the air and strangling him. It seems to me that not a few of our writers who began promisingly are now suspended in the sterile air of New York or Hollywood, wriggling ineffectually as their pristine strength leaks away. It has been too long since they touched the good earth. What I'm doing now is trying to make some sort of consensus of all I've seen and, if possible, to extract some sort of meaning from it all. These investigations and ruminations might conceivably take the form of an autobiography."[1]

FOR MORE INFORMATION SEE: Harry R. Warfel, *American Novelists of Today*, American Book Co., 1951; Walter B. Rideout, *The Radical Novel in the United States, 1900-1954*, Harvard University Press, 1956; *Chicago Daily News*, March 23, 1963; *San Francisco Chronicle*, April 2, 1963; *St. Louis Post-Dispatch*, April 13, 1963; *Chicago Sun-Times*, April 14, 1963; *Cleveland Press*, April 26, 1963; *Magazine of Books*, May 12, 1963; *Atlantic Monthly*, June, 1963; *New York Times*, April 10, 1966; *Who's Who's in America*, #35, 1968; David Madden, editor, *Proletarian Novelists of the Thirties*, Southern Illinois University Press, 1968; Jack Conroy, "Home to Moberly," *Missouri Library Association Quarterly*, March, 1968.

Jack Conroy, "Days of Anvil," *American Book Collector*, Summer, 1971; John Gordon Burke, "A Preliminary Checklist of the Writings of Jack Conroy," *The American Book Collector*, Summer, 1971; Lewis Fried, "Conversation with Jack Conroy," *New Letters*, Fall, 1972; Lewis Fried, "The Disinherited: Worker as Writer," *New Letters*, Fall, 1972; Michel Fabre, "Jack Conroy as Editor," *New Letters*, Winter, 1972; Jack Salzman, "Conroy, Mencken, and *The American Mercury*," *Journal of Popular Culture*, Winter, 1973; Jack Conroy, "Memories of Arna Bontemps," *American Libraries*, December, 1974.

JAMES FENIMORE COOPER

COOPER, James Fenimore   1789-1851 (Jane Morgan)

PERSONAL: Born September 15, 1789, in Burlington, New Jersey; died September 14, 1851, in Cooperstown, New York; buried in Cooperstown; son (and eleventh child) of William (a judge and member of the New York State legislature) and Elizabeth (Fenimore) Cooper; married Susan Augusta De Lancey, January 1, 1811; children: four daughters, two sons (one of whom died in infancy). *Education:* Attended Yale University, 1803-05.

CAREER: Novelist, social critic, historian, gentleman farmer. Served as a merchant seaman, about 1807-08; full-time writer, beginning 1820; appointed U.S. Consul at Lyons, France, 1826-29. *Military service:* U.S. Navy, midshipman, 1808-11; served on the Great Lakes. *Member:* Bread and Cheese Club (founder, 1822), writers' and artists' social club in New York City. *Awards, honors:* Honorary M.A., Yale University, 1824.

WRITINGS—Fiction: Precaution (first published anonymously), Goodrich, 1820, reprinted, Scholarly Press, 1969; *The Spy: A Tale of Neutral Ground*, Wiley & Halsted, 1821, reprinted, College & University Press, 1971 [other editions illustrated by Harold Brett, Houghton, 1924; C. LeRoy Baldridge, Minton, Balch, 1924, reprinted, Garden City Publishing, 1942; William P. Couse, Saalfield, 1936; Henry C. Pitz, Limited Editions Club, 1963]; *The Pioneers;*

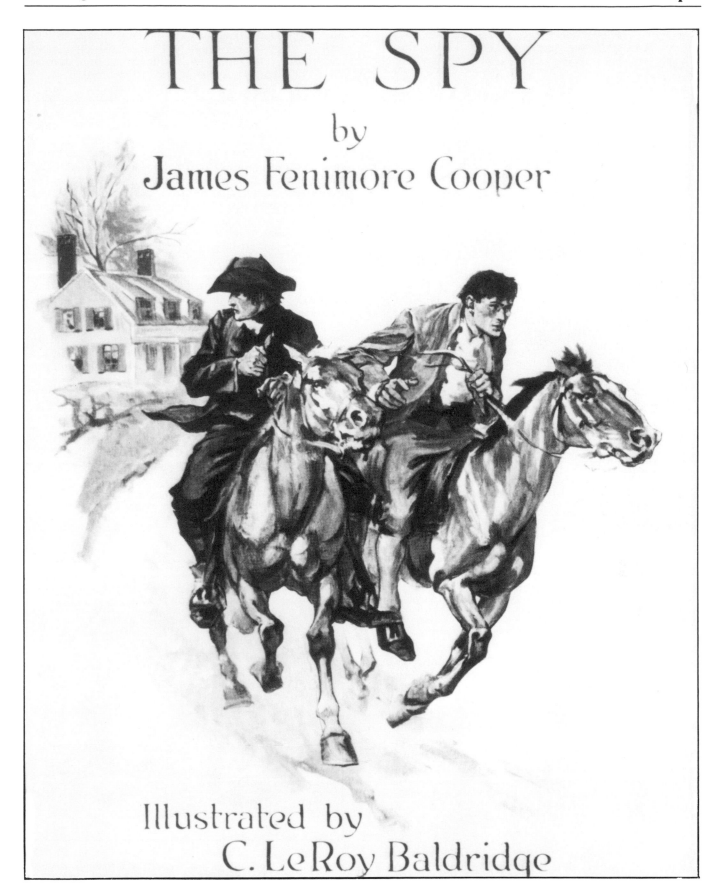

THE SPY
by
James Fenimore Cooper

Illustrated by
C. LeRoy Baldridge

In short, the law was momentarily extinct in that particular district, and justice was administered subject to the bias of personal interests and the passions of the strongest. ■ (From *The Spy* by James Fenimore Cooper. Illustrated by C. LeRoy Baldridge.)

"Then die!" shouted Magua, hurling his tomahawk with violence at the unresisting speaker. ■ (From *The Last of the Mohicans: Or a Narrative of 1757* by James Fenimore Cooper. Illustrated by E. Boyd Smith.)

or, The Sources of the Susquehanna, Wiley, 1823, reprinted, Dutton, 1970 [other editons illustrated from drawings by F.O.C. Darley, Appleton, 1872; illustrated by H. M. Brock, Macmillan, 1901; Donald S. Humphreys, Macrae Smith, 1927; Carle Michel Bogg, Nelson, 1928]; *The Pilot: A Tale of the Sea*, Wiley, 1823, reprinted (and illustrated by Robert M. Quackenbush), Heritage Press, 1968 [other editions illustrated from drawings by F.O.C. Darley, Appleton, 1873; illustrated by Donald Teague, Minton, Balch, 1925]; (under pseudonym Jane Morgan) *Tales for Fifteen; or, Imagination and Heart*, Wiley, 1823, facsimile reproduction (with an introduction by James F. Beard), Scholars' Facsimiles & Reprints, 1959; *Lionel Lincoln; or, The Leaguer of Boston*, Wiley, 1825.

The Last of the Mohicans, Carey & Lea, 1826, reprinted, Scribner, 1973 [other editions illustrated from drawings by F.O.C. Darley, Hurd & Houghton, 1871; illustrated by H. M. Brock, Macmillan, 1900; E. Boyd Smith, Holt, 1910; N. C. Wyeth, Scribner, 1919, reprinted, 1973; Edwin J. Prittie, Winston, 1925; Peter Hurd, McKay, 1928; Edward Wilson, Limited Editions Club, 1932; Brinton Turkle, Scott, Fores-

man, 1950; James Daugherty, World Publishing, 1957]; *The Prairie*, Carey, Lea & Carey, 1827, reprinted, New American Library, 1964 [other editions illustrated from drawings by F.O.C. Darley, Appleton, 1872; illustrated by C. E. Brock, Macmillan, 1900; Donald S. Humphreys, Macrae Smith, 1928; John Steuart Curry, Limited Editions Club, 1940]; *The Red Rover*, Carey, Lea & Carey, 1828, reprinted, University of Nebraska Press, 1963, an earlier edition illustrated from drawings by F.O.C. Darley, Hurd & Houghton, 1872; *The Wept of Wish-ton-Wish*, Carey, Lea & Carey, 1829, reprinted, Brown Books, 1975 (published in England as *The Borderers*, Bentley, 1849, and as *The Heathcotes*, Routledge, 1854), a later edition illustrated from drawings by F.O.C. Darley, Townsend, 1859.

The Water Witch; or, The Skimmer of the Seas, Carey & Lea, 1830, reprinted, AMS Press, 1970, an earlier edition illustrated from drawings by F.O.C. Darley, Appleton, 1874; *The Bravo*, Carey & Lea, 1831, reprinted, College & University Press, 1963, an earlier edition illustrated from drawings by F.O.C. Darley, Townsend, 1859; *The Heidenmauer; or, The Benedectines*, Carey & Lea, 1832; *The Headsman; or, The Abbaye des Vignerons*, Carey, Lea & Blanchard, 1833 [*The Bravo, The Heidenmauer*, and *The Headsman* make up a trilogy]; *The Monikins* (satire), Carey, Lea & Blanchard, 1835, a later edition illustrated from drawings by F.O.C. Darley, Townsend, 1860; *Homeward Bound; or, The Chase*, Carey, Lea & Blanchard, 1838; *Home as Found* (sequel to *Homeward Bound*), Lea & Blan-

To draw in the legs and secure the fastenings, occupied the Pathfinder but a moment. Then there existed no obstacle to their giving their undivided care to the wounded man. ■ (From *The Pathfinder or The Inland Sea* by J. Fenimore Cooper. Illustrated by N. Orr.)

chard, 1838, reprinted, Putnam, 1961 (published in England as *Eve Effingham; or, Home*, Bentley, 1838).

The Pathfinder; or, The Inland Sea, Lea & Blanchard, 1840, reprinted, Regents Publishing, 1973 [other editions illustrated from drawings by F.O.C. Darley, Appleton, 1872; illustrated by C. E. Brock, Macmillan, 1900, Donald S. Humphreys, Macrae Smith, 1926; E. F. Ward, Minton, Balch, 1928; Carle Michel Bogg, Nelson, 1928; Richard M. Powers, Limited Editions Club, 1965]; *Mercedes of Castile; or, The Voyage to Cathay*, Lea & Blanchard, 1840, a later edition illustrated from drawings by F.O.C. Darley, 1861; *The Deerslayer; or, The First War Path*, Lea & Blanchard, 1841, reprinted, Naylor, 1965 [other editions illustrated by H. M. Brock, Macmillan, 1900; N. C. Wyeth, Scribner, 1925, reprinted, 1964; Louis Rhead, Harper, 1926; Edward A. Wilson, Heritage Press, 1961]; *Imagination: A Tale for Young Women* (an excerpt from *Tales for Fifteen*), Clements (London), 1841.

The Two Admirals, Lea & Blanchard, 1842 [other editions illustrated from drawings by F.O.C. Darley, Hurd & Houghton, 1872; and illustrated by Rufus S. Zogbaum, Scribner, 1899]; *Wing-and-Wing; or, Le Feu-Follet*, Lea & Blanchard, 1842 (published in England as *Jack o' Lantern (Le Feu-Follet); or, The Privateer*, Bentley, 1842), a later

Hawkeye took a swift aim and fired. ■ (From *The Last of the Mohicans* by James Fenimore Cooper. Illustrated by H. M. Brock.)

edition illustrated from drawings by F.O.C. Darley, Appleton, 1873; *Wyandotte; or, The Hutted Knoll*, Lea & Blanchard, 1843, a later edition illustrated from drawings by F.O.C. Darley, Townsend, 1859; *Ned Myers; or, A Life before the Mast*, Lea & Blanchard, 1843; *Le Mouchoir: An Autobiographical Romance*, Wiley, 1843, also published as *Autobiography of a Pocket-Handkerchief* (under which title it had first appeared in *Graham's Magazine*, 1843), Golden-Book Press, 1897 (published in England as *The French Governess; or, The Embroidered Handkerchief*, Bentley, 1843).

Afloat and Ashore; or, The Adventures of Miles Wallingford, Burgess, Stringer, 1844 (published in two parts, the second of which is usually titled *Miles Wallingford* in America and *Lucy Hardinge* in England), a later edition illustrated from drawings by F.O.C. Darley, Hurd & Houghton, 1866; *Satanstoe; or, The Littlepage Manuscripts*, Burgess, Stringer, 1845, reprinted, University of Nebraska Press, 1962; *The Chainbearer; or, The Littlepage Manuscripts*, Burgess, Stringer, 1846, reprinted, AMS Press, 1973; *The Redskins; or, Indian and Injin: Being the Conclusion of the Littlepage Manuscripts*, Burgess, Stringer, 1846 (published in England as *Ravensnest; or, The Redskins*, 1846); *The Crater; or, Vulcan's Peak*, Burgess, Stringer, 1847, reprinted, Belknap Press of Harvard University Press, 1962 (published in England as *Mark's Reef; or, The Crater*, Bentley, 1847); *Jack Tier; or, The Florida Reef* (originally published serially in *Graham's Magazine*, 1846-48, as "The Islets of the Gulf; or, Rose Budd"), Burgess,

The Scout motioned for the females to enter. ■ (From *The Last of the Mohicans* by James Fenimore Cooper. Illustrated by Frank T. Merrill.)

"I am no scholar, and I care not who knows it; but judging from what I have seen, at deer chases and squirrel hunts, of the sparks below, I should think a rifle in the hands of their grandfathers was not so dangerous as a hickory bow and a good flinthead might be, if drawn with Indian judgement, and sent by an Indian eye." ■ (From *The Last of the Mohicans* by James Fenimore Cooper. Illustrated by James Daugherty.)

Stringer, 1848 (published in England as *Captain Spike; or, The Islets of the Gulf,* Bentley, 1848); *The Oak Openings; or, The Bee-Hunter,* Burgess, Stringer, 1848 (published in England as *The Bee-Hunter; or, The Oak Openings,* Bentley, 1848); *The Sea Lions; or, The Lost Sealers,* Stringer & Townsend, 1849, reprinted, University of Nebraska Press, 1965; *The Ways of the Hour,* Putnam, 1850, reprinted, 1969.

O-i-chee: A Tale of the Mohawk (written in 1822 and first published in the *Home Weekly* of Philadelphia, 1843), Beadle, 1865; *The Leatherstocking Tales,* Houghton, 1898-99, Volume I: *The Deerslayer,* Volume II: *The Last of the Mohicans,* Volume III: *The Pathfinder,* Volume IV: *The Pioneers,* Volume V: *The Prairie,* an abridged edition of the collected novels, edited by Allan Nevins and illustrated by Reginald Marsh, published as *The Leatherstocking Saga,* Pantheon, 1954, reprinted, 1966. Also author of "Upside Down; or, Philosophy in Petticoats," an unpublished comedy produced in June, 1850, at Burton's Theatre in New York City.

Nonfiction—Social criticism: *Notions of the Americans: Picked up by a Travelling Bachelor,* Carey, Lea & Carey, 1828, reprinted, Ungar, 1963, also published as *The Travelling Bachelor; or, Notions of the Americans,* Stringer & Townsend, 1856; *Letter to General Lafayette,* Baudry's Foreign Library (Paris), 1831, reprinted, Columbia University Press, 1931; *A Letter to His Countrymen,* Wiley, 1834; *The American Democrat; or, Hints on the Social and Civic Relations of the United States of America,* Phinney, 1838, reprinted as *The American Democrat: A Treatise on Jacksonian Democracy,* Funk & Wagnalls, 1969.

History: *The Chronicles of Cooperstown* (published anonymously), Phinney, 1838; *A History of the Navy of the United States of America,* Lea & Blanchard, 1839, reprinted, Gregg, 1970; *The Battle of Lake Erie,* Phinney, 1843; *The Legends and Traditions of a Northern County,* Putnam, 1921.

Travel sketches: *Sketches of Switzerland,* two parts, Carey, Lea & Blanchard, 1836 (published separately in England as Part I: *Excursions in Switzerland,* and Part II: *A Residence in France, with an Excursion up the Rhine, and a Second Visit to Switzerland,* both published by Bentley, 1836); *Gleanings in Europe,* two parts, Carey, Lea & Blanchard, 1837, Part I: *France* (published in England as *Recollections of Europe,* Bentley, 1837), Part II: *England* (published as *England, with Sketches of Society in the Metropolis,* Bentley, 1837); *Gleanings in Europe: Italy,* Carey, Lea & Blanchard, 1838 (published in England as *Excursions in Italy,* Bentley, 1838).

Other: *Lives of Distinguished American Naval Officers,* Carey & Hart, 1846, reprinted, Somerset, 1972.

Collections: *The Works of James Fenimore Cooper,* 32 volumes, Hurd & Houghton, 1865, later edition illustrated by F.O.C. Darley, Appleton, 1892; *Pages and Pictures from the Writings of James Fenimore Cooper* (with notes by daughter, Susan Fenimore Cooper), Townsend, 1861, also published as *The Cooper Gallery,* Miller, 1865; *The Correspondence of James Fenimore Cooper,* two volumes, edited by grandson, James F. Cooper, Yale University Press, 1922, reprinted, Haskell House, 1971; *Letters and Journals,* six volumes, edited by James F. Beard, Belknap Press of Harvard University Press, 1960-68.

Cooper in middle age. Sketch by Henry Inman.

Contributor of stories, articles, and reviews to various periodicals, including *Graham's Magazine, Naval Magazine, Knickerbocker,* and *Putnam's Magazine.*

Adaptations—Movies and filmstrips: "The Last of the Mohicans" (motion pictures), Maurice Tourneur, 1920, United Artists, 1936; "The Last of the Redmen" (motion picture based on *The Last of the Mohicans*), Columbia Pictures Corp., 1947; "Leatherstocking" (series of 10 motion pictures), Pathé Exchange, Inc., 1924; "The Pioneers" (motion picture), Monogram Pictures Corp., 1941; "The Deerslayer" (motion pictures), Republic Pictures, 1943, Twentieth Century-Fox Film Corp., 1957; "The Prairie" (motion picture), Zenith Pictures, Inc., 1950; "The Spy" (motion picture), General Television Enterprises, 1950; "The Pathfinder" (motion picture), Columbia Pictures Corp., 1952; "Hawkeye and the Last of the Mohicans" (series of 39 motion pictures), Television Programs of America, Normandie Productions, 1957.

Recordings: "The Last of the Mohicans," read by James Mason and cast (record or cassette), Caedmon.

SIDELIGHTS: **September 15, 1789.** Born in Burlington, New Jersey. "My direct male ancestor, was a friend and co-religionist of William Penn, though he was amongst those who originally settled West-Jersey—Many of his descendants subsequently crossed the Delaware, and both my father and grandfather were natives of Pennsylvania—I was born myself on the banks of the river, on the Jersey side, but completely within the influence of the mild tenets of Penn, and in fact, in the Territory which he once (had) materially controlled—I am the fifth in descent of my family, in America, (and) every individual of which, down to my own generation was born either in Pennsylvania, or on the opposite shores of the Delaware." [*The Letters and Journals of James Fenimore Cooper*, Volume VI, edited by James Franklin Beard, Belknap Press of Harvard University Press, 1968.[1]]

"My family settled in America in the year 1679. It came from Buckingham, in England, and for a century it dwelt in the county of Bucks, in Pennsylvania. It then, or rather my branch of it, became established in the State of New-York.

"My mother was the daughter of Richard Fenimore, of Burlington County, N.J. I was born in 1789, at Burlington, on the Delaware, but was carried, an infant, to Cooperstown, Ostego County, N.Y. I was sent to various grammar schools between the ages of six and twelve, and at thirteen I was admitted to Yale College, New-Haven, Conn." [*The Letters and Journals of James Fenimore Cooper*, Volume

II, edited by James Franklin Beard, Belknap Press of Harvard University Press, 1960.[2]]

He wrote to a former teacher: "I remember (a teacher) with affection. He did his duty, and more than his duty by me; and could I have been reclaimed to study by kindness, he would have done it. My misfortune was extreme youth. I was not sixteen when you expelled me. I had been early and highly educated for a boy,—so much so as to be far beyond most of my classmates in Latin; and this enabled me to play—a boy of thirteen!—all the first year. I dare say (the teacher) never suspected me of knowing too much, but there can be no great danger now in telling him the truth. So well was I grounded in the Latin that I scarce ever looked at my Horace or Tully until I was in his fearful presence; . . . If I ever write my memoir, the college part will not be the least amusing. . . . On one occassion, a tutor of the name of Fowler was scraped in the hall. Now I was charged with being one of his assailants, *by himself,* and was arraigned before you all in conclave. You presided, and appealed to my honor whether I scraped or not. I told you the truth that I did not, for I disliked the manner of assailing a man *en masse.* You believed me, for we understood each other, and I was dismissed without even a reproof."

Cooper's birthplace, Burlington, New Jersey.

[*Fenimore Cooper, Critic of His Times*, Robert E. Spiller, Russell & Russell, 1963.[3]]

1806. Expelled from Yale for pushing a rag with gunpowder through a classmate's door and exploding it.

January 1, 1808. Commissioned as a midshipman in the Navy.

1809. Father died.

May 18, 1810. Wrote to his brother: "Like all the rest of the sons of Adam, I have bowed to the influence of the charms of [a] fair damsel of eighteen—I loved her like a man and told her of it like a sailor. The peculiarity of my situation occasion'd me to act with something like precipitancy—I am perfectly confident, however, I shall never have cause to repent of it—As you are *cooly* to decide, I will as cooly give you the qualities of my mistress. Susan De Lancey is the daughter of a man of very respectable connections and a handsome fortune—amiable, sweet tempered and happy in her disposition—she has been educated in the country—occasionaly trying the temperature of the City—to rub off the rust—but hold a moment, it is enough she pleases *me* in the qualities of her *person* and *mind*—

"Like a true Quixotic lover, I made proposals to her father—he has answered them in the most gentlemanly manner—You have my consent to address my daughter if you will gain the approbation of your mother—He also informs me that his daughter has an estate in this County of Westchester in reversion, secured to her by a deed in trust to him—and depending upon the life of an aunt Aetat 72—so you see Squire *the old woman* can't weather it long.

"I write all this for *you*—you know *I* am indifferent to any thing of this nature. Now I have to request—you will take your Hat and go to mother, the boys, girls, and say to them have you any objection that James Cooper shall marry at a future day, Susan De Lancey—If any of them forbids the bans may the Lord have [no?] forgive them—for I never will—'' [*The Letters and Journals of James Fenimore Cooper*, Volume I, Belknap University Press, 1960.[4]]

January 1, 1811. Married Susan De Lancey.

1820. While reading to his wife, he said of the book (they were reading): "I could write you a better book than that myself."[3] His wife challenged him (to it), and as a result he wrote *Precaution*. "For the double purpose of employment and the amusement of my wife in her present low spirits [her mother had died]—I commenced the writing of a moral tale—finding it swell to a rather unwieldy size—I destroy'd the manuscript and chang'd it to a novel—the persuasions of my wife and the opinion of my Friend Mr. Wm. Jay—have induced me to think of publishing it—it is not yet completed and the object of this letter is to obtain some mechanical information that may regulate the size of my volumes—I am now writing the eighth Chapter of the second volume—the first contains twenty five Chapters—in the whole volume (i.e. the first) one hundred and twelve closely written pages of about eight Hundred words each—this I compute will make an ordinary volume, such as *Ivanhoe*, which I took for a guide."[4]

1821. Completed *The Spy*. ". . . By persuasion of Mrs. Cooper I have commenced another tale to be called the *Spy* scene in West-Chester County, and time of the revolution-

Engraving of Cooper by Madame Lizinska de Mirbel.

ary war—I have already got about Sixty pages of it written and my female Mentor says it throws *Precaution* far in the back-ground—I confess I am more partial to this new work myself as being a Country-man and perhaps a younger child—it will not be done however these three months at least as I propose making it somewhat longer than the last—The task of making American manners and American scenes interesting to an American reader is an arduous one—I am unable to say whether I shall succeed or not—but my wife, who is an excellent judge in every thing but her partiality flatters me with very brilliant success—to return however to the one that is done—I send you the three first chapters in order to see your style and type—that of the Monastery will do—but I should like a better paper—My writing is so bad and I am so very careless with it that unless great care is taken with the printing and orthography—the Book will be badly gotten up—The business of paragraphs is an important one and I have made little marks where I think there should be a new one."[4]

In those days it was no simple task to get a book properly printed: "[I] am afraid [the printer] does not employ competent compositors—the mistakes they make are ludicrous and since I have urged the division into paragraphs they have in several instances made them in the middle of sentences—there is a case in the accompanying proof—I should suppose the sense would teach them better—they are however undoubtedly in the worst part of the manuscript and it will grow better directly—cannot the thing be hastened—I am extremely anxious to go to Sag-Harbor and Mrs. Cooper is afraid to undertake it again in my absence—the second volume is far—far better than the first—but still they leave mistakes unnoticed—the letter S at the end of words—its omission or insertion is of great importance and there are at least a dozen mistakes of that nature most if not all of which are notic'd by me—You are

(From the movie "The Last of the Mohicans," starring Randolph Scott, Binnie Barnes, and Bruce Cabot. Copyright 1936 by United Artists Corp.)

(From the movie "The Pathfinder," starring George Montgomery. Copyright 1953 by Columbia Pictures Corp.)

(From the movie "The Last of the Redmen," starring Buster Crabbe and Jon Hall. Copyright 1947 by Columbia Pictures.)

(From the movie "The Deerslayer," starring Lex Baker, Rita Moreno, and Forrest Tucker. Copyright © 1957 by Twentieth Century-Fox.)

Lithograph of Cooper by Julian Léopold Boilly.

as much interested as myself in its appearance and I do wish you would hurry it.''[4]

Published his novel, *The Spy,* with some apprehension. There had been very little writing about Americans. ''Should chance throw a copy of this prefatory notice into the hands of an American twenty years hence, he will smile to think that a countryman hesitated to complete a work so far advanced, merely because the disposition of the country to read a book that treated of its own familiar interests was distrusted.'' [*James Fenimore Cooper,* Thomas R. Lounsbury, Houghton, 1882, republished by Gale Research.[5]]

The Spy was well received. ''I cannot conceal from myself that I owe much, if not most of my success to the desire that is now so prevalent in the Country to see our manners exhibited on paper—If I am able to create an excitement that may rouse the sleeping talents of the nation, and in some measure clear us from the odium of dulness, which the malice of our enemies, has been quick to insinuate and our apathy, or rather pursuits, have too much encouraged, I shall not have labored entirely in vain—''[4]

Cooper wrote five prefaces in *The Spy.* In the first one, he spoke on the tastes of his audience. ''We would not be understood as throwing the gauntlet to our fair countrywomen, by whose opinion it is that we expect to stand or fall; we only mean to say, that if we have got no lords or castles in the book, it is because there are none in the country. We heard there was a noble within fifty miles of us, and went that distance to see him, intending to make our hero look as much like him as possible; when we

brought in his description, the little gipsey who sat for Fanny [Frances Wharton, heroine of *The Spy*], declared she wouldn't have him if he were a king. Then we travelled a hundred miles to see a renowned castle to the east, but, to our surprise, found it had so many broken windows, was such an outdoor kind of place, that we should be wanting in Christian bowels to place any family in it during cold months: in short, we were compelled to let the yellow-haired girl choose her own suitor, and to lodge the Whartons in a comfortable, substantial, and unpretending cottage. We repeat we mean nothing disrespectful to the fair—we love them next to ourselves—our book—our money—and a few other articles. We know them to be good-natured, good-hearted—ay, and good-looking hussies enough: and heartily wish, for the sake of one of them, we were a lord, and had a castle in the bargain.''

In the third preface he discussed the American character and scene as probable material for fiction. ''Common sense is the characteristic of the American people; it is the foundation of their institutions; it pervades society, bringing the high and the low near to each other; it tempers our religion, yielding the indulgence to each other's weakness, which should follow the mandates of God; it wears down the asperities of character—but it ruins the *beau ideal.*

''The difficulty is only increased in works of fiction that are founded on the customs of America, when a writer attempts to engraft the *scions* of the imagination on the stock of history. The plant is too familiar to the senses, and the freshness of the exotic is tarnished by the connexion. This very book will, probably, be cited as an instance of the fallacy of this opinion. We wish that we could think so. *The Spy* was introduced at a happy moment, and the historical incidents were but little known, at the same time that they were capable of deep interest; but, so far as well known characters are concerned, we have been assailed with every variety of criticism, from the cock of a hat to the colour of a horse.

''Besides the familiarity of the subject, there is a scarcity of events, and a poverty in the accompaniments, that drives an author from the undertaking in despair. In the dark ages of our history, it is true that we hung a few unfortunate women for witches, and suffered some inroads from the Indians; but the active curiosity of the people has transmitted those events with so much accuracy, that there is no opportunity for digression. Then again, notwithstanding that a murder is at all times a serious business, it is much more interesting in a castle than in a corn field. In short, all that glow, which can be given to a tale, through the aid of obscure legends, artificial distinctions, and images connected with the association of the ideas, is not attainable in this land of facts. Man is not the same creature here as in other countries. He is more fettered by reason and less by laws, than in any other section of the globe; consequently, while he enjoys a greater political liberty, he is under a greater moral restraint than his European brother.''

He was articulate concerning the American novelists' problems: ''The second obstacle against which American literature has to contend, is in the poverty of materials. There is scarcely an ore which contributed to the wealth of the author, that is found, here, in veins as rich as in Europe. There are no annals for the historian; no follies (beyond the most vulgar and commonplace) for the satirist; no manners for the dramatist; no obscure fictions for the writer of romance; no gross and hardy offenses against decorum for the moralist, nor any of the rich auxiliaries of poetry. The

"What means this" said Ludlow hastily—
"She, Claudio, that you wronged, look you restore—love her, Angelo;
I have confessed her, and I know her virtue."
■ (From *The Water Witch* by James Fenimore Cooper. Illustrated from drawings by F. O. C. Darley.)

At this instant the door flew open and the fight was transferred to the platform, the light, and the open air.

A Huron had undone the fastenings of the door, and three or four of his tribe rushed after him upon the narrow space, as if glad to escape from some terrible scene within. ■ (From *The Deerslayer* by James Fenimore Cooper. Illustrated by N. C. Wyeth.)

... His frame was comparatively light and slender, showing muscles, however, that promised unusual agility; if not unusual strength. ■ (From *The Deerslayer or The First Warpath* by James Fenimore Cooper. Illustrated by Frank Schoonover.)

"William Kirby, I order you to do your duty," cried Hiram, from under the bank; "seize that man; I order you to seize him in the name of the people." ■ (From *The Pioneers* by James Fenimore Cooper. Painting by John Quidor. Courtesy of New York State Historical Association.)

weakest hand can extract a spark from the flint, but it would baffle the strength of a giant to attempt kindling a flame with a pudding-stone. . . . There is no costume for the peasant, (there is scarcely a peasant at all), no wig for the judge, no baton for the general, no diadem for the chief magistrate.''

In his fourth preface to *The Spy* he wrote: ''Of all the generous sentiments, that of love of country is the most universal. We uniformly admire the man who sacrifices himself for the good of the community to which he belongs; and we unsparingly condemn him who, under whatever plea of sophism or necessity, raises his arm or directs his talents against the land to which he owes a natural allegiance. The proudest names and the fairest hopes have fallen under the obloquy of treason. Men have admired the Roman who could sacrifice the closer tie of blood to that of country; but we overlook the courage and success of Cariolanus, in scorn of his disaffection. There is a purity in real patriotism which elevates its subject above all the grosser motives of selfishness, and which in the nature of things, can never distinguish services to mere kindred and family. It has the beauty of self-elevation, without the alloy of personal interest.''

1826. Published *The Last of the Mohicans.* ''The Mohicans were the possessors of the country first occupied by the Europeans in this portion of the continent. They were, con-

sequently, the first dispossessed; and the seemingly inevitable fate of all these people, who disappear before the advances, or it might be termed the inroads of civilization, as the verdure of their native forests falls before the nipping frost, is represented as having already befallen them. There is sufficient historical truth in the picture to justify the use that has been made of it.'' [James Fenimore Cooper, *The Last of the Mohicans,* Carey & Lea, 1826.[6]]

In his preface he writes: ''The reader, who takes up these volumes, in expectation of finding an imaginary and romantic picture of things which never had an existence, will probably lay them aside, disappointed. The work is exactly what it proposes to be in its title-page—a narrative. As it relates, however, to matters which may not be universally understood, especially by the more imaginative sex, some of whom, under the impression that it is a fiction, may be induced to read the book, it becomes the interest of the author to explain a few of the obscurities of the historical allusions.''

The final remarks in the preface are directed to his reading audience: ''With this brief introduction to his subject, then, the author commits his book to the reader. As however, candour, if not justice, requires such a declaration at his hands, he will advise all young ladies, whose ideas are usually limited by the four walls of a comfortable drawing room; all single gentlemen of a certain age, who are under the influence of the winds; and all clergymen, if they have volumes in hand, with intent to read them, to abandon the design. He gives this advice to such young ladies, because, after they have read the book, they will surely pronounce it shocking; to the bachelors, as it might disturb their sleep, and to the reverend clergy, because they might be better employed.''

After publishing *Mohicans,* he wrote to a friend on his way to Europe. ''Carey published the *Mohicans* on the 6th of February, about ten days earlier, than I had anticipated—As I sent you, however, duplicates of the 2d volume, nearly a month before, I presume you will not be far behind him—I do not know whether I desired you to sell a copy to the translators, *on your own account,* or, not; but I sincerely hope I did; for it being out of my power to profit by such a sale, I could wish you to get something for yourself—The book is quite successful, in this Country, more so, I think, than any of its predecessors—

''I intend to sail from here, some time in the month of June, either for France or Italy, which I have not yet determined—As I shall be accompanied by Mrs. Cooper, and my family it is my intention to remain in Europe a year or two—My object, is my own health and the instruction of my children in the French and Italian languages—Perhaps there is, also, a little pleasure concealed, in the bottom of the Cup—Before I go, I shall apprise you of my movements, as I intend to appear, again, in the fall—Perhaps I may be able to secure a Right in England for the next book. At all events, I hope to see you, before I return. . . .

''Will you have the goodness to get a set of the *Mohicans* neatly bound, and send it to the Hon-E. G. Stanley, the eldest son of Lord Stanley—I know no better way of distinguishing him—He is a Member of Parliament, and after his father, the next heir to the Earldom of Derby—(It is the Gentleman who was, in this Country last year—He and I, were, together, in the caverns at Glens falls, and it was there I determined to write the book, promising him a Copy—Send it with a note, saying that you were requested to do so, by the Author—''[4]

At the U.S. Consul in Europe. Upon arrival in Paris Cooper was eager to meet Lafayette, soon to become his friend. ''Though personally unknown to La Fayette, I never felt so much interest, when a boy, in any foreigner as I did in him—It is a wonderful feeling, that binds us all, so strongly to that old man—I went with, my whole family, in a boat, to see him and the balloon, at the same time—We saw the

The moon broke from behind a mass of clouds, and the eye of the woman was enabled to follow the finger of Ishmael. It pointed to a human form swinging in the wind, beneath the ragged and shining arm of the willow. ■ (From *The Prairie* by James Fenimore Cooper. Drawing by J. Hamilton.)

Portrait of Cooper by Carel Christian Anthony Last.

been here three weeks, and I am already hard at work, actually feeling less desire to go abroad, than when in New-York—

"The Booksellers are now nibbling at my book, and profess a readiness to purchase—*Mohicans* has done very well here, they tell me, and it will give *The Prairie*, a better chance—I am playing shy, but shall soon come to an arrangement as it is time to think of printing—I shall be ready by Christmas, in America, I have no doubt, allowing for the passage and all.

"I can hardly tell you how I like Paris—If I were to give an opinion at this early hour, it would be to say, that the French began to be fine before they knew how to be comfortable—There is a strange medley of finery dirt & magnificence."[4]

He described the life and manners of a diplomat. "I saw little difference in the manner of reception of our own country, excepting that every body is, as you know, announced, and that the Ladies all entered and departed in front of their beaux, instead of leaning on their arms, as with us—The freedom, gives the woman a better opportunity of showing her grace; but it has not a delicate or lady-like appear-

"Can the women and children of Pale-face live without the meat of the bison? There was hunger in my lodge." ■ (From *The Prairie* by James Fenimore Cooper. Illustrated by John Steuart Curry.)

latter, but Mrs. C—and the children returned quite disappointed, because they could not get a view of La Fayette—He passed us in the race boat, but it was calm, and my boat, which is very justly named the Van Tromp, from the Dutch formation of her bows, refused to fly as swiftly, as might be wished. I was introduced to him myself, *en passant,* but never push'd an acquaintance, because I saw very well, he was over-worked—I met him, once, alone, and where I might have had a little conversation, but it was too evident he had just fled from one annoyance, to wish to persecute him, with another—besides he did not recognize me, and It would have been awkward as well as presuming to have introduced myself—"[4]

Settled in Paris. "Here we are established for six months at least, in the garden where Mrs. Cruger resided—You may remember there was a school in that garden—I have taken *au seconde* of the Hotel and its former possessor has gone into the Pavilion—We are rather comfortably lodged for Paris—Dirt, Bugs and Fleas of course, but still a good deal of comfort—There is a large salle à manger, (that is large for lodgings) a Petit et Grand Salon—deux chambres à coucher, a cabinet, and a cuisine—For these furnished, pretty well, I pay f2600 per an. The girls are all in the school below, at the rate of f700 each, with I suppose some extra charges where they will learn to speak French, to dance, to read—to write, and special little else I fancy—They sleep in our appart[e]ment, though they eat below, for the price I pay, includes every thing—We have

"What terrors round him wait?
Amazement in his van, with Flight combined,
And sorrows faded form, and Solitude behind."
■ (From *The Deerslayer* by James Fenimore Cooper. Illustrated by J. Hamilton.)

ance—They all wore dress hats, with feathers, (and) but were not very richly attired—The men, also, were plain, with the exception of *stars*—Of these there were plenty, some of them wearing the badges of three or four orders. . . .

". . . .—The Baroness de Damas is a little *hunch'dback'd*, vulgar looking woman, of some great family, who did nothing but snigger and chat with Monseigneur le Nonce, as she called him—She wore around her neck a string of large, gold beads, perfectly plain, that I should think was near six feet long.

". . . .—There is something exceedingly imposing in the state of a King—There were five coaches, richly gilded, and gorgeously decorated otherwise, that were drawn by *eight horses* each—Nothing could be finer than the forms and action of the beasts. All the appointments were perfect, except they drew by *Dutch collars*. The Coachmen were gross looking men, fat, well fed, with cock'd hats, and in the blue and silver of the Court, and the postillions were the same—The Coachmen drove six in hand, there being only one postillion to each carriage—Two of these carriages *were cased*—it being part of the Royal etiquette that the King never stirs without an extra coach, in case of accidents; on the present occasion, there were two, as the family was all present.

". . . . The servant has just announced two *Princesses* to see Mrs. Cooper—so you see, we are going on swimmingly—Recollect they are titular Princesses, not of Royal Blood—One of the meanest looking gentlemen I have seen in France, was an English Lord—France is a charming place for a residence if you can get out of the dirt, but I think the Persian saying of, 'May your Servant eat dirt,' would not be considered as sufficiently humble for this tinselled Country—

". . . . The king eat rather heartily, and he drank several glasses of wine with a very sensible relish. The Dauphin was much more moderate; and the ladies, like all other ladies, were, I suppose, too ethereal to eat.—They laughed and talked with the attendants, and sometimes with each other, though they were seated too far asunder to converse together with ease, as the music played without intermission:—it was excellent."[4]

The myths about America became apparent to him. "A Frenchman who resided three years in New-Jersey stoutly affirmed to me that carpets were but little used in the U. States fourteen years ago! Another who passed two years *at* New-York, affirms that *peaches* are not known among us! A third, and he a fellow-traveller of La Fayette and a well-wisher to the country says there are no *cherries*! Now, I, after a residence of ten months at Paris affirm, that the two latter fruits, after you get as far South as Philadelphia are incomparably better than any thing of the kind in France—

"So difficult is it for Countries to know each other!

"It is telling you nothing new that we are a people held very cheap in the estimation of these Europeans. They think because they live under old and cherished institutions, that, as individuals, they have lived longer than we, and of course that they know more. I wish to God that our countrymen who write the famous puffing paragraphs that we see from time to time in our journals concerning the interest Europe takes in America, could get an opportunity of knowing the real opinion of these people. I find in every nation a jealousy and dislike for almost all others, and were

"I here give thee a right to shoot deer, or bears, or anything thou pleasest in my woods, forever. Leather-Stocking is the only other man that I have granted the same privilege to...." ▪ (From *The Pioneers* by James Fenimore Cooper. Illustrated by F. O. C. Darley.)

J. Hamilton's drawing of the Oswego.

it not that dislikes and jealousies nearer home occupy so much of their attention, I am of opinion that we should be the subject of a general dislike throughout all Europe, precisely for the reason that we enjoy advantages which time and chance have taken away from them.

"We never shall get to be the thoroughly manly people we ought to be and might be, until we cease to look to European opinions for anything except those which are connected with the general advancement of the race. Laziness, incapacity, and a miserable dependence upon foreign ideas destroy the dignity and half the usefulness of half the editors of newspapers. This truckling to foreigners and eagerness to know what other nations think of us, is a fault that always disgusted me when at home, but it is a hundredfold more disgusting now that I know how utterly *worthless* are the opinions they republish. I cannot conceive a greater weakness than for an individual or a people to give importance to an opinion which in the abstract is good for nothing, and which were they familiar with its origin would pass for nothing, mainly because it comes across the water."[4]

He developed a friendship with Lafayette. "In the evening at 7 o'clock Gen. La Fayette came for me, in his carriage. We drove to la rue de Rivoli, and took up Mr. McLane & Mr. Thorne. We then went to the Palais Royal to be presented. . . . It struck me there was an [e]vident desire to do honor to the American friends of the General. It was evident, however, that the presence of La Fayette gave uneasiness to a [g]reat many. The affectations and egotisms of

rank are offended by his principles and there is a pitiful desire manifested, by the mere butterflys of society to turn his ideas and habits into ridicule. I am amazed to find how very [few] men are able to look beyond the glare of things . . . The fear of losing their butterfly distinctions and their tinsel gives great uneasiness to many of these simpletons. The apprehe[n]sion is quite natural to all those who have no means of being known in any other manner, and it must be pardoned."[2]

". . . LaFayette manifested a strong desire that I should write some account of his reception in America. The good old man was so frank, and showed, mingled with his acknowledged personal interest, so strong a desire to do credit to the country, that I scarcely knew how to resist him. I am perhaps foolishly romantic enough to think that he has almost the right to command the services of an American author. At all events, be the motive what it might, I finally consented, not however to write a tame and monotonous account of La Fayette's visit, for that would put him at fault, but to attempt a sketch of the U. States which should, from time to time, touch on some of its striking incidents."[4]

November, 1826. "Well, about a week ago I was descending the stairs of our hotel, which you know are common property to everybody that inhabits the building, when I met an old man ascending, as I thought, with a good deal of difficulty. There was a carriage in the court, and from something in his countenance as well as from his air and the circumstance of the coach, I thought he was coming to see me. Indeed, I fancied I knew the face, though I could not remember the name. We passed each other, looking hard and bowing, and I was just going out of the door when the stranger suddenly stopped and said in French:

"'Est-ce que monsieur Cooper que j'ai l'honneur de voir?'

"'Monsieur, je m'appelle Cooper.'

"'Je suis Walter Scott.'

"Here was an introduction for you! worth a thousand letters, or the most formal presentations. We shook hands. I expressed my thanks for the honor, and he passed an hour with me in my cabinet. I am delighted with him. He treated me like a younger brother and spoke in the kindest and most encouraging manner. The next two days I breakfasted with him. He then paid me another visit, and we met once more at the Princess Gallitzin's, who gave him a famous soirée."[4]

1829. Americans at home criticized his social behavior. "I was told yesterday that it is said at home, that I gave myself airs in England, and did not meet civilities, myself, as they should be met. That I refused invitations that many people would be glad to accept is true, for my health and my business imperiously demanded it. You know that unless I

A series of masterly and rapid evolutions with the horses now commenced. The wheelings, the charges, the advances, and the circuitous retreats, were like the flights of circling swallows.
■ (From *The Prairie* by James Fenimore Cooper. Drawing by F. O. C. Darley.)

As he caught their glances, he drew his hard hand hastily across his eyes again, waved it on high for an adieu, and, uttering a forced cry to his dogs, who were crouching at his feet, he entered the forest. ■ (From *The Prairie* [in *The Leatherstocking Saga*] by James Fenimore Cooper. Illustrated by Reginald Marsh.)

manage my time a little, I have neither bread to eat nor stomach to digest it—Late hours not only destroy my digestion, but they make sad inroads on my ability to buy any thing to digest. But in no instance have I neglected the established forms of society, as they are practised in the several countries visited. . . . The meanness that I have witnessed among some of our people has made me sick often.''[4]

1830. ''The five years set for our absence will expire next summer, and we begin to talk seriously of returning. Still there are powerful motives to induce me to remain abroad a year or two longer. My youngest children are just beginning to reap the advantages of their position, and it seems unwise to deprive them of them, so soon. They are little linguists already, and will soon speak four languages tolerably well. Paul begins to read in three, and so I mean to push him hard; I hope he will retain their use to after life. He speaks both French and Italian far better than English, and it is amusing to hear a little fellow not yet seven talk of what he has seen in Paris, or London, or Amsterdam, or Rome, or Naples, or Venice, &c &c.''[4]

''We are now fixed for six months. It is my present intention to return home in about a year, though political events may induce me to alter my plans. . . . [My children] have not yet secured German, and it is our plan to return to Germany for that object. They prefer, without affectation both French and Italian to their own language. . . . As for their father, his progress is not so satisfactory. I am ashamed to say, that Mrs. Cooper is a much better French, Italian and German scholar than I am now, or am likely ever to be. She works hard, and goes on pari passu with the children. We have all gained something in the way of ideas, and some knowledge of men and things. Susan is a fine young woman of seventeen, and has appeared at one or two balls, in Italy."[2]

1831. Had *Bravo* and *Pioneers* printed. "Let me beg you will have the revises carefully read. I pay no attention to any of the spelling, except in words of particular signification and proper names. There is great difference in the spelling of England and America. We use one g in wagon, no u in honor and words of that class, e in visiter &c &c. The Italians spell feluca with one c, and I have corrected the proofs in that manner, but if your reader thinks there is sufficient English authority to use the two cs he is at liberty to do so—I may as well send you the Title, which will be very simple.

The Bravo
a
Tale
'Giustizzia in palazzo, e pane in piazza'
By the Author of *Spy* &c—

"Would it exceed my literary rights if I were to get a copy of each of the corrected books as they are printed. I do not own a volume of any thing I have ever written, nor have I much taste, in general, to read my own lucubrations, but I confess this task you have set me is such a punishment for my old sins, that I have some desire to see how I shall look when a little purified."[2]

Returned to America and was disenchanted. Started out on the wrong foot by making a social blunder. His friends wanted to give him a testimonial dinner, he declined.

At war with the press, fighting libel suits, personal and professional, his novels became satirical and moralistic. "Each hour, as life advances, am I made to see how capricious and vulgar is the immortality conferred by a newspaper.

"This controversy was not of my seeking; for years have I rested under the imputations that these persons have brought against me, and I now strike a blow in behalf of truth, not from any deference to a public opinion that in my opinion has not honesty enough to feel much interest in the exposure of duplicity and artifice, but that my children may point to the facts with just pride that they had a father who dared to stem popular prejudice in order to write truth."[5]

1834. Disenchanted with the American public, and their criticisms of his work, he formally resigned from fiction writing. "I came before you as a writer when the habit of looking to others for mental ailment most disqualified the public to receive a native author with favor. It has been said lately that I owe the little success I met with at home, to foreign approbation. This assertion is unjust to you. Accident first made me a writer, and the same accident gave a direction to the subject of my pen. Ashamed to have fallen into the track of imitation, I endeavored to repair the wrong done to my own views, by producing a work that should be purely American, and of which love of country should be the theme. This work most of you received with a generous welcome that might have satisfied anyone that the heart of

Otsego Hall. Engraving by H. B. Hall.

this great community is sound. It was only at a later day, when I was willing more obviously to substitute American *principles* for American *things,* that I was first made to feel how far opinion, according to my poor judgment, still lags in the rear of facts. The American who wishes to illustrate and enforce the peculiar principles of his own country by the agency of polite literature, will for a long time to come, I fear, find that *his* constituency, as to all purposes of distinctive thought, is still too much under the influence of foreign theories to receive him with favor.

"What has been here said has been said frankly, and I hope with a suitable simplicity. So far as you have been indulgent to me, and no one feels its extent more than myself, I thank you with deep sincerity; so far as I stand opposed to that class among you which forms the public of a writer, on points that, however much in error, I honestly believe to be of vital importance to the well-being and dignity of the human race, I can only lament that we are separated by so wide a barrier as to render further communion, under our old relations, mutually unsatisfactory."[3]

"The quill and I are divorced and you cannot conceive the degree of freedom, I could almost say of happiness, I feel at having got my neck out of the halter."[5]

1838. Published *Homeward Bound* and *Home As Found.* In the preface of *Home As Found* he wrote: ". . . For this country, in its ordinary aspects, probably presents as barren a field to the writer of fiction, and to the dramatist, as any other on earth; we are not certain that we might not say the most barren. We believe that no attempt to delineate ordinary American life, either on the stage or in the pages of a novel, has been rewarded with success. Even those works in which the desire to illustrate a principle has been the aim, when the picture has been brought within this homely frame, have had to contend with disadvantages that have been commonly found insurmountable. The latter being the intention of this book, the task has been undertaken with a perfect consciousness of all its difficulties, and with scarcely a hope of success." [James Fenimore Cooper, *Home as Found,* Capricorn Books, 1961.[7]]

1840. *The Pathfinder* published. In the first of two prefaces Cooper stated: "The plan of this tale is old having suggested itself to the writer many years since; though the details are altogether of recent invention. The idea of associating seaman and savages, in incidents that might be supposed characteristic of the Great Lakes, having been mentioned to a publisher, the latter obtained something like a pledge from the Author, to carry out the design at some future day; which pledge is now tardily and imperfectly redeemed."

In the second preface he stated: "That this caprice in taste and favor is in no way dependent on merit, the writer feels certain; for, though the world will ever maintain that an author is always the worst judge of his own productions, one who has written much, and regards all his literary progeny with more or less of a paternal eye, must have a reasonably accurate knowledge of what he has been about the greater part of his life. Such a man may form too high an estimate of his relative merits, as relates to others; but it is not easy to see why he should fall into this error, more than another as relates to himself. His general standard may be raised too high by means of self-love; but, unless he be disposed to maintain the equal perfection of what he has done, as probably no man was ever yet fool enough to do,

James Fenimore Cooper. Painting by C. L. Elliott.

he may very well have shrewd conjectures as to the comparative merits and defects of his own productions.

1841. *The Deerslayer* published. In the second preface he describes it as: ". . . purely fiction, no authority existing for any of its facts, characters, or other peculiarities, beyond that which was thought necessary to secure the semblance of reality."

1850. His play, *Upside Down or Philosophy of Petticoats,* was produced in New York City.

"My dear Sir,

"The comedy is written, and is now being copied. It is about as long as *The School for Scandal,* but in three acts. I have named it *The Law of Nature,* or the *Female Philosopher.* I think it will play well. Its leading character is Lovel, the old bachelor to whom you were introduced, and who fires away through the three acts. The plot is simple, but I hope sufficiently marked to keep alive the interest. Lovel is a character, and I think you may make a good deal of him. I hope there is incident enough.

"Dramatis Personae—
Richard Lovel—rich old bachelor of 66
Francis Lovel—his nephew—a devotee of
   the new philosophy

Dr. McSocial—an adventurer who sets up
for a philosopher
Gullet
Crotchet   Three of McSocial's students
Rush
Cato—an old black servant of R. Lovel's.
David—Servant of McSocial
Sophy McSocial—The doctor's sister
Emily Warrington—Old Lovel's ward and
engaged to Francis.
Dinah—Lovel's cook & Cato's wife.

Lovel, McSocial & Sophy are the leading characters. The plot, I prefer to reveal in reading the comedy.

"I wish you to keep my name entirely out of view, and I hope you can get the piece played this spring."[1]

Regardless of the controversies surrounding his life, Cooper found pleasure in his family and neighbors. "I am so much accustomed to newspapers that their censure and their praise pass but for little, but the attentions of a young lady of your tender years to an old man who is old enough to be her grandfather are not so easily overlooked. . . ."[3]

1851. Developed a liver condition. "I am in all respects better this morning, than I have been on any day since leaving home. This is the fourth day of my new attack on the bile, and it is beginning to tell. The pills are mild, and I now take but one, but so bad did the bile get that I had a compression of the abdomen, with a hardness, and coldness, almost as great as in the thigh and knees—[Dr. John W.] Francis said it was purely muscular and all came from bile, which comes from a torpid liver. The dandelion must be our *cure*, the [liniment?] may soften and appease. The tonic, or dandelion, only a tea-spoon full twice a day, or three times at most works like a charm, and must do something—Every body says I look better, and I certainly feel better."[1]

September 14, 1851. Cooper died one day before his sixty-second birthday. He asked on his deathbed that no authorized account of his life be prepared.

FOR MORE INFORMATION SEE: Felix O. C. Darley, *The Cooper Vignettes* (illustrations to Cooper's novels), J. G. Gregory, 1862; Thomas R. Lounsbury, *James Fenimore Cooper*, Houghton, 1882, reprinted, Gale, 1968; William B. Clymer, *James Fenimore Cooper*, Small, Maynard, 1900, reprinted, Haskell House, 1969; Henry W. Boynton, *James Fenimore Cooper*, Century, 1931, reprinted, Ungar, 1966; Robert E. Spiller, *Fenimore Cooper: Critic of His Times*, Minton, Balch, 1931, reprinted, Russell & Russell, 1963; R. E. Spiller and Philip C. Blackburn, *A Descriptive Bibliography of the Writings of James Fenimore Cooper*, 1934, reprinted, B. Franklin, 1968; Dorothy Waples, *The Whig Myth of James Fenimore Cooper*, Yale University Press, 1938, reprinted, Shoestring Press, 1968.

Samuel L. Clemens, "Fenimore Cooper's Literary Offenses," and D. H. Lawrence, "Fenimore Cooper's Leatherstocking Novels," and "Fenimore Cooper's White Novels," all reprinted in *Shock of Recognition: The Development of Literature in the United States*, edited by Edmund Wilson, Doubleday, 1943; Van Wyck Brooks, *The World of Washington Irving*, Dutton, 1944; James Grossman, *James Fenimore Cooper*, Sloane, 1949, reprinted, Stanford University Press, 1967; Arvid Shulengerger, *Cooper's Theory of Fiction*, University of Kansas Press,

1955, reprinted, Octagon, 1971; Marius Bewley, "Fenimore Cooper and the Economic Age," "Form in Fenimore Cooper's Novels," "Symbolism and Subject Matter," all in his *Eccentric Design: Form in the Classic American Novel*, Columbia University Press, 1959.

Leslie A. Fiedler, "James Fenimore Cooper and the Historical Romance," in his *Love and Death in the American Novel*, Criterion, 1960; Thomas L. Philbrick, *James Fenimore Cooper and the Development of Sea Fiction*, Harvard University Press, 1961; Donald A. Ringe, *James Fenimore Cooper*, Twayne, 1962; Warren S. Walker, *James Fenimore Cooper: An Introduction and Interpretation*, Barnes & Noble, 1962; A. N. Kaul, "James Fenimore Cooper: The History and the Myth of American Civilization," in his *The American Vision: Actual and Ideal Society in Nineteenth-Century Fiction*, Yale University Press, 1963; Warren S. Walker, editor, *Leather-Stocking and the Critics*, Scott, Foresman, 1965; R. E. Spiller, *James Fenimore Cooper* (Pamphlet on American Writers series, No. 48), University of Minnesota Press, 1965; Kay Seymour House, *Cooper's Americans*, Ohio State University Press, 1965; George Dekker, *James Fenimore Cooper: The American Scott*, Barnes & Noble, 1967; G. Dekker and John P. McWilliams, editors, *James Fenimore Cooper: The Critical Heritage*, Routledge, 1973; John P. McWilliams, Jr., *Political Justice in a Republic: James Fenimore Cooper's America*, University of California Press, 1973; Orm Overland, *James Fenimore Cooper's "The Prairie": The Making and Meaning of an American Classic*, Humanities Press, 1973.

For children: Elizabeth R. Montgomery, *Story Behind Great Books*, McBride, 1946; Isabel Boyd Proudfit, *James Fenimore Cooper*, Messner, 1946; Gertrude Hecker Winders, *James Fenimore Cooper: Leatherstocking Boy*, Bobbs-Merrill, 1951, reprinted, 1962; Sarah Knowles Bolton, *Famous American Authors*, Crowell, 1954; Robert Cantwell, *Famous American Men of Letters*, Dodd, 1956; "James Fenimore Cooper" (filmstrip), Encyclopaedia Britannica Films, 1958.

DORÉ, (Louis Christophe Paul) Gustave 1832-1883

PERSONAL: Surname is pronounced Do-*ray*, was originally Dorer; given name sometimes listed as Louis Auguste; born January 6, 1832, in Strassburg, Alsace-Lorraine; died, 1883, in Paris, France; brother of the composer, Ernest Doré. *Education:* Attended schools in France.

CAREER: Painter, sculptor, illustrator of books. At age fifteen, issued a set of satiric drawings entitled *Les Travaux d'Hercule* ("The Labors of Hercules"); regular contributor to *Journal Pour Rire*, 1848; began to exhibit pen and ink sketches at the Salon in Paris, 1848; helped establish the periodical, *Musee Anglo-Francais* with Philippon, 1856; instrumental in the founding of the Doré Gallery in London, 1869. Some of his well-known works include "Christ Leaving the Praetorium," 1867-72; "L'Ange et Tobie" ("The Angel and Tobias"), 1876, now in the Luxembourg Gallery; "La Vigne" (a sculpture of a colossal vase) exhibited at the Universal Exhibition in Paris, 1878. *Awards, honors:* Honorable mention for "The Battle of Inkerman" at the Salon, 1857; Chevalier of the Legion of Honor, 1862.

ILLUSTRATOR: Les Travaux d'Hercule (title means "The Labors of Hercules"), Aubert, 1848; *Desagrements d'un*

Voyage d'Agrement, Arnaud de Vresse, 1849; *Trois Artistes Incompris, Meconnus et Mecontents: Leur Voyage en Province et Ailleurs, Leur Faim Devorante, et Leur Deplorable Fin* (French wit and humor), Arnaud de Vresse, 1849; *Histoire Pittoresque: Dramatique et Caricaturale de la Sainte Russie*, J. Bry aine, 1854, translation by Daniel Weissbort published as *The Rare and Extraordinary History of Holy Russia*, reprinted Library Press, 1971; *Two Hundred Sketches, Humorous and Grotesque*, Warne, 1867; *Historical Cartoons; or, Rough Pencillings of the World's History, from the First to the Nineteenth Century*, Hotten, 1868.

Other illustrated works: Francois Rabelais, *Oeuvres de Rabelais*, J. Bry aine, 1854, translation by Thomas Urquhart and Peter A. Motteux published as *Works of Rabelais*, Hotten, 1871; Honoré de Balzac, *Les Contes Drolatiques Colligez ez Abbayes de Touraine*, [Paris], 1855, translation by Alec Brown published as *Droll Stories Collected in the Monasteries of Touraine*, Elek Books, 1958; Cecile Jules Gérard, *La Chasse au Lion*, [Paris], 1855, translation published as *Lion Hunting in Algeria*, [London], 1874; Hippolyte A. Taine, *Voyage aux Eaux des Pyrenees*, L. Hachette, 1855, translation by J. Safford Fiske published as *A Tour Through the Pyrenees*, Holt, 1874; Mary Lafou, translator, *Histoire du Chevalier Jaufre et de la Belle Brunissende: Legende Nationale*, Librarie Nouvelle, 1855, English translation published as *Sir Geoffrey the Knight: A Tale of Chivalry*, Nelson & Sons, 1869.

M. Lafou, translator, *Fierbras d'Alexandrie: Legende National*, Librarie Nouvelle, 1856; Pierre Dupont, *La Legende du Juif Errant*, Michel Levy freres, 1856, translation by G. W. Thornbury published as *The Legend of the Wandering Jew*, [London], 1857; Benjamin Gastineau, *La France en*

GUSTAVE DORÉ

Afrique et l'Orient a Paris, [Paris], circa 1856; *Histoire Complete de la Guerre d'Italie*, [Paris], 1959; Victor Adolphe Malte-Brun, *Geographie du Theatre de la Guerre et des Etats Circouvoisina*, [Paris], 1859; George Pardon, *Boldhearts the Warrior and His Adventures in the Haunted Wood: A Tale of the Times of Good King Arthur*, [London], 1859.

(With Birket Foster) William Shakespeare, *The Tempest*, Bell & Daldy, 1860; *L'Histoire des Environs de Paris*, [Paris], 1860; *Les Figures du Temps*, [Paris], 1861; Edmond Francois About, *Le Roi des Montagnes*, [Paris], 1861, translation by C.F.L. Wraxall published as *The Greek Brigand: or, The King of the Mountains*, J. & R. Maxwell, 1881; Charles Perrault, *Les Contes de Perrault*, edited by J. Hetzel, [Paris], 1861, translation by Charles Welsh published as *The Tales of Mother Goose*, D. C. Heath, 1902, new translation by A. E. Johnson published as *Perrault's Fairy Tales*, Dover, 1969.

C. Vincent and E. Plouvier, *Les Chansons d'Autrefois* (French ballads and songs), Coulon Pineau, 1861; Leon Godard, *L'Espagne: Moeurs et Paysages, Histoire et Monuments*, A. Mame, 1862; Leon de Laujon (pseudonym of Joseph Louis Duponnois), *Contes et Legendes*, [Paris], 1862; Victor Adolphe Malte-Brun, *Les Etats-Unis et le Mexique*, [Paris], 1862; Manuel (pseudonym of Ernest Louis L'Epine), *Histoire du Capitaine Castagnette*, L. Hachette, 1862, translation by Austin Dobson published as *The Authentic History of Captain Castagnette*, Beeton, 1866; X. B. Saintine (pseudonym of Joseph Xavier Boniface), *La Mythologie du Rhin*, L. Hachette, 1862, translation by M. Schele DeVere published as *The Myths of the Rhine*, Scribner, Armstrong, 1875, reprinted, Tuttle, 1957; Francois René de Chateau-

A sketch by Doré. ■ (From *The Life of Gustave Doré* by Blanchard Jerrold.)

A Doré drawing. ■ (From *The Life of Gustave Doré* by Blanchard Jerrold.)

briand, *Atala, ou les Amours de Deux Sauvages dans le Desert,* L. Hachette, 1863, translation by James Spence Harry, Cassell, 1867.

Benjamin Gastineau, *Chasses au Lion et a la Panthere,* [Paris], 1863; E. L. L'Epine, *La Legende de Croque Mitaine,* L. Hachette, 1863, translation by Tom Hood published as *The Legends of Croquemitaine and of the Chivalric Times of Charlemagne,* Cassell, 1866; Miguel de Cervantes Saavedra, *History of Don Quixote,* translated by Charles Jarvis, edited by J. W. Clark, Cassell, 1864-67, reissued as *The Adventures of Don Quixote de la Mancha,* Heron Books, 1969; Adrien Marx, *Histoires d'une Minute,* Denton, 1864.

(With Robert Dudley) John George Edgar, *Cressy and Poictiers; or, The Story of the Black Prince's Page,* Beeton, 1865; Thomas Hood, Jr., *The Fairy Realm,* Ward, Lock, 1865; Thomas Moore, *L'Epicurien* (poem), translated by Henri Butat, [Paris], 1865; Théophile Gautier, Sr., *La Capitaine Francasse,* Charpentier, 1866; John Milton, *Milton's Paradise Lost,* Cassell, 1866; Baron Munchausen (pseudonym of Rudolf Erich Raspe), *The Adventures of Baron Munchausen,* [London], 1866; Dante Alighieri, *The Divine Comedy,* Leypoldt & Holt, 1867, new translation by Lawrence Grant White, Pantheon Books, 1948, reissued, 1965; Emile Gigault de la Bedolliere, *La France et la Prusse,* [Paris], 1867.

Henry G. Blackburn, *The Pyrenees: A Description of Summer Life at French Watering Places,* Sampson, Low, 1867; Victor Adolphe Malte-Brun, *Pays Bas Belgique,* [Paris], 1867; Jean de La Fontaine, *Fables de la Fontaine,* L. Hachette, 1867, translation by Walter Thornbury published as *The Fables of de La Fontaine,* [London], 1867-70; Alfred Tennyson, *Idylls of the King,* Moxon, 1868; Jose Zorrilla, *Ecos de las Montanas: Leyendas Historicas,* [Barcelona], 1868; Thomas Hood, Sr., *Thomas Hood* (poems), edited by J. B. Payne, [London], 1870.

William Blanchard Jerrold, *The Cockaynes in Paris; or, Gone Abroad,* [London], 1871; *Fairy Tales Told Again,* [London], 1872; W. B. Jerrold, *London: A Pilgrimage,* Unwin, Grant, 1872, reprinted, Newton Abbot, 1971; Jean Charles Davillier, *L'Espagne,* L. Hachette, 1874, translation by John Thomson published as *Spain,* Sampson, Low, 1876; Louis Énault, *Londres,* L. Hachette, 1875-76; Samuel Taylor Coleridge, *The Rime of the Ancient Mariner,* Harper, 1876, reissued, Dover, 1970; Joseph Francois Michaud, *Histoires des Croisades,* Furne & Jouvet, 1877; Lodovico Ariosto, *Roland Furieux,* translated by A. J. DuPays, L. Hachette, 1878-79; *Aladdin; or, The Wonderful Lamp,* revised by M. E. Braddon, J. & R. Maxwell, 1880; Edgar Allan Poe, *The Raven,* Harper, 1883; Georgiana M. Craik, *Twelve Old Friends: A Book for Boys and Girls,* Sonnenschein, 1885; Charles Dickens, *The Life of Our Lord,* United Feature Syndicate, 1934; Olivia Coolidge, *Tales of the Crusades,* Houghton, 1970; Sophie Rostopchine Segur, *The Enchanted Forest,* retold by Beatrice Schenk De Regniers, Atheneum, 1974; Joseph McHugh and Latif Harris, *Journey to the Moon,* Celestial Arts, 1974.

Religious: *The Holy Bible,* [London], 1866, later edition edited by the Daughters of Saint Paul, St. Paul Editions, 1963; *Daily Devotion for the Household,* Cassell, 1873; *The Doré Bible Gallery,* Fine Art Publishing, 1879, reissued, Dover, 1974; Edmund Ollier, *A Popular History of Sacred Art,* Cassell, 1882; Eric Christian Matthews, *Stars of the Bible,* New Era Studio, 1963.

Collections: *A Dozen Specimens of Gustave Doré*, [London], 1866; *The Doré Gallery*, Cassell, 1870, reissued, Spring Books, 1974; *A Doré Treasury: A Collection of the Best Engravings of Gustave Doré*, edited by James Stevens, Bounty Books, 1970; *Selected Engravings*, edited by Marina Henderson, St. Martin's Press, 1973; *Illustrations to Don Quixote*, edited by Jeannie Ruzicka, St. Martin's Press, 1975; *Doré's Illustrations for the Divine Comedy by Dante*, Dover, 1976.

ADAPTATIONS—Movies and filmstrips: "The Raven" (motion picture; a visualization of Poe's poem through re-productions of drawings by Doré), American Art and History Films, 1953; "The Rime of the Ancient Mariner" (motion picture; based on the engravings by Doré for the poem by Samuel Taylor Coleridge), University of California at Los Angeles, 1953.

SIDELIGHTS: **January 6, 1832.** "I was born in Strassburg . . . and passed nearly all my earliest youth in the mountainous part of Alsatia. My father for many years held the appointment of chief engineer of roads and bridges in the department of the Rhine. It was not in Strassburg alone that I spent my childhood, but in the little communes of St. Odile and Barr, which are so near to Strassburg as to be within sight of the great cathedral.

"That part of Alsatia is very rustic and especially remarkable for the beauty of its forest and mountain scenery.

". . . Amidst those scenes were born in me the first lively and lasting impressions which determined my tastes in art, for my early attempts in drawing were all of a similar character, and for a long time I had but one wish, viz. to reproduce those sights and scenes so familiar to my boyhood, and which I love so well. More than this, a great many of my first serious efforts in painting were landscapes, always depicting the country round Strassburg.

"I was very small, but for a long time had despised the harmless water-colours, free from mineral poison, [with] which I had been so prudently supplied. I ardently longed for a box of those little tubes in white zinc, in order to squeeze real colours out of them. At last, as I was going one day into Josserond, . . . I received a famous little oaken box bound with brass and filled with tubes and brushes. I was wild with joy. Never before had I received such a present. I was for opening all the tubes and beginning at once to cover my palette with paints. . . .

"Naturally I carried my cherished box with me under my arm! say rather on my heart! . . .

"Then came a prohibition to touch my box; an order to go to bed;—and the lights were put out! All night long I never closed my eyes; and with the first grey streak of dawn I jumped out of bed, seized my box, and went downstairs into the courtyard. Alas! There was neither canvas, panels, nor pasteboard to be found. The evening before they had all been put safely away. I was dying to paint; it was a madness, an irresistible desire which I could not get rid of; and all the while, I was anxiously asking myself how I should make a beginning, and what should I paint? I began by uncorking my tubes, and decorated my palette with several appetizing clots of paints. The freshness, the gleam, the cheery look of those colours caused a delightful intoxication to run through my veins—for what in this world, to an artist, ever equals the charm of his first palette? Amongst my colours there was a

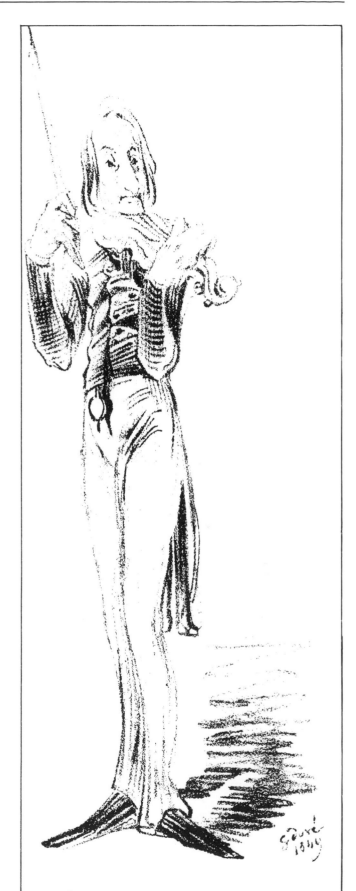

Doré's drawing of his music teacher. ■ (From *The Life of Gustave Doré* by Blanchard Jerrold.)

And, lo, the star, which they saw in the east, went before them, till it came and stood over where the young child was....(Matthew 2:9) ■ (From *The Doré Bible Illustrations,* illustrated by Gustave Doré.)

And the earth was without form, and void....(Genesis 1:2) ■ (From *The Doré Bible Illustrations,* illustrated by Gustave Doré.)

Princess Goldenhair was tired and out of breath. Her arms were scratched by the thorns. Her shoes were in tatters. She was about to tell the parrot that she could not take one more step.... ■ (From *The Enchanted Forest* retold and adapted by Beatrice Schenk de Regniers. Illustrated by Gustave Doré.)

beautiful green that delighted my eyes; what a lovely hue!—the real Veronese green in all its glory!

"But how to paint, and what? Whilst I was putting this question again and again to myself, my eyes fell upon a poor little chicken, not bad in form, but with a fearfully dirty pseudo-white plumage. This innocent creature was calmly pecking at something in the gravel not two yards distant from me. The real tone of the chicken's colour was frightful. It seemed to me an error of the Creator to have made any fowl so ugly in hue as that one, when it would have been so easy to have clad it in a gorgeous dress like that of a parrot's for instance. I determined to lose no time in rectifying this fault of Nature.

"The chicken, however, raised some difficulties in the way of my project's execution. The wretched ignoramus could not understand that I was only working for her own good, in her own interests. However, I was tenacious, and finally gained my end. In a very short time she was as verdant as spinach, and all my lovely Veronese green was used up. But—what a beautiful chicken! It was a pleasure to see her

walking about in her gorgeous new dress, so brilliant and fresh that it surpassed in vividness the loveliest spring verdure.

"I spent some time in contemplating my work; and having momentarily satisfied my longing by this brilliant success, I suddenly began to realize that I was sleepy, and should do well to make up for my restless night by indulging in a brief slumber.

"Two or three hours later I woke up with a start hearing cries, sobs, and lamentations ringing in my ears. What on earth could be the matter? Running to the window, I saw hosts of peasants and village folk stationed in front of the house. Some raised their eyes and hands towards heaven, others were crying pitifully, whilst others expressed in various ways the most profound despair. In their midst was my beautiful chicken. Whenever she attempted to move, fingers were pointed towards her in horror, and lamentations burst forth with redoubled vigour.

"After a few moments' reflection, all at once, I sounded the mystery, for I remembered a legend of that country in which a green chicken played a terrible part. Her appearance heralded floods, the loss of the harvest, a disease amongst the cattle, and a pestilent epidemic amongst the people. . . . I ran to find the master of the house, and made the most humble and complete confession. It was not really my fault; that diabolical Veronese green was at the bottom of all the trouble. Besides, why was that miserable chicken so ugly as to tempt me to make it beautiful for ever?

Doré's interpretation of Don Quixote. ■ (From *History of Don Quixote* by Miguel de Cervantes Saavedra. Illustrated by Gustave Doré.)

"I assure you it took my father's friend more than an hour to make those simple people and the superstitious Josserond peasants believe that this green bird had not been sent by some evil spirit to blight them, instead of being simply my first effort at painting. . . .

"One old woman who had been more terrified and was more incredulous than the rest, shaking her withered fingers in my face, cried out with a prophetic voice, 'Wretched youth! You have made the world weep. In its turn it will make you shed bitter tears over your painting.'" [Blanche Roosevelt Macchetta, *Life and Reminiscences of Gustave Doré*, Cassell & Co., 1885.[1]]

1841. "When I was nine years old my father was appointed chief engineer of the department of the Ain, and had the strange fortune to be transferred from a hilly country to one still more mountainous. [My father] always took me with him on his professional journeys. . . . As might have been expected from my early training in this picturesque school of education, I conceived a passionate love for mountains and mountainous scenery."[1]

September, 1847. ". . . My parents, being called to Paris by serious affairs, took me with them. Our stay was not to exceed three weeks. The idea of returning to the country after seeing this centre of light and learning troubled me much. I thought over the means of remaining; for I had already resolved, in spite of the stout resistance of my parents, on being an artist. They destined me, like my two brothers, for the Polytechnic School.

"One day I had passed the shop-window of Aubert and Philippon, on the Place de la Bourse; and, on returning to the hotel, I made some caricatures in the style of those I had seen in the window. While my parents were out, I went to the publishers, and showed them my sketches. M. Philippon looked kindly and attentively at these beginnings, questioned me as to my position, and sent me back to my parents with a letter inviting them to call upon him. They went; and M. Philippon, using all his persuasive eloquence, prevailed

Doré's impression of his school days. ■ (From *The Life of Gustave Doré* by Blanchard Jerrold.)

upon them to leave me in Paris, telling them that he could at once make use of my talent, and pay me for my work.

"From that day it was decided that I might devote myself to my drawing." [William Blanchard Jerrold, *Life of Gustave Doré*, W. H. Allen, 1891.[2]]

1848. Contributed drawings to *Journal Pour Rire;* gained reputation as a satirist. "The school of caricature was not much to my taste, and although during four or five years, I produced drawings innumerable, it was simply because the only publisher who accepted my work had but one exclusive specialty of publication.

"All my time that was not employed in working for him, I occupied with serious studies in drawing. . . ."[1]

Attended Lycée Charlemagne in Paris. Following his father's death, Doré shared his home with his mother, who cared for her son with devotion and pride for the rest of her life.

Late 1840's-early 1850's. Turned out thousands of drawings, harboring secret yearnings to be known as a painter, not an illustrator. "I have worked at these things for a fortnight, off and on; but I shall take precious good care not to tell any one else. People would immediately think that my pictures were worth nothing if they knew how long I had taken to paint them. . . .

"I can paint. . . . The fact is that no one understands me. I shall live and die misunderstood, or never comprehended at all, which is worse."[1]

1853. "At last . . . I found a way to escape apparently from the continuation of comic work which I own had begun to annoy me excessively. Seeing what a run there was upon the

Drawing by Doré at age ten, 1842. ■ (From *The Life of Gustave Doré* by Blanchard Jerrold.)

And, Lo! Toward us in a bark comes an old man. ■ (From *Inferno* by Danté Alighieri. Translated by the Rev. Henry Francis Cary, M.A. Illustrated by Gustave Doré.)

(From *The Rime of the Ancient Mariner* by Samuel Taylor Coleridge. Illustrated by Gustave Doré.)

Journal Pour Rire, which was in enormous vogue at the price of twenty centimes a copy, I begged my publisher's permission to execute an illustrated Rabelais, which should appear serially in the same form as the comic periodical. . . .

"This was the first thing of mine which made a sensation, and by eliciting praise from the press, brought me conspicuously before the notice of the public.

"I am not vain, but only grateful. God has been very good to me, and I thank Him every day of my life for His gifts. I would not change places with any man in the world. Understand me, not from vanity, but because, when I look around me and see how full the world is of hapless people and hopeless talents, I go down on my knees to thank Him for having given me so much to work with, and so much to be grateful for.''[1]

1855. Proposed series of illustrations for classic works of literature. "I conceived at this epoch the plan of those large folio editions, of which Dante [Vision of Hell] was the first volume published. My idea was then, and always has been since, to produce in a uniform style an edition of all the mas-

terpieces in literature of the best authors, epic, comic, and tragic.''[1]

"The publishers to whom I submitted my plans, were of opinion that my proposition was not a practical one. They argued that it was not at a time when the fashion was to produce at the lowest possible price they could venture upon volumes at a hundred francs. They believed there was no hope of being able to stem the current which was towards excessive cheapness.

"On my side, I contended that at a time when an art or an industry was degenerating, there were always a few hundreds of people who protested against the deluge of common things, and who were ready to buy at its fair value the first careful work that was submitted to them.''[2]

1862. Received Legion of Honor. "It is not the decoration of a button-hole that gives me pleasure. It is the official answer to the men who have tried to put me down and crush me.''[2]

1866. Unable to achieve recognition as a painter in France, Doré fretted over the possibility of seeking his fortune in

(From "Little Tom Thumb" in *Perrault's Fairy Tales* translated by A. E. Johnson. Illustrated by Gustave Doré.)

London. "It is strange, this scheme of going to London, there to open a gallery for my paintings, awakens in me an odd presentiment. You know that I hate leaving my country, my people, and my home. With the English I am not sure that I should get on. Something tells me that if I go to England, I shall break up all associations with my native land, and lose much of the influence and prestige I now possess in France. You know that I love my home, my friends, my own pot-au-feu, and that I hate to begin knowing new people, and getting into new habits. Then, too, how can I live without my beloved Paris? I have heard that England is a land of fogs; that the people are cold and the sun never shines there. They say that the channel passage will make me dreadfully sick; besides, it is a long way off, and I do not believe I shall go.

"I know what it is, I shall break up all my old associations by going to England; for after an absence one cannot easily take up the old threads again. I shall give the world here a chance to forget me; out of sight out of mind! I know I am ruining my whole life. Paris is so capricious, so athirst for new names and new faces. My friends will get out of the habit of seeing my face; others will come in, and fill my place. I shall be forgotten, but—I shall go."[1]

1867-1872. Created a twenty by thirty foot canvas entitled "Christ Leaving the Praetorium." ". . . I am not without religion and I sometimes think that if trials and sorrow are a law imposed upon us by Providence, an end to them is vouchsafed to those who without weakness have drained the bitter cup to the dregs."[2]

1869. Doré Gallery opened in London; embittered that he achieved success as a painter in England but not in France.

1871. Offered generous support to the poor during the siege of Paris. "The sad reason why I have put off my projected journey to London—a gigantic and terrible war, which puts France in a fever and on fire! You will understand how, under such circumstances, I should be disinclined to be absent from the country where all are uniting against the common danger which may come. Then, again, great news are expected from day to day; and in London they would be a day later. My brother Emile, the captain, has just written to us that his division is about to take the field!

"But, in the midst of these dark skies, an item of news has reached me . . . like a ray of sunlight. . . . The Queen of En-

She was astonished to see how her grandmother looked. ■ (From "Little Red Riding Hood" in *Perrault's Fairy Tales* translated by A. E. Johnson. Illustrated by Gustave Doré.)

gland has just done me the great honour of buying one of my works for her gallery, and I cannot express the proud pleasure that this has given me, and the gratitude I feel for this high mark of kindness.

"... For the enemy is at the gates of Paris, and we are expecting, every moment, to hear the sound of the cannon. Our misfortune is immense, and our agony is terrible. How shall we escape from the abyss of blood in which poor deserted France is plunged? No hope, no solution appears on the horizon; and yet it would be hard to think that our poor France—so innocent of this war—might be the object of universal disaffection!

"Our poor capital is in flames; its palaces destroyed—its finest streets, and all that made it beautiful. As I write, I have before me immense volumes of smoke, rising to the heavens. In the whole history of the world, I don't think there is a parallel instance of so sanguinary a drama, and of such ruin. . . . My presence is necessary in the midst of my family (part of which, however, is separated from us), in Paris, and we are without news from them for a week past."[2]

Doré's study of the Savior. ■ (From *The Life of Gustave Doré* by Blanchard Jerrold.)

Praetorium study. ■ (From *The Life of Gustave Doré* by Blanchard Jerrold. Illustrated by Gustave Doré.

" 'The Labours of Hercules,' have been designed, drawn, and lithographed by an artist fifteen years of age, who has taught himself drawing without a master, and without classical studies. It has appeared to us that this is not the least curious fact about this original album, and we have desired to cite it here, not only in order to specially interest the public in the works of this young draughtsman, but also to mark the point of departure of M. Doré, who we believe to be destined to take distinguished rank in art." ■(From *The Life of Gustave Doré* by Blanchard Jerrold. Illustrated by Gustave Doré.)

November, 1873. Suffered accident while etching. "I have had a violent shock, and a fortnight ago, I literally poisoned myself with azotique acid, in doing my etchings. . . ."[1]

1875-1880. Worked slowly and laboriously to attain skill as a sculptor.

Winter, 1881. Mother died. The artist never recovered from the shock. "I am thoroughly prostrated, and, alas! thoroughly alone; and I hardly know how to submit to the hard law which, however, spares none of us.

"Since I was born I had never ceased to live at the side of that tenderest, most devoted, and generous of mothers; and although I had lived for a very long time with my eyes fixed on this fearful predicted trial, I had not imagined so awful a void!

"I call up all my courage; but I confess to you I find the old maxim which makes work the grand restorer but partly true."[2]

"I am always . . . in the shadow of an awful solitude, which I live in since so long a time. It was a terrible trial, and I ought to have prepared myself each day for it; but how could I ever imagine the horror of such a void? In spite of all one hears about the salubriousness and all-powerful influence of work, I find none of it very true. Work does not console me; nothing consoles me; for I am alone, alone, alone, without family and almost without friends. Existence has no longer any charm for me; for I have had the improvidence not to know how to build up a home for myself, and someone to lean upon. Without that, life is but a cursed and absurd thing.

"I am alone, without assistance, without company, and with heavy cares . . . like all those in whom the splenetic sentiment is uppermost, I have a sensation of languor in the very pit of my stomach which breaks down my will and which disgusts me of all effort."[1]

Gustave Doré. Photo by Nadar.

January, 1883. Died while in the process of compiling his illustrated Shakespeare. "Ah me! how long ago is it since papa gave me five francs for my first prize at school—how small I was. I can't think of it all without crying. Oh! the days of my boyhood, those happy days when I ran and walked and played! . . . Oh for a sight . . . of my dear Strassburg, and the cathedral."[1]

FOR MORE INFORMATION SEE: Blanche Roosevelt Macchetta, *Life and Reminiscences of Gustave Doré,* Cassell & Co., 1885; William Blanchard Jerrold, *Life of Gustave Doré,* W. H. Allen, 1891, reprinted, Singing Tree Press, 1969; Millicent Rose, *Gustave Doré,* Pleiades Books, 1946; "No Sale: Long Lost Oil Paintings," *Time,* September 22, 1947; L. de Dardel, "Gustave Doré: Caricatures from His School Days," *Graphis,* No. 43, 1952; H. C. Pitz, "Gustave Doré," *American Artist,* December, 1969; Eric DeMare, *The London Doré Saw: A Victorian Evocation,* St. Martin's Press, 1973; Nigel Gosling, *Gustave Doré,* Praeger, 1974.

"Books are the quietest and most constant of friends; they are the most accessible and wisest of counsellors, and the most patient of teachers."
———Charles W. Eliot

Engraving by Gustave Doré for William Shakespeare's "The Tempest."

DRESANG, Eliza (Carolyn Timberlake) 1941-

PERSONAL: Surname is pronounced *Dree*-sang; born October 21, 1941, in Atlanta, Ga.; daughter of Gideon B. (a physician) and Ruth (a teacher and nurse; maiden name, Rudder) Timberlake; married Dennis Lee Dresang (a political science professor), August 10, 1963; children: Lee Timberlake, Steven Edward, Anna Ruth. *Education:* Emory University, B.A., 1963; University of Southern California, graduate study, 1964; University of California, M.L.S., 1966; University of Wisconsin, further graduate study, 1974, Ph.D., program (library science), 1978—. *Religion:* Christian. *Home:* 440 Virginia Ter., Madison, Wis. 53705. *Office:* University of Wisconsin, Madison Library School, Helen C. White Hall, 600 N. Park St., Madison, Wis. 53706.

CAREER: High school English teacher in Atlanta, Ga., 1963; high school Spanish teacher in Lake Mills, Wis., 1963-64; high school Spanish and French teacher in Los Angeles, Calif., 1964-65; Los Angeles Public Library, Los Angeles, Calif., children's and reference librarian at Encino-Tarzana Branch, 1966-67; Atlanta Public Library, Atlanta, Ga., head of children's department at Ida Williams Branch, 1967-68; Ford Foundation, project assistant on research done by Africans on educational topics, 1974; Madison Board of Education, Madison, Wis., director of Instruction Materials Center at Lapham Elementary School, 1974-78; University of Wisconsin, Library School, Madison, Wis., supervisor of library science student teachers, 1978-79, lecturer, 1978-80. Volunteer story teller for Head Start Program, 1967.

MEMBER: American Library Association, Association for Educational Communications and Technology, Society of Children's Book Writers, National Organization for Women, Wisconsin Women Library Workers, Wisconsin Library Association, Wisconsin Audio-Visual Association, Phi Beta Kappa, Phi Eta Sigma, Beta Phi Mu. *Awards, honors: The Land and People of Zambia* was selected by the National Council for Social Studies and the Children's Book Council for the "Notable Trade Books in the Field of Social Studies for 1975" list, Spring, 1976; named Wisconsin school librarian of the year, 1979, by the Wisconsin School Library Media Association.

Many Zambian children must scrape the pot to find even a few scraps of food. ■ (From *The Land and People of Zambia* by Eliza Dresang. Photo courtesy of National Food and Nutrition Commission.)

ELIZA DRESANG

WRITINGS: African Educational Research: A Bibliography, Ford Foundation, 1974; *The Land and People of Zambia,* Lippincott, 1975. Contributor to *School Library Journal, Wisconsin Library Bulletin, Journal of Education for Librarianship,* and *Reader in Children's Librarianship.*

WORK IN PROGRESS: Research on service to the exceptional child in the school media center; research on the use of video and cable in libraries.

SIDELIGHTS: "My writing, until I entered the doctoral program in library science, was a result of personal experience. The idea for the book on Zambia was conceived when, as a librarian, I noticed a need. The idea was nurtured through experience of living in (1967-1969) and revisiting (1972) the country of Zambia. Personal experience has been backed by extensive research.

"My article (for the *Wisconsin Library Bulletin,* March-April, 1978) on school and public library cooperation in serving exceptional children was based on my experience as a media specialist in a school which served two hundred 'regular' and one hundred 'exceptional' children. My sensitivities to individual needs and individual differences in all children have been sharpened in my present work environment. I look upon it as an extraordinarily exciting and challenging adventure."

Eliza Dresang lived in Zambia, 1968-69, and Kenya, 1971-72; she has traveled in Ethiopia, Tanzania, Uganda, Nigeria, Malawi, and Morocco, and her adopted daughter is from Korea.

HOBBIES AND OTHER INTERESTS: "Avocations, in addition to being a media specialist and author, include reading, traveling with my family, youth soccer, and working for passage of the ERA."

FOR MORE INFORMATION SEE: Wisconsin Library Bulletin, November-December, 1976, March-April, 1978; *School Library Journal,* September, 1977; "An Application of Decision-Making Theory to Curriculum Change in Library Education," *Journal of Education for Librarianship,* Winter, 1980.

DULAC, Edmund   1882-1953

PERSONAL: Born October 22, 1882, in Toulouse, France; settled in London, 1905; naturalized British subject, 1912; died May 25, 1953; married Alice May Marini, December 13, 1903 (divorced, 1908); married Elsa Bignardi, April, 1911. *Education:* Toulouse University, Litt.Ph.B.; studied law for two years; attended Toulouse Art School for three years, and Académie Julian in Paris briefly.

CAREER: Artist and illustrator of children's books. Began painting at age eight; exhibited portraits at the Paris Salon, 1904-05; exhibited annually at Leicester Galleries, London, from 1907-18. Painted portraits and caricatures of prominent people of the day, appearing weekly in the *Outlook,* 1919-20, and contributed an annual series of drawings to the *American Weekly.* He designed stage settings and costumes; designed several French and British postage stamps, including the British Coronation stamp of 1937, and modeled the King's Poetry Prize medal; composed music and made bamboo flutes; wrote and lectured on art.

ILLUSTRATOR: Lyrics, Pathetic, and Humorous from A to Z, Routledge, 1908; *Edmund Dulac's Picture-Book for the French Red Cross,* Hodder & Stoughton, 1915; *Edmund Dulac's Fairy Book: Fairy Tales of the Allied Nations,* Hodder & Stoughton, 1916; (editor) *Histoires Gasconnes: Gas-*

EDMUND DULAC

(From *Rubáiyát of Omar Khayyám* rendered into English Verse by Edward Fitzgerald. Illustrated by Edmund Dulac.)

(From *Sindbad the Sailor and Other Stories from the Arabian Nights*, illustrated by Edmund Dulac.)

(From "Cruel Kindness," by Mrs. Molesworth in *Pall Mall* Magazine. Illustrated by Edmund Dulac.)

connades, *Contes, Legendes, et Proverbes de Gascogne* (French wit and humor), Les Editions de France, 1925; *Mon Curé dans les Vignes*, Les Editions de France, 1926; *Le Tour de France Gastronomique*, Les Editions de France, 1926.

Other illustrated works: Emily Bronte, *Wuthering Heights*, Dent, 1905; Charlotte Bronte, *Jane Eyre*, Dent, 1905; *Stories from the Arabian Nights*, retold by Laurence Housman, Hodder & Stoughton, 1907; Maud Margaret Stawell, *Fairies I Have Met*, Hodder & Stoughton, 1907; William Shakespeare, *Shakespeare's Comedy of the Tempest*, Doran, 1908; Edward Fitzgerald, translator, *Rubaiyat of Omar Khayyam*, Hodder & Stoughton, 1909; *The Sleeping Beauty, and Other Fairy Tales*, retold by Arthur Thomas Quiller-Couch, Hodder & Stoughton, 1911; *Ali Baba, and Other Stories*, retold by L. Housman, Hodder & Stoughton, 1911; Hans Christian Andersen, *Stories from Hans Andersen*, Hodder & Stoughton, 1911; Edgar Allan Poe, *The Bells, and*

Other Poems, Hodder & Stoughton, 1912; M. M. Stawell, *My Days with the Fairies*, Hodder & Stoughton, 1913; *Princess Badoura*, retold by L. Housman, Hodder & Stoughton, 1913; *Sindbad the Sailor, and Other Stories from the Arabian Nights*, Muller, 1914; Mary, Queen Consort of Ferdinand, King of Roumania, *The Dreamer of Dreams*, Hodder & Stoughton, 1915.

Nathaniel Hawthorne, *Tanglewood Tales*, Hodder & Stoughton, 1918; Leonard Rosenthal, *The Kingdom of Pearl*, Nisbet, 1920; William Butler Yeats, *Four Plays for Dancers*, Macmillan, 1921; Helen de V. Beauclerk, *The Green Lacquer Pavillion*, W. Collins, 1926; Robert Louis Stevenson, *Treasure Island*, Doran, 1927; *A Fairy Garland*, Cassell, 1928; Hugh R. Williamson, *Gods and Mortals in Love*, Country Life, 1935; Alexander Pushkin, *The Golden Cockerel*, Limited Editions Club, 1950; Madaurensis Apuleius, *The Marriage of Cupid and Psyche*, Limited Editions

Club, 1951; John Milton, *The Masque of Comus,* Limited Editions Club, 1954.

SIDELIGHTS: **October 22, 1882.** Born in Toulouse, France. "My grandfather was lying dead in the next room and those who first smiled at me by the light of a lamp had tears in their eyes, save my mother who had not been told. My head was long and pointed at the back and the midwife rubbed it down with a handful of brandy. I did not cry. The house where these things took place was a large house built at the beginning of the last century on the site of an old convent destroyed during the Revolution. It belonged to my dead grandfather. His portrait, that of a handsome man with fair hair and blue eyes, hung in my grandmother's room, and sometimes, as I stood playing with odd bits of things on her lap, she would look at me and mutter, half to herself, things I did not quite understand, which meant that he was a kind man and that we would have liked each other.

"The house half enclosed a courtyard with a pump beyond which stretched a long garden. My parents lived on the first floor and when I looked down from the back windows I could see a large bed of semi-tropical plants, four enormous box trees; they were like pineapples, and three children could hide in any one of them quite easily. Then came The Garden laid out with paths and ornamental beds round a well, smothered in ivy, opening onto a long vineyard with an old barn at the end. The rest was an unknown country of gardens and houses among the trees. On the horizon, the

(From *Shakespeare's Comedy of The Tempest* by William Shakespeare. Illustrated by Edmund Dulac.)

"There is a princess in the palace not far from here. She is very clever." ■ (From "The Snow Queen," in *Stories from Hans Andersen.* Illustrated by Edmund Dulac.)

steeple of a convent and the local barracks. On the other side of the house, a straight narrow street leading to the parish church, an outer boulevard skirting the Botanical Gardens and a park. Over this wide expanse of trees and gardens came the call of bugles and the sound of church bells." [Colin White, *Edmund Dulac,* Scribner, 1976.[1]]

1890. Painted his first picture—a landscape on the lid of a wooden box, with colors borrowed from his father who dabbled in art. He was a serious child, ". . . never feeling that sense of bodily elation that is rightly described as 'full of beans.'"[1]

Entered the Petite Lycée where he produced sketchbooks adorned with caricatures of his teachers.

1899. Enrolled in the department of law at Toulouse University. Also attended classes at École des Beaux Arts.

1901. Left law school to attend art school full-time. Studied English and gained reputation as an "Anglophile."

"I have hardly closed my eyes all night." ■ (From *Stories from Hans Andersen*, illustrated by Edmund Dulac.)

Then BLUE BEARD roared out so terribly that he made the whole house tremble.

(From "Blue Beard" in *The Sleeping Beauty and Other Fairy Tales* retold by Sir Arthur Quiller-Couch. Illustrated by Edmund Dulac.)

Poster for Macbeth by Dulac in 1911.

1903. Won scholarship to Académie Julian, an art school in Paris. He loathed Paris.

December 13, 1903. Wed an American, Alice May Marini. The marriage was unsuccessful.

1904. Went to England where he was commissioned to provide illustrations for new edition of the complete novels of the Brontë sisters.

1905. Became leading contributor to *Pall Mall* magazine and produced his first illustrations for a children's story.

1907. Received major assignment—to illustrate *Stories from the Arabian Nights*.

1908. Divorced by wife on grounds of desertion.

April, 1911. Married Elsa Bignardi, who served as the model for his illustrations of *Sleeping Beauty*.

February 17, 1912. Naturalized as a British citizen.

1913. Embarked on a Mediterranean cruise during which he painted the scenery with a poet's brush. "The sea is shimmering like golden moiré, a slight mist on the horizon, ahead cerulean. Behind us the sun is being wrapped up in a changing cloth of gold, deep orange and light metallic green dropping purply incense. On the side the foam makes designs of molten lapis lazuli."[1]

November, 1915. Clawed by a cat, Dulac almost lost sight in right eye, curtailing his work.

1916. Designed costumes, props and make-up for plays derived from Japanese Noh theatre by William Butler Yeats.

October, 1916. Distressed by air raids, Dulac left London. ". . . I am sunk in the very depths of depression. It needed only one last straw—coming back from a trip tired, famished and on top of that a terrible raid. God alone knows if we have suffered. I have tried to look at it dispassionately but that evening something broke. Despite my brave outward appearance, inside I am prey to the most sickly panic. It only got worse. After four nights of raids I could not stand it any longer. I was reduced to a pathetic state. I have to get away. It was the only way of avoiding a possible breakdown."[1]

1919. Drew political cartoons for weekly newspaper, *The Outlook*. ". . . I have felt sometimes . . . that a cartoon to be a success ought to be fairly biting or very complimentary; we have, I think, steered too gently between the two. The trouble is that although I was personally ready to cartoon anybody, . . . the number of people from whom one could select was subject to all sorts of considerations, personal reasons which debarred a certain number. . . ."[1]

1922. Asked to contribute to Queen Mary's royal doll-house; designed an effigy of Queen Victoria sitting on the royal lavatory.

Black Dog disappears. ■ (From *Treasure Island* by Robert Louis Stevenson. Illustrated by Edmund Dulac.)

1923. Separated from wife. Began relationship with long-time friend, Helen de V. Beauclerk.

1923-1924. Commissioned to paint series of watercolors for covers of Sunday supplement of the New York *Weekly American.* "Always the same worries and bother, always the same imperious necessity for the ideal millionaire who will transform this slavery to unintelligent American Newspaper Editors into an economic possibility to apply one's genius to a thousand and one things, to lead a decent life and to answer one's friends' letters. Quite recently I was threatened with a complete stoppage of the only means of livelihood at present possible in a squabble with the New York *American,* settled, however, on condition that my drawings are regularly received."[1]

Described the process used in these watercolors: "... Sheets and sheets of tracing paper, some putty, rubber, pencils BB, B, H and sometimes HH. An idea for the composition is roughed out on a sheet of tracing paper with a B pencil and another and another, the paper being turned over from time to time to see whether the design does not look better from the other side. One could go on like that for ever, but one of the designs has to be chosen—it is generally the first. The figures are drawn to the required size separately; a dozen rough sketches or so for each, this time with a BB pencil and traced over again until clean lines emerge from out of chaos. The background comes last and is dealt with in the same way. The process so far is secret. No one is allowed to witness its laborious steps and the wastepaper basket in the summer and the stove in winter take care that no

DULAC, 1952

evidence of it shall remain. The clean tracings are then superimposed and twisted about until some form of satisfactory arrangement is obtained. Now appears the Whatman board, hot pressed, the figures and background are rubbed upon it in their proper order and grouping and drawn over carefully with the H pencil. All is ready for the final ceremony. The jars are cleaned and filled with fresh water, the brushes and the china pots uncovered. The Whatman board with its design is then hydropathically treated with a few pigments, not more than a blue, green, two yellows, a crimson, a red, two reddish browns, raw amber and Chinese white; lots and lots of Chinese white. And that is one way of doing a watercolour drawing."[1]

1925. Dulac's association with New York *American Weekly* was temporarily ended. "I believe I have definitely lost my American job, my drawings could not be satisfactorily reproduced for a paper that lives on 'Sensation' of every kind, murder, drugs, and the raping of young girls, the life of Los Angeles. Therefore I am open to offers from wealthy customers in view of some good steady post, or, what would be far better, prospective adoption as an only son and heir."[1]

Designed illustrations for Helen de V. Beauclerk's novel, *The Green Lacquer Pavillion.*

1932-1934. Took odd fringe jobs, designing candy boxes and playing cards. "I am certainly looking for a recipe, but for the life of me I do not know how to do it. . . . For four years all my efforts have been directed towards repairing bit by bit my little house that has been seriously shaken by a brainstorm and overwork—that is to say too much *uncongenial* work—to earn a living—(overwork, when one likes what one does, never does any harm)—a serious loss of money, etc. was bringing nervous troubles, hypersensitivity, indigestion,

(From "The Emperor's Nightingale" in *Stories from Hans Andersen.* Illustrated by Edmund Dulac.)

neuralgia and the vicious circle which is so difficult to break, a hideous nightmare in which shadows float around me at moments when the atmospheric pressure is low. For a long time I did nothing, now I am ready to fill in the holes. This is not as easy as it used to be with all the world crying poverty, meanwhile America [i.e. *American Weekly*] carries on happily. It is not a source of absolute inspiration but it is bread and butter.''[1]

1937. Designed stamp for George VI's Coronation. ''. . . Absolute madness! . . . I have signed the stamp in order to give it extra value to philatelists and it is not impossible that in twenty-five to thirty years time you might be able to sell it for five or six pence.''[1]

1940. Beset by financial woes, Dulac spent time designing ingenious collages and making toys.

1942. Aided war effort by designing stamps and banknotes to link the exiled French government and the French colonies.

1945. In ill health. Received annual commission to illustrate children's books. ''My doctor tells me that I am suffering from nervous fatigue, no wonder! What with the general sense of insecurity, the difficulties of daily life, the monotonous and scanty supply of food, only those blessed with 'food-proof' digestion and nerves of steel can survive happily.

''. . . I feel time desperately slipping by with less and less chance of catching up with it and filling it with all the good things I would like to achieve.''[1]

April, 1949. Suffered heart attack.

1953. Designed Queen Elizabeth II's Coronation stamp.

May 25, 1953. Suffered fatal heart attack—following a display of his flamenco dancing prowess.

Dulac at his painting desk, 1952.

(From *Treasure Island* by Robert Louis Stevenson. Illustrated by Edmund Dulac.)

FOR MORE INFORMATION SEE: Stanley J. Kunitz and Howard Haycraft, editors, *Junior Book of Authors,* H. W. Wilson, 2nd edition, 1951; E. Marx, "Artist as Stamp Designer: An Appreciation of Edmund Dulac," *Print,* April, 1954; Brian Doyle, editor, *Who's Who of Children's Literature,* Schocken Books, 1968; David Larkin, editor, *Dulac,* Scribner, 1975; Colin White, *Edmund Dulac,* Scribner, 1976. Obituaries: *Illustrated London News,* June 13, 1953; *New York Times,* May 30, 1953; *Wilson Library Bulletin,* September, 1953.

ELLACOTT, S(amuel) E(rnest) 1911-

PERSONAL: Born May 20, 1911, in Winkleigh, Devon, England; son of Ernest (an estate worker) and Emily (Ford) Ellacott; married Kathleen Abbott, July 12, 1937. *Education:* Studied at Royal Albert Memorial School of Art, 1927-32, Barnstaple School of Science and Art, 1932-36, Exmouth Training College, 1946-47, and Portsmouth College of Education, University of Southampton, 1965-66. *Politics:* Conservative. *Religion:* Protestant. *Home:* Pendennis, 8 Willand Rd., Braunton, North Devon, EX331AX, England.

CAREER: Teacher of English, history, and art in Devon County secondary schools at Braunton, 1947-53, and Barnstaple, 1953-71. Author and illustrator, 1952—. *Military service:* British Army, Devon Home Guard, 1940-44, became sergeant-instructor, musketry and light machine-guns. *Member:* Arms and Armour Society, Devonshire Association. *Awards, honors: Armour and Blade* named "Honours Book" by Library Association and runner-up for Carnegie Medal, 1962.

WRITINGS: The Story of Ships, Methuen, 1952, 2nd edition, 1958; *The Story of Aircraft,* Methuen, 1952, 5th edition, 1962; *Wheels on the Road,* Methuen, 1952, 2nd edition, 1956; *The Story of the Kitchen,* Methuen, 1953, 2nd edition, 1960; *Forge and Foundry,* Methuen, 1955; *Guns,* Methuen,

S. E. ELLACOTT

DEFEAT.

(From *The Norman Invasion* by S. E. Ellacott.
Illustrated by the author.)

1955; *Spinning and Weaving,* Methuen, 1956; *Rockets,* Methuen, 1959, revised edition, Criterion, 1961; *Golden Hammer,* privately printed, 1961; *Ships Under the Sea,* Hutchinson, 1961; *Armour and Blade,* Abelard (London), 1962; *Collecting Arms and Armour,* Arco Publications, 1964; *Spearman to Minuteman,* Abelard (London), 1965, Abelard (New York), 1966; *Conscripts on the March,* Abelard (London), 1965, Abelard (New York), 1966; *The Norman Invasion,* Abelard (London and New York), 1966; *A History of Everyday Things in England,* Volume 5, Putnam, 1968; *The Seaman,* 2 volumes, Abelard (New York), 1970; *Until You Are Dead,* Abelard (New York), 1972; *Here is Braunton* (mini-history), Western, 1979.

Illustrator—All by R. R. Sellman; all published by Methuen, except as indicated: *Castles and Fortresses,* 1954; *The Crusades,* 1955; *The Elizabethan Seaman,* 1957; *Civil War and Commonwealth,* 1958; John Laffin, *The Face of War,* Abelard, 1963.

WORK IN PROGRESS: A local history book, *Braunton Story;* a history of agriculture, *The Years and the Land;* a history of costume, *Clothes and the Centuries.*

SIDELIGHTS: "From my earliest days I have been interested in the social aspect of history; people's habits of life, their food, clothes, etc. My first output of this kind was insert cards, showing the history of such features as dress, armour, vehicles, etc. When I was a teacher in charge of a history department, in 1949, a farming course was organized in my school. As there was no suitable historical textbook on the subject, I wrote one, using the written material and my large-size illustrations for lessons. This was my first venture, and it is still unsold—publishers praised it highly, but thought the market too limited.

"One of the publishers asked me to co-operate in planning a series of books covering my special subjects and my first three books launched the series. After doing eight such books, I switched to larger textbooks and other publishers. I do not use a typewriter; all my books are written in round script. My drawings are done chiefly in black and white, but I do half-tone and colour work as well.

"A great part of my work is the research involved, which I have always enjoyed. In seeking original sources, I make some most interesting contacts with people in different parts of the country and of the world. My review file contains coverage from all over the world and several foreign houses have published translations, so that I have been able to see my work in German, Dutch, Portuguese, Italian, and Mexican. An American publishing house produced its own edition of *Rockets.* I must pay tribute to my wife's heroism in living my kind of life so cheerfully. She herself is a poet of remarkable talent.

"One of my most interesting commissions was from B. T. Batsford, the leading British educational publisher. They publish a famous illustrated series, *A History of Everyday Things in England,* by a husband-and-wife team, Marjorie and C.H.B. Quennell, whose volume one appeared in 1918. Three other volumes followed, the books becoming a history-room essential. In 1968 Batsford wished to publish a fifth volume to bring the series up to date and to commemorate fifty years of Quennell. However, Mr. Quennell was dead and his wife was ninety-years-old; thus, unable to do the work; so the publishers, who knew my work, asked me to do volume five.

"When the book was published, Batsford arranged a champagne launching party in London. All my expenses were paid, with top-level hotel accommodations. At the party the Minister of Education and I were photographed holding open the book. This was not my first visit to London at a publisher's expense, but it was certainly the most colourful."

HOBBIES AND OTHER INTERESTS: Rifle and pistol shooting, antique arms, historical costumes, rowing, walking, cycling, art, and village life.

EVANS, Mark

PERSONAL: Born in St. Louis, Mo.; son of Yale (an accountant) and Rea Evans. *Education:* California Institute of the Arts, B.Mus. (summa cum laude); Claremont Graduate School, M.A., Ph.D.; has studied composition with Mario Castelnuovo-Tedesco and Roy Harris, conducting with Fritz Zweig and Joseph Wagner, and piano with Helena Lewyn and Julia Bal de Zuniga. *Residence:* Los Angeles, Calif. *Office:* c/o American Federation of Musicians, Local #47, 817 Vine St., Los Angeles, Calif. 90038.

CAREER: Writer (lyricist, playwright, and novelist) and musician (composer, conductor, pianist, and organist). Creator and host of series "Mark My Words!" for National Public Radio, 1974—; Brigham Young University, Provo, Utah, consultant to Arts and Communications Archives, 1978—. *Member:* International P.E.N., American Musicological Society, American Guild of Organists, Academy of Science Fiction and Fantasy Films (chairman of music committee), California Writers Guild, Phi Mu Alpha Sinfonia, American Federation of Musicians, and American National Theatre and Academy, West. *Awards, honors:* Recipient of Ford Foundation fellowship, Disney Foundation fellowship, California State graduate fellowship, Smith-Hobson music fellowship, and his book *Scott Joplin and the Ragtime Years* was named a notable trade book, 1976, by the National Council on Social Studies.

WRITINGS: Will the Real Young America Please Stand Up?, Stackpole, 1973; *Soundtrack: The Music of the Movies,* Hopkinson & Blake, 1975, reprinted, Da Capo Press, 1979; *The Spectacular Stunt Book,* Grosset, 1976; *Scott Joplin and the Ragtime Years,* Dodd, 1976; *The Morality Gap,* Alba, 1976; (with Xavier Cugat) *Pepito: The Little Dancing Dog,* Scroll, 1979; (with Robert Stack) *Straight Shooting,* Macmillan, 1980. Author of book and lyrics and composer of stage musicals, including "Going Around in Academic Circles," based on the writings of Richard Armour, first performed in Claremont, Calif., at Balch Auditorium, March 12, 1976.

WORK IN PROGRESS: Satirical fiction and plays for stage and screen; writing for the musical theater; books in light verse for young readers.

SIDELIGHTS: "Ever since I can remember, I have been interested in words and music. When I was a small boy, my father taught me to read, and shortly thereafter, I began studying the piano. Within a few years, I was immersed in every facet of music. Since I began to improvise at the piano and organ, I turned to composing, and then began writing verses to go along with the music I wrote. I also began making up my own stories, and writing them down.

"I have always been fascinated by writers who can say something serious while making us laugh at the same time. Kenneth Grahame wasn't really just writing about Mr. Toad wanting a motor car in *The Wind in the Willows,* he was talking about all of us who occasionally want to do things we shouldn't. I am writing a story at the moment about a basset hound who wants to sing at the Metropolitan Opera. It isn't really about a bassett hound either, but about anyone who has a secret wish.

"When I see things or people who are foolish, silly, or outrageous, it is great fun to exaggerate their qualities and show how ridiculous they really are. Jonathan Swift did this in *Gulliver's Travels* and Lewis Carroll did it in *Alice in Wonderland.* Like many writers, I like to use talking animals in my books. A sad, woebegone, floppy eared basset hound always seems more melancholy than a boy or girl can ever be.

"Where do I get my ideas for books? Often from people I meet, although they do not realize that someday they may turn up as characters in my stories. (They probably will not recognize themselves, since a disagreeable person may turn up as a grumbling donkey or growling bulldog, and will think I am talking about someone else. Sometimes an idea will lit-

MARK EVANS

erally pop up, as in the case of Pepito, Xavier Cugat's chihuahua. When I first met Mr. Cugat, Pepito, popped out of his pocket, and I knew I had discovered a new character. Other ideas are the direct result of asking the question "what if?" One of my verse books concerns an incredible imaginary orchestra, and I developed the idea by asking myself "what if someone created an entirely new orchestra?"

"I plan my stories carefully, and work them out in my mind so that when I finally sit down at the typewriter, I can dash off the text very quickly. But it is the planning, plotting, and developing that is the real work and also the greatest source of enjoyment.

"Because I have spent a great deal of time writing musical shows, I am very interested in lyrics and light verse. So verse books are among my favorites.

"I am fascinated by words and think a writer should use them as a painter uses colors. Shaw's *Pygmalion* is one of my favorite plays, because he shows us how the way we speak tells the world who and what we are. I am curious about the origins of words. Mrs. Malaprop, a character created by Sheridan in his play, *The Rivals,* is funny because she uses the wrong words in the wrong places. But too many writers today lapse into jargon or fashionable cliches. Imagine Hamlet, instead of asking the question, 'To be or not to be' saying 'Right on man, I'm not sure where it's at.'

"I think a reader must care about characters. I cannot imagine two more appealing characters than Sherlock Holmes or

(From *Pepito: The Little Dancing Dog* by Mark Evans. Illustrated by Xavier Cugat.)

Mr. Chips, although they are both so very different. They are appealing because they are presented in such depth as to become real. I do not admire the anti-hero, an unpleasant fellow who is supposed to be important because he is very ordinary. It is the extraordinary character that holds my interest as reader or writer. In contrast, a well-drawn villain (Captain Hook or Ebeneezer Scrooge) may be very appealing.

"I like swashbuckling adventures, and my favorite periods of history are early American and nineteenth and early twentieth century English. I am also fascinated by satirical fantasy. Many people suggest that books, especially for young readers, should only be concerned with what really happens. But I think imagination is just as real as what you see when you look out the window. Traveling back in time is certainly more interesting than walking over to the corner hamburger stand. Improbable characters, Mad Hatters, March Hares, Cowardly Lions, and the lot, are much more exciting than probable ones.

"Elegance and style are elusive: a battle of wits between two interesting people is much more exciting than a clumsy fistfight. Think of two speakers. One speaks in a dry monotone, mumbles, and twiddles his thumbs. The other is dynamic and gives every word he chooses a special meaning. Both say the same thing, but it is the way something is said that may be just as important as what is said.

"Perhaps I can best express my feelings about writing in my own favorite way, in verse:

"'Why do I write?' I am asking myself.
Not just to place one more book on my shelf.
If I am honest, outspoken, and frank,
It's really quite easy to leave the page blank.

"Then I imagine my dreams taking flight.
Think of the things I can do when I write.
I may make a trip or fly to the moon.
I may sail a ship or ride a balloon.
Or go back in time before there were cars.
Or try leaping forward and end up on Mars.
I may meet a pirate, or dragon, or king.
Or even a basset hound trying to sing.
I may go to London, Vienna, or Rome,
by writing and still I need never leave home.
I like to imagine the lives we can lead.
By writing a story you might choose to read."

HOBBIES AND OTHER INTERESTS: Collecting books, records, and tapes (especially those relating to film music, jazz, musical theater, and classical music), spectator sports (baseball, football, basketball, wrestling, and roller derby), ballroom dancing, collecting menus, gourmet cooking, travel, classic film scores, swashbuckling adventures, Sherlock

Holmes, and Oxford accents; he particularly dislikes "television commercials, musicians who use the electric guitar as a deadly weapon, battle-axe secretaries, small dogs that make large noises, forms of any kind, and writers who take themselves too seriously."

FELDMAN, Anne (Rodgers) 1939-

PERSONAL: Born July 19, 1939, in Pittsburgh, Pa.; daughter of Bennett (a juvenile court judge) and Eleanor (Longenecker) Rodgers; married Richard Lewis Feldman (a security analyst), August 25, 1965; children: David, Mark. *Education:* Mount Holyoke College, B.A., 1961. *Politics:* Democrat. *Religion:* None. *Home:* 205 East 69th St., New York, N.Y. 10021.

CAREER: Worth Publishers, Inc., New York, N.Y., picture editor of college science textbooks, 1968—. *Member:* American Museum of Natural History, National Audubon Society. *Awards, honors: The Inflated Dormouse and Other Ways of Life in the Animal World* was chosen by *Scientific American* as one of the ten best children's science books for 1970.

WRITINGS: (With Jean Ely) *The Inflated Dormouse and Other Ways of Life in the Animal World* (juvenile), Doubleday, 1970; *The Railroad Book: Trains in America* (juvenile), McKay, 1977; *Firefighters* (juvenile), McKay, 1978.

WORK IN PROGRESS: A juvenile, *To the Rescue,* "about five disasters and the rescue personnel who cope with each."

SIDELIGHTS: "I am interested in writing good, accurate, well-illustrated nonfiction for children. All of my books are heavily illustrated with good photographs. In fact, the photographs are a very important part of the text. They are not just an 'extra.' My feeling is that a child (especially one who doesn't really enjoy reading) will examine a good, dramatic photograph carefully and, with the addition of clear text explaining the photograph, will find himself learning from both photographs and text.

"My working method for the books on trains and fires has been to research the topic thoroughly, to decide what I want to cover, to get the photographs, and then to write the text."

HOBBIES AND OTHER INTERESTS: Travel (Mexico, Israel, Greece, Italy, France, England, and the American Southwest and Rockies), animal behavior, hiking, photography, boating and camping.

Pullman dining cars in 1875 served elaborate dinners. There were no sandwiches, hamburgers, or french fries. ■ (From *The Railroad Book* by Anne Feldman. Photo courtesy of Canadian National Railways.)

**A poor old woman
lived long ago
in a quiet town on a hill.**
■ (From *Tit for Tat* by Dorothy O. Van Woerkom.
Illustrated by Douglas Florian.)

FLORIAN, Douglas 1950-

PERSONAL: Born March 18, 1950, in New York, N.Y.; son
of Harold (an artist) and Edith Florian. *Education:* Queens
College, New York, N.Y., B.A. *Home:* 147-54 Village Road,
Jamaica, N.Y. 11435.

CAREER: Free-lance illustrator.

ILLUSTRATOR: Freeing the Natural Voice, Drama Books,
1976; Dorothy O. Van Woerkom, *Tit for Tat,* Greenwillow,
1977; *Introduction to Management Science,* Prentice-Hall,
1977. Also illustrated Thomas Mallory's, *King Arthur and
His Knights of the Round Table,* edited by Sidney Lanier
and Howard Pyle, for Grosset. Work has appeared in *The
New Yorker, The New York Times, Scanlons* Magazine.

SIDELIGHTS: "For my own pleasure I paint abstract watercolors and oils, influenced by the visual patterns of nature. I was also influenced by my father."

FROST, A(rthur) B(urdett) 1851-1928

PERSONAL: Born January 17, 1851, in Philadelphia, Pennsylvania; died June 22, 1928; married Emily Phillips, October 19, 1883; children: Arthur, Jr., John. *Home:* Pasadena,
California.

CAREER: Illustrator, cartoonist, author. Exhibited his
works at the Paris Exposition, 1900.

WRITINGS—All self-illustrated: *Stuff and Nonsense,* Scrib-
ner, 1884; *The Bull Calf, and Other Tales,* Scribner, 1892,
reprinted, Dover, 1969, revised edition, Scribner, 1924;
Shooting Pictures (text by Charles D. Lanier), Scribner,
1895, reprinted, Winchester, 1972; *Sports and Games in the
Open,* Harper, 1899; *A Book of Drawings* (introduction by
Joel Chandler Harris; verse by Wallace Irwin), Collier, 1904;
Carlo, Doubleday, Page, 1913.

Illustrator: Charles Dickens, *American Notes,* Chapman,
1870; Daisy Shortcut (pseudonym of D. S. Cohen) and Arry
O'Pagus (pseudonym of H. B. Sommer) *Our Show, One
Hundred Years a Republic: A Humorous Account of the International Exposition,* Claxton, 1875; Max Adeler (pseud-
onym of Charles Heber Clark), *Elbow Room: A Novel with-
out a Plot,* J. M. Stoddart, 1876; Dickens, *The Posthumous
Papers of the Pickwick Club,* Harper, 1879; (with Henry
Holiday) Lewis Carroll (pseudonym of Charles L. Dodgson),
Rhyme? and Reason?, Macmillan, 1883; Carroll, *A Tangled
Tale,* Macmillan, 1885, reprinted, Rex Collings, 1969; Theo-
dore Roosevelt, *Hunting Trips of a Ranchman,* Putnam,
1885; Frank R. Stockton, *Rudder Grange,* Scribner, 1885;
Henry Cuyler Bunner, *The Story of a New York House,*
Scribner, 1887.

Octave Thanet (pseudonym of Alice French), *Expiation*
(novel), Scribner, 1890; Richard Kendall Munkittrick, *Farming,* Harper, 1891; Stockton, *Squirrel Inn,* Century, 1891;

A. B. FROST

(with others) *Comics from Scribner's Magazine*, Scribner, 1891; (with others) R. H. Davis, Andrew Lang, and others, *The Great Streets of the World*, Scribner, 1892; Joel Chandler Harris, *Uncle Remus and His Friends: Old Plantation Stories, Songs, and Ballads*, Houghton, 1892; (with Charles S. Reinhart and William Ludwell Sheppard) Ruth McEnery Stuart, *Golden Wedding and Other Tales*, Harper, 1893; Stockton, *Pomona's Travels*, Scribner, 1894; Thomas N. Page, *Pastime Stories*, Scribner, 1894, reprinted, Books for Libraries, 1969.

Thomas B. Aldrich, *The Story of a Bad Boy*, Houghton, 1895; Harris, *Uncle Remus, His Songs and His Sayings: Folklore of the Old Plantation*, Appleton, revised edition, 1895, later edition illustrated by Frost and Edward W. Kemble, 1920; (with Andre Castaigne, B. W. Clinedinst, Howard Pyle, and others) Page, *In Ole Virginia*, Scribner, 1896; (with E. W. Kemble and others) Stuart, *Solomon Crow's Christmas Pockets and Other Tales*, Harper, 1896; Mark Twain (pseudonym of Samuel L. Clemens), *Tom Sawyer Abroad*, Webster, 1896; Twain, *Tom Sawyer, Detective, and Other Stories*, Webster, 1896; (with C. Carleton) Thanet, *The Missionary Sheriff*, Harper, 1897; William G. van Tassel Sutphen, *The Golfer's Alphabet*, Harper, 1898, reprinted, C. E. Tuttle, 1967; Harris, *The Chronicles of Aunt Minervy Ann*, Scribner, 1899, reprinted, Garrett Press, 1969; Hayden Car-

Den ole Brer Rabbit sot de jug down in de road en let um lick de stopper a time er two. ▪ (From *The Favorite Uncle Remus* by Joel Chandler Harris. Illustrated by A. B. Frost.)

ruth, *Mr. Milo Bush and Other Worthies*, Harper, 1899; Stockton, *The Associate Hermite*, Harper, 1899.

(With Ernest Thompson Seton and Frederick Coffay Yohn) Noah Brooks, *First Across the Continent: The Expedition of Lewis and Clark*, Scribner, 1901; (with others) Charles Major, *Bears of Blue River*, Doubleday, 1901; Harris, *The Tar-Baby, and Other Rhymes of Uncle Remus*, Appleton, 1904; (with J. M. Condé and Frank Verbeck) Harris, *Told by Uncle Remus: New Stories of the Old Plantation*, McClure, Phillips, 1905, reprinted, Books for Libraries, 1972; Carroll, *Phantasmagoria and Other Poems*, Macmillan, 1911; (with J. M. Condé) Harris, *Uncle Remus Returns*, Houghton, 1918.

Contributor of illustrations and cartoons to various periodicals, including *Harper's, Collier's, Scribner's*, and *Life*.

SIDELIGHTS: **January 17, 1851.** Born in Philadelphia, the son of a historian and biographer.

1874. Worked as a lithographer. Illustrated *Out of the Hurly Burly*, which sold over a million copies.

**And swing yourself from side to side—
One soon learns how to do it.**
▪ (From the book *The Humorous Verse of Lewis Carroll* by Lewis Carroll. Illustrated by A. B. Frost.)

1875. Worked for *New York Graphic*.

1876. Began long term association with Harper and Brothers as feature draughtsman, specializing in outdoor sports.

1877-1878. Studied in London where he attracted the attention of Lewis Carroll.

1881-1882. Visited the American South and Canada to do hunting illustrations. "... My little model with the big gun came and I did all I could from him. I will have to finish it at home and get a photograph of the other child. I like what I have done pretty well—it is sunlighty. After I got through with him I found that I had an hour and a half before dinner, and went off after something to sketch and tried a barn with an apple orchard around it—I have seen worse sketches, but few; it is like a school-girl's first attempt, and I worked hard on it too." [Henry Lanier, *A. B. Frost: The American Sportsman's Artist,* Derrydale Press, 1933.[1]]

Frost's artistic endeavors were hindered by his color blindness. "I still stick to the sketches without body color and do all I can in wash. The new one I did Tuesday is the best sketch from nature I have ever made and I feel very proud of it. I was looking at it today and wondering how I did it. ... I went up on top of the ridge and tried a sketch in color. I want a background for my hunter with the turkey, and I got a buckwheat field with a line of trees beyond it; my sketch is very yellow and brown, I am afraid, for I sketched it as I saw it, and if it is monotonous in color it is my fault. I can work it up.

"I am in a game country at last. ... It is the most desolate place I have ever seen. ... If you can imagine a landscape covered with telegraph poles you have this place. I made a sketch in water-color this morning but not very successfully. I am going to leave my water-colors here. It takes me too long to make a sketch in color, so I will work in Payne's grey.

"Well, I've killed a deer, and I'm not proud of it. Not being a butcher I am not elated over the affair. ...

"He was a young buck, only half grown with the little dappled spots on him yet. I felt thoroughly ashamed of myself. ... There was no excitement, no sport in it and I want no more of it. If I can kill deer by still-hunting I will do it, or even on a runway, where the deer has a chance if you miss him; but to drive him into the water and then butcher him is not to my taste and I'm through with it.

AS THE COACH STOPS A GENTLEMAN IN A STRAW HAT LOOKS OUT OF THE WINDOW—Chap. xiv.

(From *American Notes* by Charles Dickens. Illustrated by A. B. Frost.)

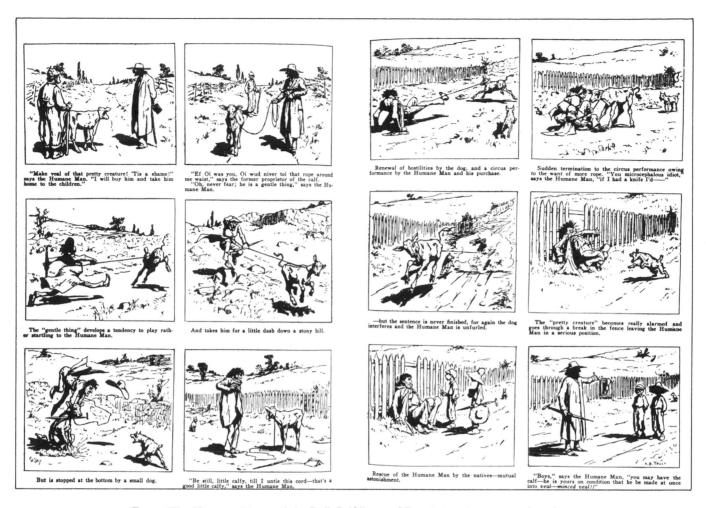

(From "The Humane Man and the Bull Calf," one of Frost's best-known comic strips.)

"This afternoon I paddled myself down the lake a little and made a sketch in color. . . . It did not come as well as when I saw it first, but I remembered pretty well the effect, and have got it, I think. . . . The sky is not good; I am never careful enough with my skies."[1]

October 19, 1883. Married Emily Phillips and moved to Long Island. Became a busy illustrator. "Things are just booming; I haven't been in such a good humour for fifteen years. First, Mr. Parsons was *very* much pleased with the drawings. Thinks they are the best things I have done yet. He said a good deal about them and was very complimentary. Says he thinks I am getting the real thing for illustration. Next my comic page was a big success. They laughed over it a great deal and want a lot more as soon as I can do them: next, I got thirty dollars for the two comics, which wasn't so bad as they took me about three hours to do. Next, they want me to draw cartoons for them; offer me a mighty good price and will give me every help they can. . . . It will certainly pay me over a hundred dollars a week and leave me time for other things. . . ." [Henry M. Reed, *The A. B. Frost Book,* Charles E. Tuttle Co., 1967.[2]]

1884. Published *Stuff and Nonsense,* his own book of comic sketches and verses.

December 11, 1887. A. B. Frost, Jr. born at "Prospect Hill" Farm in Pennsylvania.

1890. Moved to "Moneysunk" farm in New Jersey. "The studio is going up; the frame is nearly all up and I think I can use it by August first; I am making some changes in it which will improve it, I think. It will be like the last one, the hottest place on the farm, but I can't help that.

"I have not touched a pen yet. I am out all day, going from one job to another, and am needed, I tell you; such damnable stupidity as these trained mechanics show is wonderful.

"Mrs. Frost and the babies are very well, and very comfortable—Good! Won't I be glad to get them here!!—"[2]

1891. Became pupil of impressionist painter, William Merritt Chase. "I am going to Chase every Tuesday and Chase really seems to like what I do. He told me last Tuesday that I was *painting.* He said 'that is painting that is not straining.' I have a great respect for his knowledge. He certainly knows a lot that a painter ought to know. . . .

"I am, as usual, driven wild by my work. I am doing Broadway for Scribner's and in a devil of a hurry. I never seem to get time to do decent work, always in a rush. This is the last article on hand, and I mean to make it the last for some time. I have a lot of schemes and mean to try to carry some of them out, painting a little now and then."[2]

Sketch by A. B. Frost. ■ (From *A Book of Drawings* by A. B. Frost.)

1892. Illustrated *Uncle Remus and His Friends.* Joel Chandler Harris' direction: "Be as comic as you choose, or as commonplace as you choose," inspired Frost.

1895-1896. Worked on his "Shooting Pictures," famous series of hunting illustrations. "I have not got these damned shooting things done yet. They drag, and are a mill stone 'round my neck,' and the reproductions are enough to make a dog sick. . . .

"We have had a tough time since Christmas. The Boys were taken sick the same day soon after Christmas, influenza. Then Mrs. Frost got it. About the time the boys got well I went down and was sick just a month, in bed over a week, and am only now feeling like myself again. We were pretty blue too, for I worked on those shooting pictures all the Fall, and got no money and we got behind hand; and it wasn't pleasant. We are better off now for I am at work again and there is 'mon' coming in."[2]

December, 1905. Suffered from failing eyesight and a desire to become a painter rather than an illustrator. Planned to

He fixed up a contraption that he called a Tar-Baby

He fixed up a contraption that he called a Tar-Baby. ■(From "The Wonderful Tar-Baby Story" in *Brer Rabbit: Stories from Uncle Remus* by Joel Chander Harris. Illustrated by A.B. Frost.)

take his family abroad. "This Christmas time is hard on a man whose eyes are not good. I am having more trouble with my eyes, head-ache and nervousness and I can write but little at a time.

"I am working hard for *Colliers* and saving money to live on when we go abroad. I am going to say goodbye to illustration when we go. There will be no brass bands and fuss when we go, but when I go I go out of illustration for good, *I think*! You can't tell, I may be teaching a young ladies school next."[2]

1906. Took up residence in Paris. Enrolled his sons, Arthur and Jack, in art school. Desperately tried to break away from illustration and gain attention as a painter. "We take French

(From *The Story of a Bad Boy* by Thomas Bailey Aldrich. Illustrated by A. B. Frost.)

lessons but Mrs. Frost and I are pretty slow, the boys do well. I am making illustrations because I can't paint out of doors. As soon as I can paint I will drop it pretty nearly altogether, only doing what I can do from nature. We will probably be in the country all summer and I will find plenty of stuff to do.

"I had planned a lot of work and here I am knocked out of a month, for I won't be able to work for another week and the shooting season has been open ever since I went to bed. I had been looking forward to the shooting all summer as my one chance to get any fun. I haven't had any pleasure since I came to this country, no golf, no anything, and this was to be my chance, it is rotten hard luck. Jack goes out quite often and has killed quite a number of partridges and rabbits. He is not shooting as well as he used to and I think he needs someone to steady him and tell him what he is doing, but he makes some good shots. He got a double on partridges the other day. There is a good deal of game. Jack has seen pheasants and hare and two deer, but did not get shots at them. Deer and boar come quite close in the houses here after the shoot-

**It's delightfully easy to fish—
But harder than blazes to catch 'em.**
■ (From *A Book of Drawings* by A. B. Frost. Illustrated by the author.)

ing on the preserves opens. We have had pretty good fun, fishing all summer.

"I paint all the time but it is poor stuff and I destroy it all. . . . We had to go where it would do Emily the most good. I am counting on this summer to work. I hope nothing will prevent it, with a house in the country I ought to be able to paint something worth while. . . ."[2]

1911. Discovered that both his sons suffered from tuberculosis. "The main thing at present is that Jack is sick. Too much work in unaired studios and growing fast have used up his strength and he is in bed for a time. I feel anxious about him, he is not strong constitutionally. I am afraid Jack will be on the sick list for some time and his Mother and I are worried. We have had a hard winter in the matter of health. We all have had very bad colds and Arthur still has his, I am just about over mine. I lost three weeks' work, didn't go to the studio in that time and as I have all the illustrating I care to do it was rather a loss. . . .

"Arthur looked wretchedly and has had a succession of colds all winter. Dr. Turban examined him and found his lungs were in an inflamed condition and advised him to take a preventive cure. They have taken an X'ray of Arthur's

lungs and it confirms their diagnosis exactly. . . . I am doing absolutely nothing. I will try to get some painting going soon. I was so knocked out and upset by this terrible thing that I felt fit for nothing for a while. I had made arrangements to work for *Colliers* and Scribners and would have been making a fair income and have a good time, but I have to give it all up for I can't work here. I will have a big studio when we get settled and get to work again."[2]

May, 1914. Returned to America.

December, 1917. A. B. Frost, Jr. died shortly before his thirtieth birthday, after a period of "bohemian" living. Frost, Sr. went into a prolonged period of mourning. "We will have no Christmas. We could not have it without our boy."[2]

January, 1918. ". . . The Christmas holidays. They are over for us, it is the saddest time of the year for us and always will be. We have no Christmas and never will have again.

"My poor boy's birthday and Christmas came close together and we made a great day of it. Jack feels as his Mother and I do about it and we pass the day as the other days. We gave Jack some money and some to the servants and that was all.

"One night Miss Meadows en de gals dey gun a candy-pullin', en so many er de nabers come in 'sponse ter de invite dat dey hatter put de 'lasses in de wash pot...." ■ (From *Uncle Remus: His Songs and Sayings* by Joel Chandler Harris. Illustrated by A. B. Frost.)

Dey wuz times,...w'en de creeturs 'ud segashuate tergedder des like dey aint had no fallin' out. Dem wuz de times w'en ole Brer Rabbit 'ud p'ten' like he gwine quit he 'havishness, en dey'd all go roun' des like dey b'long ter de same fambly connection. ■ (From *The Favorite Uncle Remus* by Joel Chandler Harris. Illustrated by A.B. Frost.)

'...You has done commit a pen'tentiary offence, and I kin put you in the pen'tentiary for it,' says I. And she bet me a dollar she hadn't and I couldn't; and I says, 'I bet you two dollars I kin and I will....' ■ (From *Pastime Stories* by Thomas Nelson Page. Illustrated by A. B. Frost.)

LOOKING FOR LIKELY CATS

(From *Mr. Milo Bush and Other Worthies* by Hayden Carruth. Illustrated by A. B. Frost.)

"Jack is doing *very* well, he has gained a great deal of weight and looks remarkably well. Much better than he did before he was taken sick. The Doctor won't let him do much, but he works with me in my studio every morning for a while, about two hours. He has a story for Scribner's and plenty of time to do it in. I think we will go South in a few weeks and get away from the bad weather that is sure to come. So far the weather has been perfect. The three warm days last week were bad for Jack and he felt the effect, showing that he is not well yet.

"Mrs. Frost and I are very well, I have no ailments and if I did not smoke I would feel quite up to the mark. I must stop for it does not suit me.

"I have given up working in tone and am at work with a pen. I can't see well enough to work in tone, and can't get a suitable glass. I have just finished some golf drawings and am going to take up caricaturing with a view of getting into the syndicate job. If it goes at all it means better pay than I could get in any other way.

"Caricature is with me a separate thing from my life. I can draw absurd things that amuse others but do not affect me. I am wretchedly unhappy and always will be but I can make 'comic' pictures just as I always did. I know when they are funny but they do not amuse me in the least.

Then old Brer Rabbit he gathered up his foots under him and he danced out of that garden and he danced home. ■ (From "Brer Rabbit and the Little Girl" in *Brer Rabbit: Stories from Uncle Remus* by Joel Chandler Harris. Illustrated by A. B. Frost.)

"I have a hard time these days. I *must* be cheerful for Jack's and his Mother's sake and it is not easy. I wish with all my soul I were dead and with my boy and I must grin and chatter. It can't go on much longer. I will soon be 68 and my time will come some day.

"No, we are not planning to go back to Phila. I would like to go but it is not the place for Mrs. Frost. She does not like it. We will stay where we are for another year. That is far enough ahead for us to look. I try to live from day to day, I wish I could stop thinking and be a machine.''[2]

December, 1919. Moved to California. "I have no doubt that the California influence will appear in my work, though I see

He felt it was his turn to speak,
And, with a shamed and crimson cheek,
Moaned "This is harder than Bezique!"
■ (From *Rhyme? and Reason?* by Lewis Carroll. Illustrated by Arthur B. Frost.)

a good many of my old chin-bearded friends out here, too. I understand they come out from the Middle West on every train. But a man gets most of his pictures from his head, not from the people he sees. In Paris I used to pose a Frenchman as I wished him and then draw a picture everybody would recognize as a Connecticut farmer. From the model I got the pose and perhaps expression; all the rest came from memory, from pictures in my mind as distinct and easy to draw as models, real friends I have grown to love through long association. I don't make fun of my chin-bearded friends—I love them, and simply show their whims and humours. You see, I am a bit chin-bearded myself.

"... It gets warm here in Pasadena, but there's not the humidity there is back East. My son, John, the painter, was pretty run down after he had the influenza, but when he came to California he grew stronger at once so Mrs. Frost and I came out, and—well, it's the most beautiful region we ever saw. And it makes me feel like working. So here we are for life.

"Southern California should have a great future as an art center. It has everything Italy has in climate. One can work here in the year round and there is plenty of perfect stuff for landscape and marine artists. Back East the spring and autumn are the only seasons when one can work. This region might well become the American painters' paradise."[2]

1928. "Mrs. Frost is pretty well most of the time but she has had bad attacks of heart trouble which alarm us, she keeps up wonderfully and is fairly well most of the time. I am very seedy, I sleep very badly, lie awake half of the night and feel very tired and seedy all the next day."[2]

June 22, 1928. Died.

FOR MORE INFORMATION SEE: Henry W. Lanier, *A. B. Frost: The American Sportsman's Artist,* Derrydale Press

A. B. FROST

(New York), 1933; Bertha E. Mahony and others, compilers, *Illustrators of Children's Books: 1744-1945,* Horn Book, 1947; Loring H. Dodd, *A Generation of Illustrators and Etchers,* Chapman & Grimes, 1960; *Horn Book,* June, 1966; Henry M. Reed, *The A. B. Frost Book,* C. E. Tuttle, 1967.

GARELICK, May
(Garel Clark, a joint pseudonym)

PERSONAL: Born in Vobruisk, Russia; emigrated to the United States at age nine months; married Marshall (Mike) McClintock (an author). *Education:* Attended public schools in New York City, and college for two years.

CAREER: Author and editor. Has worked in the publishing business for all of her life, with jobs ranging from clerical worker to production manager. Editor of children's books for William R. Scott Company for 15 years; children's European editor for E. P. Dutton. *Awards, honors:* Children's Book Showcase Title, 1976, for *About Owls.*

WRITINGS: (With Ethel McCullough Scott, under joint pseudonym, Garel Clark) *Let's Start Cooking* (illustrated by Kathleen Elgin), W. R. Scott, 1951; (with E. M. Scott, under joint pseudonym, Garel Clark) *The Cook-a-Meal Cook Book* (illustrated by Leonard Kessler), W. R. Scott, 1953; *What's Inside?,* W. R. Scott, 1955, reissued as *What's Inside: The Story of an Egg That Hatched,* Scholastic Book Services, 1970; *Manhattan Island* (illustrated by John and Clare Ross), Crowell, 1957; *Double Trouble* (illustrated by Arthur Getz), Crowell, 1958.

The sky grew darker and darker. It was only by straining our eyes through the unnatural twilight that we could keep the Dolphin in sight. ■ (From *The Story of a Bad Boy* by Thomas Bailey Aldrich. Illustrated by A. B. Frost.)

Where Does the Butterfly Go When It Rains? (illustrated by Leonard Weisgard), W. R. Scott, 1961, reissued, Scholastic Book Services, 1970; *Sounds of a Summer Night* (illustrated by Beni Montresor), Young Scott Books, 1963; *Here Comes the Bride* (illustrated by Joe Lasker), Young Scott Books, 1964; *Wild Ducks and Daffodils* (illustrated by Clare Ross), Young Scott Books, 1965; *Winter's Birds* (illustrated by Clement Hurd), Young Scott Books, 1965; *What Makes a Bird a Bird?* (Junior Literary Guild selection; illustrated by L. Weisgard), Follett, 1969; *Look at the Moon* (Junior Literary Guild selection; illustrated by L. Weisgard), Young Scott Books, 1969; *Just Suppose* (illustrated by Brinton Turkle), Scholastic Book Services, 1971; *Who Likes It Hot?* (illustrated by Brinton Turkle), Four Winds, 1972; *Runaway Plane* (illustrated by Józef Sumichrast), J. P. O'Hara, 1973; *Down to the Beach* (illustrated by Barbara Cooney), Four Winds, 1973; (contributor) *Cricket's Choice,* Open Court Publishing, 1974; *About Owls* (illustrated by Tony Chen), Four Winds, 1975; *It's About Birds,* Holt, 1978.

ADAPTATIONS—Filmstrip: *Where Does the Butterfly Go When It Rains?,* Weston Woods.

SIDELIGHTS: "I was born in Vobruisk, a small town in Russia, in a log cabin my father had built with the help of some neighbors. But I don't remember any of this because I was nine months old when my family came to the United States. We lived for several years in Rochester, New York, moved to Newark, New Jersey, and then to New York City, where I have lived ever since. The elementary school I went to was probably the first school built in New York City; it was called Public School #1. This no doubt makes you think that I should be hundreds of years old or at least one hundred! I'm not! And since I am as vain as most women, I won't tell you my age. I won't tell you a wrong age, but I just won't tell.

"When I was about 12 years old, I decided I would read every book in the library. The books were arranged alphabetically by author. I started with the ''A'' authors but got restless and began to skip around. By this time the librarian was helping me choose books. I didn't read them all but did read a good many. I went to high school in New York City, continuing on to college for two years. My family couldn't afford to keep me in school, so I quit and went to work, trying to continue my college education at night. It was too hard to work and try to be a good student. I had to work, so I gave up school.

"Maybe it's because I was brought up in a city that I became so aware of things in the country. As a child I wondered about a good many things but, I didn't ask questions; therefore, I grew up without knowing many of the answers. But I did develop a sense of observation and found out that you can always look up the answers if you know the question. I wrote *Where Does the Butterfly Go When it Rains?* to encourage children to notice things and ask about them!

This mob of crows swirls angrily around the owl to frighten it, and drive it away. ■ (From *About Owls* by May Garelick. Illustrated by Tony Chen.)

MAY GARELICK

"It's funny, children don't seem troubled by the question, 'Where does the butterfly go when it rains?' I've had a lot of trouble with grownups though who ask continuously, 'But where DOES the butterfly go? Where? Tell me!' Children have given many answers voluntarily—'under a leaf,' 'under a rock,' 'in a tree.' One five-year-old remarked to his teacher, 'Mrs. Johnson, I think I know where the butterfly goes when it rains: He climbs way down inside a flower and then the flower closes up and he stays nice and dry until the sun comes out again.' This child knew the important thing—wet wings don't work! Really and truly, does it matter where a butterfly goes when it rains? No! But to think creatively, to make your own discovery, that's pretty important. I like to pose a question in each of my books, to encourage readers to make their own discoveries in nature and in the world around them." [Lee Bennett Hopkins, *Books Are By People,* Citation, 1969.[1]]

One of Garelick's books, *Look at the Moon,* resulted from a question asked by a four-year-old girl on a moonlit night. "We were on the Normandy coast. The moon was full, the night enchanting. We were walking in silence, when Shula asked me, 'Do you have a moon in America?' I assured her we did. 'But is it like our moon—as lovely?' She was startled to find that it was the same moon. After all she had a reason for doubting since we lived in different countries and spoke different languages. I wrote this book, as I wrote my other young nature books, in response to a question. When I write, I always try to keep my audience in mind. I ask myself, what is it that the child wants to know about this? What is the *question?*"[1]

Her most recent book, *About Owls,* was reviewed by a *Horn Book* critic who said, "Even when the illustrations show a Great Horned Owl preying on a snake or an Elf Owl careening through the air after a butterfly, they tend to accentuate the beauty of the lemuroid creatures rather than their viciousness. Presenting small tidbits of information about the owl's hunting, eating, and sleeping habits, its anatomy, its peculiar relationship with crows, and its much celebrated wisdom, the text merely supplements the illustrations which give the book its luster. . . ."

Of *Down to the Beach, Horn Book* commented, "Simple, rhythmic prose enumerates the wonders of the seashore as a preschooler might see or hear them . . . [together with] luminous, uncluttered watercolor illustrations." *Library Journal* said, "Young beachcombers will become even more aware of the mysteries and delights of the ocean. . . . This is a gentle vision of the sea. . . ."

In writing about *Look at the Moon,* a *Library Journal* critic called it, "[A] simple poetic picture book that the very young can understand and enjoy. The dark illustrations, in midnight blue and black with touches of green, show a big full moon shining on a boy, his cat, the forest full of animals, the city, the sea, and on other lands, creating a continuity of mood that conveys the general idea perfectly."

All of Garelick's books are "child-tested" before they go to the publisher. She usually reads them to a classroom of children, accepting their criticism and enjoying their comments.

HOBBIES AND OTHER INTERESTS: People, music, theater, and books. "I'm really interested in everything!"[1]

FOR MORE INFORMATION SEE: Lee Bennett Hopkins, *Books Are by People: Interviews with 104 Authors and Illustrators of Books for Young Children,* Citation, 1969; *Horn Book,* October, 1973, August, 1975, August, 1976.

GARRISON, Barbara   1931-

PERSONAL: Born August 22, 1931, in London, England; daughter of Murray (a film executive) and Dorothy (Littman) Silverstone; married Michael Garrison, June 17, 1955 (deceased, 1965); children: Brian Steven. *Education:* Wellesley College, Wellesley, Mass., B.A., 1953; Columbia University, Teachers College, M.A., 1956. *Home:* 12 East 87th St., New York, N.Y. 10028.

CAREER: Artist; illustrator; art teacher. The Spence School, New York, N.Y., art teacher, 1963-69; Harriet Beecher Stowe, art teacher, 1969-70; Nightingale-Bamford School, New York, N.Y., art teacher, 1970—. *Exhibitions*—Group shows: Arena Open, Binghamton, N.Y.; Audubon Artists, New York, N.Y.; Contemporary American Graphics Traveling Exhibits; Hunterdon Art Center National Print Exhibitions, Clinton, N.J.; International Miniature Print Exhibitions, Pratt Graphic Center, New York, N.Y.; Miniature Painters, Sculptors and Engravers Society of Washington, D.C.; Miniature Art Society of Florida; Miniature Art Society of New Jersey; National Academy of Design, New York, N.Y.; National Arts Club National Graphics Exhibitions, New York, N.Y.; National Association of Women Artists, New York, N.Y.; National Cape Coral Annual, Fort Meyers, Fla.; The New School, New York, N.Y.; Oklahoma Art Guild Annual National Exhibition,

(From *The Sultan's Perfect Tree* by Jane Yolen. Illustrated with etchings by Barbara Garrison.)

BARBARA GARRISON

Oklahoma City, Okla.; Print Club of Albany National Exhibitions, Albany, N.Y.; Print Club of Philadelphia Biennial International Exhibition, Philadelphia, Pa.; Prints by Pratt Printmakers, New York, N.Y.; Purdue University National Small Print Exhibition, West Lafayette, Ind.; The Contemporary Miniature, University of Michigan, Ann Arbor, Mich.

Invitational, one and two-person shows: New Collectors Fifth Annual Show, Community Church Gallery, New York, N.Y.; Printed Quilts and Quilted Prints, Pratt Graphics Center, New York, N.Y.; Printmakers 12, Atlantic Gallery and Long Island University, Brooklyn, N.Y.; Spring Mills, Fort Mill, S.C.; Women Artists Award Winners Exhibition, Community Church Gallery, New York, N.Y.; Watermill Gallery, Watermill, N.Y.; The Gallery, Fort Wayne, Ind. Galleries: Gallery 101, Stamford, Conn.; Fine Arts Gallery of Ardmore, Pa.; Graphics 1 and Graphics 2, Boston, Mass.; 2nd Street Gallery, Charleston, Va.; Maine Coast Artists Gallery, Rockport, Me. Work is also in the public collection of The New York Public Library Print Collection, New York, N.Y.

MEMBER: National Association of Women Artists, Artists Equity of New York. *Awards, honors:* John Carl Giogri Memorial Prize and Walter Giger Memorial Prize, National Association of Women Artists 85th Annual Exhibition, 1974; The Doris Kemp Purchase Prize, National Arts Club Graphics Exhibition, 1975; Second highest merit: Graphics, Miniature Art Society of New Jersey, 1975; Purchase Prize, Arena '75, Binghamton, N.Y., 1975; Bicentennial Award and Silver Medal, National Arts Club Graphics Exhibition, 1976; Bicentennial Award, Miniature Art Society of New Jersey, 1976; Central Savings Bank Award, New York Outdoor Art Fair, 1976; Second Prize, Gracie Square Art Show, New York, N.Y.; Second prize, Art in the Aisles, Church of

Heavenly Rest, New York, N.Y., 1977; Honorable Mention, Washington Square Outdoor Art Exhibition, New York, N.Y., 1977.

ILLUSTRATOR: Jane Yolen, *The Sultan's Perfect Tree,* Parents' Magazine Press, 1977.

GAY, Zhenya 1906-1978

PERSONAL: Born September 16, 1906, in Norwood, Massachusetts; died August 3, 1978. *Education:* Columbia University, student, 1919-22; later studied in New York City under Solon Borglum and Winold Reiss, and in Paris under Gaston Dorfinant. *Address:* R.D. 2, Box 189D, Saugerties, New York 12477.

CAREER: Author and illustrator. Began as a free-lance artist for motion picture posters and newspaper advertisements; worked as a costume designer, Brooks Theatrical Costumes; traveled in Central America, Europe, and Mexico, laying the groundwork for future book illustrations. Her works have been exhibited in many galleries and museums, including Davis Galleries, Mexico City, 1927, Montross Gallery, New York City, 1930, and American Museum of Natural History, New York City, 1935.

WRITINGS—All self-illustrated: (With Jan Gay) *Pancho and His Burro,* Morrow, 1930; (with J. Gay) *The Goat Who Wouldn't Be Good: A Story of Norway,* Morrow, 1931; (with J. Gay) *The Shire Colt,* Doubleday, 1931; *Sakimura,* Viking, 1937; (with Pachita Crespi) *A Fish Story,* Garden City Publishing, 1939; (with P. Crespi) *Happy Birthday,* Viking, 1939; (with P. Crespi) *170 Cats,* Random House, 1939; (with P.

ZHENYA GAY

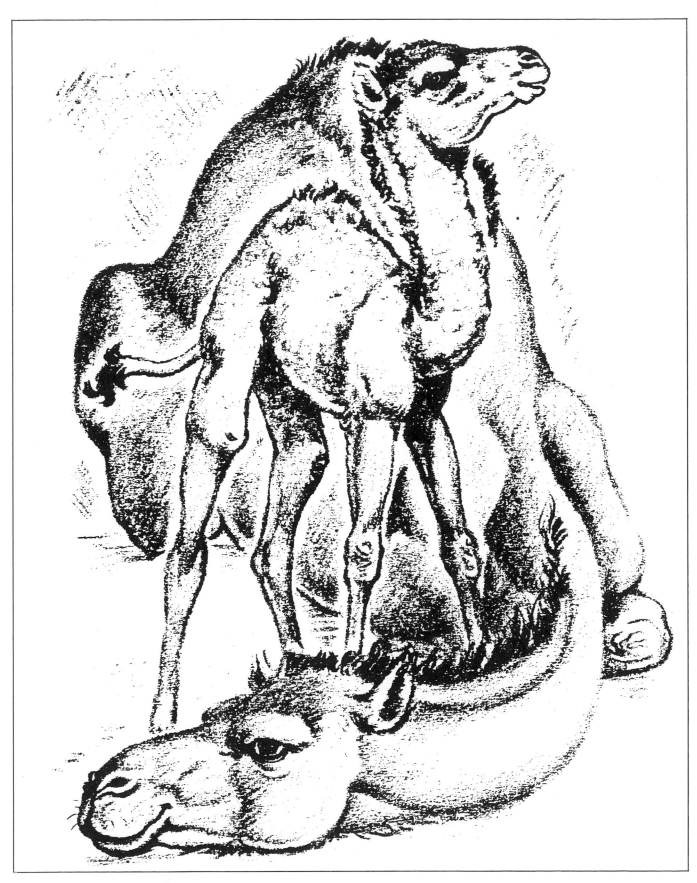

One morning there was a great surprise.

When the Major went to feed the camels he saw that there was a new camel on board. It was a baby camel which had been born in the night. ■(From *The Major and His Camels* by Miriam E. Mason. Illustrated by Zhenya Gay.)

In a flash, Tiny was off at top speed. He ran so fast that not one of them, not even Anne, could keep up with him. ■ (From *The Fairies of the Glen* by Agnes Fisher. Illustrated by Zhenya Gay.)

Crespi) *Manuelito of Costa Rica,* Messner, 1940; *Look!,* Viking, 1952; *Jingle Jangle,* Viking, 1953; *Wonderful Things!,* Viking, 1954; *What's Your Name?,* Viking, 1955; *Who Is It?,* Viking, 1957; *Bits and Pieces,* Viking, 1958; *Small One,* Viking, 1958; *The Dear Friends,* Harper, 1959; *The Nicest Time of Year,* Viking, 1960; *I'm Tired of Lions* (Junior Literary Guild selection), Viking, 1961; *Who's Afraid?,* Viking, 1965.

Illustrator: Nikolai Vasilievich Gogol, *Taras Bulba* (translation from the Russian by Isabel F. Hapgood), Knopf, 1915; Thomas De Quincey, *Confessions of an English Opium-Eater,* Limited Editions Club, 1930; Jan Gay, *Town Cats,* Knopf, 1932; Gaius Valerius Catullus, *Poems* (English translation by Horace Gregory), Covici-Friede, 1933; Frances Clarke Sayers, *Mr. Tidy Paws,* Viking, 1935; Idwal Jones, *Whistler's Van,* Viking, 1936; Oscar Wilde, *Ballad of Reading Gaol,* Limited Editions Club, 1937; Eleanor Hoffmann, *Travels of a Snail,* F. A. Stokes, 1939; Gretchen McKown and Florence S. Gleeson, *All the Days Were Antonia's,* Viking, 1939.

E. Hoffmann, *Cat of Paris,* F. A. Stokes, 1940; Rutherford George Montgomery, *Troopers Three,* Caxton, 1940; Panchita Crespi, *Cabita's Rancho: A Story of Costa Rica,* Messner, 1942; Antoni Gronowicz, *Bolek,* Thomas Nelson, 1942;

Melicent H. Lee, *Village of Singing Birds,* Harper, 1942; Agnes Fisher (pseudonym of Jessie Evelyn McEwen) *Once Upon a Time: Folk Tales, Myths, and Legends of the United Nations,* Thomas Nelson, 1943; Arkadii Petrovich Gaidar, *Timur and His Gang* (translation by Zina Voynow), Scribner, 1943; Walt Whitman, *There Was a Child Went Forth,* Harper, 1943; Helen Acker, *Three Boys of Old Russia,* Thomas Nelson, 1944; (with Edmund Monroe) Raymond Will Burnett, *To Live in Health,* Duell, Sloan & Pearce, 1944; Janette S. Lowrey, *In the Morning of the World,* Harper, 1944; Irving Robert Melbo and others, *Young Neighbors in South America,* Silver Burdett, 1944; Hilda T. Harpster, *Insect World,* Viking, 1947; Irma (Simonton) Black, *Toby: A Curious Cat,* Holiday House, 1948.

Ruth Tooze, *Tim and the Brass Buttons,* Messner, 1951; Elizabeth Helfman, *Milkman Freddy,* Messner, 1952; Joseph Eugene Chipperfield, *Beyond the Timberland Trail,* Longmans, Green, 1953; Frances Louise Lockridge, *Lucky Cat,* Lippincott, 1953; Miriam Evangeline Mason, *Major and His Camels,* Macmillan, 1953; M. E. Mason, *Sugarbush Family,* Macmillan, 1954; Jane Quigg, *Jiggy Likes Nantucket,* Oxford University Press, 1954; Elizabeth Jane Coatsworth, *Peddler's Cart,* Macmillan, 1956; Christine (Brown) Von Hagen, *Pablo of Flower Mountain,* R. Hale, 1956.

SIDELIGHTS: As a child Gay gave up her piano lessons to devote more time to sketching—her first love. "In common with all children, my interest in art began as soon as I could see, hear, and touch. Like many children, my attempts at expressing myself through the media of pencil, colored crayon, and paintbrush began as soon as I discovered the superiority of these implements to my rattle. Like some children, this early interest developed with the years into a conviction that painting, drawing, and kindred forms of delineation were what I wanted above all to do. I avoided conventional schooling and studied only that which seemed to me to be essential to my chosen work—a thorough knowledge of human and animal anatomy under the tutelage of the sculptor, Solon Borglum, and an absorption of the principles of color, design, and media from observation of, and discussion with, mature and established artists." [Bertha E. Mahoney and others, compilers, *Illustrators of Children's Books: 1744-1945*, Horn Book, 1947.[1]]

Gay's first work in the publishing world was a lithograph portrait of Thomas Hardy for a frontispiece of an essay on Hardy. This led to further illustrating of adult books. After having spent several years in Europe, Mexico, and Central America, Gay turned to illustrating children's books and eventually, to writing her own children's stories. Her favorite subjects were animals, and her move from New York City to the country near the Catskill Mountains enabled her to be close to them. "I had been spending long summers in the country, true country, far from a main road and other houses. The old farm house in which I lived had been unoccupied long enough for the animals native to the region to have reinstated themselves in nearby trees, holes, and caves. Some field mice and chipmunks lived in the house itself! This seemed to me to be a wealth of material not to be ignored, and . . . I moved into the old house for good." [B. M. Miller and others, compilers, *Illustrators of Children's Books: 1946-1956*, Horn Book, 1958.[2]]

Gay died on August 3, 1978 in Saugerties, N.Y. Her works are included in the Kerlan Collection at the University of Minnesota.

The *Christian Science Monitor* said of *I'm Tired of Lions,* "The familiar theme of wanting-to-be-somebody-else is here rather freshly used to introduce members of the animal kingdom." The *New York Herald Tribune* added that, "This is a little gem for the smallest children. After many picture books with delightful animal drawings in them but no story at all to hold the interest of youngsters, Zhenya Gay has written a perfectly delightful tale with the most sympathetic characters, and of course, her illustrations are exactly right."

Of *Dear Friends,* *Kirkus* commented that the book, ". . . emphasizes the appealing nature of its creatures, resting lightly on possibility, darting here and there in caprices of whimsy and tenderness. Gay's black and white illustrations admirably capture the sympathy and tenderness with which she regards animals. . . ." The *Christian Science Monitor* said, "The animals act like people, and all play together in a most unnaturalistic way, but the stories are good fun, the sketches most delightful, and a certain amount of authentic nature lore is run in by the way. . . ."

Commonweal described *Small Ones* as, "Just enough danger to thrill a small child and plenty of motherliness to reassure him. . . ." *Kirkus* commented that, "Zhenya Gay's drawings of Small One and his family and her quiet, believable text, tenderly portray that fluffyness and softness of the rabbit which make him a favorite animal of all children."

FOR MORE INFORMATION SEE: Bertha E. Mahony and others, compilers, *Illustrators of Children's Books: 1744-1945,* Horn Book, 1947; B. M. Miller and others, compilers, *Illustrators of Children's Books: 1946-1956,* Horn Book, 1958; Muriel Fuller, editor, *More Junior Authors,* H. W. Wilson, 1963.

(Died, August 3, 1978)

GLINES, Carroll V(ane), Jr. 1920-

PERSONAL: Born December 2, 1920, in Baltimore, Md.; son of Carroll Vane and Elizabeth M. (Cross) Glines; married Mary Ellen Edwards, October 1, 1943; children: Karen Ann, David E., Valerie Jean. *Education:* Part-time student at Drexel Institute of Technology, 1938-41; University of Oklahoma, B.B.A., 1952, M.B.A., 1954; American University, M.A., 1969. *Home address:* 7212 Warbler Lane, McLean, Va. 22101. *Office:* Air Line Pilots Association, 1625 Massachusetts Ave., N.W. Washington, D.C. 20036.

CAREER: Production expediter, General Electric Co., 1938-41. Entered military service as flying cadet in 1941, commissioned second lieutenant in 1942; served during World War II as flying instructor, and squadron and group commander; command pilot with more than 6,000 hours flying time in thirty-five different types of aircraft. Postwar assignments include Panama Canal Zone, 1946-48; Germany, 1948-49; University of Oklahoma, Norman, assistant professor of air science; Command and Staff College, Air University, Maxwell Field, Ala., student, then member of faculty, 1955-58; Air Material Command Headquarters, Wright-Patterson Air Force Base, Dayton, Ohio, weapon system project officer, and chief, Plans Branch, Quality Control, 1958-59.

U.S. Air Force, Washington, D.C., 1960-64; Office of Assistant Secretary of Defense for Public Affairs, 1964-66; Elmendorf AFB, Alaska, Chief of Public Affairs, Alaskan Command, 1966-68; retired from Air Force as colonel, 1968; National Business Aircraft Association, Director of Publications, 1968-69; *Armed Forces Management* Magazine, associate editor, 1969-70; *Air Cargo* Magazine, editor, 1970-71; *Air Line Pilot* Magazine, editor, 1971—. Free-lance writer, 1954—. *Member:* Aviation/Space Writer's Association, Order of Daedalians, Sigma Delta Chi, Explorers Club, National Aviation Club.

WRITINGS: (With Elizabeth Land) *The Complete Guide for the Serviceman's Wife,* Houghton, 1956; *Our Family Affairs,* Walker, 1956; (with W. F. Moseley) *Grand Old Lady: The Story of the DC-3,* Pennington, 1959; (with W. F. Moseley) *Air Rescue!,* Ace Books, 1961; *Helicopter Rescues* (teenagers), Scholastic, 1963; *The Modern U.S. Air Force,* Van Nostrand, 1963; *The Compact History of the U.S. Air Force,* Hawthorn, 1963; *Doolittle's Tokyo Raiders,* Van Nostrand, 1964; *Polar Aviation,* Watts, 1964; *Lighter-Than-Air Flight,* Watts, 1965; *The DC-3: The Story of a Fabulous Airplane,* Lippincott, 1966; *Minutemen of the Air: The Story of the Civil Air Patrol,* Random, 1966; *Four Came Home,* Van Nostrand, 1966; *The First Book of the Moon,* Watts, 1966; *The DC-3: The Story of the Dakota,* Deutsch, 1967; *The Wright Brothers: Pioneers of Power Flight,* Watts, 1968; *From the Wright Brothers to the Astronauts,* McGraw-Hill, 1968; *The Saga of the Air Mail,* Van Nostrand, 1968; *Jimmy Doolittle: Daredevil Aviator and Scientist,* Macmillan, 1972;

Doolittle had only a few flights in a pontoon-equipped plane before he won the Schneider Cup Race in 1925 in this Curtiss R3C-2. This aircraft can be seen at the Air Force Museum, Wright-Patterson Air Force Base, Ohio. ■ (From *Jimmy Doolittle* by Carroll V. Glines. Photo courtesy of U.S. Air Force.)

The Legendary DC-3, Van Nostrand, 1979. More than three hundred articles on aviation, management, and personal affairs in national magazines.

WORK IN PROGRESS: Several books on aviation.

GOLDSBOROUGH, June 1923-

PERSONAL: Born May 30, 1923, in Paragould, Ark. *Education:* Attended Southwestern Missouri College, Cape Gardaru, Mo., one year; St. Louis School of Fine Arts, Washington University, St. Louis, Mo., three years. *Agent:* Carol Bancroft, 185 Good Hill Road, Weston, Conn. 06880. *Office:* 443 Bronxville Road, Bronxville, N.Y. 10708.

CAREER: Illustrator; designer. New York Telephone, New York, N.Y., designer of promotion, 1958-61; free-lance illustrator of children's books, 1961—. *Exhibitions:* St. Louis Art Museum, St. Louis, Mo.; Topeka Art Museum, Topeka, Kan.; Kansas City Art Museum, Kansas City, Mo.

WRITINGS—Self-illustrated: Happy Helper A.B.C., Western, 1971; *Real Book of First Storys,* Rand McNally, 1973; *What's in the Woods?,* Prentice-Hall, 1976.

Illustrator: Mary E. Lloyd, *Glad Easter Day,* Abingdon, 1961; Caary Jackson, *Uniform for Harry,* Follett, 1962; Jean H. Richards, *Why Do People Pray?,* Rand McNally, 1965; Charles Tritten, *Heidi Grows Up,* Whitman, 1966; Selma Gordon, *Amy Loves Goodbyes,* Platt & Munk, 1966; Charles

Tritten, *Heidi's Children,* Golden Press, 1967; Jean H. Richards, *When God Imagined a World,* Rand McNally, 1967; Lawrence S. Lowery, *Peter & the Rocks,* Western, 1969; Beatrix Potter, *Story of Peter Rabbit,* Platt & Munk, 1969; Lawrence S. Lowery and Albert B. Carr, *Sweet as a Rose,* Western, 1969; Carol Woodard, *Busy Family,* Fortress, 1969.

Carol Woodard, *It's Fun to Have a Birthday,* Fortress, 1970; Norah Smaridge, *Raggedy Ann: A Thank You, Please & I Love You Book,* Western, 1970; Eric W. Johnson, *Stolen Ruler,* Lippincott, 1970; Lois Raebeck, *Who Am I? Activity Songs for Young Children,* Follett, 1970; M. Kelley, *Greenup: The Story of a Buffalo,* McGraw, 1971; Jane Britten, *House for Willie: A Story About Time,* Western, 1971; Ruthanna Long, *Ten Little Chipmunks,* Western, 1971; Eric W. Johnson, *Escape Into the Zoo,* Lippincott, 1971; Mary Carey, *Raggedy Ann & the Sad & Glad Day,* Western, 1972; Eleanor G. Vance, *From Little to Big,* Follett, 1972; Valerie Pitt, *Let's Find Out About the Community,* Watts, 1972; Ray Sipherd, *The White Kite,* Bradbury, 1972; Barbara S. Hazen, *Raggedy Ann & Andy & the Rainy Day Circus,* Western, 1973; Norah Smaridge, *Raggedy Andy—The I Can Do It, You Can Do It Book,* Western, 1973; Jane W. Watson, *Tanya & the Geese,* Garrard, 1974; R. J. Lefkowitz, *Push! Pull! Stop! Go! A Book About Forces & Motion,* Parents' Magazine Press, 1975.

Barbara Hazen, *Raggedy Ann & the Cookie Snatcher,* Western, 1977; Polly Curran, *Raggedy Ann & Andy: The Little Grey Kitten,* Western, 1977; Jean Tymme, *I Like to See: A*

"Oh, dear!" said Tanya.
"I left the gate open."
■ (From *Tanya and the Geese* by Jane Werner Watson. Illustrated by June Goldsborough.)

Book About the Senses, Western, 1978; Judy Delton, *It Happened on Thursday,* edited by Kathy Pacici, Whitman, 1978; *Mother Goose on the Farm,* Western, 1978; Marjorie Schwaljie, *Raggedy Andy & The Jump-up Contest,* Western, 1978. Also illustrated *Gingerbread Boy,* Platt & Munk.

SIDELIGHTS: "I give talks to children in elementary schools in Westchester on being a children's book illustrator. I do a great deal of educational aids—films, etc. besides text books.

"I have an abiding interest in animals. I have two dogs, a female bull mastiff and a male poodle, Penny and Tony.

"I studied with Fred Conway and Philip Guston."

GREENFELD, Howard

EDUCATION: Holds a M.A. degree; attended the University of Chicago, New York University, and Columbia University. *Residence:* Camaiore, Italy.

CAREER: Taught English in Rome, Italy; worked under Bennett Cerf at Random House, New York City; established Orion Press (publishing company; now a part of Viking Press), Florence, Italy; J. Philip O'Hara (publishing company), Chicago, Ill., editor, beginning 1971; author of books for young people. *Awards, honors:* Follett Award, 1968, for *Marc Chagall; Gertrude Stein* was selected for the Children's Book Showcase in 1974; *Books: From Writer to Reader* was selected for the American Institute of Graphic Arts Book Show in 1976 and was a Junior Literary Guild selection, September, 1976.

WRITINGS—Nonfiction: *Marc Chagall* (illustrated with reproductions of the artist's work), Follett, 1967; *The Waters of November,* Follett, 1969; *Pablo Picasso: An Introduction,* Follett, 1971; *The Impressionist Revolution,* Doubleday, 1972; *Gertrude Stein: A Biography,* Crown, 1973; *F. Scott Fitzgerald,* Crown, 1974; *They Came to Paris,* Crown, 1975; *Books: From Writer to Reader* (Junior Literary Guild selection), Crown, 1976; *Chanukah,* Holt, 1976; *Gypsies,* Crown, 1977.

SIDELIGHTS: Howard Greenfeld was raised in New York City and in neighboring New Rochelle. He attended the University of Kansas, University of Chicago, and New York University before completing a masters degree at Columbia University. "After graduation from high school I felt that I needed a change and headed west to the University of Kansas. After a year there, I moved on to the University of Chicago, where I also stayed a year. This need to change, this restlessness, continued until I finally—and somewhat miraculously since I was a poor student—completed my M.A. at Columbia University. The one thing that remained constant was my fascination with the world of books."

This fascination for books led Howard Greenfeld, after graduation from Columbia, to the editorial department of Random House, a New York publishing company. There he learned the publishing business and all its phases—he proofread, copy edited, read manuscripts and wrote reports. After a few years he left Random House and started his own publishing business. "After a few years . . . my restlessness returned, this time combined with an ambition to start my own publishing house. So I moved to Florence, Italy, where I

founded The Orion Press. Why Europe? For two reasons: one, I had always wanted to live in Europe and was especially drawn to Italy; and two, printing, binding, and overhead costs were considerably lower than they were in America. My goal was an ambitious one: to publish serious works of literature, beautifully produced, at a reasonable price.

"If I had known the difficulties involved, I would probably have abandoned the project before I began, but I am now grateful for my youthful ignorance since for eight years I think I did what I set out to do. I am very proud of the books I published." [Jean F. Mercier, "Howard Greenfeld," *Publishers Weekly,* September 3, 1973.[1]]

The company that he founded, Orion Press, is now a part of Viking Press. Greenfeld, the publisher, then turned his direction toward writing books. His first book, a biography of Marc Chagall, was published in 1967. "After a while it seemed that there was only one thing that I hadn't done, and that was to write a book. Thus, I was very happy, as well as somewhat apprehensive, when another publisher asked me to write a biography of Marc Chagall for young people. This was my chance to learn about publishing from another and most important point of view—that of the author. I enjoyed the experience so much that I've gone on to write eight more books, have given up working in an office, and now spend most of my time writing in a small farmhouse in Camaiore, a beautiful little town in central Italy."

In 1968 *Marc Chagall* won the Follett Award. In writing biographies for young people Greenfeld researches his subjects thoroughly. "I have to know the people I'm writing about and to care about them. I couldn't do it any other way."[1]

Familiar with all areas of book publishing, Greenfeld wrote *Books: From Writer to Reader,* published in 1976. "Of all the books I've written, none has given me more satisfaction than *Books: From Writer to Reader.* It has given me a chance to answer the questions asked me throughout the years and it has also allowed me to pass on the knowledge and experience I've gained in the course of my fascinating years in the world of book publishing."[1]

Marc Chagall was the result of Greenfeld's first effort in saturating himself in the life and times of a well-known person. "Mr. Greenfeld loves his subject; that is evident on every page. He wants his readers to appreciate the genius of Chagall and this book will certainly set them on the right road. . . . Young people should appreciate the beauty of this book—the illustrations, the painter himself, and the author's warm style," noted a critic for *Young Readers' Review.* A reviewer for *Book World* observed, "The fantasy, gaiety and brilliant color that mark the work of . . . Marc Chagall, have made him a special favorite of young people, who should welcome this penetrating biography. . . . Writing with clarity and warmth, the author traces Chagall's life. . . . The book itself is well printed, handsomely designed and illustrated. . . ."

One of Greenfeld's more recent biographical studies is *They Came to Paris.* In this book the author focuses on Americans living in Paris during the 1920's. A reviewer for *Booklist* wrote, "In what he calls 'a collage of events and portraits,' the author . . . affords a real sense of the colorful decade of the twenties. . . . Although not all the personalities will be familiar to teenagers, this is a vivid overview that complements standard biographies of the major figures of the period."

Gertrude Stein in her sitting room at 27, rue de Fleurus. Above her head is the portrait Picasso painted of her. ■ (From *Gertrude Stein* by Howard Greenfeld. Photo courtesy of *Pictorial Parade*.)

The author did not restrict himself to writing biographies however, and in *The Waters of November*, Greenfeld gave an account of the flood that struck Florence, Italy in 1966. "[The story is] vividly told and illustrated with stunning pictures of the flood. . . . Almost as moving is the description of the restoration now . . . in progress," commented Zena Sutherland in a *Saturday Review* article. "A large, fascinating book with numerous, beautifully printed photographs . . . ," wrote a critic for *Commonweal*.

Commenting on *Books: From Writer to Reader*, a reviewer for *Horn Book* noted, "Every facet of bookmaking . . . receives careful, evenhanded coverage. . . . The author maintains a particularly good balance between the often opposing demands of commercial success and artistic integrity and includes an excellent discussion of the financial problems involved in the publication of a book. . . . Useful and informative. . . ."

FOR MORE INFORMATION SEE: Young Readers Review, March, 1968; *Book World,* June 2, 1968; *Saturday Review,* November 8, 1969; *Commonweal,* November 21, 1969; *Horn Book,* April and June, 1973, February, 1976, April, 1977, June, 1978; Jean F. Mercier, "Howard Greenfeld," *Publishers Weekly,* September 3, 1973; *Booklist,* November 15, 1975.

GREENFIELD, Eloise 1929-

PERSONAL: Born May 17, 1929, in Parmele, N.C.; daughter of Weston W. and Lessie (Jones) Little; married Robert J. Greenfield (a procurement specialist), April 29, 1950; children: Steven, Monica. *Education:* Attended Miner Teachers College, 1946-49. *Agent:* Curtis Brown Ltd., 575 Madison Ave., New York, N.Y. 10022.

CAREER: U.S. Patent Office, Washington, D.C., clerk-typist, 1949-56, supervisory patent assistant, 1956-60; worked as a secretary, case-control technician, and an administrative assistant in Washington, D.C. from 1964-68. Co-director of adult fiction of District of Columbia Black Writer's Workshop, 1971-73, director of children's literature, 1973-74; writer-in-residence with District of Columbia Commission on the Arts, 1973. *Awards, honors:* Carter G. Woodson Award for *Rosa Parks,* 1974; Irma Simonton Black Award for *She Come Bringing Me That Little Baby Girl,* 1974; A.L.A. Notable Book, *Me and Neesie,* 1975, *Honey, I Love,* 1978; Jane Addams Children's Book Award for *Paul Robeson,* 1976; Coretta Scott King Award for *Africa Dream,* 1978; received citations for body of work from Council on Interracial Books for Children, 1975, District of Columbia Association of School Librarians, 1977, and Celebrations in Learning, 1977.

WRITINGS—Children's books: (Contributor) Alma Murray and Robert Thomas, editors, *The Journey: Scholastic Black Literature,* Scholastic Book Service, 1970; *Bubbles* (picture book), Drum & Spear Press, 1972, reprinted as *Good News,* Coward, 1977; *Rosa Parks* (biography), Crowell, 1973; (contributor) Karen S. Kleiman and Mel Cebulash, editors, *Dou-*

ELOISE GREENFIELD

I couldn't play with her all the time, even if she was my best friend. ■ (From *Me and Nessie* by Eloise Greenfield. Illustrated by Moneta Barnett.)

ble Action Unit Book 1, Scholastic Book Services, 1973; *Sister* (novel), Crowell, 1974; *She Come Bringing Me That Little Baby Girl* (picture book), Lippincott, 1974; (contributor) Joseph Claro and Katherine Robinson, *Love,* Scholastic Book Services, 1975; *Paul Robeson* (biography), Crowell, 1975; *Me and Neesie* (picture book; ALA Notable Book), Crowell, 1975; *First Pink Light* (picture book), Crowell, 1976; *Mary McLeod Bethune* (biography), Crowell, 1977; *Africa Dream* (picture book), John Day, 1977; *Honey, I Love* (poetry; ALA Notable Book), Crowell, 1978; (with Lessie Jones Little) *I Can Do It by Myself* (picture book), Crowell, 1978; *Talk About a Family* (novel), Lippincott, 1978; (contributor) William K. Durr, John Pescosolido, Willie Mae Poetter, *Encore,* Houghton, 1978; (contributor) Louise Matteoni, Wilson H. Lane, Floyd Sucher, Thomas D. Yawkey, *Daystreaming,* The Economy Co., 1978; (contributor) Matteoni, Lane, Sucher, Yawkey, *Forerunners,* The Economy Co., 1978; (contributor) Zena Sutherland, *Burning Bright,* Open Court Publishing, 1979; (with Lessie Jones Little) *Childtimes: A Three-Generation Memoir* (autobiography), Crowell, 1979. Contributor to *Black World, Ebony Jr!, Negro History Bulletin, Scholastic Scope, Ms., The Horn Book, Interracial Books for Children Bulletin.*

SIDELIGHTS: "I was born during the early days of the Great Depression, the second oldest of five children, and grew up during its worst years. People were starving. Jobs were scarce and paid little more than nothing. While I was still an infant, my family moved to Washington, D.C., where my father was able to find work, and though money was far from plentiful, we managed. I remember my childhood with pleasure. Family, neighbors and friends made it an enjoyable time.

"Writing was the farthest thing from my mind when I was growing up. I loved words, but I loved to read them, not write them. I loved their sounds and rhythms, and even some of their aberrations, such as homonyms and silent letters, though the pluralizing of 'leaf' as 'leaves' annoyed me. I could think of no good reason for getting rid of that f.

"Until I was fourteen, there was no library within close walking distance of our house, so every few weeks my father would take us in the car to the nearest one to get a supply of books. Finally, though, a branch of the public library was opened in the basement of a nearby apartment building. For the next few years, I practically lived there, and I worked there part-time during the two years that I was in college.

"I wish I could remember just what it was that made me sit down one day and write my very first rhyme. But I can't. I remember only that I was a young wife and mother working full-time as a clerk-typist, and that for some reason I began to write. First, rhymes that I hoped were humorous, then songs. There was a television program called 'Songs for Sale' that invited the viewing audience to send in original songs, the best of which would be played on the air, and I submitted one of mine. I waited anxiously for a favorable reply, but instead the song was returned with the information that the show was going off the air. I've always had the unpleasant suspicion that after looking at my song, the musical director had flung it across the room, lifted his arms and his eyes heavenward, and quit, followed by the rest of the staff.

"My next attempts were short stories. I wrote three, and they were promptly rejected. It was obvious that I had no talent, so I gave up writing forever.

"Forever lasted five or six years, during which time I learned what writing was—that it was not the result of talent alone, but of talent combined with skills that had to be developed. So I set about practicing them.

"Writing is now, along with my relationship with my husband, son and daughter, an important and enriching part of my life. I make it the major pursuit of most of my days. Writing and rewriting. Trying always to write a book that children will want to live with, live *in,* for as long as it takes them to read it; hoping that some part of the book will stay inside them for the rest of their lives. Reading can generate a special kind of excitement that I call word-madness, and it is this that I try to create. The attempt itself is exciting. Moving words around on paper. Accepting gratefully the miracle of words that come without effort. Struggling to find those that don't.

"And then, there's that added dimension—a cause. There's a desperate need for more Black literature for children, for a large body of literature in which Black children can see themselves and their lives and history reflected. I want to do my share in building it."

FOR MORE INFORMATION SEE: Negro History Bulletin, April/May, 1975; *Living Black American Authors,* 1973; *Encore* Magazine, December 6, 1976; *Horn Book,* April, 1977; *Essence* Magazine, June

HALLIBURTON, Warren J. 1924-

PERSONAL: Born August 2, 1924, in New York, N.Y.; son of Richard H. and Blanche (Watson) Halliburton; married Frances Fletcher; children: Cheryl, Stephanie, Warren, Jr., Jenna. *Education:* New York University, B.S., 1949; Columbia University, M.Ed., 1975. *Home:* 22 Scribner Hill Rd., Wilton, Ct. 06897.

CAREER: Prairie View Agricultural and Mechanical College, Prairie View, Tex., instructor in English, 1949; Bishop College, Dallas, Tex., instructor in English, 1951; Institute of International Education, associate, 1952; *Recorder* (newspaper), New York, N.Y., reporter and columnist, 1953; teacher and dean in Brooklyn, N.Y. high school, 1953-60; coordinator for New York City Board of Education, and associate of New York State Department of Education, 1960-65; McGraw-Hill, Inc., New York, N.Y., editor, 1967; Hamilton-Kirkland Colleges, Clinton, N.Y., visiting professor of English, 1971-72; Teachers College, Columbia University, New York, N.Y., editor, research associate, and director of scholarly journal, government program, and Ethnic Studies Center, 1972-77; currently editor and writer, *Reader's Digest,* New York, N.Y.

WRITINGS: (Editor with Mauri E. Peklonen) *New Worlds of Literature,* Harcourt, 1966; (adapter) *Negro Doctor,* McGraw, 1968; *The Heist* (novel), McGraw, 1969; *Cry, Baby!* (novel), McGraw, 1969; *Some Things that Glitter* (novel), McGraw, 1969; (with William L. Katz) *American Majorities and Minorities: A Syllabus of United States History for Secondary Schools,* Arno, 1970; (with Laurence Swinburne and Steve Broudy) *They Had a Dream,* Pyramid Publications, 1970; (editor and contributor) *America's Color Caravan,* four volumes, Singer Graflex, 1971; *The Picture Life of Jesse Jackson,* Watts, 1972; *The History of Black Americans,* Harcourt, 1973; (with Ernest Kaiser) *Harlem: A History of Broken Dreams,* Doubleday, 1974; *Composing* with Sentences, Cambridge, 1974; *Pathways to the World of English*, Glove, 1974; *The Fighting Red Tails: America's First Black Airmen*, Contemporary Perspectives, 1979; *Flight to the Stars: The Life of Daniel James, Jr.*, Contemporary Perspectives, 1980.

Editor of text editions of Jack London's *Call of the Wild*, Douglas Wallop's *The Year the Yankees Lost the Pennant*, and Paddy Chayefsky's *Marty* and *Printer's Measure*, all McGraw, 1968. Contributor of about one hundred short stories, adaptations, and articles to periodicals; writer of fifteen filmstrips and a motion picture, "Dig!"

SIDELIGHTS: "Writing is a sanctuary of self-realization, affording me the opportunity for adventure and discovery of my relation with the world. This is a rare if not unique privilege in today's pigeon-holing society."

HOBBIES AND OTHER INTERESTS: Jogging, a follow-through of Halliburton's days in track and field competition.

HANN, Jacquie   1951-

PERSONAL: Born May 18, 1951, in New York; daughter of Walter and Irmgard (Pach) Hann. *Education:* University of Wisconsin, Madison, B.S., 1972; also attended Parsons School of Design, 1973-74, and School of Visual Arts, 1974. *Home address:* 40 Harrison St., Apt. 34D, New York, N.Y. 10013.

CAREER: Instructor, Brooklyn College; writer and illustrator, 1975—. *Member:* Graphic Artists Guild (board of directors).

WRITINGS—Self-illustrated children's books: *That Man Is Talking to His Toes,* Four Winds, 1976; *Where's Mark?,* Four Winds, 1977; *Up Day, Down Day,* Four Winds, 1978; *Big Trouble,* Four Winds, 1978; *Crybaby,* Four Winds, 1979.

Illustrator: Mary Blount Christian, *J. J. Leggett, Secret Agent,* Lothrop, 1978; Elizabeth Levy, *The Tryouts,* Four Winds, 1979.

JACQUIE HANN

(From *That Man Is Talking to His Toes* by Jacquie Hann. Illustrated by the author.)

WORK IN PROGRESS: Writing and illustrating children's books.

SIDELIGHTS: "As a child, I never was interested in reading books, but I always wrote stories and drew pictures. I never wanted to be told anything. I wanted to experience everything for myself. Doing children's books intrigued me for a long time—it was an even blend of words and pictures, and it was art for a purpose.

"I wrote my first children's book in college with a friend. I illustrated it, set the type, printed it, and bound it. We had fantasies of being sent on a world tour for our 'Caldecott winner'—but of course it never even got published.

"I think the most important component in children's books is humor. It can be in any form—whimsy, satire, nonsense.

"I try to write books about kids as they really are, and I usually do that by delving into my own childhood to remember what I thought and felt. I don't believe in preaching morals to kids. I think kids have a great deal of common sense and just need the encouragement to think for themselves and use their imaginations."

FOR MORE INFORMATION SEE: Publishers Weekly, February 28, 1977.

JON HASSLER

HASSLER, Jon (Francis) 1933-

PERSONAL: Born March 30, 1933, in Minneapolis, Minn.; son of Leo Blaise (a grocer) and Ellen (a teacher; maiden name, Callinan) Hassler; married Marie Schmitt, August 18, 1956; children: Michael, Elizabeth, David. *Education:* St. John's University, Collegeville, Minn., B.A., 1955; University of North Dakota, M.A., 1960. *Religion:* Roman Catholic. *Home address:* 721 N. 8th St., Brainerd, Minn. 56401.

CAREER: High school English teacher in Melrose, Minn., 1955-56, Fosston, Minn., 1956-69, Park Rapids, Minn., 1959-65; Bemidji State University, Bemidji, Minn., instructor in English, 1965-68; Brainerd Community College, Brainerd, Minn., instructor in English, 1968—. *Awards, honors:* Creative Writing fellowship, Minnesota State Arts Board, 1977; Friends of American Writers Novel of the Year Award, 1978, for *Staggerford.*

WRITINGS: Four Miles to Pinecone (novel for young adults), Warne, 1977; *Staggerford* (novel), Atheneum, 1977; *Simon's Night* (novel), Atheneum, 1979; *Jemmy* (novel for young adults), Atheneum, 1980. Contributor of short stories to literary journals.

WORK IN PROGRESS: The Love Hunter, a novel.

HOBBIES AND OTHER INTERESTS: "Landscapes (gazing at them, walking through them, and painting pictures of them)."

FOR MORE INFORMATION SEE: New York Times Book Review, 1977; *Publishers Weekly,* February 28, 1977.

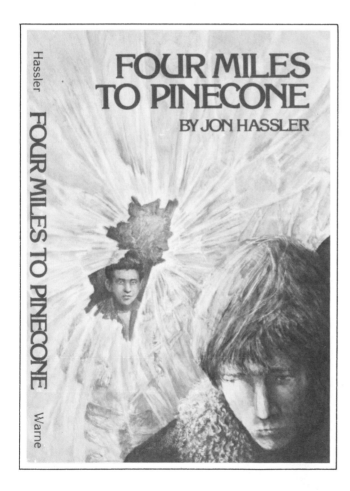

How can you turn in your best friend? How can you condone breaking the law? ▪ (From *Four Miles to Pinecone* by Jon Hassler. Jacket illustration by Ronald Himler.)

ARTHUR HAWKINS

HAWKINS, Arthur 1903-

PERSONAL: Born April 9, 1903, in Cumberland, Md.; son of Arthur Hanson (a surgeon) and Louise (Price) Hawkins; married Patricia Laporte, 1930; married Nancy Pilson (a writer), June 28, 1940; children: Arthur III, Barbara (Mrs. Julian Palmore III), Nancy (Mrs. Richard N. Field), Gilbert Huston. *Education:* University of Virginia, B.S., 1925; studied at Art Students League of New York, 1925-27. *Politics:* Independent Democrat. *Religion:* Episcopalian. *Home and office:* 396 Allaire Ave., Leonia, N.J. 07605.

CAREER: Designer, painter, art director; currently working as consulting art director in book publishing and advertising sales promotion fields. Speaker on advertising arts and judge of exhibitions. *Member:* Society of Illustrators (life member), Art Directors Club (life member and past president; New York), Authors Guild.

WRITINGS: (Editor with Edward N. Gotshall) *Advertising Directions: Trends in Visual Advertising,* Art Directions Book Co., 1959; (editor) *The Art Director at Work: How Fifteen Medal-Winning Exhibits Were Conceived and Executed,* Hastings House, 1959; (editor) *Illustrators '59,* Hastings House, 1959; *The Steak Book,* Doubleday, 1966; *Who Needs a Cookbook: How to Make 222 Delicious International Dishes with a Minimum of Direction,* Prentice-Hall, 1968; *The Antisocial Cookbook,* Madison Laboratories, 1968; *The Complete Seafood Cookbook,* Prentice-Hall, 1970; (with Aileen Paul) *Kids Cooking,* Doubleday, 1970; *Cook It Quick: 203 Delicious Half-Hour Recipes,* Prentice-Hall, 1971; (co-author) *Chef's Special,* Prentice-Hall, 1972; (co-author) *Chef's Magic,* Prentice-Hall, 1972; (with wife, Nancy Hawkins) *The Low Cost Meat Book: First Class Fare with Economy Meats,* Doubleday, 1974; (with Aileen Paul) *Candies, Cookies, Cakes,* Doubleday, 1974; (with Nancy Hawkins)

American Bi-Centennial Cookbook, Prentice-Hall, 1975; *The Architectural Cookbook,* Architectural Record, 1975; (with Nancy Hawkins) *Nantucket and Other New England Cooking,* Hastings House, 1976; (with Nancy Hawkins) *The American Regional Cookbook: Recipes from Yesterday and Today for the Modern Cook,* Prentice-Hall, 1976.

SIDELIGHTS: "After spending most of my life as a designer I found myself, quite accidentally, designing a series of cookbooks, among them *The Treasury of Great Cooking* by Vincent Price. I became interested in food and visited many of the great haute-cuisine restaurants in France, Italy and Spain. I decided to have a go at a cookbook and wrote *The Steak Book* which enjoyed considerable success. I followed with others and eventually was joined by my wife—a great cook—and we have produced a number of reasonably successful books as a team ever since.

"I continue to do advertising design, which was my first love, and will do it as long as I have a client who wishes to employ me.

"Between jobs and books, I paint. Although I had academic training at the Art Students League in New York, my work is all abstract."

Hawkins has also designed more than one thousand book jackets.

ROBERT E. HAYDEN

HAYDEN, Robert E(arl)   1913-

PERSONAL: Born August 4, 1913, in Detroit, Mich. *Education:* Wayne State University, B.A.; University of Michigan, M.A. *Home address:* 1201 Gardner Ave., Ann Arbor, Mich. 48104. *Office:* Department of English, University of Michigan, Ann Arbor, Mich. 48104.

CAREER: Fisk University, Nashville, Tenn., 1946-69, began as assistant professor, became professor of English; University of Michigan, Ann Arbor, professor of English, 1969—. *Awards, honors:* Jules and Avery Hopwood Poetry Awards from University of Michigan, 1938 and 1942; Julius Rosewald fellowship in creative writing, 1947; Ford Foundation fellowship in Mexico, 1954-55; grand prize from World Festival of Negro Arts, 1966, for *A Ballad of Remembrance*.

WRITINGS: Heart-Shape in the Dust (poems), Falcon Press, 1940; *Figure of Time* (poems), Hemphill Press, 1955; *A Ballad of Remembrance* (poems), P. Bremen, 1962; *Selected Poems,* October House, 1966; (editor and author of introduction) *Kaleidoscope: Poems by American Negro Poets* (juvenile), Harcourt, 1967; (contributor) Alain LeRoy Locke, editor, *The New Negro,* Atheneum, 1968; *Words in the Mourning Time* (poems), October House, 1970; (with David J. Burrows and Frederick R. Lapides) *Afro-American Literature: An Introduction,* Harcourt, 1971; *Night-Blooming Cereus* (reissue of book originally published as *Poems*), Broadside Press, 1972; (editor with James Edwin Miller) *The United States in Literature,* Scott, Foresman, 1973; *Angle of Ascent: New and Selected Poems,* Liveright, 1975. Also author with Myron O'Higgins of *The Lion and the Archer,* 1948.

Work represented in anthologies. Contributor to literary magazines.

HINTON, S(usan) E(loise)   1950-

PERSONAL: Born in Tulsa, Okla.; married David Inhofe, September, 1970. *Education:* Graduated from the University of Tulsa, 1970. *Residence:* Tulsa, Okla.

CAREER: Began writing at the age of sixteen; lived for six months in southern Spain. *Awards, honors: That Was Then, This Is Now* was chosen as a Notable Book by the American Library Association; *The Outsiders* was chosen by the New York *Herald Tribune* as one of the best teen-age books for 1967, and received the *Media & Methods* Maxi Award in 1975; both books were selected as Honor Books in the *Chicago Tribune Book World*'s Children's Spring Book Festival.

WRITINGS—Fiction: *The Outsiders,* Viking, 1967; *That Was Then, This Is Now* (ALA Notable Book), Viking, 1971; *Rumble Fish,* Delacorte, 1975.

ADAPTATIONS—Recording: "Rumble Fish," Viking Press.

SIDELIGHTS: Hinton was born and raised in Tulsa, Oklahoma in 1950. Her first book, *The Outsiders,* was published when she was seventeen, and was written the summer she was sixteen. "I felt the greasers were getting knocked when they didn't deserve it. The custom, for instance, of driving by a shabby boy and screaming 'Greaser!' at him always

(From *Rumble Fish* by S. E. Hinton. Jacket painting by Gary Watson.)

made me boil. But it was the cold-blooded beating of a friend of mine that gave me the idea of writing a book; I wanted to do something that would change people's opinion of greasers. Some 'socs' (the abbreviation of socials) didn't like the way my friend was combing his hair, so they beat him up! Another friend of mine never got enough to eat and frequently slept in the bus station because his father was always beating him up. The socs teased *him* because of his grades. Grades!

"The *Outsiders,* like most of the things I write, is written from a boy's point of view. That's why I'm listed as S. E. Hinton rather than Susan on the book; since my subject was gang fights I figured most boys would look at the book and think, 'What can a chick know about stuff like that?' None of the events in the book are taken from life, but the rest—how kids think and live and feel—is for real. The characters—Dallas, who wasn't tough enough; Sodapop, the happy-go-lucky dropout; Bob, the rich kid whose arrogance cost him his life; Ponyboy, the sensitive, green-eyed greaser who didn't want to be a hood—they're all real to me, though I didn't put my friends into the book. The characters are mixtures of people I know, with a bit of myself thrown in.

"Many of my friends are greasers, but I'm not. I have friends who are rich too, but nobody will ever call me a soc—I've seen what money and too much idle time and parental approval can do to people. That's why I tried not to be too hard on the socs in the book. The thing is, they are so cool. Cool people mean nothing to me—they're living behind masks, and I'm always wondering, 'Is there a real person underneath?'

S. E. HINTON

"It's great when people come up and say, 'I read your book and liked it.' But I've always been a quiet person, the kind who takes her time about things. Schedules and details are beyond me—I nearly flunked creative writing because I couldn't spell and couldn't write under pressure. And I'm shy around older people, which doesn't make publicizing the book much fun. I do the best I can but sometimes I wish I'd never written the thing. Then I remember why I wrote it and I don't mind so much.

"My younger sister hasn't once said she's sick of hearing about the book although I know she must be. My mother, after the first shock of reading it ('Susie, where *did* you pick up all of this?'), is selling it to everyone she meets. But it's the reaction of my greaser friends I'm happiest about. 'Did you put me in it?' is the question they ask most, not 'What could you know about the way we feel?' They have confidence in me." ["Face to Face," *Seventeen*, October, 1967.[1]]

In 1970 Hinton was graduated from the University of Tulsa and in September of that year, married David Inhofe. In 1975 her third and most recent book, *Rumble Fish*, was published. "The gang that inspired my book is gone now, and I'm too old to go around in jeans and carry a knife. But I don't need to anymore; I can still be a friend in dresses and make-up. Maybe not a buddy, but a friend. And if I ever forget how it is to be a teen-ager in a savage social system, I've got it all written down."[1]

While Hinton's first book was acclaimed by book critics and applauded by the younger generation, many parents objected to the characters' unruly and often violent nature. Some adults became concerned that the storyline might encourage teens to idolize a life of lawlessness and destruction, while others felt it was wrong for young people to be exposed to violence in literature under any circumstances. Nevertheless, it was the publication and success of *The Outsider* that enabled Hinton to attend the University of Tulsa.

Hinton's latest book, *Rumble Fish*, continues the theme of delinquent youths. A reviewer for *Horn Book* observed, "The Dialogue and the boy's monologue are vibrant and authentic, and the narrative moves quickly and dramatically from one event to another." In addition however, the critic noted, "[Hinton's] writing has the same style and the same perception as it had when she was seventeen. Instead of becoming a vehicle for growth and development, the book, unfortunately, simply echoes what came before. . . ."

FOR MORE INFORMATION SEE: New York Times Book Review, May 7, 1967; *Saturday Review*, May 13, 1967; *Seventeen*, October, 1967; Zena Sutherland, "The Teen-Ager Speaks," *Saturday Review*, January 27, 1968; *Horn Book*, August, 1971, December, 1975.

JAMES, Will(iam Roderick) 1892-1942

PERSONAL: Born June 6, 1892, near Great Falls, Mont.; died September 3, 1942, in Hollywood, Calif.; son of William (a rancher; died, 1896); orphaned at age four; adopted by Jean Beaupré (a French Canadian trapper and prospector); married Alice Conradt, 1920. *Education:* Had no formal education. *Home:* 12,000 acre ranch in Billings, Montana.

CAREER: Western writer and illustrator. Began working at age thirteen on horse and cattle ranches, and later on western and Canadian ranges helping to capture wild horses. He also performed in rodeos; began writing and drawing while convalescing from a fall from a bucking horse. *Military service:* U.S. Army, Mounted Scouts during World War I. *Awards, honors:* Newbery Medal, 1927, for *Smoky*.

WRITINGS—All self-illustrated and published by Scribner except as noted: *Cowboys North and South*, 1924, reprinted, Arno, 1975; *The Drifting Cowboy*, 1925; *Smoky: The Cowhorse* (novel), 1926, reprinted, 1965; *Cow Country*, 1927, reissued, University of Nebraska Press, 1973; *Sand*, 1929; *Lone Cowboy: My Life Story* (autobiography), 1930, reprinted, 1963; *Big-Enough*, 1931; *Sun Up: Tales of the Cow Camps* (short stories), 1931; *Uncle Bill: A Tale of Two Kids and a Cowboy*, 1932; *All in the Day's Riding* (short stories), 1933; *The Three Mustangeers*, 1933; *In the Saddle with Uncle Bill*, 1935; *Home Ranch*, 1935; *Scorpion: A Good Bad Horse*, 1936, reissued, University of Nebraska Press, 1975; *Look-See with Uncle Bill*, 1938; *Flint Spears: Cowboy Rodeo Contestant*, 1938; *The Dark Horse*, 1939; *My First Horse*, 1940; *Horses I've Known*, 1940; *The American Cowboy*, 1942; *Book of Cowboy Stories*, 1951.

Other: *Young Cowboy* (excerpts from *Big-Enough* and *Sun Up*), Scribner, 1935; *Cowboy in the Making* (excerpts from

Lone Cowboy), Scribner, 1937; *The Will James Cowboy Book,* edited by Alice Dalgliesh, Scribner, 1938; (contributor) "I Learned to Ride," in *Montana Margins,* edited by Joseph K. Howard, Yale University Press, 1946.

ADAPTATIONS—Movies: "Lone Cowboy," Paramount Pictures, 1933; "Smoky," Fox Film Corp., 1933, Twentieth Century-Fox, starring Fred MacMurray, 1946; "Sand," starring Rory Calhoun, Twentieth Century-Fox, 1949; "The Education of Smoky" (excerpts from the Twentieth Century-Fox motion picture, "Smoky"; 11 minutes, black and white, with a teacher's guide), Teaching Film Custodians, 1952.

SIDELIGHTS: **June 6, 1892.** Born in Judith Basin County near Great Falls, Montana. "No tag was needed around my neck where I came into the world at, for I don't think there was another child to within thirty miles of there. I was born close to the sod, and if I could of seen far enough I could of glimpsed ponies thru the flap of the tent on my first day while listening to the bellering of cattle and the ringing of my dad's spurs.

"My dad was a Texan, born and raised in West Texas. My mother was from Southern California. Both was of the Scotch-Irish nation, with some Spanish blood on my mother's side. I was about a year old when I lost my mother, and by the time I was four, my dad went and joined her acrost that Range Beyond.

"I remember the time of my dad's death, but to go back on my earlier childhood I have to use the tally of what an old timer told me, the Old-timer who adopted and raised me. He seemed to know my dad mighty well.

"According to what he told me, My dad had come up trail from Texas with many herds of the southern cattle during the 'eighties.' He'd delivered some herds as far north as Canada. After the last drive, he'd come to figger that for a cow country the North was sure enough all of that. It was colder up there but the grass was sure a plenty, so was the water, and there was no droughts, like there was in the South, no tick fever and it sure was the place to mature beef.

"So, early one spring he sells out what holdings he has in Texas, hooks up four horses to a wagon, has my mother take the lines, and he himself brings up the rear with ten head of picked saddle horses. (The Old-timer often said that the brands on some of them horses was sort of hard to read.)

"It was my dad's and mother's first intentions to keep going till they reached some place in Alberta, Canada, and start over again in the cow business up there. Then I comes along and stops the outfit in Montana. If I'd been born a month later I'd been a Canadian, and four months sooner would of made me a Texan.

"... I was lonesome. I was often calling for someone, and I'd set down for long spells and just stargaze. It was during them lonesome spells that I would often pick up things and want to make marks, tracing something in the dirt with a stick, or, with a hunk of charcoal I'd pick up from the last fire at the branding pen, I'd go and mark up the rough boards of the bunk-house porch.... That winter, while the cold winds blowed outside and the snow piled up and I couldn't go out, is when I first got acquainted with a pencil and some blank paper, and I spent many hours a day making funny marks which, to anybody else, didn't mean nothing but to

WILL JAMES

me meant a lot. To me they was all pictures of animals, mostly horses. My dad would say they was sure fine and once in a while he'd criticize and pass such remarks as 'The hind legs on that horse are a little too straight, son' or 'you forgot the dew-claws on that steer.'" [Will James, *Lone Cowboy: My Life Story,* Scribner, 1930.[1]]

1896. Orphaned at age four. "As it was [my father] was peacefully prodding cattle thru the chutes to the squeezer when his time come. There was quite a herd of cattle in that same corral where he was working, and amongst that herd was a big 'staggy' steer that'd just broke a horn. The blood from that broken horn was running down that steer's face to his nose and he was on the fight, not with his own breed, but with anything strange, like a human.

"He seen my dad a standing there, and my dad, being busy, wasn't paying no attention. He'd just stooped down for the prodding stick he'd dropped when the big steer caught him broadside with his one good horn, hoisted him in the air, took him on a ways and then flung him against the chute. The horn had pierced him thru the stomach like as if it had been done with a knife, only worse.

(From *Smoky the Cow Horse* by Will James. Illustrated by the author.)

"The cowboys rushed to him, straightened him from the crumpled position he was in, and, so they told the Old-timer, they seen at a glance that nothing could be done. But, they said there was a smile on my dad's face when, after a while, he opened his eyes, and the first words he'd said was, 'Well, boys, I'm due to join her soon now'. . . . Then, after a while, he'd added on, 'The only thing I regret is to leave little Billy behind. . . . Tell old trapper Jean that all my gatherings are his and to see that my boy is well took care of. I leave him to him.'

"He'd talked on for a little while and within an hour from the time the steer had picked him up he'd closed his eyes and went on the Long Sleep.''[1]

Adopted by Jean Beaupré or "Bopy" as James affectionately called him. "The Old-timer went on talking and then I got the drift that him and me was going to be pardners, pardners for good, and that made me feel still bigger. He told me of what my dad had said before he died and I knowed then why he took me away. This wasn't going to be no little camping trip, and I was glad, for I liked to roam and, next to my dad, there was no one I'd rather roamed with than the Old-timer.

"Jean Beaupré was his name, or one of his names, as I found out years later. My dad called him Trapper Jean, and that's what he was, a trapper during winters and he'd make a stab at prospecting during summers. He was a French Canadian from away up in the far Northwest Country, and of the breed that was first in all countries. . . . Right to-day you can see traces of that same breed all thru the West, from Alaska to Mexico, and they was here even before the eighteenth century came in. They was roaming trappers and traders, could talk sign language with all Indian nations and manage somehow to get along with 'em. There's many creeks, mountains and rivers that they named, and long before Lewis and Clark came West.

"My horse was a lot of company to me. I used to like to fool around his legs and his chest, that was as high as I could reach, and feel the muscles under the smooth hide. I guess that's where I received my first lessons in the anatomy of a horse and the reason why I draw horses without every once sketching one from life.

"I know I was glad [when Bopy] left [to prospect] because it's at such a time, when I have something in my chest, whether it's good or bad, that I want to be all alone with what I put down on the paper or board in front of me. Someone around about then, whether that someone talks or keeps quiet, is just like a stranger butting in when you're talking confidential to an understanding friend.

"I layed flat on my belly and, propped on my elbows, hat away back on my head, I drawed till the sun, beating down on my backbone, made me hunt a tree for shade. With my back against the tree and using my knees for a table, I drawed some more. I was good in that position for a long time, specially right then because I was stumped. A horse's leg was bothering me and no matter how often I erased that leg it wouldn't fit the horse I had drawed. Finally I erased the whole horse and kept the leg and made another horse that would fit it. It worked out all right.

"I do that often right to-day, but what I can't understand is why, while I was trying to draw that horse under the tree and working so hard to get it right, I never thought of looking at the four horses that was grazing to within fifty yards of me and study from them for help to get that leg right.

"I went right into drawing again the next morning, but I waited till after breakfast and then I drawed only for a couple of hours. I begin to find lots of faults with the drawings I'd done the day before, and which I thought had been so fine then, and the ones I drawed the second day struck me as worse. So, for the time being, I put my tablet and pencils carefully away between the under soogans of the bed and went to the creek to watch and talk to Bopy while he panned out his would-be pay dirt.

"My drawing from then on was kind of in spells like. As before, I went along with Bopy again on prospecting trips and seldom would my tablet and pencils hold me in camp. By this time, with the tablet, Bopy, my horse and outfit, the country around and all that was new and strange, I was having my hands full taking everything in that interested me and I was beginning to forget my lonesomeness for what all is natural but which I'd never knowed, the love of a mother and the steady companionship of a father.

". . . We'd struck a home camp . . . where we was to hole-up for the winter.

"Inside of the camp, a dirt-roofed, one-roomed log cabin, and under a wide long bunk, was about a hundred traps and of all sizes from the small one-spring muskrat trap up to the cayote and wolf trap, and to the fifty-pound lock bear trap. But after looking around some, them traps didn't interest me none much. They was just like so much steel and nothing more as compared to what I'd spotted in one corner of the cabin. There, and all stacked up, was a pile of magazines, newspapers and books. The pile was higher than me, but it sure wasn't long before I made camp right there in that corner and took the top off that pile till it was reduced, or scattered, to my size.

"I don't know how old them magazines and papers was and I didn't care because I couldn't read anyway, but I do know they was a heap older than me. They'd been gathered and stacked there for many years. The pictures is what took my eye. They was pictures of all things I'd never seen and which was as strange to me as anything strange could be. I remember seeing pictures of people dressed in clothes of the kind I'd never seen before, whiskers cut sort of queer, pretty women with lots of hair, and ponies without tails nor manes.

"Bopy spent many a long evening explaining all which stumped me in them pictures and I know that after he got thru, which was never, I still didn't understand, for I'd never seen what them pictures pictured.

"I went thru that stack of printed work mighty quick. It was my first acquaintance with such and I found a heap from that first acquaintance which wouldn't allow me to linger with one so I could get to the other. When I went thru that stack the second time I was a little slower and more watchful, the third time was still more slow, and then I settled down to really seeing what was between the leaves of what I picked up.

"I didn't get to do no drawing for quite a spell along about then, and after I had looked at all the pictures over and over again about sixteen times I begin to wonder what all them funny marks was that was under them, the writing, that's what Bopy said it was, but I didn't know what he meant,

It hadn't been easy to see on account of being so surrounded with tall cottonwoods and other trees, but once Kip seen it and begin to look, the idea had of a sudden come to his mind of fixing up the place and making his camp there.... ■ (From *Look-See with Uncle Bill* by Will James. Illustrated by the author.)

and, as he told me, he couldn't understand nor explain it. Bopy couldn't read English and very little French.

"The trees went bare of leaves, snows came and covered up the grass, a dry-log shelter was built for the ponies and hay was stacked up alongside. Bopy drug out his traps, seen that the chains, pins and anchors would hold, and scattered 'em out on the trail of drifting herds and beaver-damned streams. I didn't see none of the goings-on much, my nose was buried in things printed and only once in a while, when my bones would ache from laying or setting on the floor and when I couldn't see no more, would I get out and look at the great world which was all around me that *couldn't* be printed.

"Being Bopy couldn't read English, I think them first few lessons in grammar was near as hard for him to teach as they was for me to learn. He knowed the letters by name in French and that was all. From them letters picked here and there on the page, we'd build up a French word and started to work that way. I printed all the letters the same as they was in whatever magazine we'd work from. One day we'd work on letters and the next day on numbers and Bopy seen to it, once he got me started, that I done at least an hour's studying every day.

"That was the start of my schooling from the only teacher I ever had. I took to grammar natural-like and I got so that it was very seldom I misspelt a word, I was more apt to do that on common words, as I still do.

"My schooling was limited to grammar and arithmetic only. That was all Bopy could begin to handle, but he stayed with me pretty steady on them two subjects. Then one evening that spring he rides back to camp from the post office with a big package of books, French thin-leafed books full of small writing. There sure was a lot of reading in them. He'd also brought me a couple more tablets and some pencils. I was all set.

"The winter went on mighty peaceful and without any events out of the ordinary happening, not excepting maybe one, one that was a great surprise and pleasure to me. A rider had come by our camp and left a package and when he'd rode on, I was right on the job watching Bopy open that package. A cardboard box was unwrapped. He handed it to me and said, as he'd said more times afterwards:

"'C'est pour toi, Billee. Bonne et heureuse nouvelle année.' (It's for you, Bill, Good and happy New Year.)

"I don't think I hardly heard him as a I took the cover off that box and looked inside. There, all shining, was the copper toes of a little pair of boots. Part of the top was red and a star was designed in the center of that.

"That was my first New Year's present from Bopy, and whenever he was where he could get me a present he'd always pick on New Year's day to give it to me, for according to his bringing up, that was the big day for cheer and to celebrate and give presents on. Christmas was a day for quiet and peace. All he'd do on Christmas day was to spread out the best meal he could and he was sure a bear at doing that. He'd start on it the day before.

"I think I had a natural interest in watching animals, what they done, and how they might of felt. Cattle interested me the least. I liked to see a big herd and watch the cowboys work, brand and round 'em up when I was a kid, and even try to help when I had the chance, but, to me, cattle was just beef, an animal to raise and ship to market and set up on the table in a big platter a smoking hot. With a horse it's very different, he was a pardner to work with, and I think I felt that from the first. I got to feeling for the horse and never thought about the cow. . . .

"Most of my drawings was of horses, about four out of every five. I'd draw them running, standing, and bucking, and from all angles, most of the time with a cowboy a setting on top of 'em and with a rope in his hand, then maybe a few cattle somewhere around. From the start, I always liked to draw something with a little story in it. It always made it more interesting for me to draw while trying to put that story over.

"When I drawed a horse I'd a lot of times stick in a bear or a wolf for him to spook up at or run away from. I knowed even then that horses didn't like them animals. Or I'd have horses or cattle drifting with the storm and maybe a rider alongside, like I'd once in a while seen that winter.

"I kept most of the drawings which I thought was good at the time I made 'em. They'd be shabby at the edges and wrinkled from being packed, and sometimes I'd sure surprise myself at seeing the improvement I'd made from the earlier to the later ones. I'd laugh at the old ones and show 'em to Bopy, who agreed with me that the new ones was better. Then I'd tear up the most of the old ones.

"I sure got back to playing cowboy again that winter. The visit at the ranch had stirred up what was in my blood which I'd inherited from the generations before me. My rope begin to get a lot of use and got stretched many a time.

"I had a lot of fun that winter and I was treated rough. I was dared to ride big husky calves and colts and there wasn't a day passed when I wasn't bucked off at least once. If I piled off to often I'd get another kick and the cowboys would talk amongst themselves, loud enough so I could hear, and say, 'We'd better kill him, he'll never be a cowboy.'

"I used to take that to heart and the result would be, when I'd make a better ride that 'they had hopes for me and maybe I would be a cowboy yet.' That sure used to please me.

"What used to give the cowboys a lot of pleasure is that I was so sensitive to what they said. They took a lot of delight in stirring me up and get after me if I didn't do a thing just right, and they'd have a lot of fun in seeing me get peeved and trying to do better. I got no compliments from them but when one or two of 'em was alongside of me and throwed a paw on my shoulder, that meant a heap more than all the words in the world.

"From what I've seen of how most kids are treated since, I guess many folks would of thought, seeing how the cowboys handled me, that I was being framed to a fast death, but that sure wasn't it. Them boys knowed what they was doing. They didn't see nothing soft about me and they noticed that if I did buck off I wouldn't get hurt easy, and there was no whining. Instead I asked as to where my critter went and I'd climb on some more. If my elbows or shins or nose was skinned I'd pass that off and say it was 'nothing.' Not that I wanted to play tough but I knowed then that no cowboy, that is one, ever whined.

"As I remember the town now it must of been about three hundred size and there might of been about fifty people in sight all along the wide street, but it looked to me then like there was thousands. We passed a few store windows and that sure got my eye, but what got my eye the most was when I spotted two little boys about my size and a playing at the back end of a wagon.

"I'd never figgered there was little people like me, all I'd ever seen was big people like my dad, Bopy and the cowboys. The boys jabbered at me as I rode by, and stared too, but they wasn't staring at me, they was staring at my horse and outfit. They'd never seen such an outfit before.

"This town and country was away to the north of the range land. Cattle was few there and what few there was was close to the town and kept under fence and put in some stable in the winter. It wasn't a cow country, too cold and too much snow and timber. No cowboys ever came there and nobody ever hardly rode. When they did, it was on some work-horse and bareback.

"That's how come the kids was so curious about mine and Bopy's outfit, but I don't think they was near as curious about our outfits as I was about them. They came along and followed us. Pretty soon they run acrost some other kids, and then one little one that was dressed just like I remembered Mommy dressing. Of the half dozen kids that gathered, that one with the skirts drawed most of my attention. It was the first girl I'd ever seen.

"Them wolves was a lot of company to me that winter. They'd lay by me while I drawed and read and I'd never make a move but what they did too. If I jumped up sudden, they'd jump up too, and bristle up and look at the door of the cabin, and growl. They'd sure look mean at them times and it wouldn't been to shoot right quick. Bopy realized that, and

Bill, all bundled up and playing in the snow. ■(From *Big Enough* by Will James. Illustrated by the author.)

he never came in from his trap lines like he used to. He'd whistle a bit first and after he thought I got thru talking to them wolves he'd ease in, and the tone of his voice as he spoke to me had all to do with his welcome. They never got used to him because he'd be gone too long at the time.

"Of course Bopy could of made away with them wolves mighty quick, but seeing how they was so much company to me, how they followed me around and partnered with me so well, he figgered they was sure worth having around, even if he did have to whistle a bit before drifting into camp and watch his step after he got inside.... Them wolves was mighty ferocious but Bopy knowed that I was the last person they'd ever show a fang to."[1]

1906. "The sun being so high made me wonder why Bopy hadn't stirred me. I sat up in bed on the ground. I counted the horses that was picketed and hobbled out a ways. They was all there. Then I looked at the fire, it was down to smudging coals. I wondered why Bopy hadn't cooked the morning bait for he always had that done by sun-up,—the sun was way high now.

"I jumped up, feeling that something was wrong. I hollered for Bopy but got no answer, only echoes. I hollered all the louder then, and slipping on my boots, I run out to the river and hollered some more. No answer, and nothing of Bopy was in sight. But glancing a ways down the river I noticed a bucket he used to get water with. It was along the bank and a big hunk of ice manipulated by a swift whirling current, was sure doing a good job of battering and flattening it.

"I stared at that bucket. It hinted to something. I didn't want to think of what it hinted. I kept a saying to myself as I turned away, 'He's out hunting.' . . . But as I walked thru the cottonwoods along the river, a hollering and listening, the sight I'd got of the bucket followed me, and the further I went and the more I hollered and listened, the more I thought of the bucket and of the story it told.

"I tried to forget that and, to help me that way, I went back to camp, throwed more wood on the fire and started throwing grub together, *for two.* 'Bopy ought to be back any minute now.'

"But Bopy didn't come back. He never did come back and I never seen him no more. . . . The bucket had made things plain. Bopy had been drowned.

"For a couple of weeks I kept a riding around and everywhere. I didn't care where I was going as long as I went fast. I was just hunting and I think I covered every foot of the country for forty miles each way from camp. I'd meet riders and come acrost ranches along the river and it strikes me queer, *now,* that I never asked any of the riders if they'd seen any man like Bopy. I never stopped at the ranches either as I rode by them.

"The lady of a ranch house would wonder at what a kid like me was doing running around loose in that country. I'd keep quiet and ride on. The chink at some of the bigger outfits' cook house would wonder too, but I'd just snicker at him and go on some more.

"I had a secret. It wasn't so much of a secret but Bopy had brought me up to never ask any questions and to never let out anything, especially about him. So I went along a riding and looking and hollering, kept everything to myself, and asked for no help.

"I don't know how many days or weeks I rode and hunted and hollered. It was quite a spell, then there come a time when my riding for Bopy seemed more and more useless. I begin to quit hollering and finally I got so I rode just to be riding. I'd near lost all hope.

"Finally, one day, I tore a piece of canvas, wrote on it as to the general direction of where I would be headed, and with some loose nails which I pulled out of the wagon box, I nailed the canvas on a big tree near where the camp was. Then I gathered up the whole outfit, hooked up the team, tied the saddle horses behind the wagon, climbed up on the seat and, taking a last long look around where the camp had been, I started the team.

"Going by what I wrote on the canvas before leaving camp, I hit for the river crossing and from there as straight south as I could for the border of good old United States again. My idea was to find that last big cow outfit where Bopy had trapped that winter before going North. I'd also wrote the name of that outfit on the canvas and that I would stop there.

"The few hundred miles of that trip was a lot of help in making me forget my lonesomeness for Bopy. Being altogether dependant on myself and having all the responsibilities of taking care of my outfit, making camp, cooking my meals and getting the wagon acrost bad places, all had me watching out and kept me busy. If it hadn't been for missing Bopy at times, I know I'd had a lot of fun. I was used to having to take care of myself and of the outfit, and there was nothing along with that that I didn't know how to do, from setting up camp, cooking, picketing or hobbling the horses and picking out the trail when starting out of camp in the morning. Old Bopy had given me plenty of education that way.''[1]

James arrived at the cow camp he and Beaupré had visited years earlier.

"That night . . . I told the whole of what I'd kept to my chest. It sort of done me good to let it out, like as if the load I'd packed was shared around. The boys thought I sure had tough luck. It took me quite a spell to tell my story because I hadn't spoke nothing but French in the last four or five years and my mother tongue was pretty well forgot.

"All the men on that outfit sure treated me fine. Most likely it was because they felt sorry and wanted to make it easy for me. The foremens, cowboys, ranch hands, and even the chink cook, catered to me like I was a long lost brother. Then to make things more pleasant, the next day the range boss asks me if I wanted a job. My clothes was a little ragged and he figgered I must of needed some money. But I was well fixed for money. I had the four or five hundred dollars that Bopy had left on the wagon seat and which I'd later rolled up in my bed. Anyway, when I found out that the job was to wrangle horses on one of the round-up wagons I sure was tickled to take it. Besides I wanted to stay on that spread because of that note I'd left on the tree at Bopy's last camp. If he ever seen that note he'd knowed where to find me and his outfit. I still wanted to hope that he would some day.

"I left the wagon and outfit and horses at the ranch and went to riding on the round-up. It was my first job on a big cow outfit and I felt mighty proud and sure enough cowboy. I finished wearing out my saddle there, the stirrup leathers was wore down till they was as thin as paper and the riggin' too, and both of them important pieces was so all patched up that they'd keep breaking, and most always at a bad time. The saddle tree was too small for me now too, I'd outgrowed it and lucky it was that I shot up more in length and very little in thickness because I'd never been able to get in it. I was tall enough now that I'd come near to most any of the boys' shoulders.

"I worked pretty hard on that first job, but I had a great time doing that work. The only part I didn't like was to have to cut wood and carry water for the cook and not being able to go with the boys on the circle. But the rest was fine. I had five good saddle horses in my string and I had a 'Remuda' of two hundred saddle horses for company the whole day long. Then I'd get to see the boys three and four times a day, whenever they changed horses, and when the 'Nighthawk' (night-wrangler) took my place in herding the horses for the night, I'd see the boys again and get in on the talks and songs that went around the fire at camp.

"There was a bar adjoining the lobby. I seen the swinging door and I walked in one time, figgering to get me a drink of soda pop, but I no more than got in and started to speak when the bartender pointed up to a sign and said:

" 'Do you see that, young feller?'

" 'Yes,' I says in my broken talk, 'but I can't read it.'

"Then he explained it to me. It said 'No Minors Allowed' . . . and that was my first time to learn the difference between minors and miners. I didn't get no soda pop there and I went out on the street again.

"I had a hard time getting away from that ranch. The old lady, widowed, had two boys but she seemed to figger like she ought to have one more. One of the boys was not many years older than me and the two of us had a lot of fun to-

In the fastest gait he'd ever been put to she rode him to the corrals. ■ (From *Scorpion: A Good Bad Horse* by Will James. Illustrated by the author.)

gether. To begin with he liked my saddle and outfit a whole lot and when he learned that I'd rode for that big spread to the north he sure hung on to everything I said. Neither of these boys had ever been away from home only to do their fall shipments. They'd had to take care of their mother and the ranch and, like all boys of their age, they sort of hankered to drift a bit. My talk of the prairie country to the north and what all I'd been doing sure interested 'em, and before I got thru telling 'em and showing 'em different things in ways of knots and general cow work, they made me feel as if I was many years older than they was.

"The mother said she had a plenty to keep me on if I would only stay, but I felt I had a plenty too, plenty to learn, and I was aching to see what was ahead. Experiencing my freedom kept me going."[1]

1907. "It'd been a year now since I started drifting alone. I didn't miss Bopy so much no more and I think that my roam-

ing around, seeing all that was new, strange people, in a country to my liking, had a lot to do in making me forget him pretty well, and when I hit out that spring, asetting on top of a good feeling pony, the morning sun ashining on fresh green sod, trees abudding and millions of birds asinging everywhere, there was no room in my chest for anything excepting what was all around, under, above, and ahead of me.

"I was by the corral as the last man was catching their horses. The foreman was coiling up his rope when I walked up to him and asked.

"'Are you taking on any more riders?' . . . Just like that.

"He looked at me and grinned. 'Why yes, Son,' he says, 'when I can find any. . . .'

"I didn't say anything to that, then after a while he asks.

"'Looking for a job?'

"'Yessir,' I says.

"At that outfit was where I first got initiated with rough ponies. The others I'd tried to ride before had been just for fun and that makes a big difference, I was handed gentle old horses while 'wrangling' for the big outfit to the North, but now I wasn't wrangling no more, I was on circle, dayherd, nightguard and being a regular hand.

"I felt mighty proud of that, but I found out right there that there was grief and sweat on the way to any ambition. My string furnished me with plenty of that. Thinking of what horse I had to ride was the cause of me eating mighty light breakfasts and other meals. The thought of what they might do to me sort of made me lose my appetite."[1]

1908. "I was about sixteen when I first heard of a Rodeo, and when I found out what it was, that it was where cowboys could win a prize for riding or roping I caught my own horse, quit the whole outfit flat and hit the sixty miles for where the Rodeo was to be pulled off. I had a lot of confidence in my riding ability by then, I hadn't been bucked off for the last six months and got to be a pretty good rider, I thought, forgetting the hundred times I'd been bucked off before.

"The Rodeo and gathering was to be pulled off in the main street of the town and was to last one whole afternoon. I entered for bucking horse riding (it's called bronk riding now) and drawed my horse's name out of a hat where the names of all the bucking horses was wrote down on little folded pieces of paper.

"My first horse must of took pity on me because every time he'd send me up where there was no chance of me coming back in the saddle only by a miracle he'd produce the miracle and come right under where I was a hanging on thin air. Well, I passed, or qualified on that first horse.

"But the second one I drawed didn't take as good a care of me and on about the fifth jump I looked down to see my shadow on the ground instead of a horse and soon my shadow came up and met me.

"Well, I'd entered in a couple other events such as roping and the wild mule race and after getting all skinned up I finally came out the winner of ten whole dollars, after spending a hundred dollars and losing three days work. I sure had a lot of fun tho, and on the fourth day I rode the sixty miles back to the outfit." [Will James, *All in the Day's Riding*, Scribner, 1933.[2]]

"I drifted on down the country, South, always South. I passed and stopped at many places. No jobs was offered me and I didn't ask for none. The outfits struck me as too small. After me riding for a few big outfits like I had, I couldn't think of riding for the small ones. To me, that struck me as bad as going back to wrangling, and I felt that I was above that.

"Like most kids of fifteen or sixteen, I had a pretty high opinion of myself about then. I hadn't been knocked down yet and I was like any yearling in any herd, kind of holding my head high. That all was brought on I think by the fact that people sort of quit looking at me as a kid and want to take me in and take care of me. When I rode up to a place now I was treated pretty well like as if I was a grown-up. I was grown up pretty well as far as height was concerned, even tho I sure wasn't very big around. I felt all the bigger when I'd come to some little ranch and begin talking to a kid of my age and size. And after I'd get thru telling of all the big outfits I'd rode for and so on, I'd sometimes swell up quite a bit. Then to put on the finishing touches, I'd roll up a neat cigarette.

"I don't know what Bopy would of thought if he'd knowed of me hiring out as a 'long rope' artist. Maybe he'd felt the same way I did at the time, because then in that country it seemed like the only big wrong in appropriating cattle was getting caught doing it. It was still less wrong to steal cattle from a sheep outfit. Anyway, that's how I was made to feel, and it wasn't long when I was as much against the sheepman as any cowman could of been.

"All around, I got to thinking I was pretty smart. The old man would ride with me once in a while and sort of coach me as to the tricks of the rustling game. He knowed many tricks and I don't think I could ever got a better teacher in that line. His work wasn't coarse in nothing he done, wether it was picking out the cattle or making over an iron. In picking out cattle, he warned me never to take a 'marker' (an animal that could easy be recognized by odd markings). When he changed a brand he didn't use no knife, no hot iron, nor wet blanket. He had a little bottle of some acid, which parts he'd get at different stores and mix. By dripping a twig in that acid he could work over the old brand and spread out with the new one. In a few hours the new brand would show up in a scaly ridge and look as old as the first one it blended with. There'd even be gray hairs showing and that brand would stand inspection from the outside of the hide as well as from the inside, in case trouble come and the animal would have to be killed and skinned to show evidence. It takes a burned brand a few months before it shows a ridge inside a hide.

"But the old man didn't do much brand altering. He would had to have too many registered brands and that would throw suspicion, with as little a herd as he had. He done most of his work on young stock, 'sleepering.'"[1]

1914. Enjoyed a brief career as an extra in Western films. "'Get ready,—Camera. . . . Come on, boys.'

"It was the director hollering at us thru his megaphone, and when he said 'come on, boys,' we *came*. Six of us rode down a steep hill for all we was worth. The hill was more than steep, it was near straight up and down, and down for a long ways. Two horses turned over before they got halfways down it and rolled the rest of the way with their riders rolling after 'em. My horse didn't fall till he got to the bottom and where he struck sudden level ground. All riders and horses piled up in a heap there. . . . But, according to the story in the picture, we was chasing some bad hombres and we didn't linger at the bottom of the hill long. We untangled ourselves, caught any horse we could get a hold of, and rode on till we heard the director holler 'all right, boys.'

"That was my first acquaintance with the moving-picture game."[1]

1916. Enlisted in the Army during World War I. "I had registered while I was with the movie outfit. I wrote down to find out, and I found out plenty quick. A rider from the home ranch brought me a telegram which said that I'd been called a month before and for me to report *immediately* to a certain town for examination.

(From the movie "Smoky," starring Fred MacMurray, Anne Baxter, and Burl Ives. Copyright 1951 by Twentieth Century-Fox Film Corp.)

"I sold my horses and outfit, all but my saddle and boots and spurs, I always took that with me, and within twenty-four hours from that time I received the telegram I was in the town where I'd be run thru the chute and inspected.

". . . When I was asked who I wanted to make my insurance to I couldn't tell. I finally gave the name of a good friend of mine, a cowboy.

"It made me laugh when I was asked if I wanted to claim exemption and if I had any dependents. I didn't know of even a far-away relative. . . . But even tho there was no one to grieve over me, there was something that I missed as I got in file after file of men. That was the range I was leaving, the big open country,—and somewhere there was my little horse Smoky. I'd never forgot him. As it was now, I was jammed in crowds again and hearing talk that was strange. I felt about as bad as I did when I was took to prison.

"In my life I'd never 'punched a clock,' I wasn't used to regular hours and time for everything, nor to take orders from anybody. A cowboy, if he knows his work, never gets no orders on the range. He's pretty well his own boss and there's no time set for anything he does. He's also mighty independent.

"But there was no such a thing as being independent nor free when I went thru the second examination and, filing along with long strings of men that was handled like a herd, I went from one desk to another a collecting my O D outfit, leggings and shoes. The shoes was sure some contrast to my light riding boots, with every step I took I felt like them shoes covered and crushed a whole acre of gravel.

". . . After a while I was transferred to that company as a mounted scout. That was fine, and even tho I was informed that mounted scouts was the first to get shot when they got acrost, I didn't worry about that. I'd be a horseback, anyway, and not crawling along the ground like a terrapin. As I was told, the mounted scout is the one that's the first to investigate a place or town where the enemy is supposed to've just left, and as the enemy always leaves a few sharpshooters behind, I would be in a fine way of getting it quick. This company I was with was due to go acrost the pond in another couple of months.

"The couple of months went by and we didn't budge from the cantonment. We was told we'd be going in another month, but that time went by, and more time, and when we was finally due to go acrost sure enough and was all prepared we got a last word to hold on a spell longer. There was a few more days and then the armistice was signed.

"I was by the stables a trying to get one of the spoiled horses into his stall when I hears a commotion and noise and hollers like I've never heard before or since. Thousands and thousands of soldiers was war-whooping and acting like as if they'd kicked a hornet's nest. I had no idea of what the commotion was about, but it sure looked and sounded exciting, so I saddled the horse I'd been trying to lead in and lined him out towards the parade grounds. I never seen so many crazy-acting fellers in my life as I did when I got there, and when I got the news of what they was acting up about, that the war was over, I went just as crazy-happy as any of 'em did."[1]

1918. "I was only twenty-six years old when I started to draw the line on the raw ones, and by then I'd spent many years on the backs of fighting ponies. I sat on my first horse when I was about four, and I remember 1900 as the year I got bucked off for the first time and was sent rolling down a hill. I was seven going on eight years old at the time, and I remember the year on account of my foster father buying me my first saddle, all for my own self.

"With all the events that followed one another after that I felt by the time I was twenty-six that I'd sure enough done my share in the bronk-fighting game. By then my thoughts kept a going back to different happenings every time I'd climb onto a bowed-back horse, and when finally my spur rowels got to ringing a reminder of my lost nerve—was when I got to thinking of a job with gentler horses, a job where I'd get paid for being a cow-hand and not so much for being a bronk stomper."[2]

James was thrown by a particularly wild horse. "The boys told me afterwards how they was sure scared that I was a dead one. They said I was all twisted, chest down, face up to the sky, and half of my scalp tore up and hanging over the rail.

"But I fooled 'em, and after they straightened me up, and got air in my lungs, it wasn't long when I begin to grin at 'em—The first thing I thought of was how I'd spoiled the fun by going to work and getting hurt, and I figgered of making up for that in a way so it wouldn't strike 'em as very serious. I went on grinning, started to brush the dirt off my clothes unconcerned like, and even went to singing an old song the cowboys all know, 'Bury me not on the lone prairie.'

"A little crowd had gathered around by then, and one feller hearing me sing, remarked, 'He's out of his head.'

"'You'd be out of your head too,' I come back at him, 'if you'd tried to bend a railroad track with it.'

"The boys kidded me about that for a long time afterwards and said that the railroad company was going to sue me for damages, but they wasn't kidding much when the accident happened, and I couldn't fool 'em none as to how bad I was hurt. Blood was streaming down from my head plum down to the toe of my boots, and after trying to put all the hide back in place over that dome of mine, somebody around who had a car was kind enough to offer to take me to a doctor.

"That was the wind up of the last bucking horse I rode. I felt the effects of that for a couple of years afterwards on account that during that last ride an old internal injury had been stirred, and it begin to bother me again.

"And that's how come I didn't go to Oregon, as I'd first planned. 'Happy' [the wild bronc] had proved to be my turning point, a mighty rough one maybe, but my turning point sure enough. While I was recuperating I happened to think of a mining man I'd met who said he'd give me a grand letter of introduction to an editor of a magazine on the west coast. This mining man knowed the editor well, and being he'd seen some of the drawings I'd made and which I'd packed 'round from cow camp to cow camp, he'd thought I was foolish not to try and get some of that work in the magazines and make a living that way instead of riding.

"I didn't pay no serious attention to that man's good advice right then, most likely if I hadn't met up with 'Happy' I'd forgot all about it, and right to-day I'd still be riding for a living—not that I'd mind that so much, but this ain't so bad either, and being a has-been I'd rather draw and write about that life than take a back seat as a rider.

"So, if I'm to be thankful, 'Happy' is the one who'd get the first thanks. He's the one who jolted the mining man's advice back to my memory, and fixed me so I'd have time to think about it afterwards. He's the one that showed me for sure that I'd rode one too many bronks, and that it was high time for me to quit and be sensible."[2]

Visited a professional western artist to gather some advice. ". . . He kept right on a working and only grunted once more as I got thru talking, and when I told him I'd brought over some drawings, he just kept his eye on the canvas, never layed his brush down, and only held out his free hand for me to pass 'em to. He layed the drawings on his lap for a long time and kept right on working at his picture. Finally he layed his brush down and begin looking thru my little pencil drawings.

"It was then I reared back and grinned to myself in expecting a look of surprise, hearing compliments and then being told of a way where I could sudden make a gunnysack full of money before sundown and keep right on just that way. I figured I'd first buy me a nice cow outfit with that money, big enough so I could use a couple of round-up wagons. I'd also get all the boys I thought a lot of and have 'em come and work for me. Then maybe once in a while I'd ride in one of them coaches that traveled on rails. I'd never been in one of them yet.

"I was thinking mighty fast right for a minute or so, and now that I'd come to the end of my trail, met the artist and delivered my drawings in his hand, I figured I had no more to worry about. . . . Well, hadn't the cowboys told me that I'd make a mint with them drawings of mine, hadn't they told me that I could get at least ten dollars apiece for a drawing? . . . I figgered I could make at least twenty drawings a day, that would be two hundred dollars. That would be easy to get now because I'd figgered that to be only about half of what I'd really get, just to be on the safe side.

"I was grinning right along and sort of proud as the artist shuffled my drawings. He was handling 'em as if they was cards, getting ready to play stud poker and deal out a hand, and just as quick as he shuffled 'em, and while I was waiting for surprised remarks, my deck of drawings was handed back to me, and he went to work on his picture again, just as tho I still wasn't around and like he'd never seen them pictures of mine.

"He never even gave me a smile or a grunt, and when I finally asked him what he thought of 'em, he just said 'good.'

(From the movie "Smoky," starring Fess Parker. Copyright 1933 by Fox Film Corp., 1946 by Twentieth Century-Fox Film Corp.)

When I asked him what I should do with 'em, and where I could sell 'em, he explained that in a very few words too.

"'Just scatter 'em around in saloons,' he says. 'Somebody might buy 'em.'

"He'd kept right on working as he spoke, and when he. got thru with them few words there was a sound of grand final about them that gave me to understand he was thru on the subject of my pictures and couldn't say no more.

"I said good-bye to him and walked out in the cold air. The trails from there, as I stood out on the sidewalk, seemed very dim and scattering, and thru the fog of my thoughts it came to me that I wouldn't be an artist, not on that day at least.

"I was talking to a clerk in a hotel, showing him my drawings and asking him if I could stick a few around the lobby, I thought maybe I would sell some that way. . . . I was talking along with the clerk when a big well dressed man edged in to the desk and put his name on the register. When that was done he happened to glance over my drawings. That one glance made him take a good look, and as the bell-hop hopped to get his baggage he asked me to come up to his room with him.

"Once in the room, and when we got to talking, I found that the big man was also a big man in the mining business. He was sure interested in my drawings, and even tho he didn't seem to want to buy any right at the time, he done something else which meant a heap more to me. He said he had a good friend who was Editor of a magazine in a big city of the west Coast, and that he was sure I could sell him some drawings to use in the magazine. He would give me a letter of introduction to him, and that all I'd have to do would be to catch a train and go see him.

"It was a great event to me when I finally located the building where the magazine was published and where the Editor was that I was to see. The sight of it struck me as a landmark where I'd be starting on an entirely different trail. I opened the big door, walked in and eased around to a desk where I told a girl that I wanted to see the Editor and that I had a letter of introduction to him. The girl asked my name, talked to somebody over a phone and then asked me to sit down and wait, the Editor would see me 'in a few minutes.'

"I sat down and waited. The few minutes went by, many more minutes went by and till a whole hour had gone. I was getting mighty nervous by that time and wondering if the Editor hadn't forgot about me, but finally the phone buzzed once more, the girl called my name, said the Editor would now see me and told me how to find him. It was another great event when I came face to face with that feller and I handed him my letter of introduction, but the greatness of that event dwindled down a considerable after I'd unwrapped and showed him the drawings I'd brought. He seemed sort of fidgitive and like he didn't have much time to waste, and while he glanced at the drawings he didn't act like he was seeing 'em. His mind was a whole lot on something else. He didn't say a word while he shuffled the drawings. When he got thru he had to blink a couple of times so he could get back on the subject of 'em. Then he spoke.

"'We couldn't use such drawings as these,' he says. 'They would have to be a lot better . . . come around again some other time.'

"'When?' I asks.

"'Oh, in a few months or so, when you have something else to show me. . . . Good-bye.'

"Well, there's no use of saying that I was disappointed with my visit to the Editor. I was more than that, I was peeved. He'd treated me as if I'd just come from acrost the street to see him and like as if I had nothing else to worry about but get back there, better my work and show up again, and he'd said, in a few months or so. That sure was a long ways from the reception I'd expected.

"I had no way of knowing then that editors are more than pestered by many beginners with writings and drawings, some good ones and many that just think they're good ones, and if the Editor was to waste time on all beginners he would never get his magazine out.

"Everything is up to the beginner, and I sure was one. It would of been easier for me if I'd been used to the city because then I'd been more apt to know something about magazines and editors, but I'd just come out of the brush and all I knowed was horses and cow foremen. I would of got to know some more horses and cow foremen too, after the Editor said 'good-bye,' but I wasn't in no shape to ride no more, not for a long spell.

"I went to a little hotel close by, was given a gloomy room, and there I stretched out on the bed and begin to do some tall thinking. The first thought was that I didn't have much money, enough to last me just a few days, then what would I do? . . . A little voice at the back of me said, 'Work, of course.' 'Work at what?' I asks. I didn't know nothing but cows and horses and range. Now I was in the heart of a big city and about as hard a work as I could do would be to sell ribbons behind a counter or some such like job where I wouldn't be wanted. The future sure didn't look so good.

"But as I think back to that dark spell of time, feeling bad both in mind and body, I don't remember of being discouraged nor giving up in wanting to be an artist. I had to make up my mind to that because there was nothing else I could do.

"There was a few magazines in the room where I was put and I begin studying 'em, studying 'em for an idea of what I could do that would fit in the pages. It was then I got to fig-

guring on some subjects in my line of work which would interest the Editor, something of the life I knowed and which would also interest the folks in general. I got to working for ideas where I could draw pictures of happenings on the range, pictures that would tell a story by themselves and which would bring a laugh or a tear, and explain things in range life that folks never heard tell of. . . . Sometimes I'd get an idea for a drawing which I thought would be good, and I sketched it down on a pad so I wouldn't forget.

"As I was studying on such subjects, and near wore out the magazines in wondering how my stuff would work in this and that page, I run acrost a few Western stories and illustrations of them that made me pretty sore. They was all out of whack and showed where neither the writer nor the artist knowed a thing of what they was doing. They was misrepresenting the cowboy,—and me being one, I felt that pretty deep. They knowed as much about the cowboys as I did about Wall Street and what went on there.

"One day, after I'd been hauling beets for a few weeks, I run onto a brand new magazine which had been put out by none other than the Editor I'd been to see. His name was on one of the front pages, and I camped on that magazine from evening till late in the night, studying what was in it, what it all meant, and where I could maybe edge in. It was while I was thumbing the pages of that magazine that I run acrost some Western drawings I figgured I could sure improve on. They was illustrations for a would-be Western story, and the sight of them started me to boiling. I noticed many things in the drawings that was worse than wrong, the cowboy, horse and rope was all wrong-side-out and looked like something that'd been starched and then went out in a heavy rain.

"I had quite a few sketches made. I stuck 'em in that latest issue of the magazine and went to get my time check. I was back to the big town in a few hours, there was another hour of waiting to see the Editor, and then I came face to face with him again.

"He sort of grinned as he listened to what I had to say, but I noticed that this time he was listening. I was peeved, and went on to remark that if he wanted to have real Western work in his magazine I'd make up for how little I could draw by what I knowed. While I was talking I begin shuffling him the sketches of the ideas I'd thought of. He looked at the sketches in the same way as I would look at a bunch of scrub ponies and he took in my jabbering like I would take in their nickering.

"As he glanced at the drawings, I thought sure he'd say 'good-bye' to me again, run off and tell me to come back in a few more months. I think he was just about to do that, when one sketch seemed to catch his knowing eye. He looked at it once, twice, and a third time, then he begins to studying it and the idea there. He was fumbling it like I'd fumble a rope while wondering if I should make a throw or not. Finally he says,

"'If you can make a good drawing of this sketch I'll pay you twenty-five dollars for it. Good-bye.'

"That 'good-bye' sounded like a million dollars to me. I went out of the building, hunted me up something to draw on and with, got me a room in the gloomy little hotel, and went to work on the drawing of the sketch. The sketch which the Editor had hung back on was from what the thoughts of Smoky had inspired me to do. I'd missed him, often thought of him and of the range country he reminded me of. . . . Out

(From the movie "Lone Cowboy," starring Jackie Cooper. Copyright 1933 by Paramount Productions Inc.)

of imagination I'd make a sketch of that horse standing over me after I'd been shot by a sheriff. It showed Smoky on the fight, on guard, and where he wouldn't let the sheriff come near me. It was something I'd figgured Smoky would of done if I'd got in a fix where he thought he could help. The idea might of been a little sentimental, but it would happen with men and horses if they was as me and Smoky had been. . . . Some day I'm going to model a monument to that horse."[1]

1919. Sold his first drawing to *Sunset* magazine for $25. "I made the drawing with a common pencil and on a cardboard I didn't know nothing about. I worked hard, maybe too hard, because I wanted to do a good job, and all I thought of in that time was Smoky, getting him down on paper, and of the new game I was trying to break into.

"I more than held my breath when I took the finished drawing to the Editor, and I hoped I wouldn't get sore if he refused to take it. I'd put everything I had in that drawing.

"I finally got to see the Editor again. He looked at the drawing, grunted and smiled. I liked him when I seen that smile,—I hadn't ever pictured him smiling. He looked the

drawing over good, and after a long while he says, 'We'll take this one.'

"That sure went fine with me. . . . But I wasn't thru yet. I showed him another sketch I'd thought of after drawing the picture of Smoky standing guard over me. He squinted at that one a spell, and then he says, 'Yes, make a finished drawing of this, too.'

"I was started in the art game."[1]

1920. Married Alice Conradt. "[The editor] begin to suggest that I should go to school and learn to draw real well. I didn't want to go to school, but after he made me acquainted with a great artist, the both of 'em doubled up on me and made me feel that I should. They got me a free scholarship in a Fine Arts university, and I went, more to please them than to please myself. . . . Far as they know, I went regular, but I seldom went, and when I did I'd be drawing a steer, a horse or a cowboy instead of the clay and life models I was supposed to copy. I could never copy. I went to that art school about ten times.

"I stayed in the big Coast town all one winter and till away along in the following summer. I was getting pretty daggone homesick for range country by then, and there was more than that to make me hanker to get back, it was a girl, the girl I married. She's the sister of one of the cowboys I was running around with when I got busted up, and I first met her thru him. We'd corresponded all winter, and when I got back to the country I met her again. I'd recuperated pretty well by that time and I could now ride a gentle horse easy enough. I done my courting on horseback, dressed in a plain white shirt and 'Mexican serges.' She didn't see me in a regular suit of clothes till the day before we was married, a couple of months after I got back.

"Pickings was pretty slim for a time. I'd furnished the Editor of the magazine with enough of my drawings to last him three or four years, and now he didn't want to take any more till the most of 'em was used. They was all drawings telling their own story. Once in a while the Editor would send me a story to illustrate but there was long spells between them. Then I begin to try and connect up with some Eastern magazines which I thought might use my work. I painted some covers for 'em, drawed 'em some pictures, and the most of the work was returned.

"Being married now, I rented a house on the outskirts of a little town, and come a time when the rent was due I couldn't pay it. We hit out, and I took a job on a ranch where I had a pretty fair place to stay and watch over some stock and do a little branding once in a while. I had plenty of time to keep on drawing and painting and now I didn't have to worry about rent and food; that was furnished.

"But I wanted to do a heap better than just that, and I kept a figguring for ways to break into the art game right. But that took time and plenty of hard work.

"Then one day I thought a good chance come. It was while up the high mountains of a great cow country, another place I went to where I didn't have to pay no rent, that I met the Dean of a big Eastern university. He liked mountains and open country and come out as a guest of the company I was with. Him and me got to talking and it was decided that I should go East. He helped me get there and fixed things up at his university so I could go to Art school. I sure appreciated that, but somehow I couldn't take any interest in that school either. I went there three times, to draw more steers, horses and cowboys instead of the models that was before me and which I was supposed to work from. I never liked to draw anything that was standing still and posing."[1]

"There's many a cowboy married and living happy on some spot he picked out for home and range, the wife as a rule is as happy as he is, she can have her pet horses, ride with him, help him take the cattle to the shipping point, ride by his side on the wagon seat when going to town for a new supply of grub and when the fourth of July comes along her and him will both saddle their top horses, lope in and take in a few days' celebrations and shows and the rodeos which is in most western towns at that time. They'll also ride a long ways for winter gatherings that last three and four days at a time.

"Mrs. Cowboy can find a plenty to keep her busy and happy at her ranch home, and I've noticed that them who can't are pretty well the kind that's short on vision and with plenty of empty space in the upper story. That kind might come from most anywhere, but are more apt to be from some hick place . . . places where everybody hopes to some day go to the big city and where nobody ever gets to really know the country. They're living neither in town nor the country and so they don't get the benefit of what either would learn them."[2]

James and Alice Conradt were later divorced. James claimed the reason for it lay in his nature—that of the "lone cowboy."

1920-1921. Went to New York City where he did magazine covers (including *Life*) as well as magazine illustration. "After leaving the second university I went to the Big City and there I begin making the rounds and seeing art editors of many magazines. I thought of getting acquainted with 'em, come back West and do work for 'em from here. I landed a few little jobs, but most of the time as I made my regular rounds it was a case of where they'd just put my name down and forget about it. When I came back West I got less of the little jobs than ever. Most of the editors liked my work pretty well but they said I was too far away."[1]

1921. Returned West, to Montana. "I've often wondered what power keeps drawing a human or animal back to the place where daylight was first blinked at. Many a time a man will go back to the country of his childhood when there's not near as much for him at that home spot as where he just left. I've seen horses leave good grassy range and cross half a state to get to a home range where feed and water was scarce and the country rocky.

"That same power must of drawed me, but I was hitting for better country instead of worse when I, so natural like and without thought, drifted to where I first stood up and talked."[1]

1923. In bad financial shape, a friend suggested he include writing with his drawings. Soon, he sold his first article, "Bucking Horses and Bucking Horse Riders" to Scribner.

He once referred to the work of his editor at Scribner as "Englishing Will James." [*Newbery Medal Books: 1922-1955*, edited by Bertha E. Miller and E. W. Field, Horn Book, 1957.[3]]

"I kept a pegging along, doing the best I could and drawing to suit myself. Me and my wife somehow managed to live and I could once in a while buy a few clothes and boots for me and slippers for her. I drawed till sometimes I couldn't see any of the drawings I made, and I got to thinking that I'd never get no further in the art game than where I was. My drawings all told of things, things that I knowed, but of things that not many folks are familiar with.

"Then, after about three years of fishing around for a good start, I got to thinking of writing,—writing of things I wanted to tell of and which no picture could be made of, only with words. But thinking is as far as I got to writing for a long while. I'd never been to school and I figgured that whatever I would write would only bring a return slip and a laugh. Then one day, after I'd told my wife for the hundredth time how I intended to write, she talked that idea over with me well, so well that just to prove to her that I couldn't write and what I sent in would be returned right quick I buckled down and wrote a mixed-up thing on a few sheets of yellow paper, in long hand, made a half a dozen pen-and-ink drawings to illustrate the writing and sent the whole outfit in to a high-class magazine. It was sent to the best.

Some will go up in the air and let their feet go out from under them as they come down, and turn a somerset; sometimes two or three, before they stop rolling. A man ain't got much chance there. ■ (From *The Drifting Cowboy* by Will James. Illustrated by the author.)

"The writing was about something I knowed well. It was about bucking horses and bucking-horse riders. It was accepted, and when I got word of that I went pretty wild with joy. My wife was close second in keeping up with me. When the check come I bought her a new saddle and I took mine out of hock, where it had been for quite a spell.

"I was told, afterwards, how that story had barely made the grade, that the drawings I'd sent with it was all that carried it over. The Art Editor had liked 'em, and he'd worked to get the story thru so he could get the drawings in the magazine. . . . I'll sure be always mighty thankful to the Art Editor for that, because without him, I don't think my first story would ever have been accepted. And if it'd been returned I'd

never wrote another. . . . (My wife don't agree with me on that last. She says that I was headed towards writing anyway and I'd tried my hand again at it, even if I'd failed at my first, or tenth try.)

"I sold five stories straight-hand running and to three of the best magazines. I got to thinking that none would ever be returned, and when the sixth one came back to me I couldn't quite figure out why. There was more returned off and on after that, but I've been lucky and managed to sell 'em sooner or later, and as it is now, I've only got two that didn't sell.

WILL JAMES

"A feller wrote a review of my books one time, without being asked, and he said something about my language not being true cowboy language. As I found out afterwards, that feller had been a cowboy all right enough but I also found out that he'd only rode in one state all his life. He'd compared his language with mine and mine had been picked up and mixed from the different languages from different parts of the whole cow country. The languages of the cow country is just as different as the style of the rigs and ways of working."[1]

1924. Published his first full-length book, *Cowboys North and South*. "What I've wrote in this book is without the help of the dictionary or any course in story writing. I didn't want to dilute what I had to say with a lot of imported words that I couldn't of handled. Good english is all right, but when I want to say *something* I believe in hitting straight to the point without fishing for decorated language.

"Me, never being to school and having to pick up what I know in grammar from old magazines and saddle catalogs scattered in cow camps would find plenty of territory for improvement in the literary range, but as the editors and publishers seem to like my efforts the way I put 'em out, which is natural and undiluded, and being that them same editors and publishers make a successful practice of putting out work that'll suit the readers makes me feel confident enough to give my pen full swing without picking up the slack." [Will James, *Cowboys North and South,* Arno Press, 1975.[4]]

1927. Won the Newbery Medal for his book, *Smoky*. On hearing of the honor, his laconic reply was: "I don't know about that medal . . . but it's fine with me."[3]

". . . I was riding none other than Smoky, the horse that led me to write the story by that name only a few years ago. He was all the horse I wrote of in the story. The happenings was none less as was in it, but they was a little different. Like for instance, I was a heap younger than Clint, the cowboy in that story, and instead of the horse being a 'company horse' he was my own. He was one of the bronks I had such a hard time to ride when I started to work for the old cowman where I done the 'sleepering,' and one of the two he'd given me. And another difference was that, instead of me being with one outfit like Clint in the story, I was everywhere, and Smoky was under me in many a cow country State. But, as in the story, he was stolen from me; he turned out as a bucking horse; after many years I found him again."[1]

His writing helped him acquire a 12,000 acre ranch outside Billings, Montana. "This might sound like just a story, but I think any man that sticks to one work as long and steady as I stuck to mine, and from the time he begins to walk away after he quits growing, will live that work even if he changes to other works, and till he draws his last breath. It's been about ten years since I quit hard riding, and if I walk the streets of a town today I'm still apt to shy when a piece of paper or anything flies up that would scare a horse. I at least always think about it. Many a time, while home on my ranch and walking from the house to the corrals, I catch myself holding my left hand out a bit and like I had bridle-reins in it. I've reined myself around many a sagebrush without knowing I was doing it. Others with me would sometimes remark about that. Mixing with horses as much as I have and often feeling that I'm still on a horse, while I now might be sitting in a chair or walking, makes me laugh and wonder sometimes if I ain't part horse. And I don't think it would surprise me much to look at myself in a glass some day and see a combination of man and horse together, like a drawing I remember seeing where from the shoulders of a horse there sprouts a man. I think that's called a centaur.

"People often ask me how I get to catch horses in action, or how I get my models for my drawings and paintings. I've never sketched from life and never watched any animal with intentions of sketching it."[1]

September 3, 1942. Died in Hollywood, California. ". . . I can't write fiction, and as far as my writing being in cowboy vernacular, as some say, it strikes me as being only as anybody would talk who got his raising and education outside, and where university roofs is the sky and the floors prairie sod."[2]

"What I write is built around facts, from things I've seen happen or experienced myself. I don't hunt up material nor local color, and I'm glad I've found a way to put down the life I know, proud to tell of it in my writings and drawings. I don't claim to know anything about writing, but if folks keep on going to the trouble of reading my work that's all I'll ever need to make me very happy in doing it."[1]

FOR MORE INFORMATION SEE: Will James, *Lone Cowboy: My Life Story,* Scribner, 1930; William James, *All in the Day's Riding,* Scribner, 1933; F. Scully, "James," in his

Rogues' Gallery: Profiles of My Eminent Contemporaries, Murray & Gee, 1943; Bertha E. Mahony and others, *Illustrators of Children's Books: 1744-1945,* Horn Book, 1947; Elizabeth Rider Montgomery, *Story Behind Modern Books,* Dodd, 1949; Stanley J. Kunitz and Howard Haycraft, editors, *Junior Book of Authors,* second edition, Wilson, 1951; Robert Patterson and others, editors, *On Our Way,* Holiday House, 1952; A. Dalgliesh, "Will James, 1892-1942," in *Newbery Medal Books, 1922-1955,* edited by Bertha E. Miller and E. W. Field, Horn Book, 1955; S. J. Kunitz, editor, *Twentieth Century Authors,* first supplement, Wilson, 1955; Anthony Amaral, *Will James: The Gilt Edged Cowboy,* Westernlore Press, 1967; Will James, *Cowboys North and South,* Arno Press, 1975.

JANEWAY, Elizabeth (Hall)   1913-

PERSONAL: Born October 7, 1913, in Brooklyn, N.Y.; daughter of Charles H. (a naval architect) and Jeanette F. (Searle) Hall; married Eliot Janeway (an economist and author), October 29, 1938; children: Michael Charles, William Hall. *Education:* Attended Swarthmore College, 1930-31; Barnard College, B.A., 1935. *Politics:* "Disturbed." *Home and office:* 15 East 80th St., New York, N.Y. 10021. *Agent:* Paul R. Reynolds, 599 5th Ave., New York, N.Y. 10017.

CAREER: Critic, novelist, and lecturer. Judge, National Book Awards, 1955; member of board of trustees, Barnard

ELIZABETH JANEWAY

(From *The Vikings* by Elizabeth Janeway. Illustrated by Henry C. Pitz.)

College, 1970—; judge, Pulitzer Prizes in Letters, 1971; member of board of directors, MacDowell Colony, 1971—; Berkeley Fellow, Yale University, 1971—. *Member:* Authors League of America (member of council, 1961—; vice-president, 1973—), Authors Guild (president, 1965-69). *Awards, honors:* D.Litt., Simpson College, 1972, Cedar Crest College, 1974, Villa Maria College, 1976; Delta Kappa Gamma Educators award, 1972.

WRITINGS: The Walsh Girls (novel), Doubleday, 1943; *Daisy Kenyon* (novel), Doubleday, 1945; *The Question of Gregory* (novel), Doubleday, 1949; *The Vikings* (juvenile), Random House, 1951; *Leaving Home* (novel), Doubleday, 1953; *The Early Days of the Automobile,* Random House, 1956; *The Third Choice* (novel), Harper, 1958; *Accident* (novel), Harper, 1964; *Ivanov VII* (juvenile), Harper, 1967; (editor with others) *Discovering Literature,* Houghton, 1968; (editor) *The Writer's World,* McGraw, 1969; *Man's World —Woman's Place: A Study in Social Mythology,* Morrow, 1971; (editor) *Women: Their Changing Roles,* Arno, 1973; *Between Myth and Morning: Women Awakening,* Morrow, 1974. Contributor to numerous literary and popular journals.

ADAPTATIONS: Daisy Kenyon was filmed by Twentieth Century-Fox in 1947.

WORK IN PROGRESS: Powers of the Weak, a study of power as a process of human interaction.

SIDELIGHTS: "The breakthru is here and will continue. I don't think the women's movement is a trendy, faddy thing that will go away. My intention is different from Kate Millet's and Germaine Greer's. They're making arguments —useful and needed arguments, but I'm doing something else. I am trying to explore the social context of change which has produced the women's movement." Of *Man's World—Woman's Place,* Margaret Mead writes: "This is a lucid and fascinating book, a book that draws so skillfully on the best of our fragmented social science, that, as a social scientist, it gives me renewed faith that we may in time, produce an integrated understanding of the world."

FOR MORE INFORMATION SEE: Chicago Tribune, April 23, 1972.

JOHNSON, Gerald White 1890-

PERSONAL: Born August 6, 1890, in Riverton, N.J.; son of Archibald (a country newspaper editor) and Flora Caroline (McNeill) Johnson; married Kathryn Hayward, April 22, 1922; children: two daughters. *Education:* Wake Forest College, B.A., 1911. *Politics:* Democrat. *Address:* 217 Bolton Place, Baltimore, Md. 21217.

CAREER: Thomasville Davidsonian, Thomasville, N.C., founder and editor, 1910; newspaperman, *Lexington Dispatch,* Lexington, N.C., 1911-13, *Greensboro Daily News,* Greensboro, N.C., 1913-24; University of North Carolina, Greensboro, N.C., professor of journalism, 1924-26; *Baltimore Evening Sun* (later the *Baltimore Sun*), Baltimore, Md., editorial writer, 1926-43; free lance writer, 1943—. News commentator, WAAM-TV, Baltimore, Md., 1952-54; contributing editor, *New Republic,* 1954—. *Military service:* U.S. Army, 321st Infantry, 81st Division, 1917-19, American Expeditionary Force, France, one year. *Member:* Phi Beta Kappa, West Hamilton Street Club, Century Club (New York City). *Awards, honors:* DuPont Commentators' award, 1953; Sidney Hillman Foundation award, 1954; George Foster Peabody award, 1954; runner-up for the Newbery medal, 1960, for *America Is Born,* and 1961, for *America Moves Forward;* Gold medal of the State of North Carolina, 1964; Andrew White medal from Loyola College, Baltimore, 1969; Litt.D. from Wake Forest College, 1928, Goucher College, 1969; LL.D. from College of Charleston, 1935, University of North Carolina, 1937, University of North Carolina at Greensboro, 1966; D.C.L., University of the South, 1942.

WRITINGS: (With W. R. Hayward) *The Story of Man's Work,* Minton, Balch, 1925; *What Is News?,* Knopf, 1926; *Andrew Jackson: An Epic in Homespun,* Minton, Balch, 1927; *The Undefeated,* Minton, Balch, 1927; *Randolph of Roanoke: A Political Fantastic,* Minton, Balch, 1929; *By Reason of Strength,* Minton, Balch, 1930; *Number Thirty-Six,* Minton, Balch, 1933; *The Secession of the Southern States,* Putnam, 1933; *A Little Night Music: Discoveries in the Exploitation of an Art* (illustrated by Richard Q. Yardley), Harper, 1937, reprinted, Greenwood Press, 1970; *The Wasted Land,* University of North Carolina Press, 1937, reprinted, Books for Libraries, 1970; (with Frank R. Kent, H. L. Mencken, and Hamilton Owens) *The Sunpapers of Baltimore,* Knopf, 1937; *America's Silver Age: The Statecraft of Clay-Webster-Calhoun,* Harper, 1939.

Roosevelt: Dictator or Democrat?, Harper, 1941 (published in England as *Roosevelt: An American Study,* H. Hamilton, 1942); *American Heroes and Hero-Worship,* Harper, 1943, new edition, Kennikat, 1966; *Woodrow Wilson: The Unforgettable Figure Who Has Returned to Haunt Us,* Harper, 1944; *An Honorable Titan: A Biographical Study of Adolph S. Ochs,* Harper, 1946, reprinted, Greenwood Press, 1970; *The First Captain: The Story of John Paul Jones,* Coward-McCann, 1947; *Liberal's Progress,* Coward-McCann, 1948; *Our English Heritage,* Lippincott, 1949, reprinted, Greenwood Press, 1973; *Incredible Tale: The Odyssey of the Average American in the Last Half Century,* Harper, 1950; *This American People,* Harper, 1951; *The Making of a Southern Industrialist: A Biographical Study of Simpson Bobo Tanner,* University of North Carolina Press, 1952; *Pattern for Liberty: The Story of Philadelphia,* McGraw-Hill, 1952; *Mount Vernon: The Story of a Shrine,* Random House, 1953; *The Lunatic Fringe,* Lippincott, 1957, reprinted, Greenwood Press, 1973; *The Lines Are Drawn: American Life since the First World War as Reflected in the Pulitzer Prize Cartoons,* Lippincott, 1958; *Peril and Promise: An Inquiry into Freedom of the Press,* Harper, 1958, reprinted, Greenwood Press, 1974.

The Man Who Feels Left Behind, Morrow, 1961; *Hod-Carrier: Notes of a Laborer on an Unfinished Cathedral,* Morrow, 1964; *Politics: Party Competition, and the County Chairman in West Virginia,* Bureau of Information, University of Tennessee, 1970; *The Imperial Republic: Speculation on the Future, If Any, of the Third U.S.A.,* Liveright, 1972; *America—Watching: Perspectives in the Course of an Incredible Century,* Stemmer House, 1976.

For young people: *America: A History for Peter* (illustrated by Leonard E. Fisher), Morrow, Volume I: *America Is Born,* 1959, Volume II: *America Grows Up,* 1960, Volume III: *America Moves Forward,* 1960; *The Supreme Court* (illustrated by L. E. Fisher), Morrow, 1962; *The Presidency* (illustrated by Fisher), Morrow, 1962; *The Congress* (illustrated by Fisher), Morrow, 1963; *Communism: An American's View,* Morrow, 1964; *The Cabinet* (illustrated by Fisher), Morrow, 1966; *Franklin D. Roosevelt: Portrait of a Great Man* (illustrated by Fisher), Morrow, 1967; *The British Empire: An American View of Its History from 1776 to 1945,* Morrow, 1969.

SIDELIGHTS: Born August 6, 1890, in Riverton, North Carolina, a village so small that Johnson once remarked: "population six kin." His father was the editor of a country newspaper.

Johnson was already editing his own newspaper, *The Thomasville Davidsonian,* before he graduated from Wake Forest College in 1911. Following graduation he went to work for the Lexington North Carolina *Dispatch.*

In 1913 he became the music critic for the Greensboro, North Carolina *Daily News.* Johnson was, like his father, an amateur musician. When World War I broke out, Johnson suspended his duties on the *News* and joined the Army for two years, later resuming his work for *Daily News* until 1924.

In 1922 Johnson married Kathryn Dulsinea Hayward. It was during the twenties that H. L. Mencken from the Baltimore *Sun* recognised Johnson's talents and urged the young editor to contribute to the Baltimore *Sun.* Mencken described Johnson as "the best editorial writer in the South, a very excellent critic, and a highly civilized man." By 1926 Johnson moved his wife and two small daughters to Baltimore where he had become a regular editor writing for the city's *Evening Sun.*

Besides his newspaper work Johnson began to write history books and in 1927 his third book, *Andrew Jackson, an Epic in Homespun,* established his reputation as an American historian. Modestly, Johnson never admitted to being a scholar although he was recognised as one—around the Baltimore papers a favorite phrase used to be "Ask Gerald."

In 1943 Johnson became a free-lance writer, author and news commentator. For his work as a news commentator, Johnson received (in 1954) a Peabody Award. Robert Lewis Shayon described Johnson as: "A biographer-historian-essayist, and the mental 3-D color TV, big screen, and stereophonic sound which he brings to the news is a fusion of this triad of non-journalistic disciplines. As a biographer he sees events in life-size, psychological scale; as an historian he illuminates these with the perspective of rear-projection; and as an essayist he shapes his views with humor, satire, and literary form. Harness these forces in a dry, almost a crackerbarrel, delivery of plain-talk simplicity of expression, and you have an arresting combination. Spice it with a courageously liberal cast of mind, and you have a refreshment of the air waves which is audacious, stimulating, and vastly entertaining, not to mention useful.

"Mr. Johnson's mind is liberal in the Greek sense of being 'fit for a free man'; he gives no blind devotion to any creed." [Robert Louis Shayon, "Comment on a Commentator," *Saturday Review,* July 11, 1953.[1]]

Johnson's literary career has spanned nearly six decades. One of his first books, *Andrew Jackson: An Epic in Homespun* was critiqued in *Saturday Review of Literature:* "No reader of this book is likely to complain that Johnson has failed to make the most of his dramatic material, or has suffered many of the dramatic silences in the play to go unabridged. . . . It is to Johnson's credit that, while he offers us no new facts, but turns on all the lights, works up a great color scheme, shifts the scenery with rapidity and skill, and keeps the orchestra hard at work, he remains a realist." This book made him famous and established him as an authority on American history and government.

The birth of his first grandson in 1950 was the stimulant for the trilogy, *America: A History for Peter.* As a grandfather, Johnson thought it was his responsibility to make Peter aware of his American heritage. In a review of the first book, *America Is Born,* a *Horn Book* critic observed: "Humor and remarkable perspective on people as well as events are here and the story flows as easily as if Mr. Johnson were indeed telling it to Peter, with excitement and a steady interest that holds the reader as it would the listener. . . ." Added the *New York Herald Tribune Book Review:* "The outstanding qualities of this book are a humorous forthrightness that avoids the commonplace and the involved explanation, an ability to select the significant incident and give it color and reality, making it seem as fresh as if it were told for the first time. . . ." On the other hand the *New York Times Book Review* noted, "Mr. Johnson oversimplifies historical causes. Youngsters would appreciate his learning insight all the more if they do not suspect they are being patronized, just slightly. This is, though, a really good book, dramatic and free from commonplace. . . ." Of the second book, *America Grows Up,* a *Chicago Sunday Tribune* reviewer wrote, "Written by

an experienced senior citizen for the youthful, this personalized essay is highly interpretative . . . , graphic and delightful . . . , [and] impartial and thoughtful. Much has been omitted, unfortunately, and incidental detail too often obscures the magnitude and magnificence of our story. . . . Over-simplification and archness of style limit the audience. The teen-age historian should and must cut his teeth on more historical bone and less interpretative meringue." The last book, *America Moves Forward* was reviewed by the *New York Herald Tribune Book Review:* "Simple, fresh, and exciting enough for a child to read with pleasure yet heartily recommended for his elders, it is filled with his strongly expressed opinions presented candidly but fairly."

Encouraged by the success of the first trilogy, Johnson wrote a second, describing the three branches of the U.S. government. *The Presidency, The Congress,* and *The Supreme Court* received the same favorable reviews as the earlier trilogy. Three years later, Johnson added a fourth volume, *The Cabinet.* These books have been translated into more than thirty languages.

FOR MORE INFORMATION SEE: Saturday Review of Literature, November 5, 1927, July 11, 1953; Stanley J. Kunitz, editor, *Twentieth Century Authors,* first supplement, H. W. Wilson, 1955; *New York Times Book Review,* November 1, 1959; *New York Herald Tribune Book Review,* November 1, 1959, and November 13, 1960; *Horn Book,* December, 1959; *Chicago Sunday Tribune,* May 8, 1960; Doris de Montreville and Donna Hill, editors, *Third Book of Junior Authors,* H. W. Wilson, 1972.

STEVEN KROLL

KROLL, Steven 1941-

PERSONAL: Born August 11, 1941, in New York, N.Y.; son of Julius (a diamond merchant) and Anita (a business executive; maiden name, Berger) Kroll. *Education:* Harvard University, B.A., 1962. *Politics:* "Committed to change." *Religion:* Jewish. *Home and office:* 64 West 11th St., New York, N.Y. 10011. *Agent:* Jean Davies, 59 East 54th St., New York, N.Y. 10022.

CAREER: Transatlantic Review, London, England, associate editor, 1962-65; Chatto & Windus Ltd., London, England, reader and editor, 1962-65; Holt, Rinehart & Winston, New York, N.Y., acquiring editor in trade department, 1965-69; full-time writer, 1969—. University of Maine, Augusta, instructor in English, 1970-71. *Member:* Harvard Club (New York), Authors Guild.

WRITINGS—All juveniles: *Is Milton Missing?* (Junior Literary Guild selection), Holiday House, 1975; *The Tyrannosaurus Game,* Holiday House, 1976; *That Makes Me Mad!,* Pantheon, 1976; *Sleepy Ida and Other Nonsense Poems,* Pantheon, 1977; *Gobbledygook,* Holiday House, 1977; *If I Could Be My Grandmother,* Pantheon, 1977; *Santa's Crash-*

Bang Christmas, Holiday House, 1977; *T. J. Folger, Thief,* Holiday House, 1978; *Fat Magic,* Holiday House, 1978; *Space Cats,* Holiday House, 1979; *The Candy Witches,* Holiday House, 1979; *Monster Birthday,* Holiday House, 1980; *Are You Pirates?,* Pantheon, 1980. Contributor of book reviews to *New York Times Book Review, Book World, Commonweal, Village Voice, Listener, Spectator, Times Literary Supplement,* and *London Magazine.*

SIDELIGHTS: "When people ask how I go about writing for children, my answer is always the same. Children themselves help with the details, but what is most important is the feeling that I am somehow in touch with my own childhood.

"When I write about a child's room, that room is often my own—the one in the Manhattan apartment house where I grew up. When I write about an urban street or an urban school, it is often my street or my school, taken out of time into a situation I have invented. And sometimes, if I'm writing about a suburb or a small town, that place will resemble the home of a summer camp friend I visited once, and longed to see again.

"To be in touch with your own childhood is to be, in some way, touched with wonder, and when I write for children,

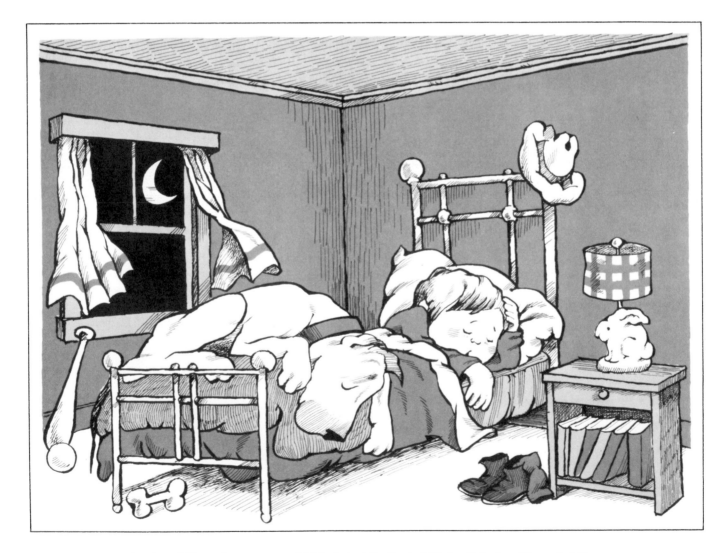

At night, Milton slept on a special blanket at the foot of Richard's bed. ■ (From *Is Milton Missing?* by Steven Kroll. Illustrated by Dick Gackenbach.)

(From *That Makes Me Mad* by Steven Kroll. Illustrated by Hilary Knight.)

that is what I feel. It is the wonder that makes things happen on the page.

"The ideas can come from almost anywhere. *That Makes Me Mad!* began with a phrase I saw penciled on an envelope. When I was writing *Sleepy Ida*, nonsense poems just popped into my head. I did poems while shaving, poems in the shower, poems waiting at the airport, poems walking down the street. And they were poems about anything, poems about noses, turkey sandwiches, crazy cats, cabbage. *If I Could Be My Grandmother* came out of observing my niece Odile's relationship with my mother. *Space Cats* began with a strange-looking shirt I saw on the subway.

"It is wonderful to be able to explore the fanciful and the real, as I do, with so little fear of limitation. Occasionally I go too far, become too extravagant, need to be restrained, but it is mostly outside the realm of children's books that I find limits, limits set by an adult world that is entirely too grown up.

"I really love writing for children. I love starting the fireworks, love that explosion of emotion, of excitement, terror, and enthusiasm that comes with putting those words on paper and sometimes, if the mood is right, doing a whole picture book story in one sitting. I wasn't always involved in children's books. I started almost by accident—as a breather between other projects when I was living in the Maine countryside—but it's part of me now and I'd like other adults to let down the barriers and feel the wonder in their own lives that I feel in these books.

"Language—what we say and what we write—defines us. But no one is taught that truth in school, and through the mass media language has been everywhere debased. If we are to escape our current confusion, we must regain some sense of our use of language. I have always felt this way, was drawn to writing for that reason as well as by the need to tell stories. I also play a lot of tennis and squash, walk all over New York, and travel wherever I can. Sometimes I think languid thoughts about cruising down the Mississippi on a riverboat."

FOR MORE INFORMATION SEE: Publishers Weekly, February 23, 1976, February 28, 1977; *New York Times Book Review*, 1977.

KUPFERBERG, Herbert   1918-

PERSONAL: Born January 20, 1918, in New York, N.Y.; son of Moses (an importer) and Augusta (Lasserwitz) Kupferberg; married Barbara Gottesman, January 24, 1954; children: Seth, Joel, Natalie. *Education:* Cornell University, A.B., 1939; Columbia University, M.A., 1940, M.S., 1941. *Religion:* Jewish. *Home:* 113-14 72nd Rd., Forest Hills, N.Y. 11375. *Agent:* Shirley Burke, 370 East 76th St., New York, N.Y. 10021. *Office: Parade*, 750 Third Ave., New York, N.Y. 10017.

CAREER: New Bedford Standard Times, New Bedford, Mass., copy editor, 1941-42; *New York Herald Tribune*, New York, N.Y., copy editor, 1942-46, assistant to editor of European edition, 1946-47, reporter, 1948-50, editorial writ-

HERBERT KUPFERBERG

No. 3 Chester Place, London—a drawing made by Mendelssohn. His friend Moscheles lived in the house. ■ (From *Felix Mendelssohn* by Herbert Kupferberg.)

er, 1950-62, record critic, 1952-66, lively arts editor, 1962-66; *Parade,* New York, N.Y., senior editor, 1967—. Fordham University, instructor in journalism, 1960-69. *Atlantic,* music critic, 1958-68; *National Observer,* music critic, 1968-77; *The Trib,* New York, N.Y., music critic, 1978—. Also advisory editor of *Dance News* and a regular contributor to the programs of Lincoln Center and Kennedy Center. *Member:* Overseas Press Club of America (chairman of music committee).

WRITINGS: These Fabulous Philadelphians: The Life and Times of a Great Orchestra, Scribner, 1969; *The Mendelssohns: Three Generations of Genius,* Scribner, 1972; *Felix Mendelssohn: His Life, His Family, His Music* (juvenile), Scribner, 1972; *A Rainbow of Sound: The Instruments of the Orchestra and Their Music* (juvenile), Scribner, 1973; *Opera,* Newsweek Books, 1974; *Tanglewood,* McGraw, 1976. Contributor to *Harper's, This Week,* and other national magazines.

SIDELIGHTS: "I have never been a fulltime music critic, but writing about music has become perhaps the most important aspect of my professional career. My interest in music began to develop in my high school years, and was nurtured first through low-priced performances at the Salmaggi Opera in New York and later through studies at Cornell University, but I went into journalism as a non-specialized writer and editor, and only later added music to the subjects I was covering. I think it makes sense for a critic to approach music through journalism rather than journalism through music; too many critics tend to write in a specialized way, losing sight of the need for direct, jargon-free communication with their readers.

"My books are an extension of my musical journalism. I wrote my history of the Philadelphia Orchestra because there was a need for an up-to-date account of this great organization and the colorful creative personalities associated with it; my book about the Mendelssohns resulted from my fascination with the composer, Felix, and his philosopher-grandfather, Moses. My *Opera* and *Tanglewood* books were suggested by the publishers.

"Because I hold a fulltime job, I write my books evenings and especially weekends. I find it advisable to combine my research and writing activities so they overlap; thus, while I was still researching and studying Felix Mendelssohn I was busy committing my findings about Moses to paper. I think too many books never get written because their authors insist on assembling all their data and material before they actually begin to write. I find the pressure of a deadline makes for clarity as well as speed—this, too, may be the result of my journalistic experience."

FOR MORE INFORMATION SEE: New York Times, October 18, 1969; *Book World,* November 2, 1969.

LA FARGE, Oliver (Hazard Perry) 1901-1963

PERSONAL: Born December 19, 1901, in New York, N.Y.; son of Christopher Grant (an architect and lecturer on architecture) and Florence Bayard (a worker in nursing training schools; maiden name Lockwood) La Farge; married Wanden E. Mathews, September 28, 1929 (divorced, 1937); married Consuelo O. C. de Baca (a literary agent), October 14, 1939; children: (first marriage) Povy (daughter), Oliver Albee; (second marriage) John Pendaries. *Education:* Harvard University, B.A., 1924, Hemenway Fellow, 1924-26, M.A., 1929. *Religion:* Roman Catholic. *Home:* Santa Fe, N.M.

CAREER: Tulane University, New Orleans, La., assistant professor of ethnology, 1926-28; Columbia University, New York, N.Y., research fellow in anthropology, 1931-33, teacher of the technique of writing, 1936-41; during the above years, La Farge made three archaeological expeditions to Arizona for Harvard, one to Mexico and Guatemala for Tulane, and one to Guatemala for Columbia. Director of the Eastern Association in Indian Affairs, 1930-32, and of the Intertribal Exhibitions of Indian Arts, 1931; president of the National Association on Indian Affairs, 1933-37, and of the American Association on Indian Affairs, 1937-42, 1946-63; field representative for the United States Indian Service, 1936; Alliance Book Corp., editorial adviser, 1940-41; appointed to the ten-man advisory committee to the Government on Indian Affairs, 1949; member of the U.S. Department of Interior's Committee on Indian Arts and Crafts; official adviser to the Hopi Indians. Trustee for the W.E.B. DuBois prize for Negro Literature, 1932-34; member of the advisory board of the Laboratory of Anthropology, Santa

Fe, N.M., 1935-41, 1946-63; member of the committee of awards of the Opportunity Fellowships of the John Hay Whitney Foundation.

MILITARY SERVICE: Served in the U.S. Army Air Command as chief historical officer, 1942-45; became lieutenant colonel. *Member:* American Association for the Advancement of Science (fellow), American Anthropological Association, National Institute of Arts and Letters, P.E.N., Authors' League (New York City), Century Club, Coffee House Club. *Awards, honors:* Pulitzer Prize for fiction, 1929, for *Laughing Boy;* O. Henry Memorial Prize, 1931, for *Haunted Ground;* M.A., 1932, from Brown University; Guggenheim fellowship for writing, 1941; Legion of Merit (military); Commendation Ribbon (military).

WRITINGS: (With Frans Blom) *Tribes and Temples,* Tulane University Press, 1927; *Laughing Boy* (novel), Houghton, 1929, reissued, Barrie & Jenkins, 1972; (with Douglas Byers) *The Year Bearer's People,* Tulane University Press, 1931; *Sparks Fly Upward* (novel), Houghton, 1931, reissued, Popular Library, 1959; *Long Pennant* (novel), Houghton, 1933; *All the Young Men* (stories; includes *Haunted Ground*), Houghton, 1935, reprinted, AMS Press, 1976; *The Enemy Gods* (novel), Houghton, 1937, reissued, University of New Mexico Press, 1975; *As Long as the Grass Shall Grow* (nonfiction), Longmans, Green, 1940; (editor) *The Changing Indian,* University of Oklahoma Press, 1942; *The Copper Pot* (novel), Houghton, 1942; *Raw Material* (autobiography), Houghton, 1945; *Santa Eulalia: The Religion of a Cuchumatan Indian Town,* University of Chicago Press, 1947; *The Eagle in the Nest,* Houghton, 1949, reprinted, Arno, 1972.

Cochise of Arizona: The Pipe of Peace is Broken (juvenile; illustrated by L. F. Bjorklund), Aladdin Books, 1953; *The Mother Ditch* (juvenile; illustrated by Karl Larsson), Houghton, 1954; *Behind the Mountains,* Houghton, 1956, reprinted, Gannon, 1974; *A Pictorial History of the American Indian,* Crown, 1956, revised edition, 1974, special edition for young readers published as *The American Indian,* Golden Press, 1960; *A Pause in the Desert* (short stories), Houghton, 1957; (with Arthur N. Morgan) *Santa Fe: The Autobiography of a Southwestern Town,* University of Oklahoma Press, 1959; *The Door in the Wall* (stories), Houghton, 1965; *The Man with the Calabash Pipe: Some Observations* (selections from the author's weekly newspaper column from 1950-63; edited by Winfield Townley Scott), Houghton, 1966.

Author of a weekly newspaper column in the *Santa Fe New Mexican,* 1950-63; contributor of articles and book reviews to many periodicals, including the *New York Times Book Review.*

SIDELIGHTS: **December 19, 1901.** Born in New York City. La Farge's background was distinguished—ancestors included Benjamin Franklin and Commodore Oliver Hazard Perry. His grandfather, John La Farge, was a famous painter and artist in stained glass and Christopher La Farge, his father, was a noted architect.

Although La Farge was born in New York where the family lived during the winter, he considered himself a Rhode Islander. Summers were spent in Saunderstown on the Rhode Island coast. "At earliest memory, at the farthest back that I can take myself, the waters of Narragansett Bay were long familiar. From then till now it continues—stability, security, happiness. . . .

OLIVER LA FARGE

"The shore is always a place on which a group of boys, or one boy alone, can become utterly absorbed and self-forgetful. Exploration of the little basins, the animals, the rocks, is never completed or exhausted. As soon as we could swim, we put out in rowboats for ourselves. With a complexity like Worry Wart's in 'Out Our Way' we rigged sails for anything that would float, slowly learning how to make the most unlikely tubs move to windward, acquiring unconsciously the feel of wind, boat, and water.

"Growing a little older, we progressed to canoes, and then to sailing dories, the most seaworthy of small craft when properly handled, and the most easily capsized. Although we thought little of it, we must have become pretty skillful, for now I can see that in all innocence we performed some surprising feats. We had no intention of being foolhardy, but, for instance, felt as boys will that we really should get home somewhere around the time at which we were expected, rather than lying over in a safe place, waiting for a bad blow to pass. It never would have occurred to any of us to tie canoe or dory up and telephone for someone to fetch us by land.

". . . Home was in many ways a child's heaven, a happy, roaring democracy with a touch of anarchy, ruled by reason and justice tempered with indulgence. We were allowed to argue about anything that came up, and argue we did, particularly at table, be it over the depth of the channel in Narragansett Bay or what was the matter with the Darwinian theory. We were always getting up from the table to find a reference book. At times we nearly drove my father mad, for he liked quiet; how my mother survived I don't know. She got it all the time, and what was more, she treated our childish logics seriously, umpiring the disputes, barring the *argu-*

mentum ad hominem until she had cured us of it, deciding when points were well taken, forestalling the resort to temper.

"Even punishment was arguable; one might say that we enjoyed the right of trial by jury. Nor was it thought ridiculous for a ten-year-old to have an opinion, backed by reasons, on the values of Spartan culture (we disliked it, the Athenians were our meat) or the two-party system. We roamed the countryside on horseback or afoot, we occasionally stole sheets to make sails for our rowboats, we wrangled unbelievably, we were chronically late for meals, we read everything we could lay our hands on, and we stood in awe of no one save only my father. It was a good life, too good as a matter of fact, somewhere along the line discipline was bound to catch up with us. It certainly was no preparation for adjustment to a totalitarian community." [Oliver La Farge, *Raw Material*, Houghton, 1945.[1]]

1914. After attending St. Bernard's School in New York, La Farge continued his college preparatory training at Groton in Massachusetts. The conformity Groton demanded of the "ideal Groton boy" was in direct conflict with the liberal atmosphere of La Farge's home; therefore, his years at Groton were difficult ones. "About ten years ago, when it was still impossible for me to talk honestly about School and I avoided the thought of it as much as possible, I found the diaries I had kept there. . . . A glance at them revealed calf love, turmoil, foolish adolescence, calling up those times and that state of being so vividly that I burned them. It was a stupid thing to have done, unworthy of a writer. If I had them now, perhaps I could recapture what it was really like.

"It is difficult, perhaps impossible, for anyone to think clearly about his school days, whatever his attitude may be. He received his impressions at an age when detached, proportioned judgement could hardly be expected; later he must not only look back upon events grown dim, but into a personality which is no longer his, and which he may have lost the capacity really to understand. Perhaps none of what I have to describe can be attributed to Groton at all, but in one form or another would have befallen me anywhere; all I know is that certain things happened there, and that it is there I first can spot, tracing back, certain major lines of my life.

"I had funny ideas about myself when I entered Groton. One was that I was a pretty fine physical specimen, a good athlete, tall. A day or two after school opened we had our first gym class. We were told to line up according to height. There were three outstandingly tall boys in the Form; I figured I came next to them or one below. But something, I don't remember what, had already suggested to me that it was well to be cagey, and there flashed through my mind the Bible story about 'Friend, go up higher.' I decided to place myself modestly in the middle of the line and have the satisfaction of being moved up by the instructor. This I did. The boy next below me objected, but I paid no attention to him.

"The instructor looked over the line, and with only a mildly humourous remark moved me to where I belonged, forth from the bottom in a Form of about twenty-five. There was a laugh against me.

"The incident was tiny, but significant. It has remained specific and clear-cut in a memory of a period which is mostly vague, primarily the memory of a growing bewilderment and uncertainty rather than of events. While the Form was still

discovering itself, uncrystallized, I had been unfavourably prominent. Those things mount up.

"I was awkward, small, not strong. My feet were too big, and pigeon-toed. They flopped when I ran, and I was slow. These physical realities were slowly but forcefully brought home to me, both through competition and through comment. Add spectacles which dominated my face, a cowlick, and a chronic incapacity (I still suffer from it) to keep ink from getting on my fingers and thence on my nose, and you have a classic picture. As increasingly the possessor of these attributes was made to be conscious of them, you can see how easily imagination could find in them points of identification with the antithesis, the Ungroton Boy.

"At Christmas I got my first suit with long pants. It was a brown tweed, a good colour and becoming; I think my father helped me choose it. About half the Form was still in knickers; I came back for the beginning of the Winter Term feeling cocky. That first day, unpacking in the dormitory, inspiration came to Robinson [the school bully]. I don't remember just what set him off; there was some chance connection, it was not quite whole cloth, there would always be a thread. Perhaps I had wrapped something in toilet paper when I was packing. I was quite capable of doing that in all innocence.

"'Bumwad Inky,' he said, his eye lighting up. (Inky is my ancient, family nickname.) 'Bumwad Inky is his bumwad suit.'

"I recognized that hot look in his eyes, the way his face lighted up, his weaving motion. I should have socked him then and there, but I was even smaller and feebler than he, I knew I should be licked, and I lacked the simple guts.

"Through the day he worked on his new idea, through Bumwad Inks to Bumptink, to Bump, and finally to the *chef d'oeuvre* of his career, Bop. I am describing a genius in his own line. He immediately associated this elementary noise with the action and alleged sound of my awkward feet, and at the same time he kept the original meaning alive. I fought him, and was licked, that evening, and several times more in the next few days. It was too late then, I was Bop.

"That first night when I went to bed, I knew that it had happened. My mind being what it was, I had already figured out the existence of definite classes within the Form, and particularly the bottom one, the slums, containing the two or three wretched individuals on whom there was always an open season, the exposed failures, the—dread word—*unpopular*. I had seen, too, that another group stood just within the bounds of belonging, and could at any time be pushed down into the slums. I had been one of those, I knew; now I had joined the outcasts.

"In my Fourth Form year I was becoming a tolerable physical specimen. I had no idea of this. My incapacity and awkwardness had been so thoroughly drummed into me by then, via my nickname and otherwise, that I had a fixed mental image of myself which remained dominant, though slowly giving way, until I was thirty, and of which I find traces still remain. Yet actual trial showed that I had some capacity for high-jumping, so I worked at it.

"I went out for things partly because I was damned if I would admit myself licked, and not to try was to admit it, since I knew I feared the jeering as much as I did merely not succeeding. This stubbornness was reinforced by a different urge, a truly hopeless quest which continued through college and far beyond. There was the desire to prove to the world, and to myself, that I really was like others, the vain attempt to replace a failure in being by achievement in doing. So long as I was convinced of my internal inferiority, so that winning my letter or being editor of the school magazine merely seemed surprising exceptions rather than parts of my real pattern, no honour won could do me any good, but each one turned to ashes as soon as it was in hand, leaving always the restless ambition to go higher and prove at last that I was really all right; the next achievement would do it. At the same time, and running directly contrary to all this, was a vast elaboration of all the techniques of escape. Escape, and the wedding of escape to this urge for doing, produced the dominant motifs of my adult life and in one form or another will run through many sections of this story. This now is merely the anatomy of an inferiority complex—I suppose it's that—the formation of an individual.

"By my Sixth Form year my record of performance had, in fact, formed a pattern which in the eyes of the others showed me as far from unsuccessful. I did not become exactly popular, but I was accepted, I formed certain friendships, I carried some weight. I enjoyed my change of status, but I thought I was merely fooling public opinion, for I knew that I, myself, had not changed from the person who had been so despised. The idea of the mask had become a conscious one; from there on for fifteen years or more I was to live with it."[1]

1920. Graduated from Groton and entered Harvard. "We went on to Harvard, to the bliss of a new start among strangers. Without word from me, by common consent my classmates from Groton dropped my hated nickname. It was a very decent thing of them to do, the biggest assist they could have given me, and it must be remembered of them. . . .

"But Groton and the Groton Boy were not easily shaken off. . . . I strove ridiculously at Harvard for surplus honours. Thus, having joined one utterly sufficient club, I was glad to get into two others for which I had no use at all, simply because it might prove to me that I was really all right. Being President of *The Advocate,* the college literary magazine, I nonetheless submitted wormlike to all the hazing involved in heeling for the *Lampoon,* although I didn't have much respect for it, didn't like most of the editors on it, and knew that they didn't like me. They had to elect me finally, whereupon I dropped the thing like a hot potato. At no time had I really wanted it, in a way I had committed an indignity against my own publication, which I loved, and all because to be editor of *two* magazines seemed more outstanding.

"Along with all this running furiously and getting nowhere, were the familiar phenomena of the inferiority complex, the touchy arrogance, self-assertiveness, and withdrawal, the behaviour which made people think me a swelled-headed nuisance, and so forth. . . ."[1]

1921-1922. During his sophomore year went to Arizona as an assistant on an archeological expedition. "When I was ready for college I thought of becoming an historian. I had fallen upon Hakluyt's *Voyages,* read them nearly straight through, and embarked upon a two-fold study of Elizabethan seafaring and the history of the sailing vessel. This might have been the most natural choice I could have made, its alliance to writing is obvious, and already my secret ambition was to be a writer. Had I made it, my life would have been unthinkably different. But, I had read *Men of the Old Stone Age* first. The other was a delightful occupation, Science stood forth as a vocation. Even in that there were manifold choices—Paleontology, Evolutionary Biology, Physical

Anthropology and Archaeology, all were pertinent to my interest. *The Origin and Evolution of Life* had been just a little too tough for me, *Men of the Old Stone Age* reread was well within my grasp. I chose Archaeology, and specifically the archaeology of palaeolithic France. In this I was conscious of a gentle pressure, my mother's feeling about a professor in the family. My real decision was that I should start in this direction and see what happened.

"The authorities at Harvard tested the strength of my interest by the simple method of sending me on an expedition to Arizona, to see what long hours wielding a shovel in the hot sun would bring out of me. Various other factors came into play at the same time that the Navajos dawned upon me, and without even being conscious of having made a vital change I settled upon Ethnology. I also fell in love with the Southwest and made the first steps in breaking out of the protected, secure provincialism of the nicely brought up Northeastern American."[1]

1924. Graduated from Harvard where he had been elected class poet.

1925. Assistant in charge of ethnology and linguistics of a Tulane University anthropological expedition to Guatemala and southern Mexico. "By sheer chance I met a Dane, Frans Blom, who was going to Mexico and Guatemala for Tulane University. He took a shine to me and hired me as his assistant. He was a fine scientist, a real explorer, and a natural teacher. New Orleans became my home, my specialty the Mayan Indians of the high, mountain country, Spanish became my second tongue, so much so that I can no longer speak Italian and my French is sadly corrupted. Those Indians remain my special subject to this day; had I continued earning my living as an anthropologist I should have visited those mountains year after year; as it is, I know them better than I do the northern half of my native state. . . ."[1]

1926-1928. Assistant professor of ethnology at Tulane University. "My second expedition outside the United States, in 1927, was to the Jacalteco Indians of the Cuchumatán Highlands in Guatemala. With me went Douglas Byers, now head of the Andover Museum. Byers had been with me in Arizona, he was an ideal companion for a long, difficult assignment, he seemed about to become a banker, and I was in hopes of seducing him back into anthropology.

"Casual information which Frans Blom and I had picked up when we passed through Jacaltenango in 1925 proved to us that here in secret there was a rich and rare survival of the ancient Mayan religion. To learn about that I came back with Byers.

"One descended upon the village from the high backbone of the Cuchumatanes, firs, pines, and tall cedars above on the crest, more great evergreens across the gorge a couple of miles away, alongside the trail manifold patches of corn and wheat on slopes so steep that falling would be a genuine hazard of farming. The houses, hundreds of them, sprawled over the delta-like hanging valley, straw-thatched huts, scattered higgeldy-piggeldy with the big, white church and municipal buildings at the centre, here and there the deep green of coffee groves or the yellower colour of bananas. The valley was open to the west, falling off at the edge of the village in a cliff, then below the cliff the land dropped away, ridged and rugged, a thousand feet and another thousand and another, down to the Mexican border ten leagues away. Far beyond the Sierra Madre rose again, a jumbled, blue formation over which the red sunsets formed. Late afternoon light came yellow over the houses, in its bath the smoke seeped through the thatched roofs so that each house carried a trailing, sun-shot nimbus. There were wild, white roses along the trail; in the village, hibiscus by the doorways.

"Here were seven thousand people of whom I knew virtually nothing. I had done a little work among related tribes the other side of the border. I had heard tales that, pressed hard enough, the men of these tribes will kill to protect their gods. I knew what one could see in passing through. The men were slender, small, golden-skinned, neatly made. They wore a heavy, black wool tunic over white cotton shirts and trousers, kept their hair short, occasionally carried blowguns. The women were handsome, they too were slender, their long skirts of green cotton with an all-over blue and white design wrapped in a narrow sheath, showed that, unlike our Indians, they did not spread as they grew older. They wound their dark hair in a crown around their heads with wide ribbons of native weave, rich and lustrous in colour.

"As one looked down over the steep edge of the trail one could see in front of the church the great cross, seventy-two feet high, slender, grey-weathered, skeletal. Its base I knew was a crude, square altar containing a number of fire pits. In the dusk I had seen a file of some six men go to that altar. Instead of the ordinary tunics they wore long ponchos of black wool, on their heeds and also over their shoulders like stoles were kerchiefs with a striped design, predominantly dark red. They carried long staves. They had gone quickly and quietly to the base of the cross and prayed there while the clouds of *copal* incense billowed up from the fires they kindled. The dull flames of the pitchwood licked into the base of the rising smoke. Then they had risen and moved on to another part of the village, quiet, intense, oblivious.

"These things I knew. We were riding down to face a strange personality and attempt the ridiculous task of persuading it that two young men, unknown to it, alien in race, should be accepted by it to the inner limits of confidence. This was my big chance, this if it succeeded would wipe out past failures, it would forestall the drudgery of getting a Ph.D. It would say something important to me about myself. The tales one had heard of that personality were strange and streaked with violence. The horses continued moving steadily, mechanically, down upon the village. I felt the gun under my leg and wondered if I should need it, I speculated upon failure.

"By the time I got through with these Indians I neither loved nor hated them. Culturally and linguistically I could think of them in the mass, but emotionally they had become many people; the sense of separation which enables one to generalize freely had grown dim and they were a number of human beings, some of whom I liked, some of whom I didn't. . . . It was around these Indians, as I prepared to write at some length about their relation to the whole social structure of Guatemala, that I did my first broad social thinking, it was from them that I derived the theory of social conditions which one accepts perforce but which never cease to irritate, which I later applied to Negroes and which led me on to new political and social concepts."[1]

1928. Returned to Harvard to do research on linguistics in the Mayan language. "For a short time I was at Harvard, digging up the real, inside dope on the mutations of the letter *k* in the Mayan family. I also worried hard about my future, and only on rare occasions, as a special indulgence, did I allow myself to work on the novel. I had to get down to brass tacks."[1]

1929. M.A. degree from Harvard. Wrote his first novel, *Laughing Boy,* which received the Pulitzer Prize for that year. "*Laughing Boy* was written for myself alone as nearly as that is possible in an attempt at a work of art. All my friends were agreed that no book about Indians could ever be sold. It was a rare bit of luck that enabled me to place one Indian short story in *The Dial*. . . . Negroes one could write about, Latin America perhaps, but Indians, absolutely not. I was pretty well persuaded of this. But I had the idea, and once conceived the idea carried with it the necessity that it be written. With that, too, was the emotion of longing and farewell to a beloved country which I might never see again. In this book I should pour out all my love. Self-expression? Perhaps, but indirectly through the expression of a beauty seen.

"Ferris Greenslet of Houghton Mifflin got in touch with me. He told me he had liked my Navajo short story in *The Dial,* and wondered if I had any idea of anything of book length along those lines. I joyfully outlined my novel. He said that Houghton Mifflin would like to see it. This word was like coming across a life-preserver when one was all but spent from swimming. It set me free and it gave me a new, incredulous hope.

"So I went back to New Orleans and finished the book, making it my main occupation now, tasting for the first time the full delight of writing, the luxury of absorption. And they really did take it. Good Lord, the hope came true. A book, with a regular binding and a dust jacket and everything, and OLIVER LA FARGE on it, was sent to me. I put it on the mantelpiece and walked around studying it from all angles. With the conviction which that carried I upped my estimate of its probable sales to two thousand five hundred, which would make me more money than I had ever seen in one lump in my life. And, at last *I was a writer.*

"*Laughing Boy* expressed the point which I had reached. I saw our own Indians as inexorably doomed, I saw that they must come increasingly into contact with our so-called civilization, and that (I then thought inevitably) contact meant conflict and disaster. I put this idea into the book, along with anger at certain evil things that I had seen, and then I let myself out by sending my hero, after the final tragedy, back into my own dreamland, the untouched, undisturbed Navajo country where the white man was not a factor and would not become one within my time. The whole treatment was specific, personal to the characters involved. It might prove good publicity for the Navajos, but it could lead to no reforms.

"*Laughing Boy* catapulted me into the spotlight. Suddenly I was somebody, and prosperous to boot."[1]

September, 1929. Married Wanden Esther Matthews.

1930-1932. Served as director of the Eastern Association on Indian Affairs and supervisor of its Inter-Tribal Exhibition of Indian Affairs in 1931. "I was just past thirty years old, *Laughing Boy* had sold to the movies, my second book was doing well, and I was beginning to hit the *Saturday Evening Post.* I had been undergoing a series of revelations concerning Indian affairs, I was sincere, brash, and young. So I expressed my ideas in a polite way, and as a result found myself president of an Association with eighteen paid-up

An Arapaho Ghost Dance. ■ (From *The American Indian* by Oliver La Farge. Photo courtesy of the Smithsonian Institution.)

members and nothing in the treasury, and a whale of a fight on my hands."[1]

1931. Son, Oliver Albee, born.

1933. Elected president of the National Association on Indian Affairs. That same year daughter, Povy, born.

1937. Marriage ended in divorce. Wrote to his brother: "Shocking and upsetting to fixed ideas as it was, [the divorce] has been the shedding of an incubus, the end of years of struggling against a steady resistance." [D'Arcy McNickle, *Indian Man: A Life of Oliver La Farge,* Indiana University Press, 1971.[2]]

Summer, 1937. Divided time between New York where his writing went poorly and Saunderstown where his father was dying. Described his home in a letter to a friend: "The family picture here is rather grim, as father has an attack of neuritis, which has stopped all his progress and he is naturally depressed by it. I go up at regular intervals and converse with him. I must say, he's game as the dickens. . . .

"My God, this place is certainly family. I forget about it until I see the look of bewilderment crossing Oliver's [his son's] face as yet one more individual is introduced to him as a cousin or an aunt, and he finds cousins who are old and grey-haired, as well as contemporaries, and so forth. He has two great aunts here right now, one aunt and one uncle, two first

cousins, four first cousins once removed, five second cousins, two more firsts once removed due over the weekend, and three elderly cousins whom I'm not savvy enough to classify."[2]

October, 1938. Father died after a long illness. "For more than a year we visited with him in the room. Each of us received the same impression. Neither self-deceived nor a coward, he was visibly making himself ready for death. He let go, one by one, of minor interests and particularly of those, such as improvements in the place, which could be considered only in terms of years from now. He kept up those which were rewarding in themselves and out of them made himself a lively life. He entertained himself with us.

"I still do not know if there is a smell of death. There was something in that room which had the emotional effect of a smell, one felt the presence of the old skull and bones. To him it must have been perched on the foot of the bed. It might come in ten minutes and it might not come for a year or more, there was no way of knowing. It could come quietly, instantly, or it could strike as a searing, unbearable pain in the full fury of a heart attack. None of this could be foreseen. It simply was always there, waiting. And he knew it."[1]

October, 1939. Married Consuelo de Baca. "Consuelo is a swell wife for an artist. . . . She has a quick grasp of a sound general conception of work, and she would rather see me put out good stuff than make money on poorer stuff or in a regular job. And this is quite realistic in her, [since] our non-making of money has direct effects upon her—she cannot get a dress, she runs short on stockings, she does the cooking, our Christmas is run on a shoestring."[2]

1941. Relinquished his part-time teaching position at Columbia University. A Guggenheim fellowship made the break possible and almost immediately he and his wife moved West. "Since we must make up our minds to live in one place only, New Mexico is the place."[2]

1942. Served in the U.S. Army Air Command as chief historical officer. "I am assigned to a fascinating outfit, made up to an exceptionally high degree of men bent on outdoing themselves in a tremendous undertaking. In my Command discipline is joined with informality and flexibility in a most effective union, and the bond between man and man is strong. I've had many lucky breaks in my life. Of these, next to being accepted by my wife, this is the biggest of all. I have fallen in love with a bomber; quite literally, a new world has been opened to me."[1]

January, 1944. Promoted to Major. Wrote to his brother: "I am really very pleased about it, especially as, by special request of General George [his Commanding Officer], I was promoted when I was still two months short of the length of service in grade usually required."[2]

August, 1945. Promoted to Lieutenant Colonel. The Army was a beneficial experience for La Farge. "The important thing was the total change. Writers and scientists are solitary workers. They are inclined to associate principally with their own kind. They control their own hours and methods of work. The Army Air Force provided a violent contrast. I was a member of a large headquarters, I had to learn to play on the team. I had to learn to work with men from totally alien backgrounds, and had the delight of becoming fast friends with many of them. Aviation had never interested me; it was essential that I become something of an expert on it. I had to become an administrator, an organizer, and something of a politician. . . . Nothing better, I think, could happen to a man in his forties."[2]

1946. Discharged from the Army. "There's a curious let-down to being in uniform once the shooting's stopped. You begin to wonder when people will start asking you why you aren't doing something useful.

"In the army one is not self-starting; either one is told what to do, or the situations as they arise or the mail coming in have the same effect. I found myself terrified at the thought of sitting down with nothing before me but time and blank paper and proceeding to make something all on my own."[2]

May, 1948. Elected president of the Association of American Indian Affairs, Inc. Long a champion of the rights of the American Indians, La Farge expressed the association's position: "We do not believe that Indians 'must be assimilated.' We believe that assimilation should be a matter of their own free choice, and it is our observation that these level-headed and practical people, where they have been able to make an intelligent choice, go at the question of what cultural values of their own to retain and what to abandon in favor of ours in a realistic manner. They should be given not only the academic education but the general understanding of our world which will enable them to make these choices soundly."[2]

1951. Son, John Pendaries, born. "Calling the infant 'Pen' is proving profitable, as we have made a house rule that anyone who makes a joke about 'Pen and Ink' sticks a dime in his piggy bank. It will be a miracle if I can lay up the money to send him to Harvard."[2]

Wrote a weekly column for the Santa Fe newspaper, *The New Mexican*.

1953. Penned his first juvenile. "What we set before our children's eyes and what we pour into their minds is just as important as what we put in their mouths. Juvenile books should be the most carefully screened and the most choosily selected of all forms of publication. Instead they are a deluge of almost anything that anyone thinks can be sold.

"Having long held a highly dubious opinion of the whole business of writing and publishing juveniles, it is with mixed feelings that I read the announcement of a forthcoming juvenile of my own [*Cochise of Arizona*] in a publisher's catalogue. No author can properly judge his own work; only indirectly by reflection from reviewers (who must always be taken with a discount), acquaintances (usually much too kind), and chance remarks, may I finally form some idea whether I have avoided the very vices I so dislike.

"Certainly, the sales of this book will be no test. The juvenile business, one might almost say the juvenile racket, exists for sales. It frequently achieves them, and, as in the case of books for adults, popularity is as yet no proof of quality. At least, that goes for immediate popularity. There is the long-term popularity, enjoyed alike by *Hamlet* and *Peter Rabbit*, that is, I think, proof. The author, unfortunately, does not last long enough to learn of it.

"The publishers, when they engaged me to write this book, sent me others they were proudly bringing out, to give me an idea of how the thing is done. They stressed two things to me: That I should stick to a simple, Anglo-Saxon, subject-predicate-object sentence structure, and that the ideas presented should be equally simple.

"The books they gave me to read only confirmed the impression I had so long had—that the great majority of juveniles are written by people to whom writing is merely business, and who have neither artistic gift nor the true writer's conscience. In what were supposed to be educative works, accurately true to life, I found not only wooden, stock characters and character behaviors that were basically untrue, but also such gross impossibilities as a boy who rode his horse a hundred miles in one day, with two hours out for lunch. The ideas and the style were certainly simple, the stories maintained constant action, and no doubt the youths who read them will like them. I still find the business on the disreputable side.

"There is a challenge in juvenile writing for writers who take their profession proudly as an art. One is required to be simple in style, statement, and vocabulary, but this does not mean that one may not try to write beautifully and even passionately. It is possible, within these limits, to achieve fine writing, to offer the reader an artistic experience. . . .

"Further, that business about simple ideas is false. Children think. Children, by the time they are around ten, are thinking about extremely complex things. A book worthy of being put in their hands is not one that contains nothing to stretch their active minds, but rather one that has accepted and won the challenge of presenting tough ideas in simple, clear terms.

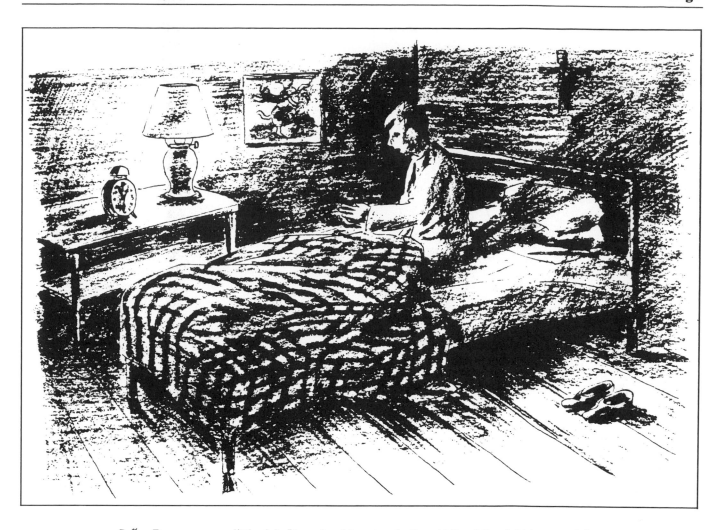

Señor Romero gave a little sigh. It was hard to get up in the middle of the night to spread the water. Then he said, "Well, we have to take the water when it comes." ■ (From *The Mother Ditch* by Oliver La Farge. Illustrated by Karl Larsson.)

"Each of these last two paragraphs contains the word 'challenge.' The word is frequently abused, but it is still valid. All writing, every undertaking in the arts, should be a response to challenge, although much of it (mea culpa) is not. When it comes to writing for children, the sense of being challenged, the sense of artistic responsibility, should be especially great.

"All of which, written in connection with a forthcoming juvenile of my own, sounds as smug as one of those numbered pieces by my old friend, Dr. Crane. I am not feeling smug. I seriously doubt that I have been able to meet my own standards, and one reason for writing this particular piece at this particular time is to get it off before anyone can throw my own book at me in refutation. It is, as it were, a confession before the act." [Oliver La Farge, *The Man with the Calabash Pipe,* edited by Winfield Townley Scott, Houghton, 1966.[3]]

Winter, 1957. Afflicted with emphysema; underwent removal of a section of his lung.

April, 1957. Second lung operation. "I spent the first half of this year hopping in and out of hospitals with bouts of pneumonia, and these resulted in the collapse of a lung on account of which it was necessary to carve and stitch me up in a very large way."[2]

October, 1962. Health deteriorated. Requested, therefore, that the executive committee of the Association of American Indian Affairs, Inc. find a presidential replacement for him. "I have been in very poor condition ever since last spring. In the beginning of September I underwent a thorough examination. It turns out that, in addition to a pair of lungs that I would not wish on the tomcat next door, I have a peptic ulcer and a somewhat enlarged heart. I am now on a very severe regimen."[2]

Spring, 1963. Condition became grave. Made preparations for an orderly withdrawal from the Indian Association. "I am faced with the likelihood of an early, rather slow, and expensive death, which cannot be covered by insurance.... It is not easy for me to make this withdrawal. With the exception of the interlude 1941-47, I have carried the burden of this Association since 1933, seldom, of course, without co-workers. If at times the load has been galling, and of recent years increasingly so, the work has also been an integral part of my life. It goes back to my first intimate association with Indians in 1921, and has woven through many personal rela-

Now his mind was opened a tiny crack. He had to entertain the thought that among them there was some decency. ■ (From *Cochise of Arizona* by Oliver La Farge. Illustrated by L. F. Bjorklund.)

tionships and rich experiences. However, I have no choice."[2]

June, 1963. Surgery was attempted, but his strength failed entirely. ". . . It occasionally happens that I think about my own death, and pray that it will be sudden. And if it comes slowly I wonder and doubt if I could turn the old skeleton into a mere visitor sitting to one side while I entertained myself by fascinating my friends."[2]

August 2, 1963. Died at the age of sixty-one in Albuquerque, N.M. "I doubt that I, Oliver La Farge, that inner essence of individuality, that spark distinct from all other sparks to which we cling so desperately and without which it is difficult even to imagine a universe in existence, that centre and self which we denote so aptly by the single, narrow, upright stroke of a capital I, will continue as such. The loss of that belief is the loss of one of the greatest of the comforts of religion, it makes it a little more difficult to face growing old and to contemplate death. The answer to it is to contemplate and

become accustomed to the idea of the extinction of the ego, hand in hand with contemplating the nature of God. This can be done, although it does not come easy to a full-living, sinful white man."[1]

Former Secretary of the Interior Stewart L. Udall once described La Farge as knowing "more about the American Indian than any non-Indian." During his life, La Farge championed numerous Indian causes. When Congress passed an $88 million Navajo-Hopi rehabilitation bill in 1949, La Farge urged President Truman to veto it on the premise that two of the bill's amendments destroyed Indian rights and jeopardized their land. Through La Farge's insistence the bill was reworked, and when passed by Congress in 1950, the new legislation supported a ten-year expenditure of $88 million to alleviate poverty, illiteracy, and high disease among the Navajo and Hopi Indian populations in the United States.

La Farge's first literary effort, *Laughing Boy,* won a Pulitzer Prize in 1929. Among the comments from the critics included *Bookman's:* "An almost perfect specimen of the sustained and tempered, the lyrical, romantic idyll. It moves among conceptions of life so foreign to those of our naturalistic fiction that it would seem to belong to a different kind of writing. It is filled with love, with nature; it is also filled with morals and religion. The love and nature are ours, as they are anybody's; the morals and religion are those of the Indian. We are thus transported into a strange, foreign, and rather pleasant civilization. . . ." "Oliver La Farge is a welcome addition to the ranks of our younger fictionists," wrote a *New York Evening Post* critic, "His first novel reveals an ability considerably out of the ordinary. It reveals a style devoid of stylism, a gift of simple, straightforward statement which is at the same time lyrical and colorful, and a quite adequate inventive power. . . ." Added the *New York Times:* "Mr. La Farge has infused the romance of *Laughing Boy* with a lucid beauty, with a vital, artistic imagination and a clear, almost hypnotic style." The film version of the book was produced in 1934 by Metro-Goldwyn-Mayer.

HOBBIES AND OTHER INTERESTS: Riding, hunting, sailing, camping, and archery.

FOR MORE INFORMATION SEE: New York Evening Post, September 7, 1929; *New York Times,* November 24, 1929; *Bookman,* January, 1930; Oliver La Farge, *Raw Material,* Houghton, 1945; *Current Biography,* H. W. Wilson, 1953; *Time,* February 8, 1959; Oliver La Farge, *The Man with the Calabash Pipe,* edited by Winfield Scott, Houghton, 1966; Everett A. Gillis, *Oliver La Farge,* Steck-Vaughn, 1967; D'Arcy McNickle, *Indian Man: A Life of Oliver La Farge,* Indiana University Press, 1971; Thomas M. Pearce, *Oliver La Farge,* Twayne, 1972.

Obituaries: *New York Times,* August 3, 1963; *Time,* August 9, 1963; *Newsweek,* August 12, 1963; *Publishers Weekly,* August 12, 1963; *Current Biography,* 1963; *Americana Annual,* 1964; *American Antiquity,* January, 1966.

(Died August 2, 1963)

LASELL, Elinor H. 1929-
(Fen H. Lasell)

PERSONAL: Born May 15, 1929, in Berlin, Germany; daughter of Werner (a city-planner) and Ida Belle (Guthe) Hegemann; married John Lasell (an actor; divorced); children: John, Michael, Holly. *Education:* Bennington College, student, 1947-49; Boston University, student in theater design division, 1957-59. *Home:* San Miguel de Allende, GTO., Mexico.

CAREER: Designer of theater sets and costumes, mostly in the Boston area, 1949-59.

WRITINGS—Under name Fen H. Lasell: *Michael Grows a Wish,* Houghton, 1962; *Fly Away Goose,* Houghton, 1965; *Kiya the Gull,* Addison-Wesley, 1968.

Illustrator: Lee Kingman, *Peter's Pony,* Doubleday, 1963; Miska Miles, *Teacher's Pet,* Little, 1966.

SIDELIGHTS: "For me writing has the element of wish fulfillment. If you spend a lot of time wishing something would happen, and it doesn't happen, you can write a book in which it does happen and feel satisfied."

HOBBIES AND OTHER INTERESTS: "My principal interest of late is writing, presently novels for adults. Painting, rebuilding houses, and always the garden, are my other obsessions."

LEA, Alec 1907-
(Richard Lea)

PERSONAL: Born in March, 1907, in Nova Scotia, Canada; married May Verna (a lecturer in health education), 1958; children: Judith Verna, Kenneth Richard. *Education:* Attended Oxford University. *Politics:* Socialist. *Religion:* Society of Friends (Quakers). *Home:* The Barn, Town End Bolton Le Sands Carnforth, Lancs. LA5 8JF, England. *Agent:* Laura Cecil, 10 Exeter Mansions, Shaftesbury Ave., London, England.

CAREER: Dairy farmer in Sussex and Devon, England, 1937-70; writer, 1937—. *Awards, honors: Temba Dawn* was named a "Children's Book of the Year" for 1975 by the Child Study Association.

WRITINGS: The Outward Urge, Rich & Cowan, 1944; *A Bid for Freedom,* Rich & Cowan, 1946; *Roots of a Man,* Stockwell, 1951; *To Sunset and Beyond,* Hamish Hamilton, 1970, Walck, 1971; *Temba Dawn,* Bodley Head, 1972, Scribner, 1975; *A Whiff of Boarhound,* Dobson, 1974; *Kingcup Calling,* Dobson, 1976; *Deep Down and High Up,* Dobson, 1976; *Beth Varden at Sunset* (sequel to *To Sunset and Beyond*), Dobson, 1977.

ADAPTATIONS: A prize winning amateur film was made of *To Sunset and Beyond* by Colin Gregg in 1971.

WORK IN PROGRESS: "[A novel for children] about the future, describing the only way in which mankind can be prevented from destroying the earth in nuclear war . . . has been finished but, as I feared, is proving too controversial to please any publisher. It describes how, with the help of extra-terrestrial beings, young people take power throughout the world and prohibit *all* means of killing people at a distance. It is unlikely ever to get published."

SIDELIGHTS: "I am worried by the fact that the bulk of children's fiction, including my own books, are nostalgic and glorify the past, whereas it is essentially the future which belongs to today's children. Those writers who do try to imagine the future in books for children seem to lack hope and produce work which may be very exciting and realistic, but is basically depressing.

"At the age of five I was a witness to the killing of my father by a party of drunken men. My main life-motivation has been a search for a way to do without killing, to banish wars, and to convince people that Jesus meant what he said. We shall eventually have a world without armies and guns and bombs—or else no world at all."

FOR MORE INFORMATION SEE: Horn Book, April, 1972, December, 1975; *Times Literary Supplement,* December 2, 1977.

LEVIN, Betty 1927-

PERSONAL: Born September 10, 1927, in New York, N.Y.; daughter of Max (a lawyer) and Eleanor (a musician; maiden name, Mack) Lowenthal; married Alvin Levin (a lawyer), August 3, 1947; children: Katherine, Bara, Jennifer. *Education:* University of Rochester, A.B., 1949; Radcliffe College, M.A., 1951; Harvard University, A.M.T., 1951. *Home:* Old

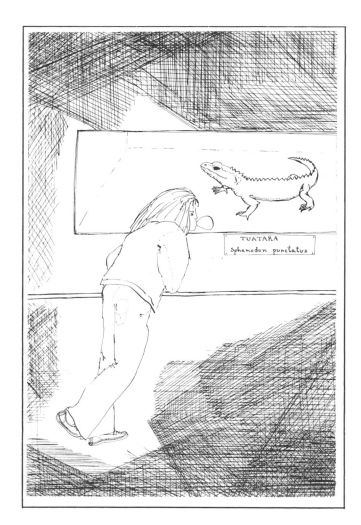

Benjamin the tuatara was such a rare animal that the zoo tours always paused at his cage so that he could be explained. ■ (From *The Zoo Conspiracy* by Betty Levin. Illustrated by Marian Parry.)

Winter St., Lincoln, Mass. 01773. *Office:* Center for the Study of Children's Literature, Simmons College, Boston, Mass. 02115.

CAREER: Museum of Fine Arts, Boston, Mass., assistant in research, 1952; Pine Manor Open College, Chestnut Hill, Mont., instructor in literature, 1970-75; instructor at Emmanuel College, 1975, and Radcliffe College, 1976—; Center for the Study of Children's Literature, Simmons College, Boston, Mass., special instructor, 1977—. *Member:* Authors Guild, Masterworks Chorale, Middlesex Sheep Breeders Association, Society of Radcliffe (institute fellows), Children's Books Authors (Boston). *Awards, honors:* Fellowship in creative writing at Radcliffe Institute, 1968-70.

WRITINGS: The Zoo Conspiracy (juvenile fiction), Hastings House, 1973; *The Sword of Culann* (young adult fiction), Macmillan, 1973; *A Griffon's Nest* (young adult historical fiction), Macmillan, 1975; *The Forespoken* (young adult historical fiction), Macmillan, 1976; *Landfall,* Atheneum, 1979; *The Beast on the Brink,* Avon, 1980. Contributor of articles to education journals and to *Horn Book.*

WORK IN PROGRESS: Novel for young adults.

LLERENA-AGUIRRE, Carlos Antonio 1952-

PERSONAL: Born March 31, 1952, in Arequipa, Peru, South America; naturalized American citizen, 1980; son of Eduardo Llerena (a lawyer) and Susana Aguirre Dongo (a teacher). *Education:* Attended Maryknoll, 1969 and Universidad Federico Villarreal, 1970; exchange student in Sarasota, Fla.; Ringling School of Art, certificate, 1974; School of Visual Arts, New York, N.Y., B.F.A., 1979. *Home:* 105-28 65 Ave., Apt. #6B, Forest Hills, N.Y. 11375.

CAREER: Free-lance artist. School of Visual Arts, New York, N.Y., instructor, 1975-79; Syracuse University, Syracuse, N.Y., visiting professor, 1979—. *Exhibitions*—Group shows: Contacta, Festival De Arte Total, Parque De La Reserva, Lima, Peru, 1970; Concurso Nacional De Pintura, Municipalidad De Miraflores, Peru, 1971; Jacobb Ladder Gallery, Ann Arbor, Mich., 1973; Society of Illustrators, New York, N.Y., 1976, 1977; Christies Gallery, New York, N.Y., 1977; *Communication Arts* Magazine Annual Show, 1977; *Art Directions* Magazine Eighth Annual Awards Show, 1977; Art Directors' Club Annual Show, New York, N.Y., 1977; The Historical Society of New York, 1977; Overseas Press Club, New York, N.Y., 1978; Jamaica Center for the Arts, New York, N.Y., 1978; Hudson Guild Gallery, New York, N.Y., 1978; Club Peru, New York, N.Y., 1978. One-man shows: University Club, Washington, D.C., 1978; Trapecio Gallery, Peru, 1979; InterAmerican Bank for Development, Washington, D.C., 1980.

AWARDS, HONORS: Honorable Mention for the painting "31 of May," Concurso Nacional De Pintura, Municipalidad De Miraflores, 1971; Certificate of Merit for "Hunger," 1976; Certificate of Merit for "Leaping Otorongo," from the book *Sticks, Stones,* 1977; Award of Distinction from *Communication Arts* Magazine for four drawings from *Sticks, Stones,* 1977; Certificate of Distinction from *Art Directions* Magazine for "Creativity 1977," 1977; Gold Medal from the Art Directors' Club for "The Brontes' Halloween," 1977.

WRITINGS—Self illustrated: *The Fair at Kanta: A Story From Peru,* Holt, 1975; *Sticks, Stones,* Holt, 1977. Work has appeared in *Avanzada, Karate,* New York *Times, Village Voice, Harper's, Travel and Leisure, Saturday Review, MS, Politicks, Psychology Today, Esquire, Washington Post,* and *Wharton* magazine.

Illustrator: William O. Steele, *Talking Bones,* Harper, 1978.

WORK IN PROGRESS: A Peruvian folktale tentatively called *The Witch's Broom,* for Harper.

SIDELIGHTS: "I am a bilingual Peruvian and a resident of New York City. I have traveled extensively through the Peruvian Andes where I have recorded, in several sketchbooks, its people, their traditions and landscapes. During these trips I was inspired to create *Fair at Kanta, Sticks, Stones,* and *The Witch's Broom.*

"Much of my time is spent creating etchings, woodcuts, and paintings of Peruvian motifs. I want to portray my people as I see them through their individual expressions of humanity.

"As well as art, I've studied several Peruvian instruments under old masters. Among them are the Quena, and ancient notched pre-Columbian flute, the Antara, a pentatonic panpipe, and the Charango, a mandolin-like instrument made with shell of an Armadillo."

FOR MORE INFORMATION SEE: Print, July-August, 1978.

CARLOS ANTONIO LLERENA-AGUIRRE

One day, an enchanted puma from the hills wandered down into the jungle. The other animals made fun of him. They all had lovely spots and markings. But he had none. ■ (From *Sticks, Stones* by Carlos Antonio Llerena. Illustrated by the author.)

LONGFELLOW, Henry Wadsworth 1807-1882

PERSONAL: Born February 27, 1807, in Portland, Maine; died March 24, 1882, in Cambridge, Massachusetts; buried in Mt. Auburn Cemetery, Cambridge, Massachusetts; son of Stephen (a lawyer and member of the United States Congress) and Zilpah (maiden name, Wadsworth; a descendent of Priscilla and John Alden) Longfellow; married Mary Storer Potter, September 14, 1831 (died, 1835); married Frances Elizabeth Appleton, July 13, 1843 (died, 1861); children: (second marriage) two sons, three daughters. *Education:* Graduated from Bowdoin College, 1825, classmate of Nathaniel Hawthorne and Franklin Pierce (fourteenth president of the United States); further study in Europe, 1826-29. *Home:* Craigie House, Cambridge, Massachusetts (once headquarters for General Washington, now a museum in Longfellow's honor).

CAREER: Poet, educator, translator, writer of prose. While a student, had several poems published in the Portland *Gazette of Maine;* Bowdoin College, Brunswick, Maine, professor of modern languages, 1829-35, librarian, 1829-35; Harvard University, Cambridge, Massachusetts, Smith Professor of Modern Languages and Belles-Lettres, 1835-54; resigned in 1854 to devote himself to writing; traveled extensively throughout his career, receiving a private audience with Queen Victoria on his final tour through Europe, 1868-69. *Awards, honors:* LL.D., Cambridge University, 1868;

D.C.L., Oxford University, 1868; first American to be honored with a bust in the Poets' Corner at Westminster Abbey, 1884.

WRITINGS—Poems: Voices of the Night, J. Owen, 1839; *Ballads and Other Poems,* J. Owen, 1842; *Poems on Slavery,* J. Owen, 1842; *Poems,* Carey & Hart, 1845; *The Belfry of Bruges and Other Poems* (contains *The Arsenal at Springfield*), J. Owen, 1846; *Evangeline: A Tale of Acadie,* Ticknor, 1847, reissued, Washington Square Press, 1967 [other editions illustrated by Jane E. Benham, Birket Foster and John Gilbert, Ticknor, Reed, 1850; F.O.C. Darley, Houghton, 1883; Violet Oakley and Jessie Willcox Smith, Houghton, 1897; Howard Chandler Christy, Bobbs-Merrill, 1905; Arthur Dixon, Dutton, 1907; John Gilbert, Routledge, 1906; Howard Simon (edited by Mina Lewiton), Duell, Sloan, 1966]; *The Seaside and the Fireside,* Ticknor, Reed, 1849; *The Golden Legend,* Ticknor, Reed, 1851.

The Song of Hiawatha, Ticknor & Fields, 1855, reprinted, Tuttle, 1975 [other editions illustrated by John Gilbert, Routledge, 1856; George H. Thomas, Kent, 1856; Frederic Remington, Houghton, 1891, reprinted, E. & W. Books, 1969; Harrison Fisher, Bobbs-Merrill, 1906; Frederic Remington and N. C. Wyeth, Harrap, 1923; Valenti Angelo, Peter Pauper Press, 1942; Joan Kiddell-Monroe, Dutton, 1960; Gordon Laite, Garrard, 1969; adaptations for children by Marion Eleanor Gridley, Rand McNally, 1950, reprinted 1957; Allen Chaffee (illustrated by Armstrong Sperry), Random House,

Henry Wadsworth Longfellow in 1840.
From the portrait by C. G. Thompson.

1951; Mina Lewiton (illustrated by Howard Simon), Duell, Sloan, 1966].

The Courtship of Miles Standish, and Other Poems, Ticknor & Fields, 1858 [other editions illustrated by John Gilbert, Routledge, 1859; George H. Boughton, Frank T. Merrill, Charles S. Reinhart, and others, Houghton, 1888; Howard Chandler Christy, Bobbs-Merrill, 1903; N. C. Wyeth, Houghton, 1920]; *Tales of a Wayside Inn,* Ticknor & Fields, 1863, reprinted, McKay, 1961 [other editions illustrated by Birket Foster, John Tenniel, and others, (London), 1867; John Gilbert, (London), 1874]; *Household Poems,* Ticknor & Fields, 1865; *Flower-de-luce,* Ticknor & Fields, 1867; *The New England Tragedies,* Ticknor & Fields, 1868, new edition (edited by J. W. Zorn), Educators Publishing Service, 1966; *The Divine Tragedy,* Osgood, 1871; *Three Books of Song,* Osgood, 1872; *Christus: A Mystery* (contains *The Golden Legend, The New England Tragedies,* and *The Divine Tragedy*), Osgood, 1872.

Aftermath, Osgood, 1873; *The Hanging of the Crane,* Houghton, 1874 [other editions illustrated by Arthur Ignatius Keller, Routledge, 1874; Mary Hallock Foote and Thomas Moran, Houghton, 1902]; *The Masque of Pandora, and Other Poems,* Osgood, 1875; *Keramos and Other Poems,* Houghton, Osgood, 1878; *Ultima Thule,* Houghton, 1880; *In the Harbor: Ultima Thule—Part II,* Houghton, 1882; *Michael Angelo: A Dramatic Poem,* Houghton, 1883; *There Was a Little Girl,* Worthington, 1883; *Sunrise on the Hills,* Crowell, 1887; *Nuremberg,* Sampson, Low, 1888.

Excerpts published separately: From *The Seaside and the Fireside—The Building of the Ship,* Fields, Osgood, 1870 [a later edition illustrated by J. Ayton Symington, Dutton, 1908]; from *Ballads and Other Poems—Excelsior,* Osgood, 1877; *The Skeleton in Armor,* Osgood, 1877 [a later edition illustrated by Paul Kennedy, Prentice-Hall, 1963]; *The Village Blacksmith,* Dutton, 1885; *The Wreck of the Hesperus,* Griffith, Farran, 1886; *Maidenhood,* Sampson, Low, 1888.

From *Tales of a Wayside Inn—King Robert of Sicily and The Birds of Killingworth,* A. Brown, 1877; *The Falcon of Ser Federigo and King Robert of Sicily* (edited by Ethel G. Skeat), Blackie & Son, 1893; *Paul Revere's Ride,* L. H. Nelson, 1905, new edition (illustrated by Joseph Low), Windmill Books, 1973 [other editions illustrated by Leonard Everett Fisher, F. Watts, 1963; Paul Galdone, Crowell, 1963]; *The Saga of King Olaf* (edited by Beatrice E. Clay), Blackie & Son, 1907; from *The New England Tragedies—Giles Corey of the Salem Farms,* Houghton, 1900; from *Voices of the Night—A Psalm of Life,* Lovell, 1900.

Prose: *Outre-Mer: A Pilgrimage beyond the Sea* (essays), Harper, 1835; *Hyperion: A Romance,* S. Colman, 1839 [a later edition illustrated by Birket Foster, D. Bogue, 1853]; *The Spanish Student* (three-act play), J. Owen, 1843; *Kavanagh: A Tale,* Ticknor, Reed, 1849, new edition (edited by Jean Downey), College & University Press, 1965 [another edition illustrated by Birket Foster, (London), 1858]; *From My Arm-Chair* (essays), [Cambridge], 1879.

Translator: Jorge Manrique, *Coplas de Don Jorge Manrique,* [Boston], 1833; Dante Alighieri, *The Divine Comedy,* Ticknor & Fields, 1867, reprinted, Doubleday, 1961; excerpts from *The Divine Comedy* published separately—*Inferno: Canticle I of The Divine Comedy,* Collier Books, 1962, *The Antepurgatorio: Cantos I-IX of the Purgatorio,* Racolin Press, 1964; Jacques Boé Jasmin, *The Blind Girl of Castel Cuille,* E. S. Werner, 1892; Esaias Tegnér, *Poems by Tegnér: The Children of the Lord's Supper,* Scandinavian Classics, 1905.

Editor: *Manuel de Proverbes Dramatiques,* Griffin's Press, 1830; (and contributor) *The Waif: A Collection of Poems,* J. Owen, 1845; excerpt from *The Waif* published separately—*The Day is Done,* E. Nister, 1891; (and contributor of translations) *The Poets and Poetry of Europe,* Carey & Hart, 1845; (and contributor) *The Estray: A Collection of Poems,* Ticknor, 1847; *Poems of Places,* Osgood, 1867-79.

Collected works: *The Poetical Works of Henry Wadsworth Longfellow,* J. Walker, 1851, revised edition, Houghton, 1975 [other editions illustrated by John Gilbert, Ticknor & Fields, 1856; Birket Foster, F.O.C. Darley, and others, Osgood, 1872; Edwin Austin Abbey, Ernest Wadsworth Longfellow, and others (three volumes), Osgood, 1870-83]; *The Prose Works of Henry Wadsworth Longfellow,* (illustrated by John Gilbert), Routledge, 1853, new edition, two volumes, Ticknor & Fields, 1857; *The Works of Henry Wadsworth Longfellow,* edited by Samuel Longfellow, 14 volumes, Houghton, 1886-91, reprinted, AMS Press, 1966.

Selections: *The Poems of Henry Wadsworth Longfellow,* Dutton, 1900, reprinted, 1972 [other editions illustrated by Allen Lewis, A. S. Barnes, 1944; John and Clare Romano Ross (edited by Edmund Fuller), Crowell, 1967]; *Favorite Poems* (illustrated by Edward A. Wilson), Doubleday, 1947, reprinted, 1967; *The Continental Tales of Henry Wadsworth Longfellow,* edited by J. I. Rodale, Story Classics, 1948; *The Essential Longfellow,* edited by Lewis Leary, Collier Books, 1963; *Evangeline and Selected Tales and Poems,* edited by Horace Gregory, American Library, 1964; *Selected Poems,*

In the hour of darkness and peril and need,
The people will waken and listen to hear
The hurrying hoof-beats of that steed,
And the midnight message of Paul Revere.

■ (From "Paul Revere's Ride" by Henry Wadsworth Longfellow. Illustrated by Paul Galdone.)

(From *Song of Hiawatha* by Henry Wadsworth Longfellow. Illustrated by John Gilbert.)

edited by C. Merton Babcock, Peter Pauper Press, 1967; *Selections from Tales of a Wayside Inn,* Pyramid Press, 1967. For children—*The Children's Own Longfellow,* Houghton, 1908, reprinted, 1966; *The Children's Hour and Other Poems,* Houghton, 1922; *Longfellow Storybook,* edited by Albert E. Cornetti, Naylor, 1955.

ADAPTATIONS—Movies and filmstrips: "Evangeline" (motion pictures), Canadian Bioscope, 1914, Fox Film, 1919, Edwin Carewe-Feature Productions, 1929; "Evangeline" (filmstrips), Encyclopaedia Britannica Films, 1956, Brunswick Productions, 1972; "The Midnight Ride of Paul Revere" (motion pictures), Thomas A. Edison, 1914, Coronet Instructional Films, 1957, Encyclopaedia Britannica Films, 1957, Film Associates of California, 1964, Lumin Films, 1967; "The Word and the Echo" (motion picture), adaptation of *Paul Revere's Ride,* Ian Clark, 1971; "Paul Revere's Ride" (filmstrips), Brunswick Productions, 1966, Lumin Films, 1967; "The Village Blacksmith" (motion picture), Fox Film, 1922.

"The Courtship of Miles Standish" (motion picture), Associated Exhibitors, 1923; "The Wreck of the Hesperus" (motion pictures), starring Alan Hale, Pathe Exchange, 1927, Columbia Pictures, starring Edgar Buchanan, 1946; "The

Wreck of the Hesperus" (filmstrip), Brunswick Productions, 1967; "Hiawatha" (motion pictures), starring Vincent Edwards, Monogram Pictures, 1952, Lumin Films, 1967, Sterling Educational Films, 1967; "Hiawatha" (filmstrips), Encyclopaedia Britannica Films, 1952, Marian Ray, 1952, Lumin Films, 1967.

Musical works and plays: *Hiawatha* (a cantata; produced in Convent Garden at the Royal English Opera, 1861), W. S. Johnson, 1861; *Masque of Pandora* (libretto; music by Alfred Cellier; first produced in Boston at the Boston Theatre, January 10, 1881), Houghton, 1881; A. L. DeVine, *A Dramatization of Longfellow's Hiawatha* (six-act play), [St. Paul, Minnesota], 1894; *Hiawatha's Wedding Feast* (cantata; music by Samuel Taylor-Coleridge), Novello, Ewer, 1900; Edith Ashby, *Miles Standish* (play), Elkin Mathews, 1900.

Hiawatha's Departure (cantata; music by Samuel Taylor-Coleridge), Novello, Ewer, 1901; *The Blind Girl of Castel-Cuille* (cantata; music by Samuel Taylor-Coleridge), Novello, Ewer, 1901; *Melodrama of Hiawatha* (music by Saidee Knowland Coe), C. F. Summy, 1905; Valerie Wyngate, *Dramatized Scenes from Longfellow's Hiawatha* (music by Norman O'Neill), Kegan Paul, 1916; Thomas W. Broadhurst, *Evangeline* (play), Samuel French, 1926; *The Singers: A Cantata* (music by John Wesley Work), Mills Music, 1949.

SIDELIGHTS: **February 27, 1807.** Born in Portland, Maine. His father, Stephen Longfellow, was a prominent lawyer and a member of the Hartford Convention and served both in the Massachusetts state legislature and in the Congress of the United States. "Out of my childhood rises in my memory the recollection of many things rather as poetic impressions than as prosaic facts. Such are the damp mornings of early spring, with the loud crowing of cocks and the cooing of pigeons on roofs of barns. Very distinct in connection with these are the indefinite longings incident to childhood; feelings of wonder and loneliness which I could not interpret and scarcely then took cognizance of. But they have remained in my mind." [Lawrance Thompson, *Young Longfellow,* Macmillan, 1938.[1]]

1810. Entered Ma'am Fellows' schoolhouse on Spring Street, Portland.

1812. Attended town school on Love Lane near his home. Unable to cope with boisterous schoolmates, Longfellow returned to a private school under the refined guidance of Nathaniel H. Carter. It was reported that Longfellow had "gone half through his Latin Grammar" and stood "above several boys twice as old as he."[1]

1814. Continued his education at the Portland Academy. The first book to hold his fascination was Washington Irving's *Sketch Book.* "Every reader has his first book; I mean to say, one book among all others which in early youth first fascinates his imagination, and at once excites and satisfies the desires of his mind. To me, this first book was *The Sketch Book* of Washington Irving.

"I was a school-boy when it was published, and read each succeeding number with ever increasing wonder and delight, spellbound by its pleasant humor, its melancholy tenderness, its atmosphere of revery,—nay, even by its gray-brown covers, the shaded letters of its titles, and the fair clean type. . . ."[1]

November, 1820. Submitted his first poem to the Portland *Gazette*. His verses signed "HENRY" appeared in the "Poet Corner." The verses commemorated a fight with the Indians at a pond not far from Hiram.

1821. Passed entrance examination to Bowdoin College, Brunswick, Maine. Because he was only fourteen years of age, it was decided that Longfellow study his freshman assignments under the tutelage of Bezaleel Cushman at the Portland Academy.

His interest in his studies was sharpened with a desire to equal if not surpass his Bowdoin counterparts. Among the best students, there was keen rivalry, intensified by regional pride.

Fall, 1822. Entered his sophomore year at Bowdoin College, Brunswick.

"BRUNSWICK September 22nd 1822

"Dear Parents,

"As we have now got comfortably settled, I suppose it is about time to let you know how we go on here. I feel very well contented, and am much pleased with a College Life. Many of the students are very agreeable companions and, thus far, I have passed my time very pleasantly. The students have considerably more leisure than I expected, but as the season advances and the days grow shorter, our leisure moments must necessarily be considerably diminished. I expected, when I got here, that I should have to study very hard to keep a good footing with the rest of the class; but I find I have sufficient time for the preparation of my lessons and for amusement, and that I am not more deficient than some of the rest of the class. I have not been 'screwed' at recitation yet and shall endeavour not to be—So much for egotism!

"I have very little more to write, but I will not forget to mention that by some means or other, I cannot tell what, I have either lost on my passage here, or left at home, all my cotton stockings except the pair which I wore—And another thing is that I wish some one would get a brass ferrule put on to my cane and send it to me as soon as possible—If you have any good apples or pears I wish you would send me some—and tell the girls to send a whole parcel of Gingerbread with them. My box of tooth-powder may also be put into the bundle—

"Yours affectionately—

H. W. L.—

"P.S. There is another thing of considerable importance which I had like to have forgotten. You do not know how much we stand in need of a good Watch. When the chapel bells ring for recitation it is only struck a few times and then is done, so that we, living so far from the College Buildings, are liable to be late—however we must do the best we can—Give my love to all and tell the Girls to write soon."[1]

As a form of exercise: "I have marked out an image upon my closet-door about my own size; and whenever I feel the want of exercise I strip off my coat, and, considering this image as in a posture of defence, make my motions as though in actual combat. This is a very classick amusement, and I have already become quite skilful as a pugilist." [N. H. Dole, "Bio-

Vainly he strove to rise; and Evangeline,
    kneeling beside him,
    Kissed his dying lips, and laid his head on her
    bosom.
■ (From *Evangeline: A Tale of Acadie* by Henry Wadsworth Longfellow. Illustrated by F. O. C. Darley.)

graphical Sketch" in H. W. Longfellow, *Voices of the Night and Other Poems,* Crowell, 1893, 1899.[2]]

1823. A new library at Bowdoin offered greater opportunities to expand his reading. "I am reading three or four books at a time—sometimes more! A very foolish way of improving, or rather of wasting time, you will think. I know it—but when a volume grows tedious and uninteresting, I choose rather to lay it aside, than to weary my patience by poring over sleepy pages in such a manner as to derive neither advantage nor amusement. Besides I can never endure that which is dull, when that, which is entertaining is upon my shelf—and within my reach, and requires but a change of posture to be placed open before me.

"PORTLAND **Jan. 11 1824**

"My Dear Father,

"I write to you at this time to inform you of a plan I have formed for passing a part of the present College vacation. 'Amusement reigns man's great demand' as Dr. Young says, and my plan is this. To go to Boston, and spend a week there. My classmate Weld is going on in the course of a week or two, and offers me a seat in his sleigh, which invitation I feel much inclination to accept. I have written to you for your approbation of this plan, which I think is a very good

(From *Evangeline* by Henry Wadsworth Longfellow. Illustrated by Howard Chandler Christy.)

one. That you may the more readily think as I do, I would inform you that I was never fifty miles from Portland, in all my life, which I think is rather a sorrowful circumstance in the annals of my history. When I hear of others talking, as travellers are very apt to do, about what they have seen and heard abroad, I always regret my having never been from home more than I have hitherto. So that I often wish I had not been so fond of a sedentary life. I am of an opinion, that it is better to know the world partly from observation than wholly from books.

"You, who have seen so much of it, at least of one division of it, will know how this is, and I dare say, will think so too, since most others do. This visit then may on this account be advantageous as well as agreeable. Besides I do not think it will be very expensive, since if I go in the manner before-mentioned the cost of travelling will be greatly reduced. My companion that is to be, should this plan go into operation, has numerous relatives in Boston, and as he will take the horse to his own account, that expense will also be removed. He is going on for his sister, who is visiting there, in consequence of which, if he has my company, I shall be under the necessity of returning in the stage. I do not know as there is any kind of utility to arise from thus being minute in the statement of particulars, but I wish you to know everything 'pro and con.' I think you will be inclined to express your approbation of this measure. I wish you would write me as soon as convenient upon this subject, that I may know what answer to give Mr. Weld in regard to this."[1]

The adventure of entering the "Literary Emporium" was an exciting prospect. The trip to Boston reenforced a strong desire to direct his life toward a literary career. After his return to Brunswick, he determined to sound out his pragmatic father who had hoped that his son would choose law as a profession. "I feel very glad that I am not to be a physician,—that there are quite enough in the world without me. And now, as somehow or other this subject has been introduced, I am curious to know what you do intend to make of me!—Whether I am to study a profession or not! and if so, what profession? I hope your ideas upon this subject will agree with mine, for I have a particular and strong prejudice for one course of life, to which you I fear will not agree. It will not be worth while for me to mention what this is, until I become more acquainted with your own wishes."[1]

Further adding: "I hardly think Nature designed me for the bar, or the pulpit, or the dissecting-room; I cannot make a lawyer of any eminence, because I have not a talent for argument; I am not good enough for a minister; and as to Physic, I utterly and absolutely detest it."[2] The elder Longfellow possibly busy with congressional matters, did not answer the letter immediately.

December, 1824. Longfellow once again addressed his father to the unanswered question of his career direction. The elder Longfellow finally answered: "The subject of your first letter is one of deep interest, and demands great consideration. A literary life, to one who has the means of support, must be very pleasant. But there is not wealth & munificence enough in this country to afford sufficient encouragement & patronage to merely literary men. And as you have not had the fortune (I will not say good or ill) to be born rich, you must adopt a profession which will afford you a subsistence as well as reputation. I am happy to observe that you are ambitious of literary distinction, and I have no doubt but you possess genius & taste which, if properly cultivated will secure you high respectability in the literary world or in a profession if you should devote your attention to one. You have every inducement to cultivate with care & diligence the faculties which you possess, and with the blessing of a kind Providence, & a careful attention to your health & morals, I feel a comforting assurance that you will succeed.

"My ambition has never been to accumulate wealth for my children, but to cultivate their minds in the best possible manner, & to imbue them with correct moral, political, & religious principles, believing that a person thus educated with proper diligence & attention, will be certain of attaining all the wealth which is necessary to his happiness. . . ."[1]

Longfellow replied: "From the general tenor of your last letter, it seems to be your fixed desire, that I should choose the profession of the Law for the business of my life. I believe that I have already mentioned to you that I did not wish to enter immediately upon any profession. I am very much rejoiced to hear that you accede so readily to my proposition of studying general literature for one year at Cambridge. My grand object in doing this will be to gain as perfect a knowledge of the French and Italian languages as can be gained by study without travelling in France and Italy, though to tell the truth I intend to visit both before I die. The advantages of this step are obvious,—the means of accomplishing an end so desirable exertion must supply. I am afraid that you begin to think me rather chimerical in many of my ideas, and that I am ambitious of becoming a 'rara avis in terris.'—But you must acknowledge the propriety and usefulness of aiming high—at something which it is impossible to over-shoot—perhaps to reach. The fact is,—what I have previously said to you upon the subject leads me to exhibit myself without disguise,—I have a most voracious appetite for knowledge. To its acquisition I will sacrifice anything; and I now lament most bitterly the defects of my early education that are attributable in part to myself and in part to my instructers. My advantages have been from infancy almost boundless—and by reflecting but one moment I see how awfully I have neglected them. I knew neither the value of time nor of these advantages. I now refer to the years which I passed at the Academy. Of having misspent the portion of my College life already passed I cannot reproach myself so severely, although I have left undone a multitude of things that ought to have been done. But fortunately for me, as I grow older I grow more studious. Nothing delights me more than reading and writing—and although this assertion, unqualified as I have made it, may savour of vanity, yet I feel the truth of it: and nothing could induce me to relinquish the pleasures of literature—little as I have as yet tasted them.

"—But this is a wide digression. And in returning to our former subject I can only say that of all professions—I would say of the three professions which are sometimes called the learned professions—I should prefer the Law. I am far from being a fluent speaker:—but practice must serve as a talisman, when talent is wanting. I can be a lawyer, for some lawyers are mere simpletons. This will support my *real* existence, literature an *ideal* one.

"I purchased last evening a beautiful, pocket edition of Sir Wm Jones's letters and have just finished reading them. Eight languages he was critically versed in—eight more he read with a dictionary, and there were still twelve more which he had studied less perfectly, but which were not wholly unknown to him; making in all twenty eight languages to which he had given his attention. I have somewhere seen or heard the observation, that as many languages as a person acquired, so many times was he a man. Mr. Jones was equal to about sixteen men, according to that observation."[1]

Beautiful with her beauty, and rich with the wealth of her being.

■ (From *The Courtship of Miles Standish* by Henry Wadsworth Longfellow. Illustrated by Howard Chandler Christy.)

1825. Commencement from Bowdoin. Fellow students included Franklin Pierce, Horatio Bridge, and Nathaniel Hawthorne.

"Thursday, Morning, June 30.

"My appointment, they tell me, is considered the fourth in the class, having only Little, Deane & Bradbury above me—How I came to get so high, is rather a mistery to me, in as much as I have never been a remarkably hard student, touching College studies,—except during my Sophomore

'**Twas the women who in autumn...** ■ (From *The Song of Hiawatha* by Henry Wadsworth Longfellow. Illustrated by Frederic Remington.)

year, when I used to think that I was studying pretty hard—though I might possibly have been mistaken.—In five weeks we shall be set free from College—for one month—Then comes Commencement—and then—and then—I cannot say what *will be* after that.''[1]

Longfellow chose for his commencement subject "Native Writers." The words reflected his own aspirations. "To an American there is something endearing in the very sounds,—Our Native Writers.''[1]

Bowdoin College established a chair of modern languages and recommended, informally, the eighteen-year-old Longfellow for the professorship. Poorly qualified at this point, it was suggested that he prepare for the position by studying in Europe for two years, at his own expense.

Before Europe, however, the elder Longfellow decided that a few months of exposure to the study of law would prove wholesome for his son.

Fall, 1825. Longfellow settled with law books in the front-room office of his Congress Street home.

May 15, 1826. Boarded the *Cadmus* for his two year study in Europe. Longfellow's goal was to learn French, Spanish, Italian and German. "I had little else to do than to busy my-self with my own thoughts and mediations, so few circumstances were there at sea to call me away from them.''[1]

"Land" was sighted: "For to my youthful imagination the Old World was a kind of Holy Land, lying afar off beyond the blue horizon of the ocean; and when its shores first rose upon my sight, looming through the hazy atmosphere of the sea, my heart swelled with the deep emotion of the pilgrim, when he sees afar the spire which rises above the shrine of his devotion.''[1]

Experienced initial frustrations with the French language partially because of his French instructor at Bowdoin. "D'-Eon was a very poor instructor—his pronunciation very bad. It is impossible that he should have been a Parisien—He was a German. . . . And this has been not only unfortunate but absolutely discouraging:—to find myself so far speaking French with a German as well as an English accent.

"After five weeks' residence in Paris I have settled down in something half-way between a Frenchman and a New Englander:—within, all Jonathan—but outwardly a little of the Parlez-vous. That is to say, I have good home-feelings at heart—but have decorated my outward man, with a long-waisted thin coat—claret-coloured—and a pair of linen pantaloons:—and then on Sundays and other fête days—I appear in all the glory of a little hard French hat—glossy—and bushed—and rolled up at the sides:—it makes my head ache to think of it.—In this garb I jostle along among the crowds of the Luxembourg, which is the favorite promenade in St. Germain.''[1]

To his father he wrote: "The truth is, that the heavy responsibility which I have taken upon myself . . . together with the continual solicitude about the final result of my studies, and the fear that you will be displeased with my expenses—are hanging with a terrible weight upon me.

"It is now exactly eight months since my arrival in Paris—and setting all boasting aside—I must say that I am well satisfied with the knowledge I have acquired of the french [sic] language. My friends all tell me that I have a good pronunciation—and although I do not pretend to anything like perfection—yet in comparison with what others have done—I am confident that I have done well. I cannot imagine who told you that six months was enough for the French. He would have been more correct if he had said six years—that is—speaking of perfection in the language.

"I shall leave Paris for Spain on Wednesday—day after tomorrow.''[1]

February 21, 1827. Left for Spain. "Thus you see me on my way to Spain: and I cannot say that I leave France with much regret:—It may be, that my curiosity leaves no room for feelings of this kind, by painting the land to which I am going as fairer than that I am leaving—or it may be a secret disappointment lurking in my heart,—at having found more perplexities to escape—and more difficulties to encounter than I had anticipated;—but true it is that I look forward to a happier life in Spain, than I have led in France.

"In broad daylight, too, one who travels in this country has always something to remind him of the perilous ways he is treading in. The cold, inhospitable, uncultivated look of the country itself—the dark, fiendish countenances which peep at him from the folds of the Spanish cloak in every town and village, but more than all, the little black crosses which one comes upon at almost every step—standing by the roadside in commemoration of a murder or other violent death which has taken place upon the spot—these keep his fancy busy.''[1]

The lodgings for which he had waited proved more delightful than he had imagined. ''The whole house is goodness—from the mistress down to the domestic, and the daughter, a young lady of 'sweet sixteen' with the romantic name of Florence, supplies the place of a sister much better than I had anticipated could be possible. Under her attentions I hope to find the acquisition of the Spanish a delightful task.

''The daughter . . . is one of the sweetest-tempered little girls that I ever met with:—and added to this, the grace of the Spanish women and the beauty of their language makes her conversation quite fascinating. I could not receive greater kindness than I receive at the hands of this good family, who on all occasions exhibit the greatest, and most disinterested affection for me. I shall feel the most sincere regret in bidding them farewell for ever. There is also another family in the house, with which I am acquainted. It is a Malaga lady with her daughter—a very handsome young lady of about seventeen—a very white skin—light blue eyes—and fine auburn hair. She frequently reminds me of sister Anne, and by the way, has the same name. As the two young ladies are very intimate together, I have a great deal of good society. Whilst I write, I see them in the balcony below me, busy with their needles and their tongues—little dreaming that I am sending tidings of them across the sea. I confess that I feel very little desire to leave Madrid, as you may imagine.

''It will not of course be necessary to explain very fully my motives in coming to Madrid in preference to any other city in Spain—with a view of making the language my study:—because I know that the same reasons which actuated me will suggest themselves forcibly to your own mind. The metropolis of a country is always the great literary mart:—then—literary advantages are always greater—books always more numerous and more accessible . . . I dare say that I shall not regret my coming.''[1]

Fall, 1827. Travelled on to Italy. ''I suppose the very names of Florence—the Arno—and Vallombrosa are full of romance and poetry for you who have not seen them:—and that you imagine me sitting at night in the shadow of some olive grove—watching the rising moon—and listening to the song of the Italian boatman, or the chime of a convent bell! Alas! distance and poetry have so much magic about them! Can you believe that the Arno—'that glassy river'—'rolling his crystal tide through classic vales,'—is a stream of yellow, muddy water almost entirely dry in summer!—and that Italian gondoliers—and convent bells—and white-robed nuns—and all the rigmarole of midnight song and soft serenade, are not altogether so delightful in reality as we sometimes fancy them to be? But I must not tell tales! I may spoil the market for some beautiful effusion. . . .

''I shall stay but a few days longer in Florence—I feel anxious to get into Germany—at least as much so as I do to see Rome and Naples. I must confess it!—It is rather singular—but I must confess it—I am travelling through Italy without any enthusiasm—and just curiosity enough to keep me awake!—I feel no excitement—no—nothing of that romantic feeling which every body else has—or pretends to have. The fact is I am homesick for Spain—I want to go back there again—The recollection of it completely ruins Italy for me: and next to going home—let me go to Spain.

Thus the Birch Canoe was builded
In the valley, by the river,
In the bosom of the forest;
And the forest's life was in it....
■ (From *The Song of Hiawatha* by Henry Wadsworth Longfellow. Illustrated by Herbert Meyer.)

''I got quite out of humor with the language, and concluded that I would not give further attention to speaking—but would make my way through Italy with the little I had acquired—and be contented with reading:—without making much pretension to speaking it.''[1]

1828. Travelled on to Rome. ''I have been so much delighted with Rome, that I have extended my residence much beyond my original intention.

''The summer, you know, in Rome is very unhealthy for foreigners: and so it proved to me:—and I who have hardly known until this what sickness is—am now an invalid seeking my health in a little village among the hills in the vicinity of Rome. I am however happy to tell you that I am no longer in danger: and find myself gradually gaining strength and activity.

''In the beginning of July I took a violent cold, which of course gave me no alarm, as I am seldom free from some affection of the kind. Feeling, however, a little feverish at night, on going to bed I took the usual remedy of something to throw open the pores, and in a day or two felt well enough to venture out. But I had anticipated my time. For a few days afterwards I felt poorly—and took the advice of a physician. . . . For my own part I grew worse, and was at length obliged to take to my bed with a raging fever. Of course another physician was instantly called—but there was no checking the fever—we were obliged to let it have its course—and come to a crisis. It proved to be an inflamatory

Fair was she to behold, that maiden of seventeen summers. ■ (From "Evangeline," in *The Children's Own Longfellow* by Henry Wadsworth Longfellow. Illustrated by Frank Schoonover.)

Why don't you speak for yourself, John? ■ (From *The Courtship of Miles Standish* by Henry Wadsworth Longfellow. Illustrated by N. C. Wyeth.)

(From the movie "The Wreck of the Hesperus," starring Willard Parker. Copyright 1948 by Columbia Pictures Corp.)

rheumatic fever—and grew very high and dangerous. It was one of those fevers, however, which are violent and rapid in their course, and throw the die of life and death in a very short space of time. My medical aid was of the highest order—and the crisis passed favorably for me. Medical aid might however have been of no avail had I not very fortunately been situated in a very kind family, whose attentions were most zealous and unremitting. Indeed, next to the hand of Providence, it is to the care of this most excellent and kind hearted family, that I owe my life.

"I have been in the house ever since my arrival in Rome, and have always experienced from them the greatest kindness. Had I been a son of the family nothing more could have been done for me, during my sickness, than what has been done. The extent of my gratitude, it would be difficult to conceive: and more so perhaps, when I mention as an instance of the attention I received, that during the seven days I was languishing upon a sick-bed, every moment some one of the family was by me, both day and night. I am, however, most indebted to the ever-watchful care of Mrs. Julia, the oldest daughter, who having the freedom of a married woman, which the other daughters had not, was of course my nurse:—and a better one I think could not be found. It is to her, I may say, I owe my life, for having administered to me a gentle dose of medicine, as I lay almost gasping for breath, from violent oppression of the chest, and having prevented the surgeon from bleeding me a fourth time;—and this too

without orders from the doctor, who on coming in and finding me so much better and the dangerous crisis thus past—was loud in his praises.

"It is now four days since I left Rome, and am residing at this village where the air is pure and delightfully cool—even in the heat of August. My strength is slowly returning: but I shall not take a step upon my travels northward, until I find myself entirely restored. This is quite a new sphere of existence to me, who have never before been a valetudinarian."[1]

Longfellow received word that Bowdoin had voted to offer him, not the expected professorship but a mere instructorship, at a greatly reduced salary.

"VENICE, **December 19, 1828**

"My dear father,

"On receiving yours of the 15th Septemb. I left Rome immediately. I unsealed your letter with the usual delightful feelings of hearing from home: but I assure you the perusal of it caused me great pain. The tidings that the anticipated appointment at Bowdoin had been refused me, were very unexpected and very jarring to my feelings. And more so, because it was a situation, which neither yourself, nor I, had solicited, but which had been gratuitously offered me upon certain conditions—the which I have scrupulously fulfilled.

"I assure you—my dear father—I am very indignant at this. They say I am too young! Were they not aware of this three years ago? If I am not capable of performing the duties of the office, they may be very sure of my not accepting it. I know not in what light they may look upon it, but for my own part I do not in the least regard it as a favor conferred upon me. It is no sinecure: and if my services are an equivalent to my salary, there is no favor done me: if they be not, I do not desire the situation.

"If they think I would accept the place which they offer me, they are much mistaken in my character. No Sir—I am not yet reduced to this. I am not a dog to eat the crumbs, that fall from such a table. Excuse my warmth, but I feel rather hurt and indignant. It is a pitiful policy,—that, whilst other institutions send abroad their professors to qualify themselves for their stations and pay their expenses—they should offer me an uncertain and precarious office—for it is a probationary one, if I understand them,—in which the labours of six years would hardly reimburse the sum I have expended in three. I do not think so meanly of myself as to accept such an appointment. It was not necessary to come to Europe for such an office as they offer me: it could have been had at a much cheaper rate—and at an earlier hour.

"I am led to employ such language as this, because I feel no great anxiety for my future prospects. Thanks to your goodness, I have received a good education. I am ashamed to touch upon this point again: I thought that what I said in my last letter would be the last I should ever have occasion to say in my own justification. But now I feel it a duty I owe to myself to speak even more fully. I know you cannot be dissatisfied with the progress I have made in my studies. I do not speak this from any feeling of self-complacency, nor do I wish that parental partialities should bias your judgment. I speak honestly—not boastingly. With the French and Spanish Languages I am familiarly conversant—so as to speak them correctly—and write them with as much ease and fluency as I do the English. The Portuguese I read without difficulty:—and with regard to my proficiency in the Italian, I have only to say, that when I came to this city, all at the Hotel where I lodge took me for an Italian, until I gave them my passport, and told them I was an American. Do you, then, advise to accept of such a situation as is proffered me. No, I think you cannot. For myself, I have the greatest abhorrence to such a step. I beg of you not to think that this springs from any undue degree of arrogance. I arrogate nothing: but I must assert a freedom of thought and of speech.

(From the movie "Hiawatha," starring Vincent Edwards. Copyright 1952 by Monogram Pictures Corp., released through Allied Artists Pictures Corp.)

"I intend leaving Venice in a few days for Dresden, where I think of remaining until the opening of spring. I do not wish to return without a competent knowledge of German—and all that I can do to acquire it shall be done. The time is short—but I hope to turn it to good advantage."[1]

January 13, 1829. Set forth for Germany.

Longfellow wrote to his father: "For my own part, I shall remain here this vacation: and should like to, the next term, unless circumstances should render my return this summer absolutely necessary. With regard to Bowdoin College, the more I think of it, the more I am dissatisfied. So much so indeed, that I am averse to going there at all, if any other situation can be procured me. I dislike the manner in which things are conducted there. Their illiberality in point of religion—and their narrow-minded views upon many other points, need no comment. Had I the means of a bare subsistence, I would *now* refuse a Professorship there. I say *now:* I mean since they have offered me a lower office. I am inclined to think that the opposition came from the younger professors. I suppose they did not like the idea of seeing so young a man step at once into the chair of prof. without serving the usual apprenticeship. I have but one question to ask—Do the Professors of Bowdoin College speak the language they teach? No—not one of them. I have another plan to suggest to your consideration which to me holds out better inducement than the first.

"Finding Göttingen everything I had imagined it, my desire to pass a year here springs up anew. Allow me at least, then, to pass the Summer here; and in the meantime my friends can probably think of some other situation equally good for me as a professorship at Brunswick. If they cannot, upon my return I might be permitted to deliver a course of lectures on modern literature at Portland Atheneum, and in the mean time, I could look out for myself. As I have already told you, upon this point I feel not the slightest anxiety or mistrust. But I will not anticipate—at present let us speak of the present. I find living at Göttingen very cheap. As I have just arrived I cannot give you any just idea of what my expenses will be monthly: but as soon as I have been here a little longer I will send you a continuation of what my last letter contained. The Library here is the largest in Germany and is full of choice rare works and the advantages for a student of my particular pursuits are certainly not overrated in the universal fame of the University of Göttingen.

"Whilst at Dresden I felt no other desire than that of returning home once more to the bosom of the family. I had got discouraged and a little downhearted. But meeting with an old and good friend, has given new elasticity to my spirits:—they have again taken their wonted tone, and I am contented and happy. In this disposition, I am a little unwilling to give up what is now in my reach: and as I shall never again be in Europe, I should think it were better to lengthen a little my absence from home at present, than by not so doing to have subject for future regret. I brought letters to several of the Professors here from Bancroft and Ticknor: and have been well received. Göttingen is a small city—and there are no amusements here whatever: so there is no alternative but study. With regard to duelling, for which all the German Universities are more or less notorious, you will find a description of them in the *North American* for July 1828—page 87. They are considered by the students as sport: and it is not uncommon to hear of six being fought in one afternoon and on the same spot. There is however no possibility either of Preble [a Portland friend] or myself being engaged in these affairs, as we do not know the broad-sword exercise, and are of course *hors de combat*. There are about 14 or 15 hundred students here: as in all Universities some *scholars*—and others high wild fellows. He who wishes to be distinguished among the latter, must fight his way into distinction: but he who wishes to pursue his studies quietly, is no more molested here than at one of our colleges.

"I find Preble improved every way. He is everything I could wish a friend to be. His associates are entirely from the studious class:—and if his mother could see every action of his during the twenty four hours of the day, she could not wish one of them changed. This is saying a great deal, but it is so.

"Please write me immediately upon the subject of this, and tell me if you think my suggestions practicable. In the mean time, I have other literary projects in view, which shall be duly set in order and made known to you, when the time ar-

In the hour of darkness, and peril, and need,
The people will waken and listen to hear
The hurrying hoof-beats of that steed,
And the midnight message of Paul Revere.

(From *Paul Revere's Ride* by H. W. Longfellow. Illustrated by Joseph Low.)

(From the movie "Evangeline," starring Dolores Del Rio. Copyright 1929 by Edwin Carewe Feature Productions Inc.)

rives in which I can put them into execution. Pray set your mind perfectly at rest upon all points, that may have occasioned you any uneasiness. . . .

"What Preble tells me of the improvements going on in Portland delights me. It might be made one of the most beautiful cities in the world. I have never seen a finer situation in all the countries I have visited. Besides, he tells me the 'march and mind' goes forward with great strides. I see Mr. Neal attributes it to his 'preface to Niagara.' Mr. de Beaufort—who by the way refused the situation of Instructor at Bow: Coll:—has probably done something in this way.

"Most Affectionately your son"[1]

June, 1829. His father was willing to allow Longfellow to remain in Germany through the summer, but urged him home with the news of his sister Elizabeth's illness. On his journey homeward (in Paris) Longfellow received notification of Elizabeth's death.

August 11, 1829. Reached New York.

From Portland Longfellow wrote President Allen of Bowdoin College.

"PORTLAND **August 27, 1829.**

"Dear Sir,

"Your letter to my father dated Sept. 26, 1828, and enclosing a copy of the vote of the Trustees and Overseers of Bowdoin College, by which they have elected me Instructer of the Modern Languages in that institution, has been duly handed me.

"I am sorry, that under existing circumstances, I cannot accept the appointment. The Professorship of Modern Languages, with a salary equal to that of the other Professors, would certainly not have been refused. But having at great expense, devoted four years to the acquisition of the French, Spanish, Italian, and German languages, I cannot accept a subordinate station with a salary so disproportionate to the duties required.

**And children coming home from school
Look in at the open door;
They love to see the flaming forge,
And hear the bellows roar.**

■ (From "The Village Blacksmith" in *The Children's Own Longfellow* by Henry Wadsworth Longfellow. Illustrated by Howard Smith.)

"I have the honor to be, Sir,

"Very respectfully

"Your Obt Sert

"HENRY W. LONGFELLOW."[1]

Board of trustees voted to offer Longfellow the title of Professor with a request that he serve an apprenticeship before formal induction into office and a salary of $800. An additional $100 was offered with a further appointment to serve as college librarian. "Having concluded to accept my appointment as Prof. at this college, I was some time busy in making the necessary arrangements for taking up my abode here: which arrangements, together with visiting of friends in town and country—completely consumed the vacation: and since the commencement of the term I have been very much occupied—as the business of instruction is new to me, and I have also the charge of the Library, which occupies one hour every day. You know very well how the little everyday occurrances of life are linked into each other, so as to form one

long continued chain; and though each one of them separately is insignificant, yet all together make up no small portion of our existence. Besides after having corrected upwards of forty exercises from Levisac's grammar—which I have to do daily—I hate the sight of pen, ink and paper.

"I am also very busy in translating an elementary grammar from the French—intended for my own use as instructer here—and for the use of Schools. It is already in a state of forwardness—and I shall put it to press without delay. I will send you a copy as soon as it is out."[1]

Of his duties at Bowdoin, he wrote: "The Executive government have thought it advisable to introduce some considerable changes into the proposed plans of studies for the year, upon which plan we have acted thus far. The new arrangement puts a hard-laboring oar into my hands, and will give me four recitations per day, besides the hour occupied in the Library.

"The Junior Class will as usual recite French every afternoon. The Seniors will have three recitations a week in French—and three in Spanish—at noon. The Sophomore class will recite French every morning. This you perceive, gives me three recitations per diem through the week, Saturday afternoons excepted. Besides this, I am to have a private lesson in German: and the prospect before me seems thick-sown with occupations, promising me little leisure for my private studies, which on account of my busy life the last term, already begin to assume a retrograde march. Before closing this catalogue, I must add, that I have also an Inaugural Address to write for next term, and a Poem before the Phi Beta at Commencement."[1]

At the commencement of his second year of teaching at Bowdoin, Longfellow was given formal induction as Professor of Modern Languages. "I have looked forward to this day with feelings of pleasure and solicitude. Having been engaged already one year in the duties of my profession, it is natural for me to have desired an occasion on which I might express to you how grateful to my feelings has been the confidence you have reposed in me in conferring on me the Professorship of the Modern Languages in this institution. When a man's duty and his inclination go hand in hand, surely he has no small reason to rejoice, no feeble stimulus to act. The truth of this I feel. I regard the profession of teacher in a far more noble and elevated point of view than many do. I cannot help believing that he who bends in a right direction the pliant disposition of the young, and trains up the ductile mind to a vigorous and healthy growth, does something for the welfare of his country and something for the great interests of humanity.

"I cannot regard the study of a language as the pastime of a listless hour. To trace the progress of the human mind through the progressive development of language; to learn how other nations thought and felt, and spake; to enrich the understanding by opening upon it new sources of knowledge; and by speaking many tongues to become a citizen of the world; these are objects worthy the exertion their attainment demands at our hands.

"The mere acquisition of a language then is not the ultimate object; it is a means to be employed in the acquisition of something which lies beyond. I should therefore deem my duty but half performed were I to limit my exertions to the narrow bounds of grammatical rules: nay that I had done little for the intellectual culture of a pupil, when I had merely put an instrument into his hands without explaining to him its most important uses. . . . And it will be my aim, not only to teach the turns and idioms of a language, but, according to my ability and as soon as time and circumstances shall permit, to direct the student in his researches into the literature of those nations whose language he is studying.''[1]

September 14, 1831. Married Mary Storer Potter. ''I think I have formed a just estimate of the excellence of Mary's character. . . . I have never seen a woman in whom every look and word, and action seemed to proceed from so gentle and innocent a spirit. Indeed how much she possesses of all we most admire in the female character!''[1]

December, 1834. Offered the Smith Professorship of Modern Languages at Harvard with a salary of $1500 and a stipulation of spending a year to eighteen months in Europe to perfect his German. ''Well—I have concluded to accept the offer at Cambridge, and shall go to Europe in the Spring. I want to sail, if possible on the first of April; and in order to do this must dissolve my connection with Bowdoin as early as the first of March. Or would the Govt prefer that I should not enter on the duties of the next term? I will do as they think best. Mr. Greene says he is willing to supply for me till the close of the College year; so that on that point there will be no embarrassment, if the Govt wish the course of instruction to go on unchanged.

''I intend to be in Brunswick about week before the beginning of the term—probably on Monday next. I am not perfectly satisfied with all the manoeuvres of the Cambridge corporation; but have concluded after much debate to accede to their terms. This is *sub-rosa*.[1]

April, 1835. Sailed out of New York for London.

Mary Longfellow, delicate of health, had not been well since their arrival. On the trip to Heidelberg, Mary was brought to the verge of death by the premature birth of her child.

November 24, 1835. ''My poor Mary is worse to-day. Sinking—sinking. My heart is heavy; yet still I hope—perhaps too fondly.''[1]

November 29, 1835. Mary died. ''This morning between one and two o'clock, my Mary—my beloved Mary—ceased to breathe. She is now, I trust, a Saint in Heaven. Would that I were with her. This morning I have knelt beside her, and kissed her cold lips, and prayed to God, that hereafter in moments of temptation, I might recall that solemn hour, and be delivered from evil.

''. . . Our beloved Mary is no more. She expired on Sunday morning . . . without pain or suffering, either of body or mind, and with entire resignation to the will of her heavenly father. Though her sickness was long, yet I could not bring myself to think it dangerous until near its close. Indeed, I did not abandon all hope of her recovery till within a very few hours of her dissolution, and to me the blow was so sudden, that I have hardly yet recovered energy enough to write you the particulars of this solemn and mournful event. When I think, however, upon the goodness and purity of her life, and the holy and peaceful death she died, I feel great consolation in my bereavement, and can say, 'Father, thy will be done.'

''Knowing the delicate state of Mary's health, I came all the way from Stockholm with fear and trembling, and with the exception of one day's ride from Kiel to Hamburg we came the whole distance by water. Unfortunately our passage

Thus with the rising of the sun
Was the noble task begun,
And soon throughout the ship-yard's bounds
Were heard the intermingled sounds
Of axes and of mallets, plied
With vigorous arms on every side;
Plied so deftly and so well.
■ (From ''The Building of the Ship'' in *Children's Own Longfellow* by Henry Wadsworth Longfellow. Illustrated by C.W. Ashley.)

from Hamburg to Amsterdam in the Steamboat was rather rough, and Mary was quite unwell. On the night of our arrival the circumstance occurred to which I alluded in my last, and which has had this fatal termination. . . . In Amsterdam we remained three weeks; and Mary seemed to be quite restored and was anxious to be gone. To avoid a possibility of fatigue we took three days to come to this place—a distance of only forty miles; and on our arrival here Mary was in excellent spirits and to all appearances very well. But alas! the same night she had a relapse which caused extreme debility, with a low fever, and nervous headache. This was on the 23rd October. In a day or two she was better, and on the 27th worse again. After this she seemed to recover slowly, and sat up for the first time on the 11th, though only for a short while. This continued for a day or two longer, till she felt well enough to sit up for nearly an hour. And then she was seized with a violent rheumatism, and again took to her bed from which she never more arose.

"During all this she was very patient, and generally cheerful, tho' at times her courage fainted and she thought that she should not recover,—wishing only that she could see her friends at home once more before she died. At such moments she loved to repeat these lines, which seemed to soothe her feelings:—

> "Father! I thank thee! may no thought
> E'er deem thy chastisements severe.
> But may this heart, by sorrow taught
> Calm each wild wish, each idle fear.

"On Sunday, the 22nd, all her pain had left her, and she said she had not felt so well during her sickness. On this day, too, we received a letter from Margaret [her sister], which gave her great pleasure, and renovated her spirits very much. But still from day to day she gained no strength. In this situation she continued during the whole week—perfectly calm, cheerful and without any pain. . . . When I went to her on Saturday morning I found her countenance much changed, and my heart sank within me. Till this moment I had indulged the most sanguine hopes;—but now my fears overmastered them. She was evidently worse, though she felt as well as usual. The day passed without change; and towards evening, as she seemed a little restless and could not sleep, I sat down by her bedside, and read [letters] to her. O, I shall never forget how her eyes and her whole countenance brightened, and with what a heavenly smile she looked up into my face as I read. My own hopes revived again to see that look; but alas! this was the last gleam of the dying lamp. Towards ten o'clock she felt a slight oppression in the chest, with a difficulty of breathing. I sat down by her side and tried to cheer her; and as her respiration became more difficult, she said to me, 'Why should I be troubled; If I die God will take me to himself.' And, from this moment she was perfectly calm, excepting for a single instant, when she exclaimed, 'O, my dear Father; how he will mourn for me.' A short time afterwards she thanked Clara for her kindness, and clasping her arms affectionately round my neck, kissed me, and said, 'Dear Henry, do not forget me!' and after this, 'Tell my dear friends at home that I thought of them at the last hour.' I then read to her from the Church Litany the prayers for the sick and dying; and as the nurse spoke of sending for Dr. Bosworth, the Episcopal clergyman, Mary said she should like to see him, and I accordingly sent. He came about one o'clock, but at this time Mary became apparently insensible to what was around her; and at half-past one she ceased to breathe.

Grant Wood's painting of "The Midnight Ride of Paul Revere."

**Lovely the moonlight was as it glanced and gleamed
  on the water,
Gleamed on the columns of cypress and cedar
  sustaining the arches....**
■ (From *Evangeline: A Tale of Acadie* by Henry Wadsworth Longfellow, edited by Mina Lewiton. Illustrated by Howard Simon.)

''Thus all the hopes I had so fondly cherished of returning home with my dear Mary in happiness and renovated health have in the providence of God ended in disappointment and sorrow unspeakable. All that I have left to me in my affliction is the memory of her goodness, her gentleness, her affection for me—unchangeable in life and in death—and the hope of meeting her again hereafter, where there shall be no more sickness, nor sorrow, nor suffering, nor death. I feel, too, that she must be infinitely, oh, infinitely happier now than when with us on earth, and I say to myself,—

''Peace! peace! she is not dead, she does not sleep!
She has awakened from the dream of life.''[1]

Winter, 1835. In Heidelberg. ''I cannot recover my energies, either mental or bodily. I take no interest in anything—or at most only a momentary interest. All my favorite and cherished literary plans are either abandoned, or looked upon as a task which duty requires me work out, as a day-laborer. Other tastes and projects have begun to spring up in my mind; though as yet all is in confusion, in a word, sometimes I think I am crazed—and then I rally—and think it is only nervous debility:—sometimes I sit at home and read diligently—and then for days together I hardly open a book.

''. . . I am sitting alone in my new home; and yet not all alone—for the spirit of her, who loved me, and who I trust still loves me—is with me. Not many days before her death she said to me: 'We shall be so happy in Heidelberg!' I feel assured of her presence—and am happy in knowing that she

is so. O my beloved Mary—teach me to be good, and kind, and gentle as thou wert when here on earth. . . .''[1]

Longfellow's efforts were directed towards mastering German, but the tragedy of Mary's death became a turning point in his life. He showed no sign of deep intellectual or emotional development. ''I cannot study. One thought occupies me night and day. She is dead—she is dead!—All day I am weary and sad—and at night I cry myself to sleep like a child. Not a page can I read without my thoughts wandering from it.

''To-night came a letter from Boston for Mary. She is not here. My heart aches for her family and friends at home. They do not yet know that she is dead; but will know it soon.''[1]

Met and fell in love with Frances Appleton, a Bostonian, in Switzerland. ''Thus there was not one discordant thing in her; but a perfect harmony of figure, and face, and soul; in a word, of the whole being. And he who had a soul to comprehend hers, must of necessity love her, and, having once loved her, could love no other woman forevermore.''[1]

October 8, 1836. Sailed for New York.

Fall, 1836. Took up residence in Cambridge. ''My chambers are very pleasant; with great trees in front, whose branches almost touch my windows, so that I have a nest not unlike the birds, being high up—in the third story.''[1]

In his birch canoe exulting
All alone went Hiawatha.
■ (From "Hiawatha," in *The Children's Own Longfellow* by Henry Wadsworth Longfellow. Illustrated by N. C. Wyeth.)

Summer, 1837. Took new residence in Mrs. Andrew Craigie's mansion on Brattle Street overlooking the Charles River. In this room, he composed all his poems between 1837 and 1845 and the romance of *Hyperion.* ''I live in a great house which looks like an Italian villa; have two large rooms opening into each other. They were once General Washington's chambers. I breakfast at seven on tea and toast, and dine at five or six, generally in Boston. In the evening I walk on the Common with Hillard or alone; then go back to Cambridge on foot. If not very late, I sit an hour with Felton or Sparks. For nearly two years I have not studied at night save now and then. Most of the time am alone; smoke a good deal; wear a broad-brimmed black hat, black frock coat, a black cane. Molest no one. Dine out frequently. In winter go much into Boston society. The last year have written a great deal, enough to make volumes. Have not read much. Have a number of literary plans and projects . . . I do not like this sedentary life. I want action. I want to travel. Am too excited, too tumultuous inwardly.''[2]

Fall, 1838. ''A new month,—a new College year, and a new book in my Journal begins today. I am neither in good health nor good spirits; being foolishly inclined to indigestion and the most unpleasant melancholy. It is a kind of sleepiness of the soul, in which I feel a general indifference to all things.

''Perhaps the worst thing in a College Life is this having your mind constantly a play-mate for boys, constantly adapting itself to them; instead of stretching out, and grappling with men's minds.''[1]

Plagued with constant toothaches, he wrote: ''The dentist tugged merrily at my tooth for five minutes. At length it came out. He said he never knew one come so hard.

HENRY WADSWORTH LONGFELLOW

(From *The Song of Hiawatha* by H. W. Longfellow. Illustrated by Joan Kiddell-Monroe.)

''Oct. 17. Face sore and swollen. Look like King Henry VIII. A working day in College. Have I been wise to give up three whole days to College classes? I think I have; for thus I make my presence felt here; and have no idle time, to mope and grieve over that most sad and sorrowful thought, which haunts me, *Forever!*''[1]

1839. *Hyperion* published in two volumes. Frances Appleton was portrayed as the heroine of this prose romance. Longfellow wrote that the feelings of the book were true, the events of the story mostly fictional.

1842. In delicate health, decided to set out for the ''water-cure'' in Germany.

October 22, 1842. Sailed home. ''We had a very boisterous passage. I was not out of my berth more than twelve hours for the first twelve days. I was in the forward part of the vessel, where all the great waves struck, and broke with voices of thunder. In the next room to mine, a man died. I was afraid that they might throw me overboard instead of him in the night, but they did not. Well, there, 'cribbed, cabined, and confined,' I passed fifteen days. During this time I wrote seven poems on Slavery; I meditated upon them in the stormy, sleepless nights, and wrote them down with a pencil in the morning. A small window in the side of the vessel admitted light into my berth, and there I lay on my back and soothed my soul with songs. . . .''[1]

December, 1842. A thirty-page collection of poems on slavery published. He expressed his views as follows: ''I believe slavery to be an unrighteous institution, based on the false maxim that Might makes Right.

"I have great faith in doing what is righteous, and fear no evil consequences.

"I believe that every one has a perfect right to express his opinion on the subject of slavery as on every other thing; that every one ought so to do, until the public opinion of all Christendom shall penetrate into and change the hearts of the Southerners on this subject.

"I would have no other interference than what is sanctioned by law.

"I believe that where there is a will, there is a way. When the whole country sincerely wishes to get rid of slavery, it will readily find the means.

"Let us, therefore, do all we can to bring about this *will* in all gentleness and Christian charity.

"And God speed the time."[2]

1843. Frances ("Fanny") Appleton acknowledged her love for Longfellow after a stormy seven-year courtship. Scanning the words of a note she sent to him, Longfellow was off for Boston. "I walked with the speed of an arrow—too restless to sit in a carriage—too impatient and fearful of encouraging anyone!"[1] The old familiar road through Cambridgeport and across the river was transformed, that May day, even more vividly than when he had first begun to make such walks, in the Indian summer of 1837. "I received Fanny's note, and walked to town amid the blossoms and sunshine and song of birds, with my heart full of gladness and my eyes full of tears!—Oh, Day forever blessed; that ushered in this *Vita Nova* of happiness!"[1]

The first joyful note of announcement of his engagement went to his mother.

"My dearest mother,

"I write you one line, and only one—to tell of the good fortune which has just come to me—namely that I am engaged. Yes, engaged to a very lovely woman—Fanny Appleton—for whom I have many years cherished a feeling of affection...."[1]

July 13, 1843. Married Frances Elizabeth Appleton. Frances' father, Nathan Appleton, purchased the Craigie House and presented it to his daughter and her husband. Six children were born of this marriage.

Accepted a proposal to edit a work on the poets and poetry of Europe. Frances Longfellow served as her husband's amanuensis, as severe trouble with his eye sight had disabled him.

The routine of teaching galled him. "When I go out of the precincts of my study, down the village street to college, how the scaffoldings about the palace of song come rattling and clattering down.

"I am in despair at the swift flight of time and the utter impossibility I feel to lay hold upon anything permanent. All my hours and days go to perishable things. College takes half the time; and other people with their interminable letters and poems and requests and demands take the rest. I have hardly

a moment to think of my own writings, and am cheated of some of the fairest hours. This is the extreme of folly; and if I knew a man far off in some foreign land, doing as I do here, I should say he was mad."[2]

1854. Resigned his professorship to devote himself to writing. "If I wish to do anything in literature it must be done now. Few men have written good poetry after fifty."[2]

July 9, 1861. A lighted match, fallen on the floor, set Frances Longfellow's dress on fire. She died the next day. Longfellow, himself severely burned, was unable to attend her funeral. He exclaimed in his bereavement that he could "*bear the cross, yes; but what if one is stretched upon it!*"[2]

Took up the task of translating Dante which he had begun earlier.

May, 1868. With a large circle of friends, Longfellow made his last visit to Europe. Received private audience with Queen Victoria.

September, 1868. Longfellow was once again at his desk, "under the evening lamp."[2]

July, 1873. A sudden seizure befell him and deprived him of the use of his right hand and arm.

1878. Just before his seventy-second birthday he called attention to the mysterious significant part which the number eighteen had played in his life. "I was eighteen years old when I took my college degree; eighteen years afterward, I was married for the second time; I lived with my wife eighteen years, and it is eighteen years since she died.... And then, by way of parenthesis or epicycle, I was eighteen years professor in the college here, and I have published eighteen separate volumes of poems."[2]

March 18, 1882. Took a chill and was seized with peritonitis.

March 24, 1882. Died in Cambridge, Massachusetts. "Perhaps the chief cause which has retarded the progress of poetry in America, is the want of that exclusive cultivation, which so noble a branch of literature would seem to require. Few here think of relying upon the exertion of poetic talent for a livelihood, and of making literature the profession of life. The bar or the pulpit claims the greater part of the scholar's existence, and poetry is made its pastime. This is a defect, which the hand of honourable patronage alone can remedy.... It is the fear of poverty that deters many gifted and poetic minds from coming forward into the arena, and wiping away all reproach from our literature."[1]

His last verse:

"O Bells of San Blas, in vain
Ye call back the past again,
   The past is dead to your prayer.
Out of the shadow of night
The world rolls into light;—
   It is daybreak everywhere."[2]

FOR MORE INFORMATION SEE: Francis H. Underwood, *Henry Wadsworth Longfellow,* Osgood, 1882, reprinted, Folcroft, 1974; William Sloane Kennedy, *Henry W. Longfellow: A Biography, Anecdotes, Letters, Criticism,* M. King, 1882, reprinted, Folcroft, 1973; Blanche R. Macchetta, *The Home Life of Henry W. Longfellow,* G. W. Carleton, 1882, reprinted, Folcroft, 1974; Samuel Longfellow, editor, *Life of*

"The American poet was taken to Julia Margaret Cameron's studio by Tennyson in 1868. 'Longfellow, you will have to do whatever she tells you. I'll come back soon and see what is left of you.' "

Henry Wadsworth Longfellow, with Extracts from His Journals and Correspondence, Ticknor, 1886, reprinted, R. West, 1973; Eric Sutherland Robertson, *Life of Henry Wadsworth Longfellow,* W. Scott, 1887, reprinted, Kennikat, 1972; Thomas W. Higginson, *Henry Wadsworth Longfellow,* Houghton, 1902, reprinted, Folcroft, 1973; Charles Eliot Norton, *Henry Wadsworth Longfellow: A Sketch of His Life,* Houghton, 1907, reprinted, Folcroft, 1972.

William H. O. Smeaton, *Longfellow and His Poetry,* Harrap, 1913, reprinted, AMS Press, 1972; Herbert Sherman Gorman, *Victorian American: Henry Wadsworth Longfellow,* G. H. Doran, 1926, reprinted, Kennikat, 1967; James T. Hatfield, *New Light on Longfellow, with Special Reference to His Relations with Germany,* Houghton, 1933, reprinted, Gordian Press, 1970; Sabatino Ianetta, *Henry W. Longfellow and Montecassio: His Rhode Island Friendship, His Birthplace,* Humphries, 1938, reprinted Folcroft, 1974; Lawrance Thompson, *Young Longfellow,* Macmillan, 1938, Octagon, 1969; Andrew R. Hilen, *Longfellow and Scandinavia: A Study of the Poet's Relationship with the Northern Languages and Literature,* Yale University Press, 1947, reprinted, Shoe String Press, 1970; Edward Charles Wagenknecht, *Henry Wadsworth Longfellow: Portrait of an American Humanist,* Longmans, Green, 1955, revised edition, Oxford University Press, 1966.

Edward L. Hirsh, *Henry Wadsworth Longfellow* (Pamphlets on American Writers Series), University of Minnesota Press, 1964; Cecil B. Williams, *Henry Wadsworth Longfellow,* Twayne, 1964; Andrew Hilen, editor, *The Letters of Henry Wadsworth Longfellow,* Harvard University Press, Volumes I and II, 1966, Volumes III and IV, 1972; R. S. Ward, "Longfellow's Roots in Yankee Soil," *New England Quarterly,* June, 1968; Gamaliel Bradford, *Biography and the Human Heart,* Books for Libraries, 1969; Rhoda Hoff, *Four American Poets,* Walck, 1969; Edward L. Hirsh, "Henry Wadsworth Longfellow," in *Six Classic American Writers,* edited by Sherman Paul, University of Minnesota Press, 1970.

Carl L. Johnson, *Three Notes on Longfellow,* Haskell, 1970; Norah Smaridge, *Trailblazers in American Arts,* Messner, 1971; Wilson Sullivan, *New England Men of Letters,* Macmillan, 1972; Harry Hansen, *Longfellow's New England,* Hastings House, 1972.

For children: Laura Benét, *Famous American Poets,* Dodd, 1950; Frederick Houk Law, *Great Americans,* Globe Book Co., 1953; Catherine Owens Peare, *Henry Wadsworth Longfellow: His Life,* Holt, 1953; Sarah Bolton, *Famous American Authors,* Crowell, 1963; Grace Hathaway Melin, *Henry Wadsworth Longfellow: Gifted Young Poet,* Bobbs-Merrill, 1968; L. Edmond Leipold, *Famous American Poets,* Denison, 1969; Laura Benét, *Famous New England Authors,* Dodd, 1970.

MASEFIELD, John   1878-1967

PERSONAL: Born June 1, 1878, in Ledbury, Herefordshire, England; died May 12, 1967, in Abingdon, Berkshire, England; son of George Edward (a provincial lawyer) and Caroline (Parker) Masefield; married Constance de la Cherois-Crommelin (died, 1960); children: Judith (an illustrator) and Lewis Crommelin (killed in action, World War II). *Education:* Attended public schools until the age of thirteen. *Home:* Burcote Brook, near Abingdon, Berkshire, England.

CAREER: Poet, dramatist, novelist, critic, and historian. Joined the Merchant Navy at age thirteen, going to sea as an apprentice at age fifteen. Left the sea after an illness, doing various jobs in New York City, including work in a bakery, livery stable, saloon, and carpet factory. Returned to England in 1897, and joined the staff of the Manchester *Guardian,* where he originated a daily column entitled, "Miscellany." He also served as literary editor of the magazine, *The Speaker. Wartime service:* Served with the Red Cross during World War I in France and on a hospital ship in Gallipoli, Italy. *Awards, honors:* Poet Laureate of England, 1930-67; Order of Merit, 1935; Hanseatic Shakespeare Prize of Hamburg University, 1938; William Foyle Prize, 1961, for *Bluebells and Other Verses;* Companion of Literature, Royal Society of Literature, 1961; D.Litt., Oxford University, 1922; LL.D., University of Aberdeen, 1922.

WRITINGS—Fiction: *A Mainsail Haul* (stories), E. Mathews, 1905, revised and enlarged edition, Macmillan, 1913; *A Tarpaulin Muster* (stories), G. Richards, 1907, B. W. Dodge, 1908, reprinted, Books for Libraries, 1970; *Captain Margaret,* G. Richards, 1908, reprinted, Scholarly Press, 1972; *Multitude and Solitude,* G. Richards, 1909; *Martin Hyde: The Duke's Messenger* (illustrated by T. C. Dugdale), Little, Brown, 1910; *Lost Endeavor,* T. Nelson, 1910; *A Book of Discoveries* (illustrated by Gordon Browne), F. A. Stokes, 1910; *The Street of Today,* Dutton, 1911; *Jim Davis,* W. Gardner, 1911, F. A. Stokes, 1912 (also published as *The Captive of the Smugglers,* Page, 1918) [other editions illustrated by Stephen Reid, D. McKay, 1924; Mead Schaeffer, F. A. Stokes, 1924; Frances Brundage, Saalfield, 1926; Bob Dean, T. Nelson, 1932; Exell, Penguin Books, 1966]; *The Taking of Helen,* Macmillan, 1922, reprinted, Penguin Books, 1963; *Sard Harker,* Macmillan, 1924, reissued, Penguin Books, 1963 [another edition illustrated by A. R. Thomson, Heinemann, 1956].

Odtaa, Macmillan, 1926, reissued, Penguin Books, 1966; *The Midnight Folk,* Macmillan, 1927 [another edition illustrated by Rowland Hilder, Macmillan, 1932, reissued, Penguin Books, 1963]; *The Hawbucks,* Macmillan, 1929; *The Bird of Dawning; or, The Fortune of the Sea,* Macmillan, 1933, reissued, 1967; *The Taking of the Gry,* Macmillan, 1934, reissued, 1967; *The Box of Delights; or, When the Wolves Were Running,* Macmillan, 1935; *Victorious Troy; or, The Hurrying Angel,* Macmillan, 1935, reissued, 1967; *Eggs and Baker; or, The Days of Trial,* Macmillan, 1936; *The Square Peg; or, The Gun Fella,* Macmillan, 1937; *Dead Ned: The Autobiography of a Corpse Who Recovered Life within the Coast of Dead Ned and Came to What Fortune You Shall Hear,* Macmillan, 1938, reissued, Heinemann, 1970; *Live and Kicking Ned,* Macmillan, 1939, reissued, Heinemann, 1970; *Basilissa: A Tale of the Empress Theodora,* Macmillan, 1940; *Conquer: A Tale of the Nika Rebellion in Byzantium,* Macmillan, 1941.

Poems: *Salt-Water Ballads,* G. Richards, 1902 [another edition illustrated by Charles Pears, Macmillan, 1916, reissued, 1960]; *Ballads,* E. Mathews, 1903; *Ballads and Poems,* E. Mathews, 1910; *The Everlasting Mercy,* Sidgwick & Jackson, 1911, Macmillan, 1912; *The Story of a Roundhouse, and Other Poems,* Macmillan, 1912; *The Widow in the Bye Street,* Sidgwick & Jackson, 1912; *Dauber,* Heinemann, 1913; *The Daffodil Fields,* Macmillan, 1913; *Philip the King, and Other Poems,* Macmillan, 1914 [another edition illustrated by Laurence Irving, Heinemann, 1927]; *Good Friday,* Macmillan, 1915, reissued, Heinemann, 1964; *Good Friday, and Other Poems* (also published as *Sonnets*), Macmillan,

1916; *Lollingdon Downs, and Other Poems*, Macmillan, 1917; *Rosas*, Macmillan, 1918; *Reynard the Fox; or, The Ghost Heath Run*, Macmillan, 1919 [another edition illustrated by Carton Moorepark, Macmillan, 1920].

Enslaved, Macmillan, 1920; *Right Royal*, Macmillan, 1920; *King Cole* (illustrated by daughter, Judith Masefield), Macmillan, 1921; *The Dream* (illustrated by Judith Masefield), Macmillan, 1922; *The Dream, and Other Poems*, Macmillan, 1923; *Midsummer Night, and Other Tales in Verse*, Macmillan, 1928; *South and East* (illustrated by Jacynth Parsons), Macmillan, 1929; *The Wanderer of Liverpool*, Macmillan, 1930; *Minnie Maylow's Story, and Other Tales and Scenes*, Macmillan, 1931; *A Tale of Troy*, Macmillan, 1932; *A Letter from Pontus, and Other Verse*, Macmillan, 1936; *To Rudyard Kipling*, E. H. Blakeney, 1936; *Tribute to Ballet in Poems* (illustrated by Edward Seago), Macmillan, 1938; *Some Verses to Some Germans*, Macmillan, 1939; *Shopping in Oxford*, Heinemann, 1941; *Gautama the Enlightened, and Other Verses*, Macmillan, 1941; *A Generation Risen* (illustrated by E. Seago), Collins, 1942, Macmillan, 1943; *Land Workers*, Macmillan, 1943; *Natalie Maisie [and] Pavilastukay: Two Tales in Verse*, Macmillan, 1942; *Wonderings*, Macmillan, 1943; *On the Hill*, Macmillan, 1949; *The Bluebells, and Other Verse*, Macmillan, 1961; *The Western Hudson Shore*, [New York], 1962; *Old Raiger, and Other Verse*, Macmillan, 1964; *In Glad Thanksgiving*, Macmillan, 1967.

Also author of *The Cold Cotswolds*, 1917; *Animula*, 1920; *Sonnets of Good Cheer to the Lena Ashwell Players, From Their Well-Wisher, John Masefield*, 1926; and *The Country Scene in Poems*, Collins, 1937.

Plays: *The Tragedy of Nan, and Other Plays*, M. Kennerley, 1909; *The Tragedy of Pompey the Great*, Little, Brown, 1910, revised, Sidgwick & Jackson, 1964; *The Faithful: A Tragedy in Three Acts*, Heinemann, 1915; *The Locked Chest [and] The Sweeps of Ninety-Eight*, Macmillan, 1916; *Melloney Holtspur; or, The Pangs of Love*, Macmillan, 1922; *A King's Daughter*, Macmillan, 1923; *The Trial of Jesus*, Macmillan, 1925; *Tristan and Isolt: A Play in Verse*, Heinemann, 1927; *The Coming of Christ*, Macmillan, 1928; *Easter: A Play for Singers*, Macmillan, 1929; *End and Beginning*, Macmillan, 1933; *A Play of St. George*, Macmillan, 1948.

Also author of an unpublished play, "The Campden Wanderer," 1907.

Biographical and critical: *William Shakespeare*, Holt, 1911, reissued, Barnes & Noble, 1969; *John M. Synge: A Few Personal Recollections with Biographical Notes*, Macmillan, 1915, reprinted, 1973; *John Ruskin*, Yellowsands Press, 1920; *A Foundation Day Address*, Yellowsands Press, 1921; *Shakespeare and Spiritual Life*, Oxford University Press, 1924, reprinted, Folcroft, 1973; *With the Living Voice*, Macmillan, 1925; *Poetry*, Macmillan, 1932, reprinted, Folcroft, 1973; *Chaucer*, Macmillan, 1931, reprinted, Folcroft, 1973; *Some Memories of W. B. Yeats*, Macmillan, 1940, reprinted, Irish University Press, 1971; *Thanks before Going: Notes on Some Original Poems by Dante Gabriel Rossetti*, Macmillan, 1947; *St. Katherine of Ledbury, and Other Ledbury Papers*, Heinemann, 1951; *An Elizabethan Theatre in London*, Oxford University Press, 1954; *Words Spoken in Honor of William Butler Yeats, Poet*, Grabhorn-Hoyem, 1970.

Other: *Sea Life in Nelson's Time*, Methuen, 1905, reprinted, United States Naval Institute, 1971; *On the Spanish Main; or, Some English Forays on the Isthmus of Darien*, Macmil-

JOHN MASEFIELD

lan, 1906, reprinted, United States Naval Institute, 1972; (author of introduction) *Chronicles of the Pilgrim Fathers*, Dutton, 1910; *My Faith in Women's Suffrage*, Womans Press, 1913; *Gallipoli*, Macmillan, 1916; *The Old Front Line*, Macmillan, 1917, reprinted, Bourne End (England), 1972; *The War and the Future*, Macmillan, 1918 (published in England as *St. George and the Dragon*, Heinemann, 1919); *The Battle of Somme*, Heinemann, 1919, reprinted, C. Chivers, 1968; *Prologue to a Book of Pictures of Adventure by Sea*, [New York], 1925; *Any Dead to Any Living*, [New Haven], 1928; *The Masque of Liverpool*, Brown Brothers, 1930; *The Conway, from Her Foundation to the Present Day*, Macmillan, 1933; (contributor) "Cape Horn Calm," in *Hundred English Essays*, edited by Rosalind Vallance, Nelson, 1936; (contributor) "Professor Murray and the Amateur Player," in *Essays in Honor of Gilbert Murray*, Oxford University Press, 1936; *Lines on the Tercentenary of Harvard University*, Macmillan, 1936.

In the Mill (autobiography), Macmillan, 1941; *The Nine Days Wonder*, Macmillan, 1941; *I Want! I Want!*, National Book Council, 1944, Macmillan, 1945; *New Chum*, Heinemann, 1944, Macmillan, 1945; *A Macbeth Production*, Heinemann, 1945, Macmillan, 1946; (author of preface) Lewis Masefield, *The Passion Left Behind*, Macmillan, 1947; *Badon Parchments*, Heinemann, 1947; *Book of Both Sorts*, Heinemann, 1947; *In Praise of Nurses*, Heinemann, 1950; *So Long to Learn: Chapters of an Autobiography*, Macmillan, 1952; *Grace before Ploughing: Fragments of an Autobiogra-*

phy, Macmillan, 1966; *The Twenty-Five Days,* Heinemann, 1972.

Editor: (With wife, Constance Masefield) *Lyrists of the Restoration from Sir Edward Sherburne to William Congreve,* Richards, 1905; (with C. Masefield) *Essays Moral and Polite, 1660-1714,* [London], 1906, reprinted, Books for Libraries, 1971; W. Dampier, *Voyages,* Dutton, 1906; *A Sailor's Garland,* Methuen, 1906, reprinted, Norwood Editions, 1975; *Defoe* (selections), Macmillan, 1909; (and translator) Jean Racine, *Esther* (play), Heinemann, 1922; (and translator) Racine, *Bernice* (play), Macmillan, 1922; *My Favorite English Poems,* Macmillan, 1950, reprinted, Books for Libraries, 1969; (and author of introductions) William Shakespeare, *Three Tragedies: Julius Caesar, Hamlet, Macbeth,* Dodd, 1965; (and author of introductions) Shakespeare, *Three Comedies: A Midsummer Night's Dream, As You Like It, The Merchant of Venice,* Dodd, 1965; (and author of introductions) Shakespeare, *Tragedies II: Romeo and Juliet, Othello, King Lear,* Dodd, 1966; (and author of introductions) Shakespeare, *Three Histories,* Dodd, 1966; (and author of introductions) Shakespeare, *Comedies II,* Dodd, 1967.

Collections and selections: *Sonnets and Poems,* Lollingdon, Cholsey, 1916; *The Poems and Plays of John Masefield,* Macmillan, 1918; *The Collected Poems of John Masefield,* Heinemann, 1924, enlarged edition, 1932; *Recent Prose,* Heinemann, 1924, revised, Heinemann, 1932, Macmillan, 1933; *Poems,* Macmillan, 1925, revised, Heinemann, 1946, reissued, 1966, complete edition, Macmillan, 1953; *Prose Plays,* Macmillan, 1925; *Verse Plays,* Macmillan, 1925; *The Collected Works of John Masefield,* Wanderer edition, Heinemann, 1935; *Dauber* [and] *Reynard the Fox: Two Tales in Verse,* Macmillan, 1962.

Contributor to periodicals, including *Outlook, Academy,* and *The Speaker.*

ADAPTATIONS—Plays: Ruth P. Kimball, *Martin Hyde* (three-act), W. H. Baker, 1935.

SIDELIGHTS: **June 1, 1878.** Born in Ledbury, Herefordshire, England. Masefield's greatest childhood adventure was the discovery of his imagination. "From my earliest infancy, certain imaginings or fantasies were in my mind with the reality of the memories of experience. I do not know what these were, but have tried to account for them. At first (and for twenty years and more) I supposed that they were memories of a life that I had lived on earth, in another body, perhaps not long before. At other times, I have wondered if they were not half-memories of picture-books shown to me in infancy, mixed with half-imaginings of my own, based upon what I myself had seen from the various windows looking westward, in both cases well up above river valleys. In both cases the river flowed from the north, and in both valleys the western limits were distant hills." [John Masefield, *So Long to Learn: Chapters of an Autobiography,* Heinemann, 1952.[1]]

"In the course of time I came to know the town and its place under some wooded hills very well, but never knew any of it so well as the little area that I knew first in my first six and a half years. In those first years it was touched with a beauty and a glory that no later time could give. . . . What memory still exists is vivid beyond all other memories, and centres upon what I first saw in my home, there, in the last house on the west of the Hereford Road by which men then went to the station. There has been much building on that road since then, but the fields then stretched from our fence to the Hereford Road without a house.

"Somewhere in that house I began to notice and remember things, though I am not sure that I was born there." [John Masefield, *Grace Before Ploughing,* Macmillan, 1966.[2]]

"It is difficult for me to describe the ecstatic bliss of my earliest childhood. All that I looked upon was beautiful, and known by me to be beautiful, but also known by me to be, as it were, only the shadow of something much more beautiful, very, very near, and almost to be reached, where there was nothing but beauty itself in ecstasy, undying, inexhaustible.

"This feeling is probably present in most children: it was strong in me. I was sure that a greater life was near us: in dreams I sometimes seemed to enter a part of it, and woke with rapture and longing. Then, on one wonderful day, when I was a little more than five years old, as I stood looking north, over a clump of honeysuckle in flower, I entered that greater life; and that life entered into me with a delight that I can never forget."[1]

"I am told that I learned to read at an early age, and that I enjoyed reading more than most children.

"I do not know if this were so, but I know that I found that I could tell myself stories at a very early age.

"I was in the garden one day, standing near a clump of honeysuckle and looking north. As I looked, I became aware, for the first time, that I had an imagination, and that I could tell this faculty to imagine all manner of strange things, and at once the strange things, especially fantastic things, would be there in multitude to do my bidding. If I told them to put on armour and conquer France, or save Joan of Arc from being burned or Mary Queen of Scots from Fotheringay, the thing would be done, and if I disliked the doing, I had but to suggest a better method, and at once the figures for the new scene were there, perfect in form and costume, armed and horsed and with colours flying.

"The faculty was extraordinary to me, and of such inner delight that I could not mention it to anyone.

"I had some small foresight in the matter, and was presently to wish that I had had more."[2]

". . . As a little child, I was living in Paradise, and had no need of the arts, that at best are only a shadow of Paradise. Every day was filled with rapture of many kinds, every evening was touched with romance, and if night brought terrors that sometimes strayed into the day, sleep swiftly nulled them."[1]

"In that beginning of my life, I knew little of Ledbury as a seaport or as a market-town. I knew very little of it save as the scene of a great yearly marvel called the October Fair, of which I thought with hope and rapture all the year round. On that great day in early October there was joyous holiday. It was a hiring fair, where men sought employment for the coming year, and the broad main street was glad with the sports of the fair: swings, merry-go-rounds, and coconut shies. It was busy also with the work of the fair: the sale of beasts of many kinds, which came there looking their smartest, to be judged and tried, in pens in the crowded street in the tumult of noise that made the fair so wonderful.

— So he turned the mare

and rode for here —

(From *The Midnight Folk* by John Masefield. Illustrated by Rowland Hilder.)

"The sideshows: swings, merry-go-rounds, rifle booths, and so forth, kept to the west side; the pens of the beasts were east from there. In any clear space men tried the paces of the horses for sale. Under the market building, and in a paven space just south from it, there were egg and cheese and butter sellers, and the cheap-jacks, with their patter, and their piles of crockery.

"Those days were long before the days of the modern road. For the October Fair, the roads were decked in ways now seldom seen. In the road, and between paving-stones on the sidewalks, men placed wonderful painted zinnias on wooden sticks. The effect upon children was astonishing: nothing more beautiful could surely be in the world.

"The Fair Days were days of wonder. I know now that there were things that I now shall never have the chance of seeing: two teams of mummers, with their tales of wonder, some dancers, some singers, all of these men of skill now vanished; and perhaps the last performers of famous plays about the Murder in the Red Barn, or Shaw the Life-Guardsman. All the joy of that old England was there every year, and I could have known it, and did not know it.

"From my memories of those first years, which ended when I was about six years and eight months old, I can extract some half-memories of two books that I could not understand, but yet felt to be strangely beautiful and inspired. One described the death of a boy, the other the courage of a soul in shipwreck.

"I have thought of both these ghostly memories ever since, but not knowing what they were. Of death and shipwreck I was soon to know plenty.

"For many years, I have thought of these early readings, and my enjoyment of them. What greater happiness is there in life

'Than to enjoy delight with liberty?'

"I have come to see that there is no greater delight and that my delight was due to one human will, enlightened and generous beyond most, who could not be thanked then, for the child knew nothing of the gift, and so was not thanked at all. Death and shipwreck did their worst and had their day, but the gift of that early reading was alive in me, despite all shipwreck and death, which are parts of this scheme of things, in any case, and give releases and a justice, wise and unfailing."[2]

His father died while Masefield was still quite young.

**Within the cowboy's van the rat-eyed wife,
Her reddish hair in papers twisted close,
Turned wet potatoes round against the knife,
And in a bucket dropped the peeled Oes.**
■ (From *King Cole* by John Masefield. Illustrated
by Judith Masefield.)

"The blissful childhood ended suddenly; after a while a different life began for me in another home.

"We went to live at the other end of the town in my grandfather's old home. Most of his books and other possessions
were there, and though I had been in the house once or twice
in each week since I could remember, it was very strange to
go to live there, and be free to explore all over the house and
the big straggly garden, with the shrubberies and abundant
fruits.

"The churchyard gave me peculiar pleasure. I was perhaps
one of the very first (or last) to go from gravestone to gravestone reading with delight the epitaphs in verse. I believe I
examined every stone in the churchyard. The tombs were all
somewhat old, for the dead were then laid in a cemetery elsewhere; and no one had been buried there for years. I liked
much of the hopeful poetry on the stones: some of it I remember to this day, as skilful verse and touched with feelings. I have wondered who wrote it. . . .

"While I was still a child, a young clergyman told me something that impressed me profoundly. It was on a most happy
and long remembered day of picnic. He and I foregathered
about fossils; he took me to see his collection. This collection had in it other things than fossils. It had the remains,
much rusted and broken, of a small medieval dagger that had
been found stuck deep within a woman's skull at the
opening-up of a local quarry. It had also a few small silver
fourth-century Roman coins, part of a hoard of such that had
been found when men had dug to put in a gate-post. These
things would have interested any boy, but what he said impressed me deeply; I have never forgotten it. 'The strange
thing is,' he said, 'that there was an uneasy feeling about
both the places where these things were found; people did
not like to go past those places after dark though they did not
seem to know exactly what was wrong with them.' In those

words, long-remembered, and long afterwards of use in the
making of some verses, I find confirmation of my belief in the
memory of Nature and of my theory of the country people,
who know no details, perhaps never had many details, but
will guard some tradition of horror for centuries. They forget
the incident and remember the frightfulness."[1]

"Life itself is joy enough for many children, it is so full of
new experience. It is strange later in life to think that reading
must have been at one time a new experience, as vivid as life
itself, being the life of every rainy day."[2]

"Most of my grandfather's books were in a strange dark
study, packed on its western wall with shelves of old books,
and having on the south wall presses of bound modern illustrated magazines. No-one ever interrupted my reading there.

"Long afterwards, I learned that my grandfather had written
a little book, and had known, as a young man, one who
sometimes met Lamb, Hazlitt, and John Keats. I like to
think that perhaps on some occasion my grandfather went
with this man to one or other of these three.

"It was thought that I was too much given to reading. Surely
anything that takes a child's mind from the horrors that are
over, or only imagined, cannot be altogether wrong. In my
case, stories were necessary; to me, most other studies
seemed tame or foolish, or a part of the madness of grownups.

"I have often tried to remember what I then wished to do
with my life. From the first, I had a love of stories and a wish
to write them, yet, thinking it all over carefully, I am sure
that I had an even stronger wish to paint them in colours, as
the glorious Randolph Caldecott had done. With great labour, having no aptitude for drawing, I painted the story of a
day in a horse's life. He was a thrilling horse, who won a
steeple-chase and the Derby, and took part in a battle, all on
the same day. I later painted another story in a series of
water-colour panels. I longed also to be able to cut stories, or
lively incidents, in stone, like those that I saw in the Church.
Putting discreet questions, here and there, I learned that
painting and carving were only done by people with talent
'for that kind of thing,' and that that kind of thing was not at
all the kind of thing: it might be all right for the people with
the talent, but not a thing to be encouraged in anyone: and
those who had the talent were, too often, men of excess,
free-thinkers, wild livers, 'as was only too well-known.' It
was not well-known to me, nor have I found it so in life; art
needs a steady head and hand. Greatly daring, I asked if I
might be allowed to learn to draw. . . .

"I cannot remember what other crafts or professions I
wished to follow. Writing must always have been the chief of
these: but this was always made to seem hopeless to me;
indeed worse than hopeless, wicked; first, because it was
agreed that I had no talent; next, for its too certain effect for
evil upon human character. I was always far too much given
to idle reading, so I was assured, when other boys would be
doing other things. For writing, as for drawing, the outlook
was not rosy, and soon became blacker."[1]

"I have been asked, if any of my early reading turned me to
the sea.

"I was the third child in the family, and some of the books at
hand were those given at past birthdays and Christmases to
my elders.

"Among these were several sea books, which I read with pleasure, such as the prose book *True Blue*, by a well-known writer for boys. . . ."[2]

September, 1891. ". . . I was sent as a new chum to be trained on board H.M.S. *Conway* in the Mersey. . . . At the beginning of my second half, I was placed in the Class of the Seamanship-Instructor, Wallace Blair. The Seamanship Classes, or Instructions, were held below decks several times a week in afternoons when we were not at sail or spar drill. They varied, as the student progressed.

"Wally Blair told us many . . . tales, most of them shewing what could be or had been done at sea in an emergency, and what might, and did, happen if one tried too much or did too little. He made me feel that in a ship the spinning of yarns was almost a part of the craft. The sea creates stories. Even in my first half-year I had seen it create stories. Now, here was Wally, a living store of stories. Every week or so, some man came back to us from the other side of the Horn, with a strange or marvellous tale of a thing seen and shared. I loved listening to Wally: I liked learning to knot, splice and mat-make; but I had once hoped for another way of life, and that, now, seemed shut away, in a world that I could never approach. I had hoped to be a writer, that is, if you can call wild dreams of some day being able to write, a hope. Unformed dreams of the sort had sometimes been in me, had been perceived in me, and had been mocked, with energy and with system: 'What? You a writer? How can you be a writer? Only clever people are writers: and terrible lives they lead, both in this world and the next.'

"Well, if I could not be a writer (and the door to that garden seemed finally slammed), could I be a teller of stories? Here was Wally, a born story-teller, delighting all hearers with his stories: why should not I be content to be such another, a yarn-spinner, a solace in the second dog-watch? I asked myself this, having no other to ask, and the answer came flooding back, that to be a story-teller was only a part of my want. I had hoped to know a great many books, to know a great deal of knowledge and to tell all sorts of stories in all sorts of ways. I had longed to know all of my country's past, and all her ways of writing; yet now I was in a world of few books, where only one kind of knowledge mattered, though that was a precious kind and very dear to me, then and now. Somehow, these longings and wants of mine could not seem absurd to me: yet I was sorely perplexed, because they seemed absurd even to people in whose wisdom I had some belief. Everyone, of the few who perceived my inclination, told me to put 'this writing-rubbish' (that was the chosen phrase) right out of my head. Some of these spoke with a wish to screen me from a later disappointment, or from the feeling that the moods of boys change and vanish. Some spoke from their fixed conviction that all writers, painters and musicians, with the possible exception of Lord Tennyson, were children of the devil of hell. Some, perhaps, did not put it quite like that, but felt that every child was naturally a little devil from hell, and that any prompting or urge within the mind of a child was put there by the devil for his and the world's damnation. To all such (then as now), any prompting to do anything was suspect, and to be thwarted, upon social or religious grounds: so the word passed: 'Put this writing-rubbish right out of your head.' But, then, it was not in my head alone, it was in myself; and sometimes, even after a black month, after a black season, something of my very self would glimmer a little: not very much: but something. The old faculty of story-telling, that had once filled my mind with happiness, seemed dead within me: it was dark

Like stone become alive, I entered in.
Smoke drifted by: I heard a violin.
■ (From *The Dream and Other Poems* by John Masefield. Illustrated by Judith Masefield.)

there, where once there had been light. In earlier years, stories had floated up into my mind as from an unfailing spring, and had flowed from it in streams. A few moments of thought upon the theme had given greater life or colour to its incidents, but the thing had proceeded joyously, as from a source of joy, there was no trouble, no hesitancy, I could at once be enjoying delight with liberty. . . . Now, I had an inner fear that this power had vanished.

"In my last Summer Half on board, I was a Senior, and rated as a supernumerary. This brought me the privilege of slinging my hammock on the port side of the lower-deck, among others, my fellows. When after Rounds at night these fellows asked me for a yarn, I found my inner fear confirmed; the old faculty was gone. What made the loss worse to me was the feeling that something dark and sinister had come between myself and the old faculty; that it was there somewhere, but that I could not get at it, and never should get at it again; I had been thrust aside and a door had slammed . . . and I had a solitary way to go, with no Eden henceforth, no radiance, no ever glad invention flowing. I tried to yarn, when it fell to my turn, but the source was dry; no water ran; the misery to myself was acute. I could, of course, hold my hearers with things that I had read, that were new to them. I knew too many Christmas Number stories from old Victorian magazines to be without a yarn, but this did not console me. I had lost something infinitely precious. I was shut from Paradise, no less, and the question rose: Why?

"The effect upon myself is hard to describe. In part, it was a sense of loss; in part, a sense of exile; but in part also a sense of having died and gone to hell, to some 'everlasting prison remediless' such as the Inquisition in Spain sometimes gave to English sailors. It must not be thought that this despair was in any way due to the life aboard. My friends were there, many and good: the life was happy and easy, with lots of leisure. But something had happened within myself, or some things had laid me flatter than I thought: I had lost my soul, or my shadow, or something. I did not tell anybody, having nobody to tell, and knowing only that no-one could help. I had some half-belief that if I sacrificed much, something would be returned to me. What if I gave up my butter to the men I most disliked, all through the term? Perhaps that would work? But I decided against this, for various good reasons: the unrighteous went without the butter; the unhappy ate it all himself.

"Although I thought that so much had died in me, that I was practically dead, I was still about in the world and taking notice."[1]

"Deep within myself was a longing to be a writer; but this longing was very deeply buried, under the more immediate longing to read and read, and not to be so ignorant. I wanted to know all that men had thought and done. . . .

"I wanted my soul to have a chance to rise into raptures, and I longed to learn new wisdom and old, too. If I could do that, I thought, then, possibly, some day, even I might be able to write something, some sort of a story, perhaps. My friends said that only clever people could hope to make a living by writing, that it was like pugilism, 'Many are called but few are chosen,' and that those not chosen lived in garrets, and took drugs till they went raving mad and died and were buried by the parish. This seemed to me true. It was most unlikely that I should ever be able to write anything which anyone would print or pay me for; yet deep within me writing lured me, something urged me to read and read. It did not tell me what to read, and I did not know; but one of the joys of my job was that it gave me time to read, and that was a joy past telling." [John Masefield, *In the Mill*, Macmillan, 1941.[3]]

1895. Abandoned the sea; went ashore in New York City. Toyed with the idea of pursuing a career in medicine, but re-experienced literary inclinations. "I was in New York City, in summer-time, when I suddenly found that the faculty of mental story-telling had returned to me. I was walking in an uptown part of the East Side when a story suddenly became bright in my mind, in the way that I had known of old, so that I could both tell it and enjoy it. In the glaring sun and roaring avenue I walked in the old joy, that again, as ever, made all other worries nothing.

"This resurrection of my inner life was a gladness. New York City, in herself, was a gladness, that dazzling, beautiful, exciting City, the Queen of all romantic Cities, with such sparkle in her air and in her people. Still, there remained the dire drawbacks, the want of talent for writing, that everyone was so sure of; the ignorance of how to acquire a talent, or, at least, a skill; as well as the frightful ignorance in myself of the things that other men seemed to know as a matter of course. I could not open a newspaper without finding a new ignorance in myself. I said, 'Get rid of the ignorance. Find out from some paper what you ought to read and then read it.' Probably, this was the exhilarating New York working her miracle in me. Anyhow, I went into Mr. Pratt's bookstore on Sixth Avenue (near Greenwich Avenue) and bought

the first volume of a *Morte d'Arthur,* then issued in the Camelot Classics under the editorship of the late Ernest Rhys.

"I was then just seventeen. That is a good age at which to begin Arthurian study. In childhood, I had tried some of Tennyson's retellings of Malory, without any success: I was at once enchanted by Malory. I was too young and too ignorant to question what I read. I supposed that these old romances were all retellings of British history or traditions, and that all of them had been founded on fact. In the main, as I supposed, the events, or something like them, had happened, and the people, or somebody like them, had lived, in places that were sometimes known: Amesbury, Bamborough, Winchester, etc. All the story-telling instinct in me was thrilled as I read. This was a story that gave a great significance to many parts of England. This was (as I supposed) our contribution to epic, and a mine from which poets could take their fables forever. Certainly it was something about which my ignorance had to be lessened. . . ."[1]

". . . I was in a new world where incredible beauty was daily bread and breath of life. Everything that I had read until then seemed like paving-stones on the path leading to this Paradise; now I seemed to be in the garden, and the ecstasy was so great that the joy seemed almost to burn. I knew, then, that life is very brief, and that the use of life is to discover the law of one's being, and to follow that law, at whatever cost, to the utmost. I knew then that Medicine was not the law of my being, but the shadow of it; and that my law was to follow poetry, even if I died of it.

"Who could mind dying for a thing so fair?

"That was the end of my hope of being a doctor; but by no means the end of my medical studies. I have always enjoyed reading medical books and papers, and talking with doctors. From time to time, I have even worked hard at particular branches of medicine; and have then always regretted not being qualified. Certain lines of research offer such rewards in benefit to Man. There are so many mysteries which need to be resolved, so many major ailments to be made less harmful; such weight, mass and mountain of obstinate stupidity to overcome that even one more willing helper is worth the having. Men say that this or that is the enemy of Life; I say that Death is the enemy. . . ."[3]

1896. Worked in carpet factory in Yonkers and continued to pursue the possibility of becoming a writer. "My first days in the new way of life were anxious, but exciting and delightful. They were anxious, because I was doubtful whether I could keep the job, and because I still expected some of the hazing to which new-comers anywhere are usually subject; they were exciting, because the experience was big, and new; they were delightful because I found the work easy and the people welcoming. They mocked me a little for my 'English accent' and for one or two ways which they thought odd. . . .

"I know, that all through my first month in the mill, I was extremely happy. I had been able to settle down with my fellows; I had held the job, I could do it well, and heard indirect praise of myself. Then it brought with it enormous advantages, for which I had longed unavailingly for years.

"After a week in the cockroach room, I heard of, and went to, a room in a neat little white frame house close to the woods outside the town. Here I settled myself. Its only disadvantage was that it was a longish way from the Restaurant where I took my meals, so that I had about a mile and a half added to my daily walking.

Supper I had resolved to do without; I wished to keep my shilling for dinner and breakfast the next day. ▪ (From *Jim Davis* by John Masefield. Illustrated by Bob Dean.)

"I now began to take stock of the situation, and to wonder whether I could make this mill my life's work, and rise, as my friend had suggested, section by section, floor by floor, to profitable heights.

". . . What could the trials of the world matter; the world and its trials seemed illusions, all touched with death; this divine art was Life, triumphing over death. I went away to the mill, floating as it were on rosy clouds.

"The things not touched with joy drop dead out of memory. That season was a time of radiant joy, for I went more and more a-roving so late into the night, into a world of poetry which grew ever greater and more marvellous as I came to know it more. . . .

". . . I had read in one of my philosophical reviews that none could hope to think good thoughts or do worthy intellectual work without abandoning all food in which life had been. Here were two thinkers, one of them an inspired poet, proclaiming the merits of pure diet, nay, the duty of guarding the temple of the soul from the contamination of the slaughterhouse. Feeling that I was filthy with blood and thereby unfit to serve such Queens as the lovely Muses, I decided that I would give up the eating of meat, fish and eggs at once. I debated the point, might milk be drunk? There was a carnal twang about milk; it did not seem quite-quite; yet I decided that I might drink milk, because I loathed it, and that I might certainly drink butter-milk, because that seemed a more loathsome drink, if possible, than the real thing.

"The next morning I commenced vegetarian on a very rigid basis. I began to live on bread, oatmeal, vegetables, fruit and milk. I had long since given up the use of tobacco; tea and coffee were now banned; I longed to become a seeing spirit, like Gautama the Enlightened, whose body, though almost transparent, was sufficient shelter and carriage for the soul.

"In my enthusiasm for the new life, nothing in the mill could matter to me. I have always delighted in work; I did my day's work well; I was told this when my money was increased, and the praise gave me a great deal of pleasure; but it was but a part of the ecstasy in which I was living. . . .

"I had very little learning, few less, but the little that I had was of an intense joy to me; and to say that my mind was a kingdom was to understate the case. I seemed to possess a limitless universe.

"After about a week of vegetarianism, I found that I had a clearness of mind such as I had never before known. It seemed to me, that Shelley had proclaimed a way of life which might regenerate the world; for everyone might have the clearness by an act of will; and in the clearness all things shewed bright or dark, so that one knew at a glance which were good or evil. I would sit down in the evenings to write and what I took to be inspiration descended on me. To say that all this was joy is insufficient: it was rapture.

"In the height of this mood, at a time which I cannot now accurately date, a cruel blow fell upon the mill; we were all suddenly told that the works would close down for five or six weeks; almost immediately, they closed.

"We did not know the cause of the closing; we judged, vaguely, that it was due 'to the depression,' whatever that was; the effect upon us all, and upon the town itself, was black indeed.

"I passed the long leisure, writing and reading. I planned and began a novel, and wrote many poems. One of these poems, through the kindness of a friend in England, was submitted to a real author, whose sole comment was 'He writes very young.' Well, I was very young. The friend himself gave a more helpful comment: he wrote 'Get down from that high horse of yours.'

"My horse then was the magic horse of brass on which the Tartar king did ride; while he was careering through high Heaven there was no dismounting nor wishing to dismount. I was chasing the comets and finding it fun.

"Apart from that riding of the sky, there was little fun in Yonkers at that time for anyone connected with the mill. When the works re-opened at last, the faces shewed too clearly how black a time the closing had been. Even in a land of abundance and prosperity all our thousands had been living on the borders of starvation. What would have happened to us, if the mills had kept closed for a few weeks more? Would it have been reckoned our fault; or 'one of the temporary dislocations to which business must ever be subject'; or would someone have wondered, if something were not wrong somewhere with the system? For myself, I knew now what might happen to a mill-worker; I set myself to lay by money against a second shutting-down.

"My writing, which had been an intense pleasure to me for some months, had now become an anxiety; it was not improving; in some ways, no doubt, it was a good deal worse than it had been. This was partly due to the fact that I was forcing myself to make experiments of one kind or another, usually at the bidding or suggestion of some good writer lately read by me.

"It is said that cooks do not greatly care for food, that jammakers never touch jam, and that the seaman's dream is ever of a farm. But artists and craftsmen love the things of their work above all things, with passion and care. We in the mill, were all craftsmen and potential artists, the separation of hand from soul, which went on daily, by this parting of the designer from the weaver, was in every way deplorable. So far as we knew, no designer ever saw his work upon a loom or went to see it finished in the picking-room; he never talked with a setter nor with a weaver. He cared, seemingly, as little for our work as we for his.

"If we had been in touch with each other, we could have told him that his sense of colour was this or that, his twirligig-border absurd, and his main design a dreariness to the minds which had to dwell upon it. If we had little sense of design, we had, at least, vitality, which was what he mostly lacked.

"Of course, the best work of any time is very good. All through the nineties the looms of civilisation turned out some works of great splendour, rather more work of great gaiety, and some of delicate beauty, including varieties of plain-cloth, of enchanting colour. We, in the mill, turned out some work which we all knew to be superb in its strength and finish. I know that men went from my section to particu-

lar looms just to see and to touch that noble web, and to taste the delight of knowing that no weaving anywhere could be better done. They relished the honest, solid work; they saw themselves in that.

"From the first, I had felt that the place of carpets was on the wall, as tapestry and story telling. There is no need whatever for the putting of elaborate design beneath people's feet, plain-cloth suffices, or would in every way be better. I have often thought of that design of the fox, and have repented my old scorn of it. The instinct of my fellow-workers was a lot sounder than mine, they demanded action in a work of art, and by their instinct saw that nine tenths or more of the designs they helped to spread were without interest.

"I was very young then, and youth is a time of unhappiness. I was very unhappy, from youth, exile, home-sickness, the worry over a friend, and despair of being able to master the fates which offered and attracted. I was also unspeakably, radiantly and burningly happy. I had found my road. It was a deep time, such as one would not be without."[3]

1897. Returned to England, determined to pursue a career in letters. "So there I was, longing for England, urged by the blaze of the sun to cast myself on the die and take the chance, feeling that I should not live long if I didn't and might very well die if I did. Cold sense told me all the time, you have a well-paid job here which you do well. It gives you leisure; it gives you books; you can save money on it. Hot sense answered, 'the only movement worth anything in Literature now is in London; it would be better to be a proof-reader in a printer's office in that movement than an exile piling up books here until it will be too late.'

"There was a phrase which I had heard so often from sailors. 'Get out of it before the life gets you.' Beyond a certain point, no man can escape from a way of life; the life gets him. I meant to get into poetry somehow before the mill got me. Very likely I wasn't good enough for poetry, but the extraordinary beauty of that promised land was enough to call out all my hope and all my courage.

"I went to the Square, to the Bank, and drew out all my savings. I had ample money to pay my passage back to England; but 'base is the slave who pays.' I meant to work my way, if it could possibly be done. I sent a telegram to the Seamen's Mission, to say that I should be in New York on the morrow, hoping to be shipped. I bought a trunk and some clothes, and went here and there in the town, saying good-bye. Going back to my lodgings, I tore up most of the manuscripts in my possession, many poems and all that had been written of the novel. These, when torn up, filled a large bucket, weighed astonishingly, and burned with a clear flame. I gave away some books, made up a package for the sailors, and sold others for what they would fetch. They fetched a very much larger sum than I had expected. I chose about nine books to take with me; I still have some of them.

"Somebody told me, that day or the next, that the impressive thing in London had been the singing of 'God save the Queen' by the crowd, that it had been a noise 'greater than any thunder.' This thought of a Nation singing stayed with me for many years. No doubt, many of the streets were ahead of or behind others; yet that great irregular sea of sound would come washing up as feeling instead of melody with effects not often known. I have since known them. From that time, I knew that my heart was in England, and that I could not long keep away from her. Even if I were to fail, I should at least fail in England; my life was my own concern and the risks attached to it were for me to take if I thought fit."[3]

"Shortly after the celebration of Queen Victoria's Diamond Jubilee, I returned to England, and went to London.

"I could not love London as I loved New York: but her vast, dumb humane power, and the glory of her position then, as the capital of the world, impressed me more. She never had the beauty and the sparkle of New York: but in so many places she had still a strangeness and romance, such odd alleys, such thrilling lonely little houses in charming gardens, such suggestion in darkness, after rain.

"The lollops, in time, gave me some ease in writing, and possibly some help in narrative. The things seen went into memory, and sometimes came out of memory, long afterwards, and were of use in books.

"The habit of working while walking was useful in another way. On my first day in London I began to study the Elizabethan dramatic poets, having long looked forward to this study after reading Mr. Swinburne's rousing sonnets. From the first, I told myself that I must read these plays with clear mental images of the stage and the people on it. Sometimes, as I walked, I played over scenes in my mind, from plays that most delighted me. . . .

"The writing that I attempted was so much difficulty faced, and a very little of it solved or overcome. It reminded me of trying to get through a bog, with no known track, no sound footing, nothing but engulfing mud. The effort was continual, the trial never ceased; what I could do easily was done, what I could do with difficulty was attempted; some of what I wrote was printed.

"Those who seek for help in the art of writing (and even men of power must do this) should ever read much old work, that time has tested. The faults of old work should be clear to all; contemporary work has not yet been sifted bare.

"Young men sometimes write with fluency, and are unable to correct what they have done. Let such youths not try to correct: let them re-write from the beginning. Sometimes the power to correct is a mark the more of maturity.

"After a year or two of experiment, I forced myself to try to write longer stories, even full-sized novels (80,000 words or more), and during these attempts gave up the making of verses almost altogether. The attempt to write upon an ampler scale taught me much of the craft that can be only learned by trial, and gave me an opportunity for doing the things that I most liked in writing, at that time in my life.

"These things were not what I should now call essentials in story-telling, though they delighted myself. Looking at pictures had long been a joy to me. I had long felt that writers must make use of other arts than their own, whenever possible. In verse, men must try for something of music and of painting; in prose, for something of drama and of portrait."[1]

1902. First collection of poems, *Salt-Water Ballads,* published. ". . . I began an unsystematic greedy study of the literature of the sea. From boyhood, I had known some of the best of its fiction and professional books; I now tried to fill in some of the gaps by reading old books of Seamanship, accounts of voyages, records of Courts-Martial, etc., and going

"What you got to do, first off, is to sink that old hulk you were playing with. We'll sink her at anchor with Preacher-feller's cannon." ■ (From *Jim Davis* by John Masefield. Illustrated by Stephen Reid.)

much to the three marine museums where models and sea-paintings could be seen.

"I do not claim to have learned much of these difficult subjects, but the study gave and still gives me deep enjoyment. Often the dreary words of the manuals of rigging seem to become the things, and I perceive the timber hulls, with the old gear, so faulty in so many ways, being, as someone says, only vegetable secured to vegetable, yet so well thought-out; and respect the old men who with such means faced the Atlantic and every other sea."[1]

1903. Married Constance de la Cherois-Crommelin.

October, 1911. Publication of *Everlasting Memory* brought fame and controversy, due to the colorful, explicit language in the poem.

1915. Served in Red Cross during World War I.

1919-1930. Devoted himself to prodigious literary output, concentrating on fiction and poetic drama. ". . . But were not all ways of writing parts of the art, necessary, important, and to be toiled at? Slowly, it dawned upon me that no writer can neglect any great form of writing: he must practise it, acquire some skill in it, or fail, to some extent, as an artist. All ways of writing are a part of his technique. That most difficult way, of the theatre, for instance, was, surely, a most precious way to any young writer, since it offered to him that criticism of the living audience, so sure, so salutary, so swift. I determined to try to learn something of the technique, though I had no instinct for it, and almost no knowledge of it. I was a story-teller, fond of reading old poetical plays, and convinced that only William Poel knew how to produce them.

"I learned at once, and with indignation, that all my love of language, fondness for effects of style, worship of the right word, all the old dear tricks, must be cut from my attempts. It was rubbed into me, by those from whom I sought instruction, that a good mime needs no words, and that a good playwright can do without them. What a blow to a youth delighting in words, worshipping the cunning use of words, to find that, on the stage, dumb-show may be more telling than eloquence. Still, the blow told: I began to understand thrift and condensation: the merits of the method shone forth. An actor bade me prepare my frame-work as a succession of actions and situations without one spoken word. This was wise advice, whatever it may have seemed at the time. . . ."[1]

1923. Instituted Oxford recitation contests. "For myself I may say that I lived for the Recitations, longed to make them better, to make them even perfect. They were far from perfect. Poetry is joy; and Contest is not all joy; it may be anything but joy to the losers; and in these Contests what was it that caused a loss?

"Perhaps in all Contests of the sort the entrants are mostly pupils from some training college, who learn from a teacher exactly how the teacher wishes the piece to be said, and do it as told. As for the meaning, is it not poetry, 'just a poem,' as Browning said? The judges could not enjoy an hour of listening to such speech: hope supported them: genius sometimes startled them. Ah, when the genius came. . . .

"Many of the speakers were of a kind that I called 'lollipop-speakers:' they spoke every kind of verse as if it were a caramel to be sucked, without any glimmering of a notion that the words had any meaning. They would roll out difficult lines (exquisite and subtle lines) with a relish, as though a peppermint flavour warmed their hearts, yet neither they nor the proud teacher by them had any understanding whatsoever of what a great mind had tried to say in the hour of his exaltation. Such people plainly did not know that mind, greatness or exaltation had been concerned in the matter."[1]

1930. Named poet laureate of England. "I am linked to this county by subtle ties, deeper than I can explain: they are ties of beauty. . . . I know no land more full of bounty and beauty than this red land, so good for corn and hops and roses. . . ." [Muriel Spark, *John Masefield*, Peter Nevill, 1953.[4]]

1935. Received Order of Merit—England's most coveted honor.

1940's-1950's. Maintained an effort to sustain his prolific literary output. "I have learned from life (to some extent) to take what comes and be glad it's no worse: a writer must do this: he submits his work to the world, and if the world refuse it and trample on his face besides, he must know that there is no appeal."[1]

1960's. Emphasized critical works, including some studies of Shakespeare.

May 12, 1967. Died in Abingdon, Berkshire, England at the age of eighty-eight. "Now that I am coming to an end, I wish to try to set down what matters have been helpful to me in the work of my choice that has filled my days. That work has been the finding, framing and telling of stories, in verse, and prose, according to the tale and the power within me. I have done, and have enjoyed, much other work of different kinds, yet always with the love (and the hope) of story-telling deep within me, as the work beyond all other work to which my nature called.

"I believe that life to be the source of all that is of glory or goodness in this world; and that modern man, not knowing that life, is dwelling in death."[1]

FOR MORE INFORMATION SEE: Iolo A. Williams, *John Masefield: A Bibliography of His Works*, Brick Row Book Shop, 1921, reprinted, Folcroft, 1973; William H. Hamilton, *John Masefield: A Critical Study*, Macmillan, 1922, reprinted, Kennikat, 1969; W. Hamilton, *John Masefield: A Popular Study*, Macmillan, 1925, reprinted, R. West, 1973; Gilbert O. Thomas, *John Masefield*, T. Butterworth, 1932, reprinted, Folcroft, 1975; David W. Clarke, *Modern English Writers*, Longmans, 1947; Hallie E. Rives and G. E. Forbush, *John Book*, Beechhurst Press, 1947; Richard Church, *British Authors*, Longmans, 1948; Alexander H. Higginson, *British and American Sporting Authors*, Blue Ridge Press, 1949; Frank A. Swinnerton, *Georgian Literary Scene*, Farrar, Straus, 1951; Helen S. N. Cournos and John Cournos, *Famous British Poets*, Dodd, 1952; Leonard A. G. Strong, *John Masefield*, Longmans, 1952, reissued, 1968; Gilbert Highet, *People, Places, and Books*, Oxford University Press, 1953; Muriel Spark, *John Masefield*, Nevill, 1953, reprinted, R. West, 1973.

Kenneth Hopkins, *Poets Laureate*, Library Publications, 1955; Fraser B. Drew, "John Masefield and the Manchester Guardian," *Philological Quarterly*, January, 1958; D. Stanford, "Masefield at Eighty," *Contemporary Review*, July, 1958; Louis Untermeyer, *Lives of the Poets*, Simon & Schuster, 1959; Geoffrey Handley-Taylor, *John Masefield, O.M., The Queen's Poet Laureate: A Bibliography and Eighty-First Birthday Tribute*, Cranbrook Tower Press, 1961; Margery Fisher, *John Masefield*, Walck, 1963; Brian Doyle, editor, *Who's Who of Children's Literature*, Schocken Books, 1968; Corliss Lamont, *Remembering John Masefield*, with an introduction by Judith Masefield, Dickinson University Press, 1971; F. B. Drew, "Gift of Books: John Masefield and Louise Townsend Nicholl," *Literary Review*, Summer, 1973; Drew, *John Masefield's England: A Study of the National Themes in His Work*, Dickinson University Press, 1973.

Obituaries: *New York Times*, May 13, 1967; *Time*, May 19, 1967; *Illustrated London News*, May 20, 1967; *Newsweek*, May 22, 1967; *Publishers Weekly*, May 22, 1967; *Britannica Book of the Year 1968*.

MASSELMAN, George 1897-1971

PERSONAL: Born December 9, 1897, in Amsterdam, Netherlands; died October 8, 1971, in Redding, Conn.; son of Gerrit Jan and Johanna (Gebuys) Masselman; married Florence Coughlin, January 7, 1941; children: Wilhelmina Masselman Van Hemert, Georgina Masselman Fitchett, Lee Masselman Kallos. *Education:* Navigation Academy, Amsterdam, Netherlands, B.Sc., 1917. *Politics:* Democrat. *Religion:* Protestant. *Home:* Fox Run, West Redding, Conn. 06896.

CAREER: Java China Trading Co., New York, N.Y., president, 1923-36; Board of Economic Warfare, Washington, D.C., principal economist, 1941-44; U.S. Office of Strategic Services, overseas duty, 1944-45; Industrial College of the Armed Forces, Washington, D.C., geographer, 1945-48; National War College, Washington, D.C., consultant, 1947; New School for Social Research, New York, N.Y., lecturer in social science, 1948-49; Danbury State College, Graduate School, Danbury, Conn., lecturer in social science, 1963-64. Selectman, Town of Redding, Conn., 1956-59. *Member:* Economic History Association, American Historical Association, Nederlands Historisch Genootschap. *Awards, honors:* Research grant, American Philosophical Society, 1964.

WRITINGS: The Cradle of Colonialism (History Club selection), Yale University Press, 1963; *The Money Trees: The Spice Trade,* McGraw, 1967; *The Atlantic: Sea of Darkness,* McGraw, 1969. Contributor of articles to professional journals.

SIDELIGHTS: Was fluent in German and Dutch, competent in French.

(Died, October 8, 1971)

He lay down beside her, rested his muzzle in her lap, and gazed at her with eyes full of love. ■ (From *Fables of Leonardo da Vinci* interpreted and transcribed by Bruno Nardini. Illustrated by Adriana Saviozzi Mazza.)

ADRIANA MAZZA

MAZZA, Adriana   1928-
(Adriana Saviozzi)

PERSONAL: Born April 8, 1928, in Florence, Italy; daughter of Peter (an accountant) and Alma (Melani) Mazza; married Alfio Mazza (an art restorer; deceased), April 18, 1953; children: Paul. *Home:* Via Lambruschini, Florence, Italy.

CAREER: Free-lance children's book illustrator, 1948—. *Exhibitions:* Book Fair, Bologna, Italy. *Awards, honors:* List of Honor, Andersen Award.

WRITINGS: (Under pseudonym Adriana Saviozzi; self-illustrated) *Somebody Saw,* World, 1962.

Illustrator: Kathleen Daly, *Four Little Kittens,* Western, 1957; *Mother Goose,* Golden Press, 1963; Ruth Faux, *It Happened to Anita,* Dodd, 1967; Joan L. Nodset, *Where Do You Go When You Run Away,* Bobbs, 1964; Natalie S. Carlson, *Orphelines in the Enchanted Castle,* Harper, 1964; Beatrix Potter, *The Tale of Peter Rabbit,* Western, 1970; Bruno Nardini (translator), *Fables of Leonardo Da Vinci,* Hubbard, 1973; Giunti Nardini (editor), *Leonardo Da Vinci's Fantastic Animals,* Collins (London), 1977. Also illustrated *The Little Donkey of Jesus* for Centro Internazionale del Libro (Florence).

SIDELIGHTS: "I work in watercolors, tempora and black & white. I have traveled and lived in the United States, visited Switzerland, lived in Florence, Italy and the Republic of San Marino. I speak English and Italian. Have always been interested in children which brought about my work as a book illustrator for children. I am an American citizen and my son is a student at a local university."

McCORMICK, Dell J. 1892-1949

CAREER: Author of stories for young children. Mc-Cormick also worked as a log scaler in a northern Idaho sawmill, where he heard the Paul Bunyan legends that he wrote down for children years later. *Military service:* Served in the Army during World War I. *Awards, honors:* Pacific Northwest Library Association Young Readers' Choice award, 1940, for *Paul Bunyan Swings His Axe.*

WRITINGS: Paul Bunyan Swings His Axe, Caxton Printers, 1936, reissued, Scholastic Book Services, 1972; *Tall Timber Tales: More Paul Bunyan Stories* (illustrated by Lorna Livesley), Caxton Printers, 1939, reissued, 1966; (with Anne B. Malcolmson) *Mister Stormalong* (illustrated by Joshua Tolford), Houghton, 1952.

FOR MORE INFORMATION SEE: Elizabeth R. Montgomery, *Story Behind Modern Books,* Dodd, 1949.

In all the woods there was no one so kindly toward Babe as Paul Bunyan, and no ox was ever so faithful to its master as Babe, the famous Blue Ox. ■ (From *Paul Bunyan Swings His Axe* by Dell J. McCormick. Illustrated by the author.)

He towered above the trees of the forest and combed his beard with a young fir tree. With his giant ox, Babe, he roamed the forest from Maine to California. His footprints were so large they filled with water and became known as lakes. ■ (From *Tall Timber Tales* by Dell J. McCormick. Illustrated by Lorna Livesly.)

MEYERS, Susan 1942-

PERSONAL: Born November 5, 1942, in Brooklyn, N.Y.; daughter of Palmer (a writer) and Helvia (Ostman) Thompson; married former spouse, Stephen A. Meyers, October 6, 1961; children: Jessica Lauren. *Education:* University of California, Berkeley, A.B., 1965. *Home:* 11 Oxford Ave., Mill Valley, Calif. 94941.

MEMBER: Writer's Guild, Society of Children's Book Writers (board of directors). *Awards, honors: Melissa Finds a Mystery* was winner of Dodd, Mead's *Calling All Girls* Prize Competition in mystery category, 1966; Gavel Awards certificate of merit, American Bar Association, 1973, for article "Legal Supermarkets."

WRITINGS: Melissa Finds a Mystery, Dodd, 1966; *The Cabin on the Fjord,* Doubleday, 1968; *The Mysterious Bender Bones,* Doubleday, 1970; *The Truth about Gorillas,* Dutton, 1980. Has also reviewed books and written articles for various magazines.

WORK IN PROGRESS: Pearson: The True Story of a Harbor Seal, for Dutton; *P. J. Clover, Private Eye.*

SIDELIGHTS: "When I was a young girl I very definitely did not want to be a writer. My father wrote for a living and it looked to me like hard and frustrating work. I was going to be a veterinarian, or a zoo keeper, or an artist, or an actress. Yet, here I am today, writing—just as he did—and liking it very much.

"I grew up in the country and spent a great deal of time outdoors. I always had pets—dogs, cats, rabbits, hamsters, and even a goat. But until I went to school and until my sister was born—both of which happened at about the same time—I didn't have many playmates. I had to learn to amuse myself and to spend time alone. I don't remember finding this especially difficult. In fact, to this day, I enjoy being by myself—at least part of the time.

"Our house was full of books and both my parents were avid readers. I read a lot too. I remember loving *Heidi, The Swiss Family Robinson, Black Beauty, David Copperfield*, as well as *The Saturdays, Homer Price*, and *Nancy Drew*. The people and places I read about seemed very real to me. Whenever I finished a book I enjoyed, I wanted to read another one exactly like it.

"Though I wasn't aware of it at the time, I know now that I learned a great deal about writing by listening to my father talk about the plots for the radio and television scripts he wrote. I also learned from my mother. She was a great story teller and had a vivid imagination. She told me that bears lived in our attic, and though part of me knew it couldn't be true, another part of me believed it for years. She also told spooky stories complete with props and sound effects. And, she told me tales of her own childhood. I liked these true stories best of all. When I listened to them I felt as if her friends and adventures were mine, too.

"Now, when I write, I try to give my readers the same feeling. I want them to find the characters I create so alive and so interesting that they wish they were inside the book living the story with them. Of course, I don't always succeed. Writing is hard work. It takes a great deal of skill and patience to capture the people and places and things that live in one's imagination and set them down on paper so that they will live for the reader as well. No, I don't always succeed. But I never stop trying.

"I find that everything I write is connected, in some way, with my life. When I visited relatives in Norway, the country and the people seemed so interesting that I had to write about them. That was how *The Cabin on the Fjord* began.

When I saw an advertisement for the movie 'King Kong,' my sympathy for gorillas—so much maligned and misunderstood—was aroused. I wrote a non-fiction book, *The Truth About Gorillas*, in an attempt to set the record straight. *The Mysterious Bender Bones* grew out of a true story I heard about an anthropologist who kept valuable fossil bones locked in a suitcase under his bed.

"Working with words gives me great pleasure. I enjoy making sentences, deciding which should be long and which should be short, and where the commas should go. I like searching for words and phrases that say exactly what I mean. What is more, I've discovered that when you are a writer, life is rarely boring. Characters and stories are everywhere. There is always some new and fascinating subject to explore. The boundaries of your world expand and life seems full of possibilities.

"I was right when I noticed, as a child, that writing is hard and frustrating work. But I've found, as an adult, that it is also deeply satisfying and endlessly interesting. I didn't expect to be a writer, and now I can't imagine being anything else. Life is full of surprises, isn't it?"

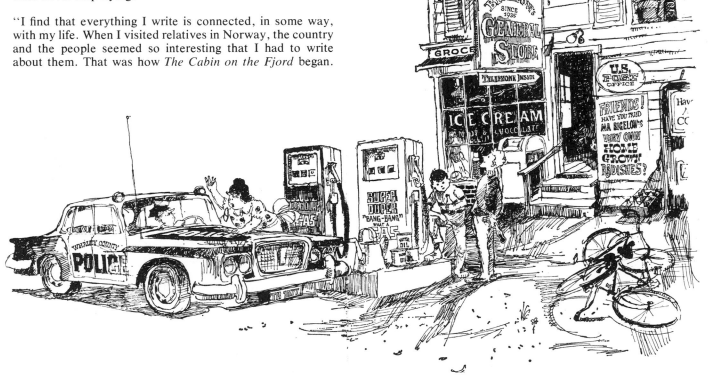

A plump little woman in a faded cotton dress was leaning on the front fender, talking a mile a minute and gesturing dramatically with her hands. ■ (From *The Mysterious Bender Bones* by Susan Meyers. Illustrated by Ib Ohlsson.)

SUSAN MEYERS

NYCE, (Nellie) Helene von Strecker   1885-1969

PERSONAL: Born June 11, 1885, in Warren County, N.J.; daughter of Cyrus William Oliver (a minister) and Vera Kern (Strecker; an author) Nyce; married Frank Hand. *Education:* Philadelphia School of Art, diploma in industrial drawing, 1906, diploma in illustration, 1910. *Home and office:* Box 231, Blue Anchor Rd., Berlin, N.J. *Agent:* Frank Katz, New York, N.Y.

CAREER: Illustrator; art and music teacher. Had three series of illustrations in the *Ladies' Home Journal*, "Flossie Fisher's Funnies," 1910-1918, and "The Adventures of the Greyfur Family," 1916-1917, both written by her mother, Vera Nyce; "The Blue Button Twins," 1912-1914, was written and illustrated by Helene Nyce. *Exhibitions:* Philadelphia Library, 1971; Ridleytownship Library, Pa., 1972; Weaton Village, Millville, N.J., 1978. *Awards, honors: A Jolly Christmas at the Patterprints* received the 1971 Book of the Year Award from The Child Study Association of America.

WRITINGS—All self-illustrated; all published by Saalfield: *The Great Big Story Book*, 1928; *Rainy Day Stories*, 1928; *Mother's Footstool Stories*, 1928.

"Picture Pasting Book" series—all written and illustrated by Helene Nyce; all published by Saalfield, 1927: *The Book of Birds, The Book of Flowers, The Book of Peter Rabbit, The Book of Mother Goose, The Book of Every Sights, The Book of Children at Play.*

"Picture Coloring Book" series—all written and illustrated by Helene Nyce; all published by Saalfield, 1928: *Fish; Butterflies; Birds; Trees; Flowers.*

Illustrator: Vera Nyce (introduction and specimen stories), *Flossie Fisher Funnies*, Frederick A. Stokes, 1913; Vera Nyce, *Little Mab and Gran-Pa Mouse*, Stecker Litho. Co., 1916; Vera Nyce, *The Naughty Piggies*, Stecker Litho. Co., 1916; Vera Nyce, *The Adventures of the Greyfur Family*, Lippincott, 1917; Vera Nyce, *The Greyfur's Neighbors*, Lippincott, 1917; *The Cutting and Pasting Book of Mother Goose*, Saalfield, 1918; Vera Nyce, *Toby and Tidy, Their Trials*, Stecker Litho. Co., 1918; (child verses by Eugene Field) *John Newbery Series*, Saalfield, 1927; Gertrude E. Heath, *When All the Birds Begin to Sing*, Saalfield, 1928; Vera Nyce, *A Jolly Christmas at the Patterprints*, Parents' Magazine Press, 1971.

Work has appeared in *Ladies' Home Journal*, *American Woman* Magazine, *Junior Home* Magazine, *Junior World Journal*, *Bible World*, *Our Little Ones*, *Story World*, *Junior Joys*, *Lutheran Boys and Girls*, *Betty Talks*, *B. Sunshine*.

SIDELIGHTS: Helene von Strecker Nyce was born and raised on a farm in New Jersey. By the age of fifteen she was

HELENE NYCE

He really couldn't go back up the chimney, for the fire had been blazed up to dry his coat, and not being used to doors he left this one wide open. ■ (From *A Jolly Christmas at the Patterprints* by Vera Nyce. Illustrated by Helene Nyce.)

creating scissor-cut silhouette with a pair of manicure scissors. In 1906 Nyce received a diploma in Industrial Arts from the Philadelphia School of Arts and in 1910 received a diploma in Illustration from the same school.

Most of Nyce's life was devoted to illustrating books and magazines and, on several occasions, she illustrated children's stories written by her mother, Vera Nyce. Nyce is perhaps best remembered for her "Flossie Fisher's Funnies," a popular series which ran in the *Ladies' Home Journal* from 1910 to 1918. Flossie Fisher dolls, jewelry, stationery, and china were created from the series and avidly collected by children all around the world. In 1913 "Flossie Fisher Funnies" was published in book form.

In 1969, the illustrator, best known for her india ink and scissor-cut silhouette and charming illustrations, died at the age of eighty-four.

NYCE, Vera   1862-1925

PERSONAL: Born July 26, 1862, in Reading, Pa.; daughter of John Kern and Emma (Griffith) Strecker; married Cyrus William Oliver Nyce (a minister), March 21, 1884; children: Nellie (Helene; Mrs. Frank Hand), Paul. *Home and office:* Box 231, Blue Anchor Rd., Berlin, N.J. *Agent:* Frank Katz, New York, N.Y.

CAREER: Author; farming and assisting her husband in his church work. Authored two series for the *Ladies' Home Journal,* both illustrated by her daughter, Helene Nyce, "Flossie Fisher's Funnies," 1910-1918, and "The Adventures of the Greyfur Family," 1916-1917. *Awards, honors:* A *Jolly Christmas at the Patterprints* received the 1971 Book of the Year Award from The Child Study Association of America.

WRITINGS—All illustrated by her daughter, Helene Nyce: *Flossie Fisher Funnies,* Frederick A. Stokes, 1913; *Little Mab and Gran-Pa Mouse,* Stecker Litho. Co., 1916; *The Naughty Piggies,* Stecker Litho. Co., 1916; *The Adventures of the Greyfur Family,* Lippincott, 1917; *The Greyfur's Neighbors,* Lippincott, 1917; *Toby and Tidy, Their Trials,* Stecker Litho. Co., 1918; *A Jolly Christmas at the Patterprints,* Parents' Magazine Press, 1971.

HELENE (left) and VERA (center) NYCE

SIDELIGHTS: Vera Nyce was born in Reading, Pennsylvania on July 26, 1862. In 1884 she married a minister (Cyrus W. O. Nyce) and subsequently spent a great deal of her life helping her husband with his ministry, farming, and raising their two children, Nellie (Helene von Strecker Nyce, an illustrator) and Paul.

When her daughter became involved in illustration and creating silhouettes, Nyce began to write the children's stories for her daughter's illustrations. She was perhaps best known as the creator of the popular "Flossie Fisher Funnies" which ran as a successful series in the *Ladies' Home Journal*. The Flossie Fisher Club was world renowned and the Flossie Fisher characters were duplicated on jewelry, china, banners, furniture, powder boxes and stationery. During the years of the series' popularity Nyce and her daughter received over fifty thousand fan letters from children in all parts of the world.

In a letter dated August, 1915, the creator of the "Flossie Fisher Funnies" alluded to the series' growing popularity: "In warm weather the stories and letters generally drop off, but this August they have increased. The club [Flossie Fisher Fan Club] is prospering too. The latest chapter—in a school—is one of a hundred and fifty members. School teachers are already writing for cut-outs to be in readiness for the opening of their schools. Last week a teacher in England wrote for the cut-outs and also to join the [Flossie Fisher Fan Club]. We now have more than fifteen thousand members; is not that splendid?"

Nyce created for her daughter's illustrations other children's books; one of which, *A Jolly Christmas at the Patterprints*, was named "Book of the Year" by the Child Study Association of America in 1971.

(Died in 1925)

OLCOTT, Frances Jenkins   1872(?)-1963

PERSONAL: Born about 1872 in Paris, France; died March 29, 1963; daughter of Franklin (a member of the United States Consular Service) and Julia (a writer and translator) Olcott. *Education:* Tutored by parents; graduate of New York State Library School, 1896. *Home:* Albany, New York.

CAREER: Librarian, author, and compiler. Began career as an assistant librarian in the Brooklyn Public Library; developed the first educational system of children's libraries while head of the children's department of the Carnegie Library of Pittsburgh; founded a training school for children's librarians known as the Carnegie Library School of Pittsburgh; retired from library service to concentrate on her literary career.

WRITINGS—All for children: Fairy Tales for Children, New York State University, 1898; *The Children's Reading*, Houghton, 1912; *Story-Telling Poems*, Houghton, 1913, reprinted, Books for Libraries, 1970; *Good Stories for Great Holidays*, Houghton, 1914; (compiled with Amena Pendleton) *The Jolly Book for Boys and Girls*, Houghton, 1915; *Bible Stories to Read and Tell: With References to the Old and New Testaments* (illustrated by Willy Pogany), Houghton, 1916; *The Red Indian Fairy Book* (illustrated by Frederick Richardson), Houghton, 1917; *Tales of the Persian Genii* (illustrated by W. Pogany), Houghton, 1917; *The Book of Elves and Fairies* (illustrated by Milo Winter), Houghton, 1918; *The Wonder Garden* (illustrated by M. Winter), Houghton, 1919.

Story-Telling Ballads, Houghton, 1920; *Stories about George Washington*, Houghton, 1922; *Good Stories for Great Birthdays*, Houghton, 1922; (editor) Jakob Ludwig Karl and Wilhelm Karl Grimm, *Grimm's Fairy Tales* (illustrated by Rie Cramer), Penn Publishing, 1922, [another edition with an introduction by Frances Clarke Sayers, Follett, 1968]; *Wonder Tales from China Seas* (illustrated by Dugald Stewart Walker), Longmans, 1925; *Wonder Tales from Windmill Lands, from the Dutch and Other Sources* (illustrated by Herman Rosse), Longmans, 1926; (editor) Zakarias Topelius, *Canute Whistlewinks and Other Stories*, Longmans, 1927; *Wonder Tales from Pirate Isles, Chiefly Translated from the Dutch* (illustrated by H. Rosse), Longmans, 1927; *Wonder Tales from Baltic Wizards, from the German and English* (illustrated by Victor G. Candell), Longmans, 1928; *Wonder Tales from Fairy Isles, England, Cornwall,*

HE TURNED HIM ROUND;
BUT STILL IT HUNG BEHIND HIM

(From *Story-Telling Ballads* by Frances Jenkins Olcott. Illustrated by Milo Winter.)

And Joseph said unto Pharaoh, "The dream of Pharaoh is one. God hath shewed Pharaoh what he is about to do." ■ (From *Bible Stories to Read and Tell* selected and arranged by Frances Jenkins Olcott. Illustrated by Willy Pogany.)

Wales, Scotland, Man, and Ireland (illustrated by Constance Whittemore), Longmans, 1929.

Wonder Tales from Goblin Hills, from the German and English (illustrated by Harold Sichel), Longmans, 1930; *Go! Champions of Light* (illustrated by D. S. Walker), Revell, 1933; *The Isles of Colored Shells* (tales and poems; illustrated by Heman Fay, Jr.), Houghton, 1934; *Our Wonderful World,* Little, Brown, 1935; *Good Stories for Anniversaries* (illustrated by Hattie Longstreet Price), Houghton, 1937, reprinted, Tower Books, 1971; (co-author with John Ernest Williamson) *Child of the Deep* (photographs by Williamson), Houghton, 1938; *The Bridge of Caravans: 625 Miles of Adventure, Cypriote, Turkish, Syrian, and Palestinian,* W. A. Wilde, 1940.

SIDELIGHTS: Born in Paris when her father, a member of the United States Consular Service, was stationed there. The city was a strong influence on Olcott during her formative years. After the family returned to Albany, New York, there followed years of private study under her parents' tutelage. Olcott's father taught her German and the classics but

it was her mother, a translator of children's stories from the French, who taught her to love writing stories.

After graduating from the New York State Library School, Olcott began her career as an assistant librarian in the Brooklyn Public Library. Later, as the head of the children's department of the Carnegie Library of Pittsburgh, Olcott developed the first educational system of children's libraries for an entire community and founded the school for children's librarians called the Carnegie Library School.

Olcott devoted herself to writing children's books after her retirement from library service. She was fascinated with travel and all things Oriental. Following a year's study in the Holy Land she devoted much of her literary work to biblical subjects for youngsters.

On March 29, 1963 Olcott died in a New York City nursing home. Her life had followed a very purposeful design—the literary education of children.

FOR MORE INFORMATION SEE—Stanley J. Kunitz and Howard Haycraft, editors, *Junior Book of Authors,* second revised edition, H. W. Wilson, 1951; E. Ward and D. A. Marquardt, *Authors of Books for Young People,* Scarecrow, 1964; (obituary) *New York Times,* April 4, 1963.

(Died March 29, 1963)

PETRIDES, Heidrun   1944-

PERSONAL: Born August 3, 1944, in Posen, Germany; daughter of Peter (an architect) and Strobel Petrides. *Home:* Bambergerst 18, Berlin, Germany.

HEIDRUN PETRIDES

When he had thought long enough, he took Peter by the hand and they went home. ■ (From *Hans and Peter* by Heidrun Petrides. Illustrated by the author.)

CAREER: Illustrator. Teacher in Hamburg, Germany, 1969-77; social worker in Berlin, Germany, 1972-76.

ILLUSTRATOR: Der Xaver und der Waste, Atlantis, 1963, published in the United States under title *Hans & Peter,* Harcourt, 1963; *Oer Orache von Avignon,* Atlantis, 1966; Jurgen Tamchina, *Dominique and the Dragon,* Harcourt, 1969; *Daniel und die Schulbaude,* Atlantis, 1973; *Jupp und Jule,* Beitelswauu, 1976.

SIDELIGHTS: "I want to make pedagogic books, which can help the children of poor people to survive (corresponding with my experience as a social worker in Berlin). I am planning a trip of one year, for myself, to Mexico."

SCHMIDERER, Dorothy 1940-

PERSONAL: Born October 26, 1940, in New York, N.Y.; daughter of Simon (an architect) and Mary (an art teacher; maiden name, Burlingham) Schmiderer. *Education:* Bryn Mawr, A.B., 1963; further study at Parson School of Design, 1964-66. *Home and office:* 238 East 58th St., New York, N.Y. 10022.

CAREER: Scholastic Magazines, Inc., New York City, designer, 1966-69; Harper & Row Publishers, Inc., New York City, book designer, 1970-76; Viking Press, Inc., book designer, 1977-78. *Awards, honors:* Children's Book Council Showcase Award, 1972, for *The Alphabeast Book;* award

Kk kangaroo

(From *The Alphabeast Book: An Abecedarium* by Dorothy Schmiderer. Illustrated by the author.)

from American Institute of Graphic Arts, 1975, for design of *Honkytonk Heroes*.

WRITINGS: (Self-illustrated) *The Alphabeast Book: An Abecedarium*, Holt, 1971.

SCHWARTZ, Stephen (Lawrence) 1948-

PERSONAL: Born March 6, 1948, in New York, N.Y.; son of Stanley L. (a businessman) and Sheila (a teacher; maiden name, Siegal) Schwartz; married Carole Ann Piasecki, June 6, 1969; children: Scott Lawrence, Jessica Lauren. *Education:* Juilliard School of Music, preparatory division, 1964; Carnegie Institute of Technology (now Carnegie-Mellon University), B.F.A., 1968. *Residence:* Ridgefield, Conn. *Agent:* Shirley Bernstein, Paramuse Associates, 1414 Avenue of the Americas, New York, N.Y. 10019.

CAREER: Composer, lyricist, director and author. *Member:* National Academy of Recording Arts & Sciences (national trustee), American Society of Composers, Authors & Publishers, Dramatists' Guild, Society of Stage Directors & Choreographers. *Awards, honors:* Two Grammy Awards from National Academy of Recording Arts & Sciences, 1971, for ''Godspell'' (original cast recording); three Drama Desk Awards for ''Godspell'' (music and lyrics), 1971, Working direction, 1978; Trendsetter Award from *Billboard*, 1971, for ''Godspell'' and ''Mass''; award from National Theatre Arts Conference, 1971, for ''Godspell''.

WRITINGS: The Perfect Peach (juvenile), Little, Brown, 1977.

Composer and lyricist for title song of ''Butterflies Are Free'' (play and film), 1969; composer of music and new lyrics for ''Godspell'', 1971; author, with Leonard Bernstein, of English texts for Bernstein's ''Mass'', 1971; composer and lyricist for ''Pippin'' (play), 1972; composer and lyricist for ''The Magic Show'' (play), 1974; composer and lyricist for ''The Baker's Wife'' (play), 1976; adapter, director, composer and lyricist of four songs for ''Working'' (play), 1978.

While Pee-chee held the tiger tight and flew like a kite.
■ (From *The Perfect Peach* by Stephen Schwartz. Illustrated by Leonard B. Lubin.)

So we held another meeting about the Queen and it was decided that one mouse would be selected to find a way with her. ■ (From *She Was Nice to Mice* by Alexandra Elizabeth Sheedy. Illustrated by Jessica Ann Levy.)

ALEXANDRA ELIZABETH SHEEDY

SHEEDY, Alexandra Elizabeth   1962-

PERSONAL: Born June 13, 1962, in New York, N.Y.; daughter of John J. (an executive) and Charlotte (a writer and literary agent; maiden name, Baum) Sheedy. *Education:* Attends high school in New York City. *Home:* 145 West 86th St., New York, N.Y. 10024. *Agent:* Charlotte Sheedy, 145 West 86th St., New York, N.Y. 10024.

CAREER: Writer and actress.

WRITINGS: She Was Nice to Mice (for children), illustrated by Jessica Ann Levy, McGraw, 1975. Contributor of articles to periodicals, including *New York Times, Seventeen, Ms.,* and *Village Voice.*

WORK IN PROGRESS: A book, *Yours Truly, Mandy.*

SIDELIGHTS: Sheedy wrote her first published book when she was twelve. ''I started writing because I used to tell stories to the children who lived nearby and when I was six I started writing them down. I write poetry and plays, too, and writing is important to me. It is important for me to express my feelings and thoughts. If I'm feeling angry or wonderful or upset or happy I just write it out and reread the feelings over and over again. When I'm depressed I read something I wrote when I was happy and I can feel a great lift in my spirits. I love writing!

''I am really close to my parents. My mother and my father do not live together. We children spend half of the week at one house and half of the week at the other house. We have been living as we do for six years. I get along well with my brother Patrick, who is ten, and my sister Meghan, who is thirteen. We have an iguana and rabbit as pets.''

LEONARD SHORTALL

SHORTALL, Leonard W.

PERSONAL: Born in Seattle, Wash.; married; children: three. *Education:* Attended the University of Washington.

CAREER: Illustrator; also worked in the field of advertising. *Awards, honors:* Garden State Children's Book Award, 1977, for *Encyclopedia Brown Lends a Hand* by Donald J. Sobol.

WRITINGS—All self-illustrated; all published by Morrow, except as noted: *Country Snowplow,* 1960; *John and His Thumbs,* 1961; *Sam's First Fish,* 1962; *Davey's First Boat,* 1963; *Danny on the Lookout,* 1964; *Ben on the Ski Trail,* 1965, reissued, Western, 1976; *The Hat Book,* Golden Press, 1965, reissued, Western, 1976; *Steve's First Pony Ride,* 1966; *Eric in Alaska,* 1967; *Andy, the Dog Walker,* 1968; *Peter in Grand Central Station,* 1969; *Jerry the Newsboy,* 1970; *Tod on the Tugboat,* 1971; *Tony's First Dive,* 1972; *Just-in-Time Joey,* 1973; *One Way: A Trip with Traffic Signs,* Prentice-Hall, 1975; *Little Toad to the Rescue,* Golden Press, 1977.

Illustrator: Jerrold Beim, *Andy and the School Bus,* Morrow, 1947; J. Beim, *Country Fireman,* Morrow, 1948; Mabel Louise Robinson, *Back-Seat Driver,* Random House, 1949; Lilian Moore and Leone Adelson, *Old Rosie, the Horse*

Nobody Understood, Random House, 1952; L. Moore and L. Adelson, *Terrible Mr. Twitmeyer,* Random House, 1952; Caary Paul Jackson, *Spice's Football,* Crowell, 1955; M. L. Robinson, *Skipper Riley,* Random House, 1955; Patricia Gray, *Heads Up,* Coward, 1956; M. L. Robinson, *Riley Goes to Obedience School,* Random House, 1956; Jeanne McGahey Hart, *Gloomy Erasmus,* Coward, 1957; Marion Renick, *Young Mr. Football,* Scribner, 1957; J. Beim, *Country Mailman,* Morrow, 1958; Doris Faber, *Wonderful Tumble of Timothy Smith,* Knopf, 1958; Jean Fritz, *How to Read a Rabbit,* Coward, 1959; Patricia Lauber, *Adventure at Black Rock Cave,* Random House, 1959.

Eleanor Cameron, *A Mystery for Mr. Bass,* Little, Brown, 1960; P. Lauber, *Champ: Gallant Collie,* Random House, 1960; Mary Stolz, *A Dog on Barkham Street,* Harper, 1960, reissued, Dell, 1973; Beth Brown, editor, *Wonderful World of Dogs,* Harper, 1961; Jacob Townsend, *Cats Stand Accused,* Houghton, 1961; J. Fritz, *Tap, Tap, Lion—1,2,3,* Coward, 1962; Scott Corbett, *Cutlass Island,* Little, Brown, 1962; Eve Rouke, *Never in a Hurry,* Guild Press, 1962; Eleanor Clymer, *Harry, the Wild West Horse,* Atheneum, 1963; L. Moore and L. Adelson, *Mr. Twitmeyer and the Poodle,* Random House, 1963; M. Stolz, *The Bully of Barkham Street,* Harper, 1963; Betty Baker, *Shaman's Last Raid,* Harper, 1963; B. Baker, editor, *Treasure of Padres,* Harper, 1964; Harold W. Felton, *Pecos Bill and the Mustang,* Prentice-Hall, 1965; P. Lauber, *Clarence Turns Sea Dog,* Random House, 1965; Daniel Mannix, *The Outcasts,* Dutton, 1965; Osmond Molarsky, *Piper, the Sailboat that Came Back,* Graphic Society Publishers, 1965; Dorothy Edwards Shuttlesworth, *ABC of Buses,* Doubleday, 1965; M. Renick, *Watch Those Red Wheels Roll,* Scribner, 1965; Jennifer Wayne, *Kitchen People,* Bobbs-Merrill, 1965.

Jean Bothwell, *The Mystery Clock,* Dial, 1966; James W. English, *Tops in Troop 10,* Macmillan, 1966; Adelaide Holl, *Colors are Nice,* Golden Press, 1966; Pauline L. Jensen, *Thicker Than Water,* Bobbs-Merrill, 1966; Elizabeth Vreeken, *One Day Everything Went Wrong,* Follett, 1966; J. Bothwell, *The Mystery Box,* Dial, 1967; B. Brown, editor, *The Wonderful World of Horses,* Harper, 1967; Naomi Buchheimer, *I Know a Teacher,* Putnam, 1967; Cliff Faulknor, *The In-Betweener,* Little, Brown, 1967; Peter Paul Hilbert, *Zoo on the First Floor,* Coward, 1967; Donald J. Sobol, *Secret Agents Four,* Four Winds, 1967; Ruth Carlsen, *Monty and the Tree House,* Houghton, 1967; Christine Govan, *The Curious Clubhouse,* Collins & World, 1967; P. Lauber, *Clarence Goes to Town,* Random House, 1967; Thoeger Birkeland, *When the Cock Crows,* Coward, 1968; C. Govan, *Phinny's Fine Summer,* World, 1968; Ross R. Olney, *Story of Traffic Control,* Prentice-Hall, 1968; Carol J. Farley, *Sergeant Finney's Family,* Watts, 1969; Wilfred McCormick, *Fullback in the Rough,* Prentice-Hall, 1969; Barbara Rinkoff, *Harry's Homemade Robot,* Crown, 1969; Emily West, *Mr. Alexander and the Witch,* Viking, 1969; Janet Fulton, *Golden Fire Engine Book,* Golden Press, 1969.

Patricia A. Anthony, *Animals Grow,* Putnam, 1970; C. Govan, *The Trash Pile Treasure,* World, 1970; Keo Felker Lazarus, *The Gismo,* Follett, 1970; Lois Duncan, *Hotel for Dogs,* Houghton, 1971; Sonia Levitin, *Rita, the Weekend Rat,* Atheneum, 1971; B. Rinkoff, *The Case of the Stolen Code Book,* Crown, 1971; Mary Jo Stephens, *Zoe's Zodiac,* Houghton, 1971; Thomas E. Tinsley, *Plants Grow,* Putnam, 1971; Hilary Beckett, *Rafael and the Raiders,* Dodd, 1972; Lee Kingman, *Georgina and the Dragon,* Houghton, 1972; Alison Prince, *The Red Jaguar,* Atheneum, 1972; Thomas

Joey turned around and saw that Billy had a spray can in his hand. "Look what you've done!" he cried. ∎ (From *Just-In-Time Joey* by Leonard Shortall. Illustrated by the author.)

Little Toad heard a great, "YAWN. HOHUMMMMM! Pardon me!" He looked up and saw Cicada high up in the elm tree.

"I've been asleep in the ground for seventeen years, but I still can't seem to wake up!" Cicada sighed. "Perhaps what I need is a little nap."

"Don't let me keep you up. I'm just passing through," Little Toad called up into the tree, but Cicada had already begun to hum her loud buzzy hum.

"That's nice. Singing herself to sleep," Little Toad said as he continued his journey. "Well, I'll have time for sleeping when I finish my important job."

(From *Little Toad to the Rescue* by Leonard Shortall. Illustrated by the author.)

"Well I'll be a zigzagging Zulu!" said Mitch slowly. "Look what old Beanie found!" ■ (From *Deadline at Spook Cabin* by Eugenia Miller. Illustrated by Leonard Shortall.)

and Gretchen Perera, *Louder and Louder: The Dangers of Noise Pollution,* Watts, 1973; Seymour Simon, *A Building on Your Street,* Holiday House, 1973; David Townsend, *The Cats Stand Accused,* Houghton, 1973; Barbara Shook Hazen, *Animal Manners,* Golden Press, 1974; David Protheroe, *More Social Science Projects You Can Do,* Prentice-Hall, 1974; Carolyn Lane, *The Winnemah Spirit,* Houghton, 1975; Martha Shapp, *Let's Find Out What Electricity Does,* revised edition, Watts, 1975; Elliott Arnold, *Brave Jimmy Stone,* Scholastic Book Services, 1975; Keo Lazarus, *The Gismo from Outer Space,* Scholastic Book Services, 1975; Stan Applebaum and Victoria Cox, *Going My Way?,* Harcourt, 1976; Wanda Cheyne, *Animal Crackers,* Rand McNally, 1976; Kathleen Savage and Margaret Siewert, *Bear Hunt,* Prentice-Hall, 1976; Charles Keller, compiler, *More Ballpoint Bananas,* Prentice-Hall, 1977; Beverly Major, *The Magic Pizza,* Prentice-Hall, 1978.

"Mishmash" series; written by Molly Cone; all published by Houghton: *Mishmash,* 1962; *. . . and Substitute Teacher,* 1963; *. . . and the Sauerkraut Mystery,* 1965; *. . . and Uncle Looey,* 1968; *. . . and the Venus Flytrap,* 1976.

"Encyclopedia Brown" series; written by Donald J. Sobol; all published by Thomas Nelson, except as noted: *Encyclopedia Brown, Boy Detective,* 1963; *. . . Finds the Clues,* 1966; *. . . and the Case of the Secret Pitch,* 1966; *. . . Gets His Man,* 1967; *. . . Solves Them All,* 1968, Scholastic Book Services, 1977; *. . . Keeps the Peace,* 1969; *. . . Saves the Day,* 1970; *. . . Tracks Them Down,* 1971; *. . . Shows the Way,* 1972; *. . . Takes the Case,* 1973; *. . . Lends a Hand,* 1974; *. . . and the Case of the Dead Eagles,* 1975; *. . . Eleven,* Scholastic Book Services, 1976.

Also illustrator for several national magazines, including *Woman's Day, Red Book,* and *Farm Journal.*

FOR MORE INFORMATION SEE: B. M. Miller and others, compilers, *Illustrators of Children's Books: 1946-1956,* Horn Book, 1958; Lee Kingman and others, compilers, *Illustrators of Children's Books: 1957-1966,* Horn Book, 1968; *Horn Book,* June, 1977.

SPANFELLER, James J(ohn)   1930-

PERSONAL: Born October 27, 1930, in Philadelphia, Pennsylvania; married wife, Patricia; children: James, Jr. *Education:* Studied at the Philadelphia Museum School of Art and the Pennsylvania Academy of Fine Arts. *Home:* Katonah, New York.

CAREER: Free-lance illustrator, 1957—. Held a one-man show, 1965, at the Society of Illustrators. *Military service:* United States Army for two years. *Awards, honors:* Named Artist of the Year by the Artists Guild of New York, 1964.

ILLUSTRATOR: Robert Paul Smith, *Where Did You Go? Out! What Did You Do? Nothing,* Norton, 1958; Penelope Farmer, *Summer Birds,* Harcourt, 1962; Clyde R. Bulla, *In-*

Spanfeller by Spanfeller.

"Home is where one starts from...." ■ (From *A Tune Beyond Us* edited by Myra Cohn Livingston. Illustrated by James J. Spanfeller.)

dian Hill, Crowell, 1963; Henry Morgan, *O-Sono and the Magician's Nephew and the Elephant,* Vanguard, 1964; Richard Parker, *Boy Who Wasn't Lonely,* Bobbs-Merrill, 1964; Julia Cunningham, *Dorp Dead,* Pantheon, 1965; Mary F. Shura, *Run Away Home,* Knopf, 1965; Flora M. Hood, *Pink Puppy,* Putnam, 1966; P. Farmer, *Emma in Winter,* Harcourt, 1966; Catherine Marshall, *God Loves You: Our Family's Favorite Stories and Prayers,* McGraw, 1967; Myra C. Livingston, editor, *Tune Beyond Us: A Collection of Poetry,* Harcourt, 1968; Robert Lamb, *Plug at the Bottom of the Sea,* Bobbs-Merrill, 1968; M. C. Livingston, *A Crazy Flight, and Other Poems,* Harcourt, 1969; Andrew Lang, editor, *The Blue Fairy Book,* Junior Deluxe Editions, 1969; Vera and Bill Cleaver, *Where the Lilies Bloom,* Lippincott, 1969; William I. Martin, *"Tricks or Treats?",* Holt, 1970; M. C. Livingston, *The Malibu, and Other Poems,* Atheneum, 1972; William H. Mooks, *Doug Meets the Nutcracker,* Warne, 1977.

SIDELIGHTS: Spanfeller was born in 1930 in Philadelphia, Pennsylvania and studied art in that city at the Philadelphia Museum School of Art and later at the Pennsylvania Academy of Fine Arts. He has been a free-lance illustrator since 1957 and has been awarded more than sixty citations for his work—from the Society of Illustrators; from the American Institute of Graphic Arts; a National Book Award; and the prestigious Artist of the Year Award from the Artists Guild of New York, to name a few. One of his children's books (he has illustrated over forty) is being considered for a major Hollywood film.

Working with a mirror, the artist uses himself as a model in much of his work. "I find I'm the most available model in my studio, especially since I prefer to work late into the night. . . . My drawings just grow and, because I want them to do just that, I can't get involved in the materials. Getting caught up in anything unrelated stops the flow. When I work,

I add a section here, cut away a section there, and let all kinds of things happen that couldn't with an approach that's restricted by worrying about other considerations—like art supplies. I splosh around with razor blade and rubber cement and have myself a ball." [Nick Meglin, *American Artist,* March, 1977.[1]]

Spanfeller lives with his wife Pat and son Jim, Jr. in Katonah, New York. Besides commissioned work, he also is an art instructor. In his classes he strives to maintain individuality in his students' work and prides himself when others can't spot a "Spanfeller students' work" in school exhibitions. Admittedly, he works them hard. "Illustration as now practiced in this country is essentially a kind of folk art for the middle class. It functions as a marketing-oriented communication art. Theoretically, at least, this structure prevents it from being a 'fine' or gallery art because of the necessity of the marketing problem-solving. Magazines, books, and agency art are all dictated to by these marketing requirements. Because of all this, illustration remains shallow and rarely is original, truthful, or speaks to the human spirit. The practice, employed by many illustrators, of tracing photographs and then, by various gimmicks, making them resemble real art demonstrates the low aesthetic level that is celebrated and too often rewarded in the profession.

(From *Joanna and Ulysses* by May Sarton. Illustrated by James J. Spanfeller.)

"... The future of American illustration is with young, dedicated people who truly wish to relate to human values and spirit and express personal ideas within the confines of a revitalized communication art."[1]

FOR MORE INFORMATION SEE: Nick Meglin, *American Artist,* March, 1977.

This story starts and middles and ends with me.
■ (From *Dorp Dead* by Julia Cunningham. Illustrated by James Spanfeller.)

SPYRI, Johanna (Heusser)   1827-1901

PERSONAL: Surname is pronounced *Spee*-ree; born July 12, 1827, in Hirzel, Switzerland; died July 7, 1901; daughter of Johann Jacob (a doctor) and Meta (Schweizer) Heusser; married Bernhard Spyri (a town clerk), 1852; children: one son (died of tuberculosis during his student years). *Education:* Attended the village school, Hirzel, Switzerland. *Home:* Zurich, Switzerland.

CAREER: Author. Wrote verses and poetry as a small child; began writing career at age 43 to help the refugees of the Franco-Prussian War, 1870.

WRITINGS—Stories: *Heidi,* [Germany], 1880, translation from the German by Helen B. Dole published as *Heidi: A Story for Children and Those That Love Children,* Ginn, 1899, reissued, British Book Center, 1977 [other editions illustrated by Maginel Wright Enright Barney, Rand McNally,

(From *Heidi* by Johanna Spyri. Illustrated by Frank Schoonover.)

(From the movie "Heidi," starring Shirley Temple and Jean Hersholt. Copyright 1937 by Twentieth Century-Fox Film Corp.)

(From the movie "Heidi," copyright 1954 by United Artists Corp.)

1921; Jessie Willcox Smith, McKay, 1922, reissued, Scribner, 1958; Gustaf Tenggren, Houghton, 1923; Dorothy Lake Gregory and Milo Winter, Rand McNally, 1925; Marguerite Davis, Ginn, 1927; Maud and Miska Petersham, Garden City Publishing, 1932; Hildegarde Woodward, Appleton-Century, 1935; Charles Mozley, F. Watts, 1943; William Sharp, Grosset, 1945; Leonard Weisgard, World Publishing, 1946; Agnes Tait, Lippincott, 1948; Vincent O. Cohen, Dutton, 1952, reissued, Penguin, 1971; Jenny Thorne, Purnell Books, 1975; another edition with illustrations from the motion picture starring Shirley Temple, Saalfield, 1937, reissued Random House, 1959].

Red-Letter Stories (translated from the German by Lucy Wheelock), Lothrop, 1884; *Rico and Wiseli* (translated from the German by Louise Brooks), De Wolfe, Fiske, 1885, reissued, Crowell, 1922, new edition translated by M. E. Calthrop published as *All Alone in the World: The Story of Rico and Wiseli's Way,* Dutton, 1959; *Uncle Titus: A Story for Children and for Those Who Love Children* (translated from the German by L. Wheelock), Lothrop, 1886 [another edition translated by Clement W. Coumbe published as *Uncle Titus in the Country,* Saalfield, 1926]; *Gritli's Children: A Story for Children and for Those Who Love Children* (translation of *Gritlis Kinder* by L. Brooks), Cupples & Hurd, 1887 [another edition translated by Elisabeth P. Stork published as *Gritli's Children: A Story of Switzerland,* Lippincott, 1924]; *Swiss Stories for Children and for Those Who Love Children* (translated from the German by L. Wheelock),

JOHANNA SPYRI

Lothrop, 1887; *In Safe Keeping* (translated from the German by L. Wheelock), Blackie & Son, 1896; *Einer vom Hause Lesa,* F. A. Perthes [Gotha, Germany], 1898.

Schloss Wildenstein, F. A. Perthes, 1900; *Was Soll denn aus Ihr Werden?,* F. A. Perthes, circa 1900; *Aus dem Leben,* C. E. Mueller [Halle, Germany], 1902; *Dorris and Her Mountain Home* (translated from the German by Mary E. Ireland), Presbyterian Committee of Publication, 1902; *Moni the Goat Boy, and Other Stories* (translation of *Moni der Geissbub* by Edith F. King), Ginn, 1906, new edition translated by C. W. Coumbe, Saalfield, 1926; *Heimatlos: Two Stories for Children and Those Who Love Children* (translated from the German by Emma Stetler Hopkins; illustrated by Frederick Richardson), Ginn, 1912; *Chel: A Story of the Swiss Mountains* (translated from the German by Helene H. Boll), Eaton & Mains, 1913; *The Rose Child* (translated from the German by Helen B. Dole), Crowell, 1916; *What Sami Sings with the Birds* (translated from the German by H. B. Dole), Crowell, 1917; *Little Miss Grasshopper* (translated from the German by H. B. Dole), Crowell, 1918; *Little Curly Head: The Pet Lamb* (translation of *Beim Weiden-Joseph* by H. B. Dole), Crowell, 1919, new edition translated by M. E. Calthrop and E. M. Popper published as *The Pet Lamb, and Other Swiss Stories,* Dutton, 1956.

Spyri's birthplace in Hirzel.

(From *Jörli: The Story of a Swiss Boy* by Johanna Spyri. Photo by J. Gaberell.)

Cornelli (translated from the German by E. P. Stork; illustrated by Maria L. Kirk), Lippincott, 1920 [another edition translated by C. W. Coumbe published as *Cornelli: Her Childhood,* Saalfield, 1926]; *Toni: The Little Wood-Carver* (translated from the German by H. B. Dole), Crowell, 1920; *Erick and Sally* (translated from the German by H. H. Boll), Beacon Press, 1921; *Maezli: A Story of the Swiss Valleys* (translated from the German by E. P. Stork; illustrated by M. L. Kirk), Lippincott, 1921 [another edition translated by C. W. Coumbe published as *Maxa's Children,* Saalfield, 1926; another edition translated by H. B. Dole published as *Castle Wonderful,* Crowell, 1928]; *Tiss: A Little Alpine Waif* (translated from the German by H. B. Dole; illustrated by George Carlson), Crowell, 1921; *Trini: The Little Strawberry Girl* (translated from the German by H. B. Dole; illustrated by G. Carlson), Crowell, 1922; *Jo: The Little Machinist* (translated from the German by H. B. Dole), Crowell, 1923; *Vinzi: A Story of the Swiss Alps* (translated from the German by E. P. Stork; illustrated by M. L. Kirk), Lippincott, 1924; *Joerli: The Story of a Swiss Boy* (translation of *Die Stauffermuehle* by Frances Treadway Clayton and Olga Wunderli), B. H. Sanborn, 1924 [another edition translated by E. P. Stork published as *Joerli; or, The Stauffer Mill,* Lippincott, 1928]; *The Little Alpine Musician* (translated from the German by H. B. Dole), Crowell, 1924 [another edition translated by C. W. Coumbe published as *A Little Swiss Boy,* Saalfield, 1926]; *The New Year's Carol* (translated from the German by Alice Howland Goodwin; illustrated by Grace

She now and then drank her milk and looked meanwhile perfectly happy. ■ (From *Heidi* by Johanna Spyri. Illustrated by Roberta MacDonald.)

Edwards Wesson), Houghton, 1924; *Veronica and Other Friends* (translated from the German by L. Brooks), Crowell, 1924.

Arthur and Squirrel (translated from the German by H. B. Dole), Crowell, 1925; *Children of the Alps* (translated from the German by E. P. Stork; illustrated by Margaret J. Marshall), Lippincott, 1925; *The Children's Carol* (translated from the German by H. B. Dole), Crowell, 1925, new edition edited by Darlene Geis published as *The Children's Christmas Carol,* Prentice-Hall, 1957; *Francesca at Hinterwald* (translated from the German by E. P. Stork; illustrated by M. J. Marshall), Lippincott, 1925; *Eveli: The Little Singer* (translated from the German by E. P. Stork; illustrated by Blanche Greer), Lippincott, 1926; *Eveli and Beni* (translated from the German by H. B. Dole), Crowell, 1926; *Peppino* (translated from the German by E. P. Stork; illustrated by B. Greer), Lippincott, 1926; *In the Swiss Mountains* (translated from the German by H. B. Dole), Crowell, 1929; *Boys and Girls of the Alps* (translated from the German by H. B. Dole), Crowell, 1929; *Renz and Margritli* (translated from the German by H. B. Dole), Crowell, 1931.

ADAPTATIONS—Movies and filmstrips: "Heidi" (motion picture), Twentieth Century-Fox, starring Shirley Temple and Arthur Treacher, 1937, Teaching Film Custodians, 1947, United Artists, 1953, Warner Brothers-Seven Arts, 1968; "Heidi" (motion picture), starring Sir Michael Redgrave, Maximilian Schell, and Jean Simmons, first presented as a television special on the National Broadcasting Network, November 17, 1968; "Heidi" (filmstrip), Universal Education and Visual Arts, 1971; "Heidi and Peter" (motion pic-

(From "Heidi," presented as a six-part drama on the "Once Upon a Classic" television series, starring Emma Blake and Dame Flora Robson. Broadcast on PBS television.)

(From the movie "Heidi and Peter," based on the novel *Heidi*. Copyright 1955 by United Artists Corp.)

ture), United Artists, 1955; "A Gift for Heidi" (motion picture), RKO Radio Pictures, 1962; "Favorite Children's Books: Heidi" (filmstrip; with phonodisc), Coronet Instructional Films, 1969; "Highlights from Heidi" (filmstrip; with phonodisc or phonotape in cassette, each with teacher's guide), Encyclopaedia Britannica Educational Corp., 1973; "Heidi: The Living Legend" (motion picture), ACI Films, 1974.

Plays: William Friedberg and Neil Simon, *Heidi* (musical), Samuel French, 1959; Beryl Marian Jones, *Heidi* (three-act), Pitman, 1965.

Recordings: "Heidi" (phonotape), Spoken Arts, 1974.

SIDELIGHTS: **July 12, 1827.** Born in Hirzel near Zürich, Switzerland, the second daughter of Dr. Johann Jacob Heusser and Meta Heusser (who won some local recognition as a gifted poet and writer of songs).

In her *Recollections of Johanna Spyri's Childhood,* Anna Ulrich, a family friend offered the following impressions: "A timid shyness caused [Spyri] to make the urgent request not to describe her life to the public, for she did not wish to have her innermost, deepest soul laid bare to human eyes. This wish we hold sacred. But we may venture to glance into her father's house on the sunny mountain height, in the earliest Spring days of her life.

"The house where Johanna Spyri was born, the doctor's house in Hirzel, seven miles distant from Zürich, stands on a green hill, one of a chain dividing the Canton of Zürich from the Canton of Zug. From the windows of the simple white country house you look over dark fir forests to the blue water of Lake Zürich, on one side, while the other looks towards the green undulating heights of Zugerland. . . .

"The sleeping-rooms on the upper floor were very fully occupied, for the doctor's white house was a family house in the best sense of the word. There lived not only Johanna's parents, Doctor Johann Jacob Heusser, and his wife Meta, who was a Schweizer, but also the grandmother, the pastor's wife, Anna Schweizer, with her two daughters, Regula and Anna, the latter, after an unfortunate marriage, having come to live here to educate the two little girls, the former as an ideal aunt. They cannot be better described than Johanna has done in *Gritli's Children.*

"... [Spyri's] oldest brother, Theodor, a very gifted and extremely lively boy, domineered over his sister sometimes as a true protector and at other times as a veritable master, which he remained all his life long. The dolls were really hidden away from him at night in the chest, for the future physician and skilful surgeon showed itself in him at an early age, and as Johanna's and Netti's beloved children [dolls] served as 'experiment-rabbits,' they were often found with amputated legs and arms, as well as with bodies leaking sawdust. Since the bodily condition of human beings interested him very early, he wrote this beautiful verse, when his three-, four- and five-year-old sisters were going through the measles:

> 'Christel, Hanni, Netti,
> Each one was a fatty,
> They all took sick
> And died very quick.'

"Fortunately it was not so bad as that, and the three recovered very well, although none of them in later life could answer to the description of fat.

(From the television musical special "The New Adventures of Heidi," starring Burl Ives and Kathy Krutzman. Presented by NBC television, December, 1978.)

"Now we come to Johanna's sister 'Netti'—the remarkable twisting, at that time, of the name Anna to Nanette and Netti. A rosy-cheeked little girl with brown curls and dark, sparkling eyes, she bore a physical resemblance to Johanna; in later years they were often taken for each other. The sisters were also very much alike mentally, only Johanna had in everything the stronger, more talented nature, which Netti always laid stress upon, she who not only loved but also admired Johanna more than anyone else. No wonder that the sisters only two years apart should be so congenial.

"Christian came as the third, a blond-haired blue-eyed boy, lively and merry and ambitious as if made to be the brother of a child so overflowing with strength and happiness as Johanna—or 'Hanni,' as she was called.

"And now Johanna herself, lively, without being at all nervous, beaming with cheerfulness, with sparkling eyes in a narrow, florid face with regular features, scintillating with the joy of life, and feeling neither cold nor heat nor weariness. . . .

"Two younger sisters followed, Ega and Meta, but Christian and Netti remained Johanna's most intimate friends. The

(From the television movie "Heidi," starring Jennifer Edwards and Sir Michael Redgrave. Presented by NBC television, 1968.)

Nothing seemed so strange or wonderful to Heidi as the mysterious sounds in the tops of the trees. ■ (From *Heidi* by Johanna Spyri. Translated by Philip Schuyler Allen. Illustrated by Maginel Wright Enright.)

care of the little sisters was more congenial to Netti than to Johanna.

"One day she was playing hide-and-seek with Christel and Netti in the barn nearby. While playing with fiery zeal, as in all her games, she saw Christel's straw-blond hair, lighted up by a slanting beam of the evening sun, suddenly emerge from a heap of hay. Hanni shouted aloud with delight and stamped around with all her might on their pile of hay, which suddenly gave way, and Hanni fell through a hole in the scaffolding down on the hard stone barn-floor. Unconscious and bleeding she lay there until her mother and aunt, warned by her sister's screams of fright, came hurrying to her and carried the badly injured child into the house. It required the faithful care of both, as well as of the doctor and father, to save the little girl's endangered life, and even after long weeks her face and arm showed the most remarkable discolorations. Fortunately Hanni bore no lasting ill effects.

"School and studying did not delight Johanna very much in her early life. At first she went with her brothers and sisters to the village school, an old farmhouse, the windows of which looked into the green of a vegetable garden. The ancient benches were decorated with all sorts of marks cut into them, and in front of the classes was the old snuff-taking teacher Strickler, who once put up the threatening prophecy; 'Hanneli, you will be a dunce!' It came about like this: Hanni, so versatile in other respects, showed no talent at all for drawing. With her the eraser worked more industriously than the pencil. So one day on her drawing-sheet there appeared a spot she had rubbed through, in the shape of a radiating sun; whereupon Hanni had to laugh so heartily and irrepressibly that her teacher was incited to make this sinister prediction.

"Instruction in the public school, however, did not last long. Netti and Hanni were very soon, together with the pastor's daughter of Hirzel, taught by him in his study. This was

...He seized the food, nodded his thanks and acceptance of her present, and then made a more splendid meal than he had known ever since he was a goatherd.
■ (From *Heidi* by Johanna Spyri. Illustrated by Greta Elgaard.)

Heidi entered...eagerly into the characters and their experiences....But she never looked quite happy, and there was no longer any merriment in her eyes.
■(From *Heidi* by Johanna Spyri. Translated by Helen B. Dole. Illustrated by William Sharp.)

much more to Hanni's taste, for the new teacher, Pastor Tobler, himself a poet and the author of 'Enkel Winkelrieds,' gave the children much stimulation. Even as elderly women they remembered by heart many of the poems which they had learned with him in Krieg's very pleasant reading-book. To be sure, they had already learned many poems at home. Aunt Regeli knew most of Schiller's and Uhland's ballads by heart and entertained the children with them.

"[Spyri's] mother, in spite of her immense love for all poetry, had little time to make the children acquainted with it. . . .

"But the sunniest child-life knows shadows. The first deep one that fell into Johanna's life was the death of her beloved grandmother, Anna Schweizer-Gessner, who lived under the same roof with her. . . .

"Now her room was empty, and Johanna experienced for the first time what she so often expressed in her books—that children can suffer as deeply and as keenly as grown people.

"In the same year her mother and aunt went to Pfäfers for the cure. The three oldest children, Theodor, Netti and

(From *Heidi* by Johanna Spyri. Illustrated by Jessie Willcox Smith.)

Christel, were allowed to visit them there. Johanna suddenly saw herself robbed of all her playmates, for the two little sisters did not as yet count as such. She went around the house somewhat sadly, and this her usually rather harsh father could not bear to see, and he exclaimed: 'The child must have some pleasure, too!' So he ordered that Hanni should go to visit the married cousin, wife of the pastor in Birch, in Wollishofen near Zürich. With great satisfaction this little nine-year-old person set out all sole alone, travelled through forest and fields over the ridge of the Zimmerberg to her destination, which was reached in about five hours. She was received with delight and still greater surprise by her extremely lively aunt and the very quiet, worthy pastor.

"Hanni was not allowed to make the journey back from Wollishofen alone; her mother and aunt were terrified when they heard in Pfäfers about this journey. But the recollection of it lived again in the numerous little travellers in Johanna's books who, like Rico, went alone on his way to Lake Garda, which he so longed to see.

"The recollections of Johanna's childhood would not be complete if no mention was made of her first relations with the two best friends of her life. One was Goethe, who had really closed his eyes a few years after she opened hers, and whom she had not known by sight; but one of the first books to influence her was the *Vertuch,* that collection of colored pictures from all provinces of life, which under Goethe's able oversight was published in Weimar. That also the *Wandering Bell* very early affected the child's lively imagination every one feels who reads in *Arthur and Squirrel* about the wandering grammar.

There were a great many other beautiful tales in the book. Reading these and looking at their pictures made the days pass very quickly and soon the time was at hand when grandmama decided to end her visit. ■ (From *Heidi* by Johanna Spyri. Illustrated by Maginel Wright Enright.)

...She would remain without moving, battling silently with her terrible homesickness until Clara sent for her again. ■ (From *Heidi* by Johanna Spyri. Illustrated by Vincent O. Cohen.)

"And now the other friend. This was a very tall, slender student at the Gymnasium, who often came up to Hirzel on Saturday with brother Theodor, his intimate friend, to spend Sunday in the hospitable doctor's house. He, who had no real home of his own, felt from the first as if sheltered under the friendly eyes of mother and aunt, and was very much delighted with the little wild creature, who never failed to give a witty and clever answer. . . .

"[Bernhard] Spyri, the earnest student, loved dearly to take part in the theatrical performances of the doctor's children. Then they walked together over mountain and valley, and [Bernhard] celebrated these excursions in long poems. Now and then the future pedagogue awoke in him and he sharply and earnestly rebuked the overflowing spirits of his little friend, who did not usually bear this patiently. But the sun of heart-felt mutual attachment soon put such little thunderstorms to flight. [Bernhard] was faithful and true, a man of honor from the crown of his head to the sole of his feet; Johanna felt this even then. And he knew just as surely that the happiness of his life depended on holding the little, impulsive hand of the sunny mountain child firmly in his own. It was a childhood love, which lasted through life.

"And what was the real foundation, on which this bright child-life grew up? We find it best in her mother's words, which she wrote at midnight between the beds of her little children:

'It is dark; life's loud tumultous chorus
    Now is silent grown as midnight breaks;
Stars are marching in their beauty o'er us;
    All the world's asleep; Love only wakes!

'Mother-love here, in darkness cherisht;
   Mother-love, too, yonder, vigil keeps;
Fear not, Heart, for if thy love e'en perisht,
   That Love surely slumbers not nor sleeps! . . .'''

[Anna Ulrich, *Recollections of Johanna Spyri's Childhood*, translated by Helen B. Dole, Crowell, 1925.[1]]

1852. At the age of twenty-five, married her childhood love, Bernhard Spyri, a town clerk in Zürich. The couple had one son who succumbed to tuberculosis during his student years.

1870. At the age of forty-three, Spyri penned her first short stories which met with such general favor that she soon embarked on a larger work, *Heidi*. The book took many years and did not appear until 1880.

December, 1884. Husband died. Spyri continued writing with a particular fervor all of the childhood memories which lay dormant.

July 7, 1901. Died in Zürich after a lingering illness. One critic wrote: "Madame Spyri, like Hans Andersen, had by temperament, a peculiar skill in writing the simple histories of an innocent world. In all her stories she shows an underlying desire to preserve children alike from misunderstanding and the mistaken kindness that frequently hinders the happiness and natural development of their lives and characters. The author, as we feel in reading her tales, lived among the scenes and people she describes, and the setting of her stories has the charm of the mountain scenery amid which she places her small actors."[1]

FOR MORE INFORMATION SEE: Stanley J. Kunitz, editor, *Junior Book of Authors*, revised edition, H. W. Wilson, 1951; "Heidi—or the Story of a Juvenile Best Seller," *Publishers Weekly*, July 25, 1953; Brian Doyle, editor, *Who's Who of Children's Literature*, Schocken, 1968.

Then he sat down on the sledge with her on his knees, well wrapped up in the sack to keep her warm. He held her tightly with his left arm and, taking hold of the bar with his right hand, pushed off with both feet. ■ (From *Heidi* by Johanna Spyri. Illustrated by Cecil Leslie.)

Loud shouts came from the pump where the three boys were washing. ■ (From *A Little Swiss Boy* by Johanna Spyri. Illustrated by Frances Brundage.)

SWIFT, Jonathan 1667-1745
(Isaac Bickerstaff, M. B. Drapier, Simon Waystaff)

PERSONAL: Born November 30, 1667, in Dublin, Ireland; died October 19, 1745, in Dublin; buried in St. Patrick's Cathedral in Dublin; son of Jonathan and Abigail (Erick) Swift; cousin of John Dryden; alleged by some to have married Esther Johnson (the "Stella" of his writings), 1716 (died, 1728). *Education:* Graduated from Trinity College, Dublin, with a degree "by special grace"; Oxford University, M.A., 1692. *Politics:* Originally a Whig; became a Tory in 1710.

CAREER: Novelist, satirist, poet, and pamphleteer. Secretary to Sir William Temple in England, 1689-94, 1696-99. Returned to Ireland, where he was ordained an Anglican priest and served at Kilroot, near Belfast, 1695; became chaplain to the Earl of Berkeley and was appointed vicar of Laracor, 1699; Dean of St. Patrick's Cathedral, Dublin, beginning, 1713. Lived in England, 1708-14; upon the death of Queen Anne in 1714 and the decline of the Tories, Swift returned to Ireland where he defended Tory economic and political interests against the English. *Member:* Scriblerus Club, formed about 1713, which included Swift, Pope, Arbuthnot, Gay, and Congreve as members. The club produced *The Memoirs of Martinus Scriblerus*, a satirical work about a fictitious character, directed against "false tastes in learning." *Gulliver's Travels* is said to have been an outcome of one of the projects of the club.

WRITINGS: A Discourse of the Contests and Dissensions Between the Noble and the Common in Athens and Rome, with the Consequences They Had upon Both These States,

J. Nutt, 1701, reissued, edited by Frank H. Ellis, Clarendon Press, 1967; *A Tale of a Tub [and] An Account of a Battle Between the Ancient and Modern Books in St. James' Library*, J. Nutt, 1704, reprinted, Garland, 1972 (includes *A Discourse Concerning the Mechanical Operation of the Spirit*); *Baucis and Philemon* (poem), H. Hills, 1709; *The Examiner, and Other Pieces Written in 1710-11*, [London], 1711, reissued, Blackwell, 1957; *The Conduct of the Allies, and of the Late Ministry, in Beginning and Carrying on the Present War*, J. Morphew, 1711; *A Proposal for Correcting, Improving, and Ascertaining the English Tongue*, B. Tooke, 1712, reprinted, British Book Center, 1975; *Some Remarks on the Barrier Treaty between Her Majesty and the States-General*, J. Morphew, 1712, reprinted, Garland Publications, 1974; *An Argument to Prove That the Abolishing of Christianity in England May, as Things Now Stand, be Attended with Some Inconveniences, and Perhaps Not Produce Those Many Good Effects Propos'd Thereby*, T. Atkins, 1717; *The Intelligencer*, [Dublin], 1720, reprinted, AMS Press, 1967.

Travels into Several Remote Parts of the World, B. Motte, 1726 (most subsequent editions published as *Gulliver's Travels*), reissued, Oxford University Press, 1971 [other editions illustrated by Jean Grandville (pseudonym of Jean-Ignace Isidore Gerard), Hayward & Moore, 1840; Thomas Morton, Cassell, Petter, 1865; Charles E. Brock, Macmillan, 1894, reprinted, University Microfilms, 1967; Arthur Rackham, Dutton, 1900; Herbert Cole, Dodd, 1900; Milo Winter, Rand McNally, 1912; Louis Rhead, Harper, 1913; Fritz Eichenberg, Heritage Press, 1940, reprinted, 1961; Aldren Watson, Grosset & Dunlap, 1947; Luis Quintanilla, Crown Publishers, 1947; Richard M. Powers, World Publishing, 1948; Robin Jacques, Oxford University Press, 1955; Hans Baltzer, Constable, 1961, reissued, Duell, Sloan, 1963; adaptations for children include those illustrated by Arthur Rackham, Dutton, 1952; Leonard Weisgard, Junior Deluxe Editions, 1954; Maraja (adapted by Sarel Eimerl), Golden Press, 1962; Willy Pogany (retold by Padraic Colum), Macmillan, 1962; Jo Polseno, Grosset & Dunlap, 1963; Don Irwin, Childrens Press, 1969].

A Modest Proposal, S. Harding, 1729, reissued, edited by Charles Beaumont, C. E. Merrill, 1969; *The Life and Genuine Character of Doctor Swift*, J. Roberts, 1733; *A Libel on Dr. D---ny, and a Certain Great Lord* (poem), A. Moore, 1730; *The Lady's Dressing Room* (poem), J. Roberts, 1732; *On Poetry: A Rapsody* (poem), [Dublin], 1733; (under pseudonym Simon Wagstaff) *A Complete Collection of Genteel and Ingenious Conversation, According to the Most Polite Mode and Method Now Used at Court, and in the Best Companies of England*, G. Faulkner, 1738, reprinted as *Polite Conversation*, Folcroft, 1975; excerpt from *Polite Conversation* published separately—*Tittle Tattle; or, Taste a-la-Mode* (play), R. Griffiths, 1749; *Directions to Servants*, R. Dodsley & M. Cooper, 1745, reissued, Scholar Press, 1971 [another edition illustrated by Joseph Low, Pantheon Books, 1964]; (under pseudonym M. B. Drapier) *A Letter to the Right Honorable the Lord *****, [London], 1754; *The Journal to Stella, 1710-13*, Bell, 1897, reissued, edited by Harold Williams, Clarendon Press, 1948, reprinted, Barnes & Noble, 1975.

Collections: *Miscellanies in Prose and Verse*, B. Motte, Volume I, 1711, reprinted, Scholar Press, 1972 (additional volumes appeared in 1727, 1732, and 1735); *The Works of D. Jonathan Swift*, nine volumes, [Dublin], 1752; *The Works of the Reverend Jonathan Swift*, 24 volumes, edited

Jonathan Swift, as a student at Trinity College, 1682.

by Thomas Sheridan, J. Johnson, 1803; *The Works of Jonathan Swift*, 19 volumes, edited by Sir Walter Scott, A. Constable, 1824; *The Poetical Works of Jonathan Swift*, three volumes, W. Pickering, 1833-34; *The Prose Works of Jonathan Swift*, 12 volumes, edited by Temple Scott, Bell, 1898-1909, reprinted, AMS Press, 1971; *The Poems of Jonathan Swift*, three volumes, edited by H. Williams, Clarendon Press, 1937, reissued, 1958; *The Prose Works of Jonathan Swift*, 14 volumes, edited by Herbert Davis, Blackwell, 1939-68, reissued, Barnes & Noble, 1968; *Collected Poems*, edited by Joseph Horrell, Harvard University Press, 1958; *Correspondence*, edited by H. Williams, Clarendon Press, 1963-65; *Poetical Works of Swift*, edited by Herbert Davis, Oxford University Press, 1967; *Rage or Raillery: The Swift Manuscripts at the Huntington Library*, edited by George P. Mayhew, Huntington Library, 1967; *The Writings of Jonathan Swift*, edited by Robert A. Greenberg and William B. Piper, Norton, 1973.

Selections: *Satires and Personal Writings*, edited by William A. Eddy, Oxford University Press, 1932, reissued, 1958; *Selected Prose and Poetry*, edited by Edward Rosenheim, Jr., Rinehart, 1959; *Poems*, edited by Padraic Colum, Collier Books, 1962; *Irish Tracts, 1720-1723 [and] Sermons*, edited by H. Davis and Louis Landa, Blackwell, 1963; *Poetry and Prose* (contains appreciations by Pope, Johnson, Scott, Hazlitt, and others), Clarendon Press, 1964; *Jonathan Swift: A Selection of His Works*, edited by Philip Pinkus, St. Martin's Press, 1965; *Selected Poems*, edited by James Reeves, Barnes & Noble, 1967; *The Best of Swift*, edited by Robert W. Jackson, Cork, Mercier, 1967; *An Annotated Edition of Five Sermons by Jonathan Swift*, edited by Carl P. Daw, [Charlottesville, Virginia], 1970.

Contributor of articles to Richard Steele's *Tatler;* editor of the Tory *Examiner,* 1710-11.

ADAPTATIONS—Movies and filmstrips: "Gulliver's Travels" (motion pictures), Paramount Pictures, 1939, Graphic Curriculum (animated cartoon; six minutes, color), 1968, AIMS Instructional Media Services (animated for primary grades; seven minutes, color), 1971, and Palm Productions is developing a screenplay from a Peter Ustinov treatment, 1978; "Gulliver's Travels" (filmstrip; color, with a teacher's guide), Young America Films, 1957; "Gulliver among the Lilliputians" (filmstrip; color, with filmstrip facts), Encyclopaedia Britannica Films, 1958; "The Three Worlds of Gulliver" (motion picture), Columbia Pictures, starring Kerwin Mathews, 1960; "Gulliver's Travels to Lilliput" (filmstrip; color, sound), Society for Visual Education, 1967; "Favorite Children's Books: Gulliver's Travels" (filmstrip; 11 minutes, sound, color, with a user's guide), Coronet Instructional Films, 1969.

SIDELIGHTS: **November 30, 1667.** Born in Hoey's Court, Dublin. Father, Jonathan Swift, Sr., married Abigail Erick. "The marriage was on both sides very indiscreet; for his wife brought her husband little or no fortune, and his death happening so suddenly before he could make a sufficient establishment for his family. [I] (not then born) hath often been heard to say that [I] felt the consequences of that marriage not only through the whole course of [my] education, but during the greatest part of [my] life." [A. L. Rowse, *Jonathan Swift,* Scribner, 1975.[1]]

He had a sister, Jane, eighteen months older than himself.

His nurse absconded with him in infancy to Whitehaven across the Irish Channel, where they both remained for three years. "The nurse was so careful of [me] that, before [I] returned, [I] had learnt to spell; and by the time [I] was three years old [I] could read any chapter in the Bible."[1]

Returned to his own family at age three.

1673. Went to Kilkenny School, which he attended for eight years. His uncle, he insisted, "gave him the education of a dog."[1]

1682. Entered Trinity College, Dublin, at age fifteen. He would have preferred Oxford: "I am not of this vile, country, I am an Englishman . . . the family of the Swifts are ancient in Yorkshire."[1]

1689. There was revolution and turmoil in Ireland. "[T]he troubles then breaking out, [I] went to [my] mother, who lived in Leicester. And after continuing there some months, [I] was received by Sir William Temple, whose father had been a great friend to the family, and who was now retired to his house called Moor Park, near Farnham in Surrey: where [I] continued for about two years."[1]

Education now began in a friendly and cultivated household. Apprenticeship there lasted a decade.

(From the movie "Gulliver's Travels," starring Richard Harris. Distributed by EMI Films, 1977.)

They had seen me cut the cables and thought my design was only to let the ships run adrift or fall foul on each other: but when they perceived the whole fleet moving in order, and saw me pulling at the end, they set up such a scream of grief and despair, that it is almost impossible to describe or conceive. ■ (From *Gulliver's Travels* by Jonathan Swift. Illustrated by C.E. Brock.)

1690. Very first writing was a congratulatory ode to King William:

> "What do sceptre, crown and ball,
> Rattles for infant royalty to play withal,
>   But serve t'adorn the baby-dress
>   Of one poor coronation day
>   To make the pageant gay:
> A three-hours' scene of empty pride,
> And then the toys are thrown aside."[1]

August, 1691. Returned to England. "I should not have behaved myself after the manner I did in Leicester, if I had not valued my own entertainment beyond the obloquy of a parcel of very wretched fools, which I very solemnly pronounce the inhabitants of Leicester to be. . . .

"A thousand household thoughts always drive matrimony out of my mind whenever it chances to come there; besides that I am naturally temperate, and never engaged in the contrary, which usually produces those effects."[1]

December, 1691. Returned to Moor Park. Spent two and a half years there. Gave himself to poetry.

> "Whate'er I plant, like corn on barren earth,
>   By an equivocal birth
> Seeds and runs up to poetry."[1]

Wrote about the universal idiocy of war:

> "War! that mad game the world so loves to play,
>   And for it does so dearly pay:
> For though with loss or victory awhile
>   Fortune the gamesters does beguile,
> Yet at the last the box sweeps all away."[1]

Foretold his future voice in this couplet:

> "My hate, whose lash just heaven has long decreed
> Shall on a day make sin and folly bleed."[1]

He suffered in his subordinate position at Moor Park and later warned a friend in power: "Never to appear cold to me, for I would not be treated like a schoolboy—I had felt too much of that in my life already. I used to be in pain when Sir William Temple would look cold and out of humour for three or four days, and I used to suspect a hundred reasons."[1]

Undoubtedly philosophers are in the right when they tell us, that nothing is great or little otherwise than by comparison. ■ (From *Gulliver's Travels* by Jonathan Swift. Illustrated by John Corbino.)

May 3, 1693. "I esteem the time of studying poetry to be two hours in a morning (and that only when the humour fits), which I esteem to be the flower of the whole day, and truly I make bold to employ them that way, and yet I seldom write above two stanzas in a week. I mean such as are to any Pindaric ode; and yet I have known myself to be in so good a humour as to make two in a day, but it may be no more in a week after; and when all done, I alter them a hundred times, and yet I do not believe myself to be a laborious writer: because if the fit comes not immediately I never heed, but think of something else. I have a sort of vanity or foibless, I do not know what to call it, and which I would fain know if you partake of. It is (not to be circumstantial) that I am overfond of my own writings (I would not have the world think so), and I find when I write what pleases me, I am Cowley to myself, and can read a hundred times over. I know 'tis a desperate weakness, and has nothing to defend it but its secrecy, and I know I am wholly in the wrong, and have the same pretence the baboon had to praise her own children."[1]

May, 1694. Decided to return to Ireland and establish his independence by taking orders in the Church. "Sir William was extremely angry when I left him—and yet would not oblige himself any further than upon my good behaviour; nor would promise anything firmly to me at all. So that everybody judged I did best to leave him. I design to be ordained September next, and make what endeavour I can for something in the Church."[1]

January, 1695. Ordained in Christ Church Cathedral, Dublin. Later that year he proposed marriage to a sister of one of his college friends. She hesitated and he continued a barrage of letters to her: "Impatience is the most inseparable quality of a lover. . . .

"I am once more offered the advantage to have the same acquaintance with greatness [i.e. from Temple] that I formerly enjoyed, and with better prospect of interest I here solemnly offer to forgo it all for your sake.

"Surely you have but a very mean opinion of the joys that accompany a true, honourable, unlimited love; yet either nature and our ancestors have hugely deceived us, or else all other sublunary things are dross in comparison. Is it possible you cannot yet be insensible to the prospect of a rapture and delight so innocent and exalted? Trust me, Heaven has given us nothing else worth the loss of a thought. Ambition, high appearance, friends and fortune are all tasteless and insipid when they come in competition. . . .

I walked with Intrepidity five or six Times before the very Head of the Cat.
■ (From *Gulliver's Travels* by Jonathan Swift. Illustrated by Fritz Eichenberg.)

"But listen to what I here solemnly protest, by all that can be witness to an oath, that if I leave this kingdom before you are mine, I will endure the utmost indignities of fortune than ever return again."[1]

The lady refused him and he never forgave her. A short while later she tried to renew his interest—his answer: "In England it was in the power of any young fellow of common sense to get a larger fortune than ever you pretended to. Are you in a condition to manage domestic affairs with an income of less perhaps than £300 a year? Have you such an inclination to my person and humour as to comply with my desires and way of living, and endeavour to make us both as happy as you can? Will you be ready to engage in those methods I shall direct for the improvement of your mind, so as to make us entertaining company for each other, without being miserable when we are neither visiting nor visited. . . .

"Without regarding whether your person be beautiful, or your fortune large. Cleanliness in the first, and competency in the other, is all I look for. I desire, indeed, a plentiful revenue, but would rather it should be of my own."[1]

January 27, 1699. Temple died. Swift settled his estate and returned to Ireland as a chaplain. During this, his last period of residence at Moor Park, Swift was in charge of affairs—a position more suited to his temperament. From this time emerged his first prose masterpiece, *A Tale of a Tub*.

Then, too, there was "Stella," (Esther Johnson) the ward of Sir William Temple. "[I] had had some share in her education by directing what books she should read, and perpetually instructing her in the principles of honour and

(From *Gulliver's Reisen* by Jonathan Swift. Translated by Paul Benndorf. Illustrated by Ernst Kutzer.)

virtue; from which she never swerved in any one action or moment of her life. She was sickly from her childhood until about the age of fifteen; but then grew into perfect health and was looked upon as one of the most beautiful, graceful and agreeable young women in London, only a little too fat. Her hair was blacker than a raven, and every feature of her face in perfection."[1]

1701. Persuaded Stella and her companion, Miss Dingley, to take up residence in Ireland. His writings began to stir up ill feelings among his readers due to his acuteness in exposing the absurd postures of people in positions of power. "The very same principle that influences a bully to break the windows of a whore who has jilted him naturally stirs up a Great Prince to raise mighty armies and dream of nothing but sieges, battles and victories. . . .

"A mighty king, who for the space of above thirty years amused himself to take and lose towns, beat armies and be beaten, drive princes out of their dominions, frighten children from their bread and butter, burn, lay waste, plunder, dragoon, massacre."[1]

He attacked the clergy: "Who that sees a little paltry mortal, droning and dreaming and drivelling to a multitude, can think it agreeable to common good sense that either Heaven

'Gave me her Hand to kiss.'

(From *Gulliver's Travels* by Jonathan Swift. Illustrated by C. E. Brock.)

or Hell should be put to the trouble of influence or inspection upon what he is about?''[1]

He attacked literary critics: ''The true critics are known by their talent of swarming about the noblest writers, to which they are carried merely by instinct, as a rat to the best cheese, or a wasp to the fairest fruit. So, when the King is a horse-back, he is sure to be the dirtiest person of the company, and they that make their court best are such as bespatter him worst.''[1]

Nor did the philosopher escape his censure: ''The philosopher's way in all ages has been by erecting certain edifices in the air . . . I think, with due submission, they seem to labour under two inconveniences. First, that the foundations being laid too high, they have been often out of sight, and ever out of hearing. Secondly, that the materials, being very transitory, have suffered much from inclemencies of air, especially in these North-West regions.''[1]

Being offered no office in England, he had returned to his fate—Ireland, but he did not go willingly or *quietly*!

1701. Took his D.D.

1704. *A Tale of a Tub* published.

April, 1710. Mother died. ''I have now lost my barrier between me and death. God grant that I may live to be as well prepared for it, as I confidently believe her to have been. If the way to Heaven be through piety, faith, justice and charity, she is there.''[1]

September, 1710. Stayed with the Vanhomrigh family in London. A daughter of this family, Vanessa, was quick to set her sights for Swift. She unrelentingly pursued him, following him to various towns in his travels. He protested—she continued. ''There is not a better girl on earth. I have a mighty friendship for her. She has good principles, and I have corrected all her faults; but I cannot persuade her to read, though she has an understanding, memory and taste that would bear great improvement. But she is incorrigibly idle and lazy—she thinks the world was made for nothing but perpetual pleasure. Her greatest favourites at present are Lady Ashburnham, her dog, and myself. She makes me of so little consequence that it almost distracts me. She will bid her sister go downstairs before my face, for she has 'some private business with the Doctor.'''[1]

Continually she would appear, sending a note asking him to call on her. Again and again he would put her off. ''I would not see you for thousand pounds if I could. . . . Why, then, you should not have come [i.e. to Windsor], and I knew

(From the animated film "Gulliver's Travels," copyright © 1957 by NTA Pictures.)

that as well as you ... I doubt you do wrong to go to Oxford. ...''[1]

However, he continued to see her as surreptitiously as possible and sent her letters. ''Remember I still enjoin you reading and exercise for the improvement of your mind and health of your body, and grow less romantic, and talk and act like a man of this world. ...

''I see every day as silly things among both sexes, and yet endure them, for the sake of amusements. The worst thing in you and me is that we are too hard to please; and whether we have not made ourselves so is the question.

''I wish you would get yourself a horse, and have always two servants to attend you, and visit your neighbours—the worse the better. There is a pleasure in being reverenced, and that is always in your powers, by your superiority of sense, and an easy fortune.

''The best maxim I know in this life is to drink your coffee when you can [i.e. enjoy yourself], and when you cannot, to be easy without it.''[1]

1711. His continued companionship with Stella marked by visits and endless letters, with the ''little language'' of endearments, was incorporated in his books.

1713. Became Dean of St. Patricks in Dublin, Ireland.

1716. Swift may have married Stella in secrecy and insisted that they remain on the same footing as before. There is historical agreement that the empty ceremony was performed.

1720. Began writing *Gulliver's Travels*.

June 2, 1723. Vanessa died.

1724. Gave his attentions to his office. ''For a divine has nothing to say to the wisest congregation of any parish in this kingdom which he may not express in a manner to be understood by the meanest among them. ... When a man's thoughts are clear, the properest words will generally offer themselves first, and his own judgment will direct him in what order to place them so as they may be best understood. ...

''Men should consider that raising difficulties concerning the mysteries in religion cannot make them more wise,

(From the movie ''The Three Worlds of Gulliver,'' starring Kerwin Matthews and Jo Morrow. Copyright © 1960 by Columbia Pictures.)

Jonathan Swift, as played by Alec Guiness in the play "Yahoo."

learned or virtuous; better neighbours or friends, or more serviceable to their country. . . .

"[There are] multiplied controversies to such a degree as to beget scruples that have perplexed the minds of many sober Christians, who otherwise could never have entertained them. . . .

"I am not answerable to God for the doubts that arise in my own breast, since they are the consequence of that reason which He hath planted in me; if I take care to conceal those doubts from others, if I use my best endeavours to subdue them, and if they have no influence on the conduct of my life.

"I look upon myself, in the capacity of a clergyman, to be one appointed by Providence for defending a post assigned me, and for gaining over as many enemies as I can.

"I hear they think me a smart Dean, and that I am for doing good. My notion is that if a man cannot mend the public, he should mend old shoes if he can do no better; and therefore I endeavour in the little sphere I am placed to do all the good it is capable of.

"We are, indeed, commanded to love our neighbour as ourselves, but not as well as ourselves. The love we have for ourselves is to be the pattern of that love we ought to have towards our neighbour. But, as the copy doth not equal the original, so my neighbour cannot think it hard if I prefer myself, who am the original, before him who is only the copy.

"Preachers now in the world, however they may exceed St. Paul in the art of setting men to sleep, fall short of him in the working of miracles."[1]

August, 1725. With the recession of his lifelong illnesses that produced dizziness and loss of hearing, he continued

his work on *Gulliver's Travels:* "I have finished my Travels and I am now transcribing them. They are admirable things, and will wonderfully mend the world. . . .

"Reading books twice over for want of fresh ones, and fairly correcting and transcribing my Travels for the public. . . .

"Expect no more from man than such an animal is capable of, and you will every day find my description of Yahoos more resembling. . . .

"I have ever hated all nations, professions, and communities, and all my love is towards individuals. For instance, I hate the tribe of lawyers, but I love Councillor Such-a-one, and Judge Such-a-one. So with physicians—I will not speak of my own trade—soldiers, English, Scotch, French, and the rest. But principally I hate and detest that animal called man, although I heartily love John, Peter, Thomas and so forth. . . .

"When you think of the world give it one lash the more at my request. The chief end I propose in all my labours is to vex the world rather than divert it. . . .

"Drown the world! I am not content with despising it, but I would anger it, if I could with safety. I wish there were an

YOU WILL GROW WEAK AND FAINT

(From *Gulliver's Travels* by Jonathan Swift. Illustrated by Jean de Bosschère.)

hospital built for its despisers, where one might act with safety, and it need not be a large building, only I would have it well endowed.''[1]

1726. Notified that Stella was dying. ''What you tell me of Miss Johnson I have long expected, with great oppression and heaviness of heart. We have been perfect friends these thirty-five years. Upon my advice they both came to Ireland, and have been ever since my constant companions. And the remainder of my life will be a very melancholy scene, when one of them is gone whom I most esteemed, upon the score of every good quality that can possibly recommend a human creature. I have these two months seen through Miss Dingley's disguises. And indeed, ever since I left you, my heart is so sunk that I have not been the same man, nor ever shall be again, but drag on a wretched life till it shall please God to call me away. . . .

''I would not for the universe be present at such a trial as seeing her depart. She will be among friends that, upon her own account and great worth, will tend her with all possible

I had always a strong impulse that I should some time recover my liberty though it was impossible to conjecture by what means or to form any project with the least hope of succeeding. ■ (From *Gulliver's Travels* by Jonathan Swift. Illustrated by Aldren Watson.)

care, where I should be a trouble to her, and the greatest torment to myself. . . .

''I am of opinion that there is not a greater folly than to contract too great and intimate a friendship, which must always leave the survivor miserable. . . . If I were now near her, I would not see her; I could not behave myself tolerably, and should redouble her sorrow. . . .

''Pardon me, I know not what I am saying; but believe me that violent friendship is much more lasting, and as much engaging, as violent love.''[1]

March, 1727. Stella rallied and as usual, he presented her with a poem for her birthday.

...Some eagle had got the ring of my box in his beak, with an intent to let it fall on a rock, like a tortoise in a shell, and then pick out my body and devour it. ■ (From *Gulliver's Travels* by Jonathan Swift. Drawings by Robin Jacques.)

...Twenty wasps, allured by the smell, came flying into the room, humming louder than the drones of as many bagpipes. ■ (From *Gulliver's Travels* by Jonathan Swift. Illustrated by Arthur Rackham.)

"This day, whate'er the fates decree
Shall still be kept with joy by me:
This day then, let us not be told,
That you are sick, and I grown old.

"Although we now can form no more
Long schemes of life, as heretofore,
Yet you, while time is running fast,
Can look with joy on what is past.

"Say, Stella, feel you no content
Reflecting on a life well spent?
Your skillful hand employed to save
Despairing wretches from the grave;
And then supporting from your store
Those whom you dragged from death before . . .
Your generous boldness to defend
An innocent and absent friend;
That courage which can make you just
To merit humbled in the dust . . .
That patience under torturing pain,
Where stubborn stoics would complain.

"Me, surely me, you ought to spare,
Who gladly would your suffering share,
Or give my scrap of life to you
And think it far beneath your due—
You to whose care so oft I owe
That I'm alive to tell you so." [1]

April, 1727. On the eve of his departure for France, a political crisis arose, George I died. "I writ to Stella the day we heard the King was dead, and the circumstances of it. . . . I was with great vehemence dissuaded from it by certain persons whom I could not disobey. . . . I believe this giddiness is the disorder that will at last get the better of me; but I would rather it should not be now. . . . I am like a great Minister, in a tottering condition." [1]

1727. Swift's proposal for educating women. "It is a little hard that not one Gentleman's daughter in a thousand should be brought to read or understand her own natural tongue, or be judge of the easiest Books that are written in it: As any one may find, who can have the patience to hear them, when they are disposed to mangle a Play or Novel, where the least word out of the common road is sure to disconcert them; and it is no wonder, when they are not so much as taught to spell in their childhood, nor can ever attain to it in their whole lives. I advise you therefore to read aloud, more or less, every day to your Husband, if he will permit you, or to any other friend, (but not a Female one) who is able to set you right; and as for spelling, you may compass it in time by making Collections from the Books you read.

"I know very well that those who are commonly called Learned Women, have lost all manner of Credit by their impertinent Talkativeness and Conceit of themselves; but there is an easy remedy for this, if you consider, that after all the pains you may be at, you never can arrive in point of learning to the perfection of a School-boy. But the Reading I would advise you to, is only for improvement of your own good Sense, which will never fail of being Mended by Discretion. It is a wrong method, and ill choice of Books, that makes those Learned Ladies just so much worse for what they have read. And therefore it shall be my care to direct you better, a task for which I take my self to be not ill qualified; because I have spent more time, and have had

more opportunities than many others, to observe and discover from what sources the various follies of Women are derived.

"Man, which is not equally so in a Woman: I do not except even Modesty and Gentleness of nature. Nor do I know one vice or folly which is not equally detestable in both. There is indeed one infirmity which seems to be generally allowed you, I mean that of Cowardice. Yet there should seem to be something very capricious, that when Women profess their admiration for a Colonel or a Captain on account of his Valour, they should fancy it a very graceful becoming quality in themselves to be afraid of their own shadows; to scream in a Barge when the weather is calmest, or in a Coach at the Ring; to run from a Cow at a hundred yards' distance; to fall into fits at the sight of a Spider, an Earwig, or a Frog. At least, if Cowardice be a sign of Cruelty, (as it is generally granted) I can hardly think it an accomplishment so desirable as to be thought worth improving by Affectation." [*Satires and Personal Writings by Jonathan Swift*, Oxford University Press, 1932.[2]]

January 28, 1728. Stella died. "This day, being Sunday, about eight o'clock at night, a servant brought me a note, with an account of the death of the truest, most virtuous, and valuable friend that I, or perhaps any other person, ever was blessed with. She expired about six of the evening of this day; and as soon as I am left alone, which is about eleven at night, I resolve, for my own satisfaction, to say something of her life and character. . . .

"I cannot call to mind that I ever once heard her make a wrong judgement of persons, books, or affairs. Her advice was always the best, and with the greatest freedom, mixed with the greatest decency. . . . There seemed to be a combination among all that knew her to treat her with a dignity much beyond her rank. . . .

"She spoke in a most agreeable voice, in the plainest words, never hesitating, except out of modesty before new faces, where she was somewhat reserved; nor, among her nearest friends, ever spoke much at a time. However, in an afternoon or evening's conversation, she never failed, before we parted, of delivering the best thing that was said in the company. . . .

"In spite of the smallness of her fortune, her charity to the poor was a duty not to be diminished. . . . She bought clothes as seldom as possible, and those as plain and cheap as consisted with the situation she was in; and wore no lace for many years . . . I have heard her say, she always met with gratitude from the poor: which must be owing to her skill in distinguishing proper objects, as well as her gracious manner in relieving them. . . .

"By returning very few visits she had not much company of her own sex, except those whom she most loved for their easiness or esteemed for their good sense. But she rather chose men for through all her modesty, whatever they discoursed on, could easily observe that she understood them very well, by the judgement shown in her observations as well as in her questions. . . . She loved Ireland better than the generality of those who owe both their birth and riches to it. She had indeed reason to love a country where she had the esteem and friendship of all who knew her, and the universal good report of all who ever heard of her. . . . She detested the tyranny and injustice of England, in their treatment of this kingdom.

"**January 29, 1728.** My head aches, and I can write no more.

"**January 30, 1728.** Tuesday. This is the night of the funeral, which my sickness wlll not suffer me to attend. It is now nine at night, and I am removed into another apartment that I may not see the light in the church, which is just over against the window of my bed-chamber."[1]

1733. "I remember, when I was a little boy, I felt a great fish at the end of my line which I drew up almost on the ground. But it dropped in; the disappointment vexes me to this very day, and I believe it was the type of all my future disappointments.

"You think, as I ought to think, that it is time for me to have done with the world; and so I would, if I could get into a better before I was called into the best, and not die here in a rage, like a poisoned rat in a hole. I wonder you are not ashamed to let me pine away in this kingdom, while you are out of power."[1]

He spoke of the condition of Ireland as: "A bare face of nature, without houses or plantations; filthy cabins, miserable, tattered, half-starved creatures, scarce in human shape; one insolent, ignorant, oppressive squire to be found in twenty miles riding; a parish church to be found only in a summer day's journey; a bog of fifteen miles round; every meadow a slough, and every hill a mixture of rock, heath and marsh. . . . There is not an acre of land in Ireland turned to half its advantage, yet it is better improved than

the people; and all these evils are effects of English tyranny.

> "*As I stroll the city, oft I*
> *Spy a building large and lofty,*
> *Not a bowshot from the College,*
> *Half the globe from sense and knowledge.*
> *Tell us what this pile contains?*
> *Many ahead that holds no brains—*"[1]

1738. Book titled, *A Complete Collection of Genteel and Ingenious Conversation according to the Most Polite Mode and Method now Used at Court and in the Best Companies of England*, published.

May, 1740. Made his will. [The Bulk of his fortune went to building and endowing]—"an hospital large enough for the reception of as many idiots and lunatics as the annual income of the said lands [recited] and worldly substance shall be sufficient to maintain; and I desire that the said hospital may be called St. Patrick's Hospital."[1]

October, 1742. Suffered a stroke or perhaps it was his old disease—in such pain, it was said, that five people could hardly hold him for a week. Yet, such was his vitality that he survived another three years, the pain subsided, and he walked up and down the great house, his mind gone—muttering, "I am what I am; I am what I am."

October 19, 1745. Died at age 77. Laid to rest in a vault close to Stella. "All my endeavours from a boy to distin-

At length he ventured to take me up behind by the middle between his forefinger and thumb, and brought me within three yards of his eyes, that he might behold my shape more perfectly.
■ (From *Gulliver's Travels* by Jonathan Swift. Retold by Padraic Colum. Illustrated by Willy Pogany.)

guish myself were only for want of a great title and fortune: that I might be used like a Lord by those who have an opinion of my parts—whether right or wrong it is no great matter. And so the reputation of wit or great learning does the office of a blue ribbon, or of a coach, and six horses.

> *"Had he but spared his tongue and pen,*
> *He might have rose like other men.*
>
> *"His satire points at no defect*
> *But what all mortals may correct."*[1]

FOR MORE INFORMATION SEE: John Boyle, *Remarks on the Life and Writing of Dr. Jonathan Swift,* A. Millar, 1752, reprinted, Adler, 1968; Thomas Sheridan, *The Life of the Reverend Dr. Jonathan Swift,* C. Bathurst, 1784, reprinted, Folcroft, 1973; Henry Craik, *Life of Jonathan Swift,* two volumes, J. Murray, 1882, reprinted, R. West, 1973; Leslie Stephen, *Swift,* Macmillan, 1882, reprinted, Gale, 1968; James Hay, *Swift: The Mystery of His Life and Love,* Chapman & Hall, 1891, reprinted, Folcroft, 1973; Samuel Johnson, "Six Chief Lives," in *Lives of the Poets,* edited by Matthew Arnold, Macmillan, 1892, reprinted, Russell & Russell, 1968; Gerald Patrick Moriarty, *Dean Swift and His Writings,* Seeley, 1893, reprinted, Haskell House, 1970.

John Churton Collins, *Jonathan Swift: A Biography and Critical Study,* Chatto & Windus, 1902, reprinted, Folcroft, 1970; Sophie Shilleto Smith, *Dean Swift,* Methuen, 1910, reprinted, Folcroft, 1973; William A. Eddy, *Gulliver's Travels: A Critical Study,* Princeton University Press, 1923, reprinted, Russell & Russell, 1963; Sidney Dark, *Five Deans: John Colet, John Donne, Jonathan Swift, Arthur Penrhyn Stanley, William Ralph Inge,* Harcourt, 1928, reprinted, Kennikat, 1969; Shane Leslie, *Skull of Swift: An Extempore Exhumation,* Bobbs-Merrill, 1928, reprinted, Books for Libraries, 1971; Francis E. Ball, *Swift's Verse,* J. Murray, 1929, reprinted, Folcroft, 1974.

Cornelius van Doorn, *Investigation into the Character of Jonathan Swift,* N. V. Swets & Zeitlinger, 1931, reprinted, Haskell 1967; Herman Teerink, editor, *A Bibliography of the Writings in Prose and Verse of Jonathan Swift,* Steckhert-Hafner, 1937, revised as *Bibliography of the Writings of Jonathan Swift,* edited by Arthur H. Scouten, University of Pennsylvania Press, 1963; Donald Maurice Berwick, *Reputation of Jonathan Swift, 1781-1882,* [Philadelphia], 1941, reprinted, Haskell House, 1965; Robert Wyse Jackson, *Swift and His Circle: A Book of Essays,* Talbot Press, 1945, reprinted, Books for Libraries, 1969; Elizabeth Rider Montgomery, *Story behind Great Books,* McBride, 1946; Bernard Acworth, *Swift,* Eyre, 1948, reprinted, R. West, 1973; Evelyn Hardy, *Conjured Spirit: A Study of the Relationship of Swift, Stella, and Vanessa,* Hogarth, 1949, reprinted, Greenwood Press, 1973.

Oliver St. John Gogarty, *Intimations,* Abelard Press, 1950; John Cournos and H. S. N. K. Cournos, *Famous British Novelists,* Dodd, 1952; William Bragg Ewald, *Masks of Jonathan Swift,* Harvard University Press, 1954, reprinted, Russell & Russell, 1967; Louis A. Landa, *Swift and the Church of Ireland,* Oxford University Press, 1954; John Middleton Murry, *Jonathan Swift: A Critical Biography,* Noonday Press, 1955, reprinted, Farrar, Straus, 1967; Phyllis Greenacre, *Swift and Carroll: A Psychoanalytic Study of Two Lives,* International University Press, 1955; Michael Foot, *Pen and the Sword,* Macgibbon, 1957, reissued, 1966;

Jonathan Swift, in 1710. Painted by Charles Jervas.

Kathleen Williams, *Jonathan Swift and the Age of Compromise,* University of Kansas Press, 1958; Irvin Ehrenpreis, *Personality of Jonathan Swift,* Harvard University Press, 1958, reissued, Barnes & Noble, 1969; Denis Johnston, *In Search of Swift,* Barnes & Noble, 1959; James A. Preu, *Dean and the Anarchist,* Florida State University Press, 1959, reprinted, Haskell House, 1972.

Bertrand A. Goldgar, *Curse of Party: Swift's Relations with Addison and Steele,* University of Nebraska Press, 1961, reprinted, Norwood Editions, 1974; Charles A. Beaumont, *Swift's Classical Rhetoric,* University of Georgia Press, 1961; Oliver W. Ferguson, *Jonathan Swift and Ireland,* University of Illinois Press, 1962; Hesketh Pearson, *Lives of the Wits,* Harper, 1962; Sybil LeBrocquy, *Cadenus: A Reassessment in the Light of New Evidence of the Relationships between Swift, Stella, and Vanessa,* Dolmen Press, 1962; I. Ehrenpreis, *Swift: The Man, His Works, and the Age,* Harvard University Press, Volume I, *Mr. Swift and His Contemporaries,* 1962, Volume II, *Dr. Swift,* 1967; Edward W. Rosenheim, Jr., *Swift and the Satirist's Art,* University of Chicago Press, 1963; Elizabeth Drew, *Literature of Gossip,* Norton, 1964; Ernest L. Tuveson, editor, *Swift: A Collection of Critical Essays,* Prentice-Hall, 1964; Nigel Forbes Dennis, *Jonathan Swift: A Short Character,* Macmillan, 1964.

Jack S. Gilbert, *Jonathan Swift: Romantic and Cynic Moralist,* University of Texas Press, 1966, reprinted, Haskell House, 1972; Richard I. Cook, *Jonathan Swift as a Tory Pamphleteer,* University of Washington Press, 1967; N. Dennis, *Jonathan Swift,* Macmillan, 1967; Alexander Norman Jeffares, editor, *Fair Liberty Was All His Cry: A Tercentenary Tribute to Jonathan Swift, 1667-1745,* St. Martin's Press, 1967; Robert Hunting, *Jonathan Swift*, Twayne, 1967; Frank Brady, editor, *Twentieth Century Interpretations of Gulliver's Travels*, Prentice-Hall, 1968; A. N. Jeffares, compiler, *Swift*, Macmillan, 1968; Brian Doyle, editor, *Who's Who of Children's Literature*, Schocken Books, 1968; Deane Swift, *Essay upon the Life, Writings, and Character of Dr. Jonathan Swift*, G. Olms, 1968; Roger McHugh and Philip Edwards, editors, *Jonathan Swift, 1667-1967: A Dublin Tercentenary Tribute*, Dufour, 1968; K. Williams, *Jonathan Swift*, Routledge, 1968; S. LeBrocquy, *Swift's Most Valuable Friend*, Dufour, 1968; Denis Donoghue, *Jonathan Swift: A Critical Introduction*, Cambridge University Press, 1969; Martin Seymour-Smith, *Poets through Their Letters*, Holt, 1969.

William Butler Yeats, *Words upon the Window Pane* (one-act play), Irish University Press, 1970; K. Williams, compiler, *Swift: The Critical Heritage*, Barnes & Noble, 1970; Denis Donoghue, editor, *Jonathan Swift: A Critical Anthology*, Penguin, 1971; Peter A. Tasch, *Dramatic Cobbler: The Life and Works of Isaac Bickerstaff*, Bucknell University Press, 1971; Morris Golden, *Self-Observed: Swift, Johnson, Wordsworth*, Johns Hopkins Press, 1972; David Ward, *Jonathan Swift: An Introductory Essay*, Methuen, 1973; Martin Price, *Swift's Rhetorical Art: A Study in Structure and Meaning*, Southern Illinois University Press, 1973; Craig Hawkins Ulman, *Satire and the Correspondence of Swift*, Harvard University Press, 1973; L. A. Landa and James E. Tobin, *Jonathan Swift*, Farrar, Straus, 1975; A. L. Rowse, *Jonathan Swift*, Scribner, 1976.

WALLACE, Beverly Dobrin 1921-

PERSONAL: Born March 16, 1921, in Chattanooga, Tenn.; daughter of Harry (an engineer) and Lillian (Zinn; a secretary) Dobrin; married Henry Wallace (an ink chemist), February 1, 1948; children: Joshua, David. *Education:* Attended Carnegie Tech (now Carnegie Mellon); Hofstra University, B.S., 1964, M.A., 1970; attended Arts Students League of New York and Pratt Center for Contemporary Printmaking. *Politics:* Liberal and Democratic. *Home:* RFD 1, Bullet Hole Road, Mahopac, N.Y. 10541. *Agent:* Toni Mendez, 140 East 56th Street, New York, N.Y. 10022. *Office:* Scotland Elementary School, Ridgefield, Conn. 06817.

CAREER: Painter; printmaker; book illustrator; teacher. Winnicomac Elementary School, Commack, Long Island, N.Y., art teacher, 1964-68; Somers Middle School, Somers, N.Y., art specialist, 1968-71; Hebrew Hospital for Chronic Sick, Bronx, N.Y.; occupational therapist, 1971-72; Scotland Elementary School, Ridgefield, Conn., art teacher, 1972—; children's book illustrator, 1970—; author, 1971—. *Member:* International Defenders of Wildlife, Common Cause, Bookeepers Association of Putnam County, National Education Association, Connecticut Education Association, Putnam Arts Council. *Awards, honors:* Emily Lowe Award for Excellence in Painting, 1963; invited to speak at reading conference at Penn State University, 1975.

WRITINGS—Self-illustrated: *Insects: The Seasons in Their Lives*, Bobbs, 1975.

Illustrator: Mary Louise Sherer, *The Secret of Bruja Mountain*, Harvey House, 1971; Barbara Williams, *Desert Hunter: The Spider Wasp*, Harvey House, 1975.

WORK IN PROGRESS: Doing research on spiders for illus-

BEVERLY DOBRIN WALLACE

trating a book; fictional story for children based on characteristics of the crow; series of articles for a magazine in the field of art education.

SIDELIGHTS: "As a child I lived in big industrial cities, first Birmingham and then Pittsburgh, because of my father's work. But the summer I was eight, our life style changed remarkably when we rented a house in the woods for the entire vacation. A boat came with the house and my big brother would take me walking in the woods and rowing on the river. Things that other kids around there took for granted were objects of wonder to us. I began to draw pictures and to develop the habit of looking hard and remembering detail.

"Wild places—woods, meadows, mountain tops, caves, river banks—still make me feel special, like someone in a story. That summer I wrote many stories. The setting was always a wild place and the hero was a friendly wild animal who saved my life.

"My fascination with nature which started during that childhood summer has increased through the years. I live now in a house right next to the woods and water and I have bee hives in my backyard.

"For years I painted and made etchings, exhibiting my work in galleries and in shows and competitions. But when I began to illustrate children's books I knew this was my favorite kind of picture making. Insects fascinated me more than ever and the magnifying lens would soon become part of my visual apparatus as I began to study entomology seriously.

"I teach art at an elementary school in Ridgefield, Connecticut and I find that the children and I share the same excitement about the mysterious hobgoblins that frequent our backyards. Often I show them the movies I make of insect activity. Much of the research for *Insects: The Seasons in Their Lives* was done with my super-eight movie camera. It has a macro-zoom lens which permits me to get as close as a half-inch to the subject of a picture. The image is magnified tremendously. A creature who appears drab and tiny to the naked eye may easily loom magnificent and terrible through the macro-zoom lens. In the cold months I was able to study the anatomy and the movements and behavior of the insects in the movies.

"I wrote *Insects: The Seasons in Their Lives* to show the influence of the yearly seasonal cycle on the lives of insects. The book also stresses a vital interdependency between insects and plants, pointing out, of course, how grateful we should be to insects for helping plants grow.

"In the summer of 1973 I set out each morning armed with my butterfly net, magnifying glass and movie camera. I always took a sketch pad and pens and I wore a large sun hat and boots. I looked fairly odd crossing the road in this get-up, but the neighbors soon got used to me and several children often came along. There were facts I had learned in my entomological studies which had to be made visual for my readers. I drew each insect activity from life. This accounts for the vitality people find in my drawings. Since the little buggers were not bent on accommodating me, it took a lot of finding, watching, photographing and sketching.

"Now I have a number of hives, but that was the year I started beekeeping in order to find out about bees. These are wonderful creatures to watch. If the hive is opened quietly and gently, the bees tolerate your presence. I spent two years writing and illustrating *Insects: The Seasons in Their Lives.*

"When I was asked to illustrate *Desert Hunter: The Spider Wasp,* the author, Barbara Williams, sent me a corpse of Pepsis Formosa (the spider wasp) from Utah, and I was able to borrow two live tarantulas from Alice Gray at the American Museum of Natural History.

Silently he slid into a green tunnel where the jungle growth crowded close on both sides of the water. It was like entering a green room, dim and peaceful. The only sound was a constant hum of the music of a million insects. ■ (From *The Secret of Bruja Mountain* by Mary Louise Sherer. Illustrated by Beverly Dobrin Wallace.)

"As a member of The International Defenders of Wildlife, I am active in conservation endeavors. I believe in writing to my Congressmen on ecological issues, and I do whatever I can as a teacher and a homemaker to recycle paper, metal, glass and wood.

"My husband and our two sons share my involvement with nature. Sometimes, when the boys come home to visit, we all four take a walk in the woods."

CUMULATIVE INDEX TO
ILLUSTRATIONS AND AUTHORS

Illustrations Index

(In the following index, the number of the volume in which an illustrator's work appears is given *before* the colon, and the page on which it appears is given *after* the colon. For example, a drawing by Adams, Adrienne appears in Volume 2 on page 6, another drawing by her appears in Volume 3 on page 80, another drawing in Volume 8 on page 1, and another drawing in Volume 15 on page 107.)

YABC

Index citations including this abbreviation refer to listings appearing in *Yesterday's Authors of Books for Children,* also published by the Gale Research Company, which covers authors who died prior to 1960.

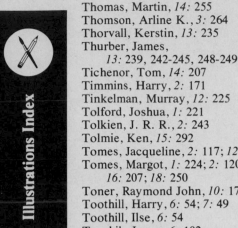

Illustrations Index

Author Index

(In the following index, the number of the volume in which an author's sketch appears is given *before* the colon, and the page on which it appears is given *after* the colon. For example, the sketch of Aardema, Verna, appears in Volume 4 on page 1).

YABC
Index citations including this abbreviation refer to listings appearing in *Yesterday's Authors of Books for Children,* also published by the Gale Research Company, which covers authors who died prior to 1960.

Brown, Vinson, *19:* 48
Brown, Walter R(eed), *19:* 50
Brown, William L(ouis), *5:* 34
Browne, Matthew. *See* Rands,
    William Brighty, *17:* 156
Browning, Robert, *YABC 1:* 85
Brownjohn, Alan, *6:* 38
Bruce, Mary, *1:* 36
Bryant, Bernice (Morgan), *11:* 40
Bryson, Bernarda, *9:* 26
Buchan, John, *YABC 2:* 21
Buchwald, Art(hur), *10:* 18
Buchwald, Emilie, *7:* 31
Buck, Lewis, *18:* 37
Buck, Margaret Waring, *3:* 29
Buck, Pearl S(ydenstricker), *1:* 36
Buckeridge, Anthony, *6:* 38
Buckley, Helen E(lizabeth), *2:* 38
Buckmaster, Henrietta, *6:* 39
Budd, Lillian, *7:* 33
Buehr, Walter, *3:* 30
Buff, Conrad, *19:* 51
Buff, Mary Marsh, *19:* 54
Bulla, Clyde Robert, *2:* 39
Bunting, A. E.. *See* Bunting, Anne
    Evelyn, *18:* 38
Bunting, Anne Evelyn, *18:* 38
Bunting, Eve. *See* Bunting, Anne
    Evelyn, *18:* 38
Burch, Robert J(oseph), *1:* 38
Burchard, Peter D(uncan), *5:* 34
Burchardt, Nellie, *7:* 33
Burford, Eleanor. *See* Hibbert,
    Eleanor, *2:* 134
Burger, Carl, *9:* 27
Burgess, Em. *See* Burgess, Mary
    Wyche, *18:* 39
Burgess, Mary Wyche, *18:* 39
Burgess, Robert F(orrest), *4:* 38
Burgess, Thornton W(aldo), *17:* 19
Burgwyn, Mebane H., *7:* 34
Burland, C. A. *See* Burland, Cottie
    A., *5:* 36
Burland, Cottie A., *5:* 36
Burlingame, (William) Roger, *2:* 40
Burman, Ben Lucien, *6:* 40
Burn, Doris, *1:* 39
Burnett, Frances (Eliza) Hodgson,
    YABC 2: 32
Burnford, S. D. *See* Burnford,
    Sheila, *3:* 32
Burnford, Sheila, *3:* 32
Burningham, John (Mackintosh),
    16: 58
Burns, Paul C., *5:* 37
Burns, Ray. *See* Burns, Raymond
    (Howard), *9:* 28
Burns, Raymond, *9:* 28
Burns, William A., *5:* 38
Burroughs, Polly, *2:* 41
Burt, Olive Woolley, *4:* 39
Burton, Hester, *7:* 35
Burton, Virginia Lee, *2:* 42
Burton, William H(enry), *11:* 42
Busoni, Rafaello, *16:* 61
Butler, Beverly, *7:* 37

Butters, Dorothy Gilman, *5:* 39
Butterworth, Oliver, *1:* 40
Butterworth, W(illiam)
    E(dmund III), *5:* 40
Byars, Betsy, *4:* 40
Byfield, Barbara Ninde, *8:* 19

Cable, Mary, *9:* 29
Cadwallader, Sharon, *7:* 38
Cady, (Walter) Harrison, *19:* 56
Cain, Arthur H., *3:* 33
Cain, Christopher. *See* Fleming,
    Thomas J(ames), *8:* 19
Cairns, Trevor, *14:* 50
Caldecott, Randolph (J.), *17:* 31
Caldwell, John C(ope), *7:* 38
Calhoun, Mary (Huiskamp), *2:* 44
Calkins, Franklin. *See*
    Stratemeyer, Edward L.,
    1: 208
Call, Hughie Florence, *1:* 41
Callen, Larry. *See* Callen,
    Lawrence Willard, Jr., *19:* 59
Callen, Lawrence Willard, Jr.,
    19: 59
Cameron, Edna M., *3:* 34
Cameron, Eleanor (Butler), *1:* 42
Cameron, Elizabeth. *See* Nowell,
    Elizabeth Cameron, *12:* 160
Cameron, Polly, *2:* 45
Camp, Walter (Chauncey),
    YABC 1: 92
Campbell, Ann R., *11:* 43
Campbell, Bruce. *See* Epstein,
    Samuel, *1:* 87
Campbell, Jane. *See* Edwards,
    Jane Campbell, *10:* 34
Campbell, R. W. *See* Campbell,
    Rosemae Wells, *1:* 44
Campbell, Rosemae Wells, *1:* 44
Canfield, Dorothy. *See* Fisher,
    Dorothy Canfield, *YABC 1:* 122
Canusi, Jose. *See* Barker, S.
    Omar, *10:* 8
Capps, Benjamin (Franklin), *9:* 30
Caras, Roger A(ndrew), *12:* 65
Carbonnier, Jeanne, *3:* 34
Carey, Bonnie, *18:* 40
Carey, Ernestine Gilbreth, *2:* 45
Carini, Edward, *9:* 30
Carle, Eric, *4:* 41
Carleton, Captain L. C. *See* Ellis,
    Edward S(ylvester),
    YABC 1: 116
Carlisle, Clark, Jr. *See* Holding,
    James, *3:* 85
Carlsen, Ruth C(hristoffer), *2:* 47
Carlson, Bernice Wells, *8:* 19
Carlson, Dale Bick, *1:* 44
Carlson, Natalie Savage, *2:* 48
Carlson, Vada F., *16:* 64
Carol, Bill J. *See* Knott, William
    Cecil, Jr., *3:* 94

Carpelan, Bo (Gustaf Bertelsson),
    8: 20
Carpenter, Allan, *3:* 35
Carpenter, Frances, *3:* 36
Carpenter, Patricia (Healy Evans),
    11: 43
Carr, Glyn. *See* Styles, Frank
    Showell, *10:* 167
Carr, Harriett Helen, *3:* 37
Carr, Mary Jane, *2:* 50
Carrick, Carol, *7:* 39
Carrick, Donald, *7:* 40
Carroll, Curt. *See* Bishop, Curtis,
    6: 24
Carroll, Latrobe, *7:* 40
Carroll, Laura. *See* Parr, Lucy,
    10: 115
Carroll, Lewis. *See* Dodgson,
    Charles Lutwidge,
    YABC 2: 297
Carse, Robert, *5:* 41
Carson, Captain James. *See*
    Stratemeyer, Edward L.,
    1: 208
Carson, John F., *1:* 46
Carter, Bruce. *See* Hough, Richard
    (Alexander), *17:* 83
Carter, Dorothy Sharp, *8:* 21
Carter, Helene, *15:* 37
Carter, (William) Hodding, *2:* 51
Carter, Katharine J(ones), *2:* 52
Carter, Phyllis Ann. *See* Eberle,
    Irmengarde, *2:* 97
Carter, William E., *1:* 47
Cartner, William Carruthers, *11:* 44
Cartwright, Sally, *9:* 30
Cary. *See* Cary, Louis F(avreau),
    9: 31
Cary, Louis F(avreau), *9:* 31
Caryl, Jean. *See* Kaplan, Jean
    Caryl Korn, *10:* 62
Case, Marshal T(aylor), *9:* 33
Case, Michael. *See* Howard,
    Robert West, *5:* 85
Casewit, Curtis, *4:* 43
Casey, Brigid, *9:* 33
Casey, Winifred Rosen. *See*
    Rosen, Winifred, *8:* 169
Cason, Mabel Earp, *10:* 19
Cass, Joan E(velyn), *1:* 47
Cassel, Lili. *See* Wronker, Lili
    Cassell, *10:* 204
Cassel-Wronker, Lili. *See*
    Wronker, Lili Cassell, *10:* 204
Castellanos, Jane Mollie
    (Robinson), *9:* 34
Castillo, Edmund L., *1:* 50
Castle, Lee. [Joint pseudonym].
    See Ogan, George F. and
    Margaret E. (Nettles), *13:* 171
Caswell, Helen (Rayburn), *12:* 67
Catherall, Arthur, *3:* 38
Catlin, Wynelle, *13:* 19
Catton, (Charles) Bruce, *2:* 54
Catz, Max. *See* Glaser, Milton,
    11: 106

Author Index

Author Index